MARKETING PLACES

MARKETING PLACES

Attracting Investment, Industry, and Tourism to Cities, States, and Nations

PHILIP KOTLER
DONALD H. HAIDER
IRVING REIN

THE FREE PRESS
A Division of Macmillan, Inc.
NEW YORK

Maxwell Macmillan Canada
TORONTO

Maxwell Macmillan International
NEW YORK   OXFORD   SINGAPORE   SYDNEY

The Free Press
A Division of Macmillan, Inc.
866 Third Avenue, New York, N.Y. 10022

Maxwell Macmillan Canada, Inc.
1200 Eglinton Avenue East
Suite 200
Don Mills, Ontario M3C 3N1

Macmillan, Inc. is part of the Maxwell Communication
Group of Companies.

Printed in the United States of America

printing number
1   2   3   4   5   6   7   8   9   10

Library of Congress Cataloging-in-Publication Data

Kotler, Philip.
    Marketing places : attracting investment, industry, and tourism to
cities, states, and nations / Philip Kotler, Donald H. Haider,
Irving Rein.
          p.   cm.
    Includes bibliographical references and index.
    ISBN 0-02-917596-8
    1. Marketing.   2. Industry—Location.   3. Industrial promotion.
I. Haider, Donald H.   II. Rein, Irving J.   III. Title.
HF5415.K6315   1993   92-46319
338.6′ 042—dc20   CIP

For
NANCY KOTLER
JEAN HAIDER
LYNN MILLER

CONTENTS

ACKNOWLEDGMENTS

The authors wish to acknowledge the contributions of a number of people who helped make this manuscript possible. Our gratitude goes to Neil Kotler of the Smithsonian Institute for his perceptive reading of the manuscript and his editorial help and suggestions. We also want to thank David Gertner for his assistance in research, editorial help, and his critical reading of the manuscript; Rick Andrews for his research and insights on image marketing; Jennifer Scott for research, word processing, and editing; and Meridith Cass for research assistance.

Ethan Markowitz edited the manuscript and his insights were crucial to the book. Lynn Miller edited the final draft and made it a better book. Ed Mills made valuable suggestions on the manuscript's contents.

We are also grateful for research aid from Mark Bloom, Susan Booth, Paul Frank, Tony Gama-Lobo, Abel Lezcano, and Mark Rothschild. We also benefited from research on Wisconsin by Kelly Abate, Jill Chessen, Kevin Gore, Jane Keller, Kris Kosup, Scott Nehs, and Rolf Nelson.

The authors wish to acknowledge Prentice Hall, Inc. for granting permission to its author, Philip Kotler, to use limited amounts of material from his *Marketing Management: Analysis, Planning, Implementation, and Control* (1991), in his book, in chapter 7. The authors would also like to thank Robert M. Ady, president of PHH Fantus, for his thoughtful advice and counsel.

1

Places in Trouble

At any moment, a large and growing number of places—cities, regions, and entire nations—are on the sick list. According to Standard & Poor's, the investment credit rating agency, "almost two-thirds of the 50 states and nearly three-quarters of America's more than 5,000 cities are confronted by a financing gap."[1] In its 1991 annual financial survey of U.S. cities, the National League of Cities found most places to be suffering from an imbalance between revenues and expenditures, which has resulted in layoffs and service reductions.[2]

Bankruptcy may be the ultimate test of a place's sickness. In mid-1975 New York flirted dangerously with bankruptcy only to experience enormous recovery following federal assistance and adoption of tough fiscal medicine. Its turnaround from huge deficits to budget surpluses ended in the late 1980s. Then, once again, it experienced a collapse of its core financial service and real estate industries, an out-migration of major employers, rising crime levels, and service reductions.

In 1978 Cleveland defaulted on its debt obligations. Philadelphia had to be refinanced in the early 1990s, while Connecticut's largest city, Bridgeport, sought the refuge of federal bankruptcy laws in 1991. In 1992 California, the nation's largest and most prosperous state, encountered a massive $10 billion budgetary shortfall whose resolution required that public employees be paid with scrip and vendors with

IOUs until a vastly reduced state budget was enacted. Place sickness is by no means restricted to the United States. In 1988 the Mayor of Rio de Janeiro declared his city bankrupt.[3] Dating from the late 1950s and the construction of Brazil's new federal capitol, Brasilia, and the shift of financial services and businesses to São Paulo, Rio experienced a loss of jobs and tax revenues. Betting recovery on increased U.S. and European tourism, its revival faltered when disillusioned tourists encountered Rio's reputation as a hotbed of pickpockets and assailants.

Sickness includes not only a place's fiscal health but also its economic condition. Nations experience both cyclical and even prolonged periods of poor health—trade imbalances, rising debt, high inflation and unemployment, and unstable currencies. Entire regions can be chronically depressed—northern England, western France, southern Italy, and Appalachia here in the United States. Economic weaknesses, commonly measured by loss of population, high unemployment, and falling income and investment, are associated with the fate of a place's particular industries or industry clusters, resources, and products—oil in the Southwest, autos and machinery in the Midwest, and agriculture in the Farm Belt. In some cases, the fate of regions and places rises and falls with specific industries, while in others industry declines may be more permanently wedded to changes in technology and competition. The East and West coasts experienced the latter in computer, semiconductor, and aerospace–defense industries.

However, a place's relative sickness or health transcends fiscal and economic measurement.[4] Places are more than budgets and businesses. They are people, cultures, historical heritage, physical assets, and opportunities. Places are ranked, rated, and evaluated today on every conceivable dimension: where to start or locate a business or plan a retirement, where to raise a family or look for a spouse, where to plan a vacation, hold a convention, or have a meal. From quality of life considerations to charm, culture, and ambience, the quest for livable, investible, and visitable places is a perpetual search for the new and vibrant, an effort to stay clear of the sullen and depressed.

In this book, we deal with the problems that places face in seeking a better future. Like nations, places can reverse their decline, can experience a rebirth and revitalization through a process of strategic market planning. The Five Tigers of East Asia—South Korea, Taiwan, Hong Kong, Singapore, and Thailand—are examples of resurgence where the component parts of strategy, marketing, and planning are concentrated in specific nations. So, too, certain places have reversed their fortunes through concerted planning and skillful execution: St. Paul,

Glasgow, Indianapolis, and Baltimore, to name a few cities. Take, for instance the case of St. Louis, which suffered severe decline through the mid-1970s that some thought to be fatal. Fifteen years later, St. Louis bills itself as an urban miracle, a renaissance city in which old commercial buildings have been rehabilitated, vacant houses restored, the downtown rebuilt and revitalized. Its ethnic vitality, historical culture, and architectural splendor have been preserved, and a spirit of rebirth permeates the city and county.

In this book we draw examples of rebirth and recovery from places throughout the United States, Canada, Europe, and Asia. These include world-class cities and smaller communities, older manufacturing centers and rural backwaters. Places in trouble are not just those whose primary businesses or industries are declining, but all places that may think tomorrow will be much the same as today. The resources, assets, and advantages that certain places enjoy today may not be those that provide the same opportunities a decade from now. This is a book about change and response. It tells how strategic market planning can help prepare places for dealing with an uncertain future.

In this chapter, we set the stage by addressing the following four questions: (1) What is happening to places? (2) Why do places fall into trouble? (3) What are places doing to solve their problems? (4) What should places do to solve their problems?

WHAT IS HAPPENING TO PLACES?

Almost all places are in trouble, but some are in more trouble than others. Their situations fall along a continuum. At the most desperate extreme are places that are *dying or chronically depressed.* They lack the resources on which to launch a recovery. Some are small towns and cities that have lost their major industry or company and are plagued with unemployment, shuttered stores, and abandoned property. People and businesses out-migrate leaving a weakened tax base on which to fund schools, hospitals, and other public services. Crime and drugs take over the life of these places, and further accelerate the decline. East St. Louis, Illinois, and Newark, New Jersey, vividly illustrate these ravaged places. Ultimately, these cities persist only on grants from outside or eventually devolve into partial ghost towns.

There are also *acutely depressed* places that have some potential for revival. Places such as Detroit, Philadelphia, and New York have entered a period of hard times. The bad news is that their debt and problems keep worsening. The good news is that these places possess historical, cultural, and political assets that could support a turnaround if the right leadership and vision emerges.

Other places have *boom and bust characteristics*. These towns and cities are highly sensitive to business cycle movements as a result of their mix of industries and growth companies. In the post-World War II period, Boston lost its textile and shoe industries, both of which fled to the South in search of lower costs. Most of Boston's revival turned on regional service and financial centers surrounded by high-tech industries and growth companies. The Massachusetts Miracle turned into the Massachusetts Mirage as its computer industry collapsed, real estate faltered, and growing service industries experienced retrenchment and downsizing. Energy-exporting states and centers in the Southeast, Texas, and Oklahoma epitomize the boom and bust cycle.

On the brighter side are some places that have undergone *healthy transformations*. These places invested heavily to create new conditions to improve their attractiveness. Indianapolis billed itself as the amateur sports capital of the nation. Baltimore launched an ambitious waterfront development and cleanup program that greatly revived its prospects. Glasgow, Scotland, turned itself from a gritty manufacturing city into an exciting European art capital. And according to one observer of St. Paul, Minnesota, "Some fifty years ago a national magazine described St. Paul as having already 'grown up, prospered, and died.'" This report of St. Paul's death turned out to be greatly exaggerated.

Finally, some places deserve the title of the *favored few*. They enjoy strong financial health and continue to attract tourists, new residents and business people. Some places have done this for centuries: Venice, Florence, Paris, and Vienna. In the United States, such places as Santa Fe, New Mexico, and Santa Barbara, California, qualify, as well as San Francisco and San Diego. Still, even these favored few face problems: pollution, congestion, water shortages, and other modern scourges. Their problem is not to find new ways to grow but quite the opposite, to prevent unmanaged growth from destroying their assets.

WHY DO PLACES FALL INTO TROUBLE?

Whatever economic circumstances a place finds itself in, it inevitably evolves into new circumstances. Every place is subject to *internal growth and decline cycles* as well as to *external shocks and forces beyond its control*. We examine these two change forces next.

Internal Forces Leading Places into Trouble

Many places experience a period of growth followed by a period of decline, which might repeat itself several times. The growth period inevitably ends, because growth lays the seeds of its own destruction. The decline period may also end, but for a different set of reasons. The processes underlying growth and decline dynamics can occur independent of the state of the business cycle, although they may be accelerated by sudden changes in the economic climate.

Figure 1-1 illustrates a well-documented *city growth dynamic*. Imagine a city that is initially attractive. It might be blessed with expanding industries, have an exceptional climate or natural beauty, and might have a remarkable historical heritage. Assuming that job opportunities are strong and the quality of life is appealing, this city inevitably attracts new residents, visitors, business firms, and investment. The inward migration of people and resources raises housing and real estate prices and strains the existing infrastructure and social service budget. The city typically raises taxes on residents and businesses to pay for the needed expansion of transportation, communication, energy, and social resources. Some residents and businesses begin to move out of the

FIGURE 1-1
City Growth Dynamics

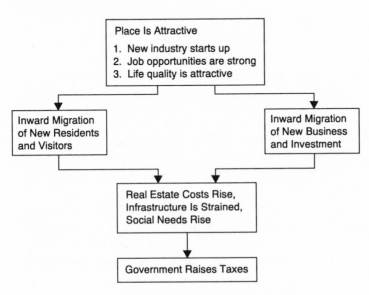

city boundaries to lower their costs, thus reducing the tax base. Thus the very state of being an attractive place may unleash forces that ultimately unravel the place's attractiveness.

Orlando was a peaceful, sleepy city before the arrival of Disney. Today, the fastest growing city in America finds itself expanding at rates it cannot control. The downtown has never really developed, natural beauty is seriously curtailed by malls and developments, and traffic is snarled. The need for schools forces children into large classes and trailers. Another attractive city, Seattle, is now facing traffic gridlocks and pollution concerns. The city recently instituted strict downtown building regulations to stem the onslaught of new companies and new residents moving up from Los Angeles in search of a more affordable life-style.

As a place begins to lose its attractiveness, forces are released that worsen the situation (see *city decay dynamics* in figure 1–2). A major company or industry in the town might falter or exit due to business mismanagement, an eroding community infrastructure, the onset of a general recession, or lower costs elsewhere. Business profits and jobs decline. Real estate prices fall. Infrastructure deteriorates. These developments accelerate the outward migration of residents and businesses and cause a sharp drop in tourism and convention business. Banks tighten credit, causing an increase in bankruptcies. Joblessness leads to more crime and drugs, and social needs increase. The city's image becomes further tarnished. The government raises taxes to maintain or improve infrastructure and meet social needs. But the higher taxes only accelerate the out-migration of resources.

Philadelphia has passed through this decay dynamic. The city reached a high point in 1976 with the celebration of the Bicentennial of the Signing of the Declaration of Independence. The city freshened its historic district, its citizens had a positive attitude, and tourists flocked to Philadelphia. During the 1980s, a building boom further revitalized its downtown. At the same time, rising city taxes and inefficient city government led many middle-class residents to flee to the suburbs, leaving behind a lower tax base to support a growing disadvantaged population facing problems

FIGURE 1-2
City Decay Dynamics

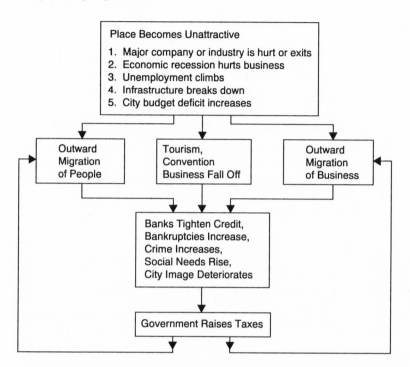

of crime, homelessness, drugs, and AIDS. Further tax increases only drove more residents and companies out of the city. The city's Moody credit rating fell, pushing the city into issuing lower-quality junk bonds and raising its borrowing costs. Meanwhile, Philadelphia spent energy trying to wrest more grant money from the state's treasury. Union contracts prevented the city administration from reducing the number of city workers. By 1990, Philadelphia faced a $229 million deficit and the prospect of bankruptcy, which simply meant that "the government may come to a standstill. . . . Trash pickup, cops, fire—all would stop."[5]

Smaller cities and towns are also prone to decline. They often find themselves too dependent on one main source of revenue; when it dries up, so does the place. Young people move away after their high school graduation, and the place starts to resemble a retirement community.

The small town of New York Mills, Minnesota, (pop. 750) is in gradual decline. As early as the mid-fifties, the town leaders, seeing the
loss of vital trade activity to larger towns, formed a boat company
around an aluminum designer. The Lund Boat Company was a hit
and the town population stabilized and began to grow. A large trailer
park prospered and new homes were built on the outskirts. In the
next two decades, the town began to slip in population again as the
creamery closed and all but one car dealer moved out of town. In
addition, a new highway now circled the town and residents found it
easier to shop at the new Pamida discount store thirteen miles out of
town. The town leaders wanted to remake the main street into a
Finnish theme town, but years of argument never convinced the citizens. The town sits in a precarious position. A good place to live, but
not unlike the ghost town of Heinola, a few miles to the west, New
York Mills faces possible extinction.

External Forces Leading Places into Trouble

Places are also shaken by major forces in the external environment over
which they have no control. The major forces upsetting the economic
equilibrium of communities are rapid technological change, global
competition, and political power shifts.

RAPID TECHNOLOGICAL CHANGE.   Technological advances unleash
the most potent changes in the way people live, work, travel, and communicate. Nineteenth-century America was an agricultural economy,
operating basically on rudimentary human and mechanical power.
Twentieth-century America became a manufacturing economy, operating on sophisticated mechanical and electrical power. In moving into
the twenty-first century, the United States will be a knowledge and service society, operating primarily on electronic and computer power.

   Technological advances inevitably hurt some industries in a process
that economist Joseph Schumpeter called "creative destruction." The
invention of the automobile made horses and carriages obsolete; on the
other hand, it also led to superhighways, gasoline stations, drive-in restaurants and movies, and the explosive growth of the oil industry. Advances in oil refinement in turn led to new synthetic products such as
nylon and rayon, which in turn depressed the demand for cotton and
wool, permanently injuring those states dependent on producing natu-

ral fibers. Technological advances in communication, transportation, and manufacturing, exemplified by microelectronic advances, have become a driving force in the world economy. A decade ago, the United States generated three-quarters of the world's scientific information; today this is down to 50 percent, and is likely to be halved again over the next decade.[6] Most of the new jobs being created are in the "thoughtware sector" which includes computer software, finance, education, medicine, telecommunications, engineering services, data base development and dissemination, innovative forms of distribution, innovative insurance, new forms of hospital management and waste collection.[7] Science and technology drive the marketplace, and their applications affect job growth. No wonder governments have assumed new responsibilities for promoting, encouraging, financing, and generating new technology and its applications.

Places are now beginning to feel the full impact of the revolution in technology and communication. Fax machines, hand-held computers, and teleconferencing allow companies to move to places with lower costs or more attractive working conditions. The old notion that Manhattan is finance, Los Angeles is film, and Detroit is automobiles is no longer valid. Financial services have recently moved to New Jersey and Kansas City, film production to Orlando and Czechoslovakia and automobile manufacturing to Tennessee and Mexico.

The automobile industry in America had no foreign plants thirty years ago. The Japanese, to avoid quotas and to take advantage of local market factors, built a large number of factories in America. The Japanese plants—some built in partnership with American manufacturers—feature rural locations, nonunion workers, and state-of-the-art manufacturing processes. The American automobile industry is now being rebuilt by outside money and the outsiders are changing the face of the communities in which they build.

GLOBAL COMPETITION. In the nineteenth century, competition in America was mainly local and regional, given the underdeveloped state of transportation and communication. Competition became more global in twentieth-century America, especially in the 1970s. In this last decade of the twentieth century, a dominant factor in any community's life is the emergence of a global economy and its consequences for the local economy and the quality of life. Previously self-contained local, regional, and national economies are being transformed into interdependent parts of an integrated world economy. As a result, global economic competition is combining with vast improvements in global communication, transportation, and finance to accelerate the pace, the intensity, and the scope of economic and social change, even in the smallest and most remote places.

In our new world economy, every place must compete with other places for economic advantage. Various communities launch drives to attract business firms and industrial plants, corporate and divisional headquarters, investment capital, tourists and conventioneers, sports teams, and so on, all of which promise increased employment, income, trade, investment, and growth.

No longer are places merely the settings for business activity. Instead, every community has to transform itself into a seller of goods and services, a proactive marketer of its products and its place value. Places are, indeed, products, whose identities and values must be designed and marketed. Places that fail to market themselves successfully face the risk of economic stagnation and decline.

Thus, the old realities of business cycles are now joined by the new realities of global competitive pressures. Nor are state-run economies spared the pressures of competition. Indeed, at the close of the twentieth century, communist economies, having labored for decades under socialist ideology, closed markets, and centralized planning, are desperately trying to stave off national bankruptcy, seeking to move toward a market or mixed welfare state/market type of economy. Nations, as well as cities, states, and regions, need to map out place investment strategies to carry them successfully into the twenty-first century.

The United States and other nations have entered into a new economic era. Older economic theories, models, and measurements designed for the industrial, smokestack era have lost their utility in explaining this new era. The policymaker's faith in various monetary and fiscal prescriptions has been shaken by the simultaneous rise of inflation and unemployment. The Keynesian consensus that served decision makers during much of the twentieth century has weakened in an era of independent economies. In the new era, few of the old road maps and compasses are of help in correcting an economic disorder. Table 1-1 contrasts the key differences between the old and the new economic eras. Places whose industries and firms operate according to the old economic era concepts are headed for hard times.

TABLE 1-1
Characteristics of Old and New Economies

Characteristics	Old	New
Scope	Domestic	Global
Driving force	Mass production	Technology, innovation
Resource	Capital	Knowledge, information
Jobs	Stable, large firms	Dynamic, smaller firms
Organizations	Centralized/hierarchical	Matrix, fluid, decentralized
Markets	Stable	Fluid
Workers	Uneducated, unskilled	Educated, skilled, adaptive
Tasks	Simple, physical	Complex, intellectual, participatory
Technology	Mechanical	Electronic, biological
Emphasis	Predictability	Innovation, creativity
Information flow	Top-down	Bottom-up, interactive
Opportunities	Limited, fixed	Fluid, rotational, mobile
Business/government	Minimal intervention	Cooperation, partnership
Symbol	Smokestack	Computer

Source: See Rosabeth Moss Kanter, *The Change Masters* (New York: Simon & Schuster, 1983), chap. 2.

All places are intimately affected by the new global forces. Consider the following:

- Between 1983 and 1988, the U.S. Bureau of Labor Statistics estimated 10 million workers lost their jobs due to plant closings and layoffs, mostly related to foreign competition. On average, any given place is likely to lose one-half of its jobs over a ten-year period as jobs come and go, are redefined or reclassified. This means that simply to stay even in employment figures, places must replace one-half of their current jobs every decade. Such change increases the pressures on communities to retain current businesses and attract new ones.[8]

- More than 80 percent of U.S.-produced goods compete with foreign products, double the amount from 1970, while goods purchased by Americans from abroad more than doubled since 1970.[9] Gone is the narrow, isolated market for products; this means that firms, large or small, must think in export terms and about foreign competition. Communities must urge their companies to undertake exporting to earn foreign exchange to pay for the growing amount of foreign imports.
- There has been a notable shift in the source of new jobs, according to the economist David Hale.[10] The last decade saw a downsizing of large businesses, an explosive growth of new companies, and a spiraling growth of self-employed. Since 1980, America's 500 largest companies have lost more than four million jobs, while small businesses have created 20 million new ones. Promoting small business would call for reversing an earlier emphasis on large business retention and attraction. If small business constitutes the engine of the job generation process, then places should promote those things that facilitate small business growth: entrepreneurs, commercialization of new technologies, research parks and business incubator centers, incentives for small business, and attracting venture capital. In the 1990-92 recession, small business formation slowed because of new restrictions and higher costs, which hampered new job growth.
- Businesses increasingly think of the advantages of international locations rather than domestic locations alone, giving rise to joint ventures, sourcing abroad within a production chain, and worldwide integration of research, development, purchasing, production, and marketing activities. Nearly one-half of the world's exports of nonagriculture products originate in companies that are units in a multinational network, and nearly one-quarter of these exports consist of exchanges among units of individual multinational firms. Businesses are footloose, more capable than ever of adjusting to changes in their environment, far more than are places.[11]
- The increased mobility of businesses has contributed to much accelerated job turnover and employment mobility. Gone are job se-

curity, the notion of several decades with a single employer, and a gold watch at age 65 retirement. Today, an estimated one in five people leaves his or her job each year—more than 20 million job turnovers—due to retirement, to layoffs, to job reclassification.[12] Competitive forces have transformed the world of work and business investment in worker training. Training costs are being driven by a shrinking product life cycle, technical job requirements, and middle management downsizing. Accordingly, PHH Fantus projects that by the year 2000 it will cost $20,000 to train a new hire for manufacturing firms opening a new U.S. plant.

INTERGOVERNMENTAL POWER SHIFTS. Technological advances and global competition have given rise to extensive debates at all government levels—city, state, and nation—about the appropriate role of government intervention into troubled places and industries. Marketplace shifts and changes have occurred at a rate far faster than government's capacity to respond. The unceasing globalization of markets has produced at least three different camps on the role of government. One group—the *protectionists*—favor high tariffs and quotas to protect America's established industries and places—usually the declining industries—from losing jobs to foreign competitors. A second group— the *government activists*—want the government to engage in active industrial policy to define and assist those growth industries deemed to constitute America's best future. A third group—the *free traders*—want the government to steer clear of both protectionism and industrial policy, leaving the sorting out to the market.

U.S. policymakers in the 1970s debated whether there should be greater federal government interventions into the marketplace to aid ailing places and industries and to abet new industries. By the late 1980s, however, such discussions not only diminished as a result of federal resource constraints and large federal deficits but more practically were also overtaken by realization of the great difficulties of identifying future growth industries in such a rapidly changing world economy. In the wake of the 1990–1992 recession, industrial policy had returned again under the rubric of "growth policies for the 1990s" with the prospect that it again would be widely debated.[13]

Greater openness of the U.S. economy, a high degree of capital mobility, and flexible exchange rates, have altered the effectiveness of macroeconomic policies on the domestic economy. U.S. policymakers readily acknowledged that policies could no longer be set independently of our major trading partners and creditors. Harvard's Robert Reich, a prominent industrial policy advocate in the 1970s, belatedly acknowledged this change, noting that the nation-state has become obsolete in its capacity to micro-manage state and localities' economic adjustments and is too large to do so effectively.[14]

A new view about the federal government's responsibilities for helping local economies grew during the Reagan administration. In the 1960s the federal government assumed greater fiscal and programmatic responsibility for states and localities. Beginning in the late 1970s direct federal fiscal assistance for these governments has been reduced, making these governments more responsible for generating funds for schools, health, and various social services. Gradually, many communities found themselves with insufficient financial resources to support many of their public services—a condition worsened by the 1990–92 national recession.

The main point is that places have been heavily affected by external forces related to rapidly changing technologies, global competition, and intergovernmental power shifts. Not only must communities respond effectively to these threats but they must also do a better job of anticipating their occurrence.

WHAT ARE PLACES DOING TO SOLVE THEIR PROBLEMS?

Troubled places are responding to these developments and changes in a variety of ways. A few do nothing because they lack leadership or are resigned to their fate. Most of them scramble for more resources, thinking that money is the solution to their problems rather then diagnosing their problems from a systematic perspective. These towns and cities lobby their state governments for bailout money. Some issue more bonds and raise taxes. Eventually, they try to cut local government costs: they slow down payment of their bills, they dismiss city workers, and in some more recent cases, they start privatizing public services to save money.

Beyond the effort to husband their financial resources, many communities roll out aggressive programs to attract industry and tourists. Their local chambers of commerce and economic development agencies hunt down leads of possible businesses they might attract with handsome inducements. Today the states of New Jersey and Connecticut keep raiding New York City for corporate headquarters, factories, investments, visitors, and tourists. The states of Wisconsin, Indiana, and Michigan compete vigorously to attract Chicago-area residents as summer vacationers. South Dakota successfully competed with Minnesota to attract meat processing plants and service facilities to its area. Kentucky competed successfully with several other American states, using tax abatements and other business incentives, to convince a Japanese auto manufacturer to build its new auto plant there. Less successfully, a number of California municipalities failed in their bid to attract a major new technology research center; instead, a consortium of corporations in the semiconductor field decided to locate their major new research and development facility in Austin, Texas. The escalating competition between states for business attraction has the marks of a zero-sum game or worse, a negative-sum game, in that even the winner ultimately becomes the loser.

Communities are also working hard to prevent their current businesses from exiting in search of lower-cost labor or taxes or higher inducements. Witness New York City's efforts to retain its businesses:

Dateline, New York City, November 1988: In the wake of losing corporate headquarters—Union Carbide, 1980 (4,000 jobs); J. C. Penney, 1987 (4,000 jobs); Mobil (1,600 jobs) and more than 10,000 back office jobs of such major financial institutions as Merrill Lynch; Bankers' Trust; PaineWebber; and Donaldson, Lufkin and Jenrette—New York City offers Chase Bank a record $235 million in financial rewards over 25 years to move 5,000 workers to Brooklyn rather than to Jersey City. To match the lower costs and other advantages offered by competing areas, NYC has developed the art of high-stakes deal making for the purpose of business retention; $50 million for Shearson Lehman (1984); $100 million for NBC, (1987); $85 million for Drexel Burnham (1988); and a yet to be disclosed amount for Citicorp (1988). Henceforth, any company, large or small, currently located in New York City, that moves above 96th street in Manhattan or to the city's four other boroughs, according to city policy, will have a standing offer to negotiate a retention package.[15]

Communities also compete by financing some expensive attractions to the area that might make it a stronger tourist or business destination.

The assumption is that if something works in place A, it is likely to work in place B. Designing downtown pedestrian shopping malls or riverfront festival markets, sports stadiums, museums, research parks, and convention centers are a few examples of what often has come to be regarded as panaceas for troubled places. This approach is generally characterized by piecemeal, ad hoc actions, that seek a single solution for multifaceted problems. Unfortunately, many of these ad hoc investments produce more expense than income. Memphis, Tennessee, started building a Great American Pyramid to house its sports arena but today is left with a cavernous thirty-two-story pyramid that stands vacant except for a basketball arena. Consider Flint, Michigan's abortive effort at revitalization:

Flint, Michigan, found itself in a deteriorating condition in the 1980s. General Motors (GM) chose to close plant production as their sales declined. While still the city with the most GM employees, the city officials needed to rethink Flint's future. One plan called for remaking Flint as a short-trip destination for midwesterners looking for a weekend of entertainment. The city financed a giant theme park called Autoworld. In addition a new Hyatt Hotel was constructed and some renovations to the downtown shopping area were undertaken. It all sounded good, but quickly failed. Autoworld was a pale imitation of Disney. The hotel and shopping improvements were too thin to present an image of a real transformation. And the surrounding deteriorated areas turned off visitors. The hotel ultimately closed down. Downtown Flint today consists of mostly shuttered stores, and a few bars and X-rated movie theaters. Flint's troubles were dramatized in Michael Moore's *Roger & Me*, a pseudo-documentary film that basically trashed GM's treatment of Flint and Flint's inept response to its crisis.

Along with these moves, places intensify their communication expenditure and image making. The communities try to float positive stories and ads, and prevent negative news stories describing their plight. These communities think they are carrying out marketing programs, when in fact they are only undertaking promotion programs. Marketing provides a more comprehensive problem-solving framework, of which promotion is only a small part.

A few communities respond to their crisis by undertaking serious *market-oriented strategic planning*. They appoint a top-level commission of public and private citizens who evaluate the community's troubles and their underlying causes, examine the place's current and potential opportunities, and establish a long-term vision of what the community can be and achieve in the long run. They recognize that a community is an *export-import center* and that the community's survival, if not prosperity, depends on figuring out what it can produce and export to earn enough revenue to buy the products and services that it must import from elsewhere.

Few cities had more problems than Cleveland in the 1970s. The lasting image was of a city besieged by incompetent leadership, financial failure, civil worker strikes, and a hopeless school system. The citizens, finding themselves unable to attract new companies or tourists, launched the New Cleveland campaign. "The campaign had three objectives:

- To identify and document Cleveland's strengths and continuing development
- To communicate these matters in a credible, creative, and effective manner commensurate with the quality of the city itself
- To restore and enhance local, regional, national and international confidence in Cleveland."[16]

The city's business and public leaders supported new construction in the deteriorating downtown area. They invested in infrastructure improvements in transportation and access. Cleveland broadcasted its revitalization story using direct mail, booklets, and newsletters, all targeted to specific opinion leaders and buyers. As a consequence of these and other initiatives, Cleveland's marketing program won All-American city honors in both 1982 and 1984. Even more significantly, public opinion began to turn in favor of Cleveland as new business moved in and citizens gained confidence and exuded a positive attitude about their city's future prospects.

WHAT SHOULD PLACES BE DOING TO SOLVE THEIR PROBLEMS?

A central proposition of this book is that marketplace shifts and changes occur far faster than a community's capacity to react and respond. Buyers of the goods and services that a place can offer (i.e., business firms, tourists, investors, among others) have a decided advantage over place sellers (i.e., local communities, regions, and other places that seek economic growth). The challenge of place marketing is to strengthen the capacity of communities and regions to adapt to the changing marketplace, seize opportunities, and sustain their vitality.

This book presents a fresh approach—called *strategic place marketing*—for the revitalization of towns, cities, regions, and nations. Strategic marketing calls for designing a community to satisfy the needs of its key constituencies. Place marketing succeeds when stakeholders such as citizens, workers, and business firms derive satisfaction from their community, and when visitors, new businesses, and investors find their expectations met. Place marketing, at its core, embraces four activities:

- Designing the right mix of community features and services
- Setting attractive incentives for the current and potential buyers and users of its goods and services
- Delivering a place's products and services in an efficient, accessible way
- Promoting the place's values and image so that potential users are fully aware of the place's distinctive advantages

The major elements in strategic place marketing are shown in figure 1-3. The initial task is to organize a planning group made up of citizens, business people, and local and regional government officials. This planning group validates the importance of collaboration between the public and private sector and the need to involve all stakeholders in shaping a place's future. The planning group's charge is threefold: First, it must define and diagnose the community's condition, its major problems, and their causes. Second, it must develop a vision of the long-term solution to the community's problems based on a realistic assessment of the community's values, resources, and opportunities. Third, it must develop a long-term plan of action involving several intermediate stages of investment and transformation.

The long-term solution involves improving four major marketing factors found in every community: First, it must assure that basic services

FIGURE 1-3
Levels of Place Marketing

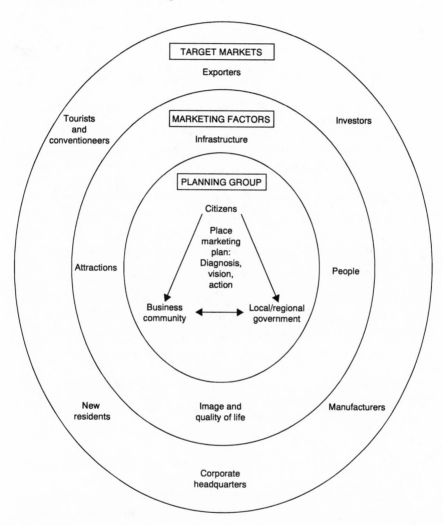

are being provided and infrastructure maintained to the satisfaction of its citizens, businesses, and visitors. Second, the place may need new attractions to improve the quality of life to sustain current business and public support and to attract new investment, businesses, or people. Third, the community needs to communicate its improved features and life quality through a vigorous image and communication program. Finally, the place must generate support from its citizens, leaders, and current institutions for making the place hospitable and enthusiastic about attracting new companies, investment, and visitors to its community.

These four marketing factors, in the final analysis, affect the place's success in attracting and satisfying its five potential target markets: goods and service producers, corporate headquarters and regional offices, outside investment and export markets, tourism and hospitality business, and new residents.

The fortunes of places depends in the final analysis on the collaboration of the public and private sectors—teamwork among governmental units, business firms, voluntary and civic associations, and marketing organizations. Unlike purely business or commercial product marketing, place marketing requires the active support of public and private agencies, interest groups, and citizens.

A place's potential depends not so much on a place's location, climate, and natural resources as it does on its human will, skill, energy, values, and organization. For a place to succeed, it must be able to carry out the following fundamental tasks:

1. Interpreting what is happening in the broad environment.
2. Understanding the needs, wants, and behavior choices of specific internal and external constituencies.
3. Building a realistic vision of what the place can be.
4. Creating an actionable plan to complement the vision.
5. Building internal consensus and effective organization.
6. Evaluating at each stage the progress being achieved with the action plan.

CONCLUSION

No two places are likely to sort out their strategies, use their resources, define their products, or implement their plans in the same way. Places differ in their histories, cultures, politics, leadership, and particular ways of managing public–private relationships Accordingly, places have to acknowledge that there are no simple panaceas, doctrinaire prescriptions, or magical elixirs. Instead, place marketers are guided by an amalgam of economic theories, demographic and industrial trend forecasts, and political understanding, case examples, and practical experience. We believe that *strategic place marketing* is the most adaptative and productive approach to the problems of places.

2

How Places Market Themselves

We have seen how places increasingly compete with other places to attract their share of tourists, businesses, and investment. The marketing of places has become a leading economic activity and, in some cases, the dominant generator of local wealth. Consider a few examples:

- After an intense competition among cities, the International Olympic Committee chose the city of Atlanta, Georgia, as the site of the 1996 Summer Olympic Games. The value to Atlanta, its businesses, and its citizens is estimated at more than $3 billion.
- The battle for the supercollider project ignited an intense competition among the states. The project offered the winning state a large number of high-tech science positions and the short-term benefit of thousands of construction jobs. The states went all out to impress the visiting federal representatives. A typical reception committee included brass bands, helicopter rides over proposed sites, banquets, museum visits, and welcoming banners draped over main street. The states also spent money on environmental impact studies, lobbying in Washington, D.C., and for public relations addressing local and national concerns. In the end, Texas won the prize after pledging millions of their own money and benefiting from their considerable influence in Washington, D.C.
- The intense competition for the United Airlines Maintenance Fa-

cility ended with the prize being awarded to Indianapolis. Two of the finalists had different views of the competition. Louisville withdrew, claiming the bidding was unfair. An Oklahoma City councilman saw the competition differently: "We had a good run at it, but we didn't get there."[1]

Economic development has long been a priority of places, states, regions, and nations. Only in the past decade have a few places shifted from a rather narrow view of economic development to a broad set of strategies to attract new businesses, retain old ones, develop overseas trade, build tourism, and attract outside investors. Places have transformed their ad hoc economic campaigns into highly sophisticated marketing strategies aimed at building competitive markets, targeting specific buyers, and positioning the community's resources to respond to specialized buyer needs and desires.

Organizing a program to develop and market a place requires a thorough grasp of target markets. In this chapter, we address three questions: (1) Who are the main target markets of place marketers? (2) How do place marketers market their place? and (3) Who are the major place marketers?

WHO ARE THE MAIN TARGETS OF PLACE MARKETERS?

Most places are interested in growth, but not growth at any cost. Places distinguish between three groups that might be drawn to a place: people and businesses worth attracting; people and businesses who are acceptable but need not be specifically targeted; and people and businesses to avoid or discourage. In the last group, for example, are ex-convicts, drug dealers, inveterate gamblers, prostitutes, and questionable or shaky businesses. Even here, Las Vegas or Atlantic City would want to attract some of these groups, such as inveterate gamblers.

When a place wants to attract a buyer category such as tourists the place must carefully define this category in order to achieve its goals. For example, Finland would like to attract more tourists during the winter and fewer during the summer, when its vacation areas are overcrowded; it would be happier attracting wealthy tourists from Switzerland rather than poor tourists from Hungary; it would like to attract Australian tourists but has a better chance of attracting British tourists.

Or consider a place such as Florence, Italy, that thrives on tourist expenditures. Possessing one of the greatest treasure houses of Renaissance art in the world, Florence attracts visitors who want to experience its art, history, and cultural life. Yet, even this market is a complex one, consisting of different age and income groups; professional groups, such as art curators, European historians, and their professional associations and conventions; students of Michelangelo, Donatello, and other great masters of painting and sculpture found in Florence; perhaps even business firms in the fields of art supply, paint manufacturing, and the graphic arts, attracted to Florence for business meetings or to create new sales branches.

Or consider New York City, where tens of thousands of square feet of office space stand vacant because of the out-migration of service industries. Surely, a major target market for New York City consists of U.S. and overseas firms in industries such as financial services, real estate management, publishing, tourism and conventions, and in industries that produce cultural products such as the visual and performing arts. New York City's target markets are broader still. For example, New York is the headquarters of the United Nations diplomatic missions and of numerous international agencies. Should it seek to attract the headquarters of other major nonprofit organizations such as relief agencies that work closely with United Nations agencies, and agencies dealing with drug abuse, homelessness, and crime control?

All said, a place can try to attract any of four broad target markets: (1) visitors, (2) residents and workers, (3) business and industry, and (4) export markets. (See table 2–1.) We comment briefly on these target markets here and examine them further in chapters 8, 9, 10, and 11.

Visitors

The *visitor market* consists of two broad groups: *business* and *nonbusiness visitors*. *Business visitors* come to a place to attend a business meeting or convention, to check out a site, to buy or sell something. *Nonbusiness visitors* include *tourists* who want to see the place and *travelers* who are visiting family and friends.

Every visitor to a place spends money on food and lodging, local products, and other goods and services. This spending has a multiplier effect on local income, employment, and on the tax revenues generated by businesses. Presumably, these visitors spend more in a given place than the cost incurred by that place in providing them with ser-

TABLE 2-1
The Four Main Target Markets

1. VISITORS
    a. Business visitors (attending a business meeting or convention, checking out a site, coming to buy or sell something)
    b. Nonbusiness visitors (tourists and travelers)

2. RESIDENTS AND WORKERS
    a. Professionals (scientists, physicians, etc.)
    b. Skilled workers
    c. Wealthy individuals
    d. Investors
    e. Entrepreneurs
    f. Unskilled workers (domestics, migrants, etc.)

3. BUSINESS AND INDUSTRY
    a. Heavy industry
    b. "Clean" industry (assembly, high-tech, service companies, etc.)
    c. Entrepreneurs

4. EXPORT MARKETS
    a. Other localities within the domestic markets
    b. International markets

vices. The greater the number of visitors attracted, and the less the cost imposed by each visitor, the greater the net income to the place they visit. Similarly, the longer the visitors stay, the more they spend. Places would, therefore, prefer to target those visitors who spend the most per day and stay the longest.

Most places attract visitors by setting up tourism and convention bureaus. In large cities, these are typically separate organizations that compete with each other for public funds. In Chicago, for example, tourism is handled by the Chicago Tourism Council while the Chicago Convention and Visitors Bureau manages business visitors. Each organization claims that it can produce more net income than the other. The Chicago Convention and Visitors Bureau claims that a trades-show visitor typically spends more than 500 percent more per stay than a tourist in Chicago; therefore, it argues that it should receive a larger share of public funds to promote these activities.[2]

Tourism bureaus must decide on how to allocate their funds to competing tourism destinations within their area. In the province of British Columbia, potential tourism destinations compete for a limited pool of grants, loans, and professional advice from the Ministry of Municipal Affairs. In the United States, 54 county-based tourism agencies in Pennsylvania compete for $7.7 million in tourism promotion grants.[3]

The tourism bureau must also decide between attracting a mass market of lowspending, short-stay tourists or a smaller market of highspending, long-stay tourists. In addition they must decide on how much to spend trying to attract tourists from their region, from other regions within the country, and from other countries. Chicago, for example, attracts most of its visitors from the Midwest; some from the East Coast; fewer from the West Coast; and some from foreign countries, particularly Ireland. Greece, a country highly dependent on tourism, carefully monitors changes over time in the composition of its visitors. As part of its marketing planning process, Greece analyzes the origin of visitors from more than thirty-five countries.

Tourism bureaus must also decide on the specific groups to attract. Israel, for example, must decide how many funds should be spent to attract Jewish visitors, Jewish settlers, Christian pilgrims, Muslim pilgrims, professional and amateur archaeologists, historians, and other scholars.

Convention bureaus, on the other hand, must decide how to allocate their funds between *improving* the place's convention and meeting facilities and *promoting* these facilities to targeted industries, business firms, and trade associations. A city with limited convention or hotel facilities, cannot compete for large national conventions such as CON-EXPO held by the Construction Industry Manufacturers Association, the National Restaurants' Show, or the annual convention of the National Association of Medical Equipment Suppliers. Even in pursuing smaller trade and professional associations, a place finds itself competing against other convention bureaus in similar size cities. Lead times for booking these conventions run three to ten years into the future; so strategies and marketing activities require well-thought-out plans. For prestige events, such as the Superbowl or the Olympics, the place wars are particularly fierce and long-term strategic marketing is critical.

In the midst of the visitor drive, there is irony in the fact that a place's citizens are often divided over the desirability of attracting large numbers of visitors. Critics cite the following social costs of visitors:

1. *The visitors might damage the environment by abusing facilities and nature.* The Finnish people, for example, resent German vacationers who often come in large numbers, stay at camping grounds, leave litter, and spend little money.
2. *Some visitors might be undesirable.* Amsterdam's reputation as a very tolerant city attracts a large number of "flower children" and drug users, with the consequence of an increasing crime rate.
3. *The visitors often come during seasons that crowd the facilities the indigenous population would normally use.* Residents living in the French Riviera complain that they can hardly use their beaches in August because of the huge influx of tourists and traffic.
4. *Tourism gives rise to low-paying jobs in service industries—restaurants and hotels—which may be less desirable than other patterns of business developments.* Andreas Papandreou, the former Greek prime minister, resisted developing Greek tourism further by saying that he didn't want to turn Greece into "a nation of waiters."

The point is that a place must develop a set of objectives and strategies toward visitors rather than promoting haphazardly. Once a place decides on which visitors and how many visitors it wants, it can begin to build up its facilities and infrastructure. It does this by researching what its target visitors seek in different destinations and what they seek in coming to the place. Many a community has built up its visitor infrastructure without clear target groups in mind, only to be left with half-empty hotels and facilities.

Residents and Workers

A second important target market for places is residents and workers. A place may want to augment its number of unskilled workers; for many years, Germany and France actively recruited foreign low-skilled laborers from Turkey, Algeria, and Morocco. Places with aging populations—such as Vienna and Sweden—work hard to attract or retain young people in the community. Some small U.S. towns are desperate to attract a physician and dentist to live in the town; otherwise the townspeople go without medical help.

On the other hand, some places are so attractive that, finding themselves overwhelmed by an in-migration of new residents and workers, they lack the facilities to accommodate all the newcomers. Some have launched no growth or "demarketing" campaigns that seek to limit their physical and population growth. Some places have even created negative images of themselves to discourage people from settling there. Oregon circulated stories to discourage new residents: "You can tell when it's summer in Oregon; the rain feels warmer."

When cities undertake to attract specific residents or workers, they must develop appropriate incentives. Young families, for example, place emphasis on schools and on public safety as major factors in choosing a place to settle in. Older households, on the other hand, are likely to pay attention to cultural and recreational facilities.

Business and Industry

Attracting business, industry, and economic investment constitutes a third category of target markets. Places typically seek to attract new businesses and industries to provide jobs for their citizens and revenues for their treasuries. In the past, places have chiefly sought "smokestack" industries such as steel and autos. Today, they are more interested in attracting "clean industries" such as banking, catalog and subscription services, and especially high-tech firms. Communities also are usually committed to retaining existing businesses and fostering their expansion.

Places need to understand how business firms make their location decisions. As a rule, business firms rate places as potential sites in terms of their business climates and regulatory environments; the caliber of the labor force; the availability of infrastructural benefits such as access to airports, good roads, and mass transportation; the quality of the school system and other types of training institutions; and the quality of life. Business firms also respond to relocation inducements and incentives such as tax concessions and tax deferrals, inexpensive land and infrastructure subsidies, and subsidized training facilities. Some states, such as Wisconsin, view the relocation decision as a call to battle; see Exhibit 2-1.

A place can maintain and strengthen its economic base in four ways: First, the place must retain its current businesses, or at least the desirable ones. Retention is a major problem for New York City in that several major corporations have moved or threatened to move important labor-intensive functions out of the city into lower cost locations. More businesses in various cities are playing the game of "holdup": If the city

---

EXHIBIT 2-1

Forward Wisconsin: Target Marketing for a Competitive Edge

Forward Wisconsin is a privately backed economic development group that runs a highly sophisticated marketing operation. Wisconsin is well known for its extremely aggressive marketing program that raids its neighbors frequently and successfully. Forward Wisconsin accomplishes its goals by using a focused approach that markets Wisconsin as a desirable business location.

There are six targets that it identifies:

Specific industries. Industries such as biotechnology, food processing, and printing that match-up well with state strengths.

Quickly growing companies. Fast-growth companies that need new facilities.

Crucial geographical targets. Prime targets are surrounding states, because they have a history of moving across state lines to Wisconsin. East and West coast areas where quality

---

doesn't meet our terms, we'll leave. These are no longer idle threats; competitive locations are becoming more active as raiders raising the ante in the bidding wars. Each place must reexamine the location value it offers to the existing companies. Places cannot wantonly raise business taxes and neglect to provide modern business services if they want to retain their critical industries and companies. The ransom game is a dual-edge sword. If a place offers too little to keep a business, it will lose the business; if it pays too much, it also loses.

Second, the place must devise plans and services to help existing businesses expand. When these businesses sell more products to more distant markets, they produce more income and jobs within the local economy. The city, for example, can sponsor training programs to help managers and workers improve their skills; improve the transportation, communication, and energy infrastructure; facilitate bank loans to

of life has deteriorated are also seen as good places to raid.

Links to Wisconsin. The program identifies executives who have vacationed or lived in Wisconsin. It checks tourism organizations for name leads.

Minority businesses. It tries to attract minority businesses to Wisconsin.

Opportunity targets. It searches for companies undergoing changes in company status, new CEO leadership, or seeking new Midwestern locations.

To reach the targets, Forward Wisconsin conducts direct mail campaigns, telemarketing, prospect visits, trade shows, and special events. Even more telling is the sheer volume of the effort. In a marketing year, it will send out 40,000 personalized letters, speak with 3,000 companies over the phone, and participate in a mix of events ranging from hosting a reception before a Milwaukee Symphony concert for executives to personal visits by teams of their economic developers to raidable places such as Minneapolis–St. Paul and Chicago.

When Forward Wisconsin visits your place, it is best to hide the children.

Source: Marketing Plan of Forward Wisconsin.

local businesses; and provide specialized amenities tailored to specific business needs.

Third, the place must make it easier for entrepreneurs to start up new businesses. David Birch of M.I.T. has documented that most new jobs in the United States have been provided by new business start-ups and not from expansion of America's largest companies.[4] Therefore, a place must understand and foster the conditions that attract and support local entrepreneurs. These include developing a strong small business agency to train and advise entrepreneurs, encouraging local banks to make obtaining loans easier for start-up businesses, providing loans, generating equity lending, bringing together venture capitalists and entrepreneurs, promoting research parks, helping secure government contracts, and using various incentives to aid business start-ups. Exhibit 2–2 describes Iowa's campaign to attract new business.

EXHIBIT 2-2
State for Sale

Iowa has a problem. The state is losing population. Between 1975 and 1985, Iowa experienced a dramatic downturn in agriculture with reductions in new housing units, nonagricultural jobs, and contract construction. Although Iowa has one of the most distinguished public and private school systems in America, Iowa graduates are moving out of state because of the lack of jobs.

Not surprisingly, Iowa has launched an all-out campaign to industrialize. In 1987, the state legislature passed a major training and benefits program for new business in Iowa, including the repeal of machinery and equipment taxes, repeal of personal property taxes (including corporate inventories), the creation of tax credits for new jobs, tax abatements for new R&D facilities, and interest buy downs on business loans. In addition, Iowa has no unitary tax on corporate income, a right-to-work law, deductibility of federal income tax, ample industrial revenue bond financing, a single factor corporate income tax, and a foreign trade zone.

"The structure of the Iowa Industrial New Jobs Training Program (INJTP) allows employees to select the trainees of their choice, train them anywhere in the world, and then receive a 50 percent wage and benefit reimbursement for up to one year."

For Iowa, no employee is untrainable, no tax structure too low, and no cost too high.

Sources: Diana C. Woods researched Iowa's marketing packages in June 1988 at Northwestern University. Quotation from advertising insert provided by the Division of Job Training, Des Moines, Iowa, March 1992.

Fourth, a place can aggressively attract outside companies or their factories to move to its location. Most states have an economic development agency or nonprofit corporation whose job it is to target, visit, and solicit outside companies to invest resources in their location. In some cases, it is questionable whether the rewards of attracting a company are equal to the incentives places offer them:

Six states competed vigorously to attract a new Japanese auto plant; Tennessee won the prize by offering a huge set of concessions. For months, [Tennessee] state officials met with Japanese envoys, granting demand after demand. They agreed to highway improvements and new sewer lines. They promised tax abatement, discounted utility rates and offered Saturday language lessons. Tennessee would throw in driving lessons, too. The deal was done.[5]

Kentucky engaged in a spirited contest to snare Toyota Motor Corporation. It spent more than $125 million—including $55 million in worker-training grants alone—to persuade Toyota to build an auto plant in Georgetown. By the time all the tax incentives are accounted for, the total bill may exceed $350 million. State and local officials vehemently defend these costs on the grounds that the current and prospective benefits far outweigh such concessions.

Fort Wayne, Indiana, invested $15 million in 1985 to provide a transportation hub for Burlington Air Express only to see Burlington shop around for more public funds in 1989. Toledo, Ohio, responded to Burlington's needs by offering to put up $50 million in 1989 to build a highway interchange, make runway improvements, and build a hub facility for the company. This subsidy worked out to at least $125,000 per job! Taxpayers are beginning to question whether these concessions are inordinate giveaways or necessary investments. Mayor Fred Helmke, on losing this battle with Toledo, commented, "We're players in economic development, but we're not suckers."[6]

Clearly the ante has risen so fast that each new concession becomes the starting point for the next negotiation. The result is inducement inflation and a negative-sum game for all except the Japanese. Businesses from other countries have followed the Japanese lead in pyramiding concessions from the place bidders.

Places need to choose the best mix of the four industry buildup strategies. They must define the types and mix of industries to pursue. Many places try to avoid attracting polluting industries, sweatshop industries, and industries that draw undesirable residents and visitors (such as gambling and prostitution). Border cities such as San Antonio, Texas, have had rousing public debates on whether to exploit the benefits of low-cost labor or to seek markets with more advanced technologies and higher paying jobs. Cities need to decide whether they should build a diversified economy or one based on a few specialized industries. Large cities such as Chicago, Philadelphia, and Boston, thrive on a diversified industry base. Other cities thrive on one or a few specialized industries such as Rochester, Minnesota, (health care and computers), Nashville, Tennessee, (health care, military, and musical entertainment), and Pittsburgh, Pennsylvania, (computer software, robots, and medical technology). As desirable as diversification may seem, most communities do not have the luxury of being able to play this game and, instead, must seek niches and specialized markets.

Export Markets

A fourth target market is exports—the ability of a city or a region to produce goods and services that other places, people, and business firms are willing to purchase. Exports are the lifeblood of city-states such as Singapore and Hong Kong, whose natural resources are too limited to produce everything they need, nor can their limited populations absorb all the goods and services they can produce. The wealth of such places depends on aggressively exporting products to other countries, and then using the export earnings to finance the imports of raw materials and other goods that they require.

Yet, Singapore and Hong Kong are the rule, not the exceptions. All cities, states, and nations must import; they need automobiles, computers, clothing, and so on. Therefore, they must produce some goods and services that can be exported. Every place must encourage its local businesses to expand their sales beyond the local market into the large domestic market as well as foreign markets.

A few places have managed to create strong brand names and images for the products and services they supply. Italy enjoys a strong image for producing high-quality fashion goods; and the Made in Japan label produces instant consumer confidence in Japanese cars and consumer electronics. Some American states have managed to brand some of their products: examples include Florida oranges, Wisconsin cheese, Kentucky bourbon, and Idaho potatoes. Once a place has established a strong brand name for one particular product line, it may be able to transfer its positive image to other related product lines.

On the other hand, certain places have poor reputations for the quality of their goods, and this inhibits exports. Thus, Yugoslavia's car, the

Yugo, did not sell well in the United States because of Yugoslavia's poor manufacturing reputation. Ford car dealers had a difficult time selling their Mexican-manufactured cars in the United States, because of Mexico's weak image. (Ironically, Ford's higher-quality cars were made in Mexico.) In general, cities, regions, and nations can project an image that either helps or hurts their manufacturers' ability to sell goods elsewhere.

Places are well advised to aim for some diversification of their industries and target markets. Diversity, however, is not always an option; smaller places have no choice but to focus on one particular market. An example are the Caribbean Islands that focus almost exclusively on tourism because they possess few other resources that can rival the appeal of their sun and sand.

A government export agency can contribute in several ways to promoting exports: The agency can offer subsidies to local businesses and insurance devices that reduce a company's risks. It can sponsor training programs and offer technical assistance to familiarize companies with export procedures. It can enlist public relations firms to improve a community's image in target export markets. Government export agencies can sponsor overseas trade shows for a community's products, open foreign offices to aid local industries, and take local business executives on foreign trade missions to make contacts and solicit orders.

HOW DO PLACE MARKETERS MARKET THEIR PLACES?

Increasingly places rely on four broad strategies to attract visitors and residents, build their industrial base, and increase exports. These strategies are image marketing, attractions marketing, infrastructure marketing, and people marketing (see table 2–2). We examine these strategies in the following paragraphs.

Image Marketing

Under an image strategy, the place hires an advertising agency or public relations firm to identify, develop, and disseminate a strong positive image for the place. This is often the least expensive of the three strategies, since the place is not investing money in adding attractions or improving its infrastructure, but only "communicating" something about its present features to others.

TABLE 2–2
Major Actors in Place Marketing

LOCAL ACTORS
  Public sector actors
    1. Mayor and/or city manager
    2. Urban planning department
    3. Business development department
    4. Tourist bureau
    5. Convention bureau
    6. Public information bureau
    7. Infrastructure managers (transportation, education, sanitation)

  PRIVATE SECTOR ACTORS
    1. Real estate developers and agents
    2. Financial institutions (commercial banks, mortgage banks, pension funds, etc.)
    3. Electricity and gas utilities
    4. Chamber of commerce and other local business organizations
    5. Hospitality and retail industries (hotels, restaurants, department stores, other retailers)
    6. Tour packagers and travel agencies
    7. Unions
    8. Taxi companies
    9. Architects

REGIONAL ACTORS
    1. Regional economic development agencies
    2. Regional tourist boards
    3. County and state government officials

NATIONAL ACTORS
    1. Political head of government
    2. Various ministries
    3. National unions

INTERNATIONAL ACTORS
    1. Embassies and consulates
    2. International chambers of commerce

The cost and effectiveness of the image strategy depends, of course, on the place's current image and real attributes. A place may find itself in one of six image situations:

1. *Positive image.* Some cities, regions, and countries are blessed with positive images. Stratford-on-Avon, Venice, Santa Fe, and Singapore all conjure up positive images in most people's minds. Though each place may have certain flaws and not appeal to everyone as a destination or place to live or a place for business, they all can be represented positively to others. They don't require changing the image so much as amplifying it and delivering it to more target groups.

2. *Weak image.* Some places are not well known because they are small, lack attractions, or don't advertise. If they want more visibility, they need to build some attractions and advertise them. Other places may have attractive features but may refrain from advertising, not wishing to be overrun with tourists. For instance, several towns along Maine's coast and Oregon's coast prefer not to broadcast their pristine virtues because their antigrowth sentiments outweigh their economic interests. They want to limit the public's awareness.

3. *Negative image.* Many places are stuck with a negative image: Detroit is the murder capital of the United States, Miami is the vice capital, Colombia, South America, is the drug capital, Lebanon is war torn, and Bangladesh is poverty stricken. These places, if anything, want to curb their image distribution. They would like less news attention, rather than more; they would like to discover some hidden gem in their makeup that might provide a launching pad for a new image that covers up the old. North Dakota, for example, considered legislation to drop *North* from its name because of its apparent negative image—a cold, barren state losing population and business at a rapid rate. Yet, if the place advertises a new image but continues to be the place that gave rise to the old image, the image strategy will not succeed.

4. *Mixed image.* Most places contain a mixture of positive and negative elements. Many people want to visit San Francisco for its many attractions, but some visitors fear it as drug-ridden and a gay center. Washington, D.C., is a beautiful city but its exploding crime rate now contends with Detroit's. Visiting

Italy is a distinct pleasure as long as one isn't there when worker strikes occur in airlines, railroads, police stations, hotels, and museums. Places with mixed images typically emphasize the positive and avoid the negative in preparing their image campaigns.

5. *Contradictory image.* A few places emit contradictory images in that people hold opposite views about some features of the place. Some people think of the Virgin Islands as a safe tourist destination and others see it as a dangerous place, remembering the tourist murders some years ago. Some people think of Pittsburgh as a polluted city because of its coal and steel industry and others know it as a clean-air, award-winning city. Los Angeles, the brunt of many smog, traffic, and crime attacks during the 1980s, had revived its downtown, reintroduced light rail, and is reforming its police department. Here the strategy challenge is to accentuate the positive so that people eventually stop believing in the opposite, no-longer-true image. Image reversals, however, are difficult to accomplish as illustrated by the negative media coverage experienced by Los Angeles during and after the South Central riots.

6. *Overly attractive image.* Some places are cursed with too much attractiveness that might be spoiled if they promote themselves further. To fight the problems of traffic congestion, crowded schools, water pollution, and other costs of development, a group called Citizens for Limited Growth is trying to stem the tide of new residents moving to San Diego. Albuquerque and Santa Fe, New Mexico, have spawned no-growth movements. Petaluma, California, became famous for a landmark U.S. Supreme Court case on efforts to limit growth by refusing to extend water and sewer lines to proposed new developments. In some extreme cases, cities have actually fabricated and disseminated a negative image to discourage visitors and fortune hunters. They may put out the word that the townspeople are unfriendly or that the weather is bad.

Some places act as if good image work involves inventing a clever slogan. New York City's "The Big Apple" and Minnesota's "Land of 10,000 Lakes" are slogans that have appeared on everything from license plates to jackets. While a catchy phrase might capture attention, it can't do the whole job of image marketing. A place's image must be valid and communicated in many ways through several channels if it is to succeed and take root.

In fact, places typically find it difficult to choose a slogan because most places are multidimensional. In a 1989 meeting, seventy Chicago movers and shakers discussed an image for Chicago; such dimensions were raised as world-class museums, friendliest people, great universities, architectural mecca, America's Riviera, my kind of town, ad infinitum. All these terms may have merit and even truth, but this doesn't make the choice easy. Nor do any of these convey a full picture of the city's riches. As much as Chicago seeks to shed its image as a gangster haven from the 1920s and the blemish of the infamous St. Valentine's Day massacre, television reruns such as "The Untouchables" and a tour of gangster hangouts and the residences of some of Chicago's more legendary gang figures perpetuate its darker image. Some places try to capitalize on a negative, as Haiti did; see exhibit 2–3.

Images aren't easy to develop or change. They require research into how residents and outsiders currently see the place; they require identifying true and untrue elements, as well as strong and weak elements; they require inspiration and choice among contending pictures; they require elaborating the choice in a thousand ways so that the residents, businesses, and others truly express the consensual image; and they require a substantial budget for the image's dissemination.

Attractions

Improving the image is not enough to ensure a place's prosperity. The place needs special features to satisfy the residents and attract outsiders. Some places are fortunate to have a natural attraction, such as the town of Bellogio sitting on Lake Como, or Aspen with its mountain range, or Hawaii with its year-round pleasant weather. Other places benefit from a remarkable legacy of historical buildings such as Athens with its Parthenon, Vicksburg with its antebellum mansions, or Bangkok with its exotic temples and statuary. Still other places have commissioned world-renowned edifices, such as Paris's Eiffel Towel and Arch of Triumph, New York's Empire State Building, India's Taj Mahal, and St. Louis's famed Gateway Arch. Attractions also come, of course, in quieter forms, such as the beautiful system of parks in Minneapolis, Chicago's lakefront, or the outdoor restaurants along Parisian boulevards. Indeed, water has a particular attractiveness for places, and

EXHIBIT 2-3

Voodoo Image

The country of Haiti has a quadruple image problem—poverty, violence, AIDS, and voodoo. The problems are fueled by a long period of nondemocratic and inefficient government. Haiti's negative image is so powerful that only 30,000 tourists are rumored to visit the island each year. It is among a handful of countries that could be considered the Fourth World. Surrounded by such tourism meccas as the Bahamas, Puerto Rico, and the Virgin Islands, Haiti also has some tough competition.

Haiti does possess several desirable attractions such as a warm climate all year round, a beautiful mountainous landscape, and three attractions of human origin: the resorts of Port-a-Prince; the massive fortress, the Citadel; and the world's largest outdoor market. These resources could be the foundation of an energetic tourism campaign if Haiti's powerful negative image could be overcome.

What could lure a visitor to Haiti? A tourism campaign was built around the slogan "Haiti, It's Spellbinding." In this attempt to turn around the image of Haiti, the government tried to capitalize on a negative—Haiti's image as a center for mystical rites. They were targeting the adventure-seeking tourist looking for an alternative to the standard sun and sand vacation experience. To communicate this new image, the new slogan appeared on all tourism posters and brochures and was part of a newspaper and magazine advertising campaign.

This campaign had only a limited effect but it represented progress in developing Haiti's image. Haiti was beginning to understand that image needs to be researched, developed, and distributed. Further research and feedback from the marketplace would lead the government to new assumptions about how to reach their potential markets. Recent political upheaval only adds to the negative image and places all future campaigns on hold.

Sources: Michael Giuliano researched Haiti's image campaign in June 1988 at Northwestern University. Interview with Collette Jefferies, Haiti Government Tourism Bureau, January 5, 1992.

nearly all major cities built on waterways are developing their water-fronts for tourism and recreation.

Today many cities are searching for new attractions to add; they want to build crown jewels. One answer in at least two dozen American cities is stadium-mania; namely, building a new sports stadium, prefer-ably a superdome, either for its present teams or in the hope of attract-ing another city's team. In Memphis, Tennessee, and Jacksonville, Florida, new stadiums sit underutilized in anticipation of major sports teams while costing millions of taxpayers' dollars.

Other attractions are regularly proposed, such as building a giant convention center, converting the downtown area into a walking mall, constructing a waterfront festival marketplace, putting up a dramatic sculpture, developing a museum, creating an entertainment district, or a major shopping street. All of these cost money and are often erected from desperation rather than deliberation. The results are uncertain, and they sometimes backfire. Funds run out before the stadium is com-pleted. The downtown walking mall ends up attracting fewer rather than more people and cries are heard to "de-mall the mall." (For an eval-uation of these "place improvements," see chapter 5.)

Infrastructure

Clearly, neither image nor attractions can provide the whole answer to a place's development. They cannot compensate or cover up for a place's deficiencies. The real fundamentals have to do with infrastructure. A place has to work: Its citizens and visitors must have good transportation, not gridlocks. The city must deliver sufficient, low-cost energy to citizens and businesses, not a series of brownouts. The schools must deliver a qual-ity education, not declining reading scores and growing student dropout rates. People must be able to walk the streets safely, not fear for their lives. The water must be safe to drink, the building codes must be enforced, recreational space must be provided, good hotels and restaurants must be available.

People

The fourth marketing strategy is for a place to market its people, and this might take several forms. South Carolina, for example, boasts about its friendly and down-to-earth folks in its efforts to entice retirees from northern states to move to South Carolina. Austin, Texas, talks about its professional work force in seeking to lure more scientific talent to move there. Salt Lake City, with its large Mormon community, advertises its highly ethical and dedicated workers in targeting certain businesses to relocate there. South Dakota mentions its low-cost, dependable workers to attract insurance and medical claims work to the state.

Other areas may suffer from the opposite problem, that outsiders have a poor image of the people living there. New Yorkers, for example, are seen by many as pushy, rude, unhelpful, and unfriendly. Southwest Airlines, for instance, vowed not to seek a New York route if this would require hiring New Yorkers. Other cities—such as Oakland, California, and Newark, New Jersey—are handicapped because their high crime rates suggest they harbor many dangerous people. Some midwesterners discourage their college-bound youths from applying to California colleges on the notion that California is overrun with con artists, surfers, and unconventional life styles.

In selecting target markets, places must consider the perceived character of their people. The image of their people affects the interest of potential target markets. Places need to encourage their citizens to be more friendly and considerate of visitors and new residents. Places also need to raise the level of their citizens' skills so that they can meet the needs of the target markets.

Now the "attractiveness dilemma" becomes clearer. If a place could, it would first fix its fundamentals (the infrastructure), add some attractions, raise the friendliness and skills of its people, and then broadcast its distinct image. But if the place's infrastructure and finances are poor, it can not raise the money to improve its infrastructure or build attractions. So with limited funds, the place ends up working on image first, and possibly encouraging its people to be friendlier. This is really a bootstrapping approach and often fails. The place needs to repair its fundamentals and yet may not have the money to do it.

WHO ARE THE MAJOR PLACE MARKETERS?

Who implants these place marketing activities to the aforementioned target markets? The work, it turns out, is carried out by legions of individuals and organizations. They are found at the local level, regional level, national level, and international level. (See table 2–2.) Here we focus on local-level actors, those in the public and private sectors.

Public Sector Actors

Typically, place marketing activities are a major responsibility of elected officials. Pressures for place marketing may originate in the private sector as when business is poor, hotels are half-empty, and unemployment is rising. But the responsibility is taken up by the city mayor, city manager, county commissioner, or other public executives. They require a planning department or economic development agency to develop place marketing strategies and plans. These agencies influence and, in some cases, decide on the mix of tourism, industry, and exports to pursue. They in turn work with the public agency managers in charge of transportation, education, recreation, and so on, to implement the plans.

Under effective mayors, cities can often succeed in dramatically improving their conditions. Former Mayor William Schaefer of Baltimore played a central role in the city's revitalization plan which included building major attractions. Mayor Richard Lugar and his successor, William Hudnut, of Indianapolis deserve much of the credit for reviving the economy of Indianapolis through positioning it as an amateur sports capital. And Mayor George Latimer of St. Paul, Minnesota, helped St. Paul shed its image as a poor cousin of Minneapolis and turned it into a vital community of its own. Of course, the mayors rarely accomplish these changes single-handedly. They provide and inspire a vision, appoint able agency heads, and win the support of the many private sector actors whose participation is vital.[7]

Private Sector Actors

In other cases, leadership may come from the private sector. In the Dutch island of Curacao, off the coast of Venezuela, private business people initiated and carried out the revitalization. Most of the credit belongs to Eduardo Halabi, a wealthy real estate and restaurant owner who managed to attract two large American hotel chains to build new hotels on the island. It is not surprising that real estate people have a vital interest in an economy's condition and play a major role in supporting positive action. Similarly, hotel and restaurant operators get involved along with retailers and other business leaders through the local chamber of commerce and trade associations. The financial institutions are also vitally interested; their funding and confidence are necessary to support the design and implementation of place marketing plans.

The real challenge is to coordinate all the public and private interest groups into a cohesive working body that agrees on the ends and the means to be pursued. Too often, within the public sector itself, agencies with overlapping and competing responsibilities lead either to inaction or cross-purpose actions. Some of the private sector actors may disagree with the vision, causing a fracturing of the total effort needed. Bringing all the disparate groups together to support a common cause takes leadership. Managing to turn a city into a successful working entity is infinitely more difficult than managing a single business or government agency (these issues are discussed further in chapter 12).

How Place Actors Sell Their Products

In this section we present two cases to illustrate the diverse and dynamic nature of the place marketing process. The first example, St. Marys, Ontario, Canada, illustrates the workings of a grass roots-led effort to improve a place. The second example, St. Petersburg, Florida illustrates a sophisticated elite-led effort to add an attraction to a place.

ST. MARYS—A PLACE OUT OF THE LIMELIGHT.   The town of St. Marys, Ontario, Canada is only twelve miles from Stratford. Stratford itself is a well-known place marketing success story: It moved dramatically from a small manufacturing city to one of the foremost Shakespearean summer festival cities in the world (see p. 204). St. Marys, with a population of 5,000 and only a ten-minute drive from Stratford, has not benefited from its proximity to Stratford. St. Marys' problem was not only how to develop the town but also whether developing it was desirable. Some St. Marys residents wanted to capitalize on the booming tourism business in neighboring Stratford by positioning St. Marys as a complementary attraction for Stratford tourists. A small number of St. Marys citizens, however, enjoyed the tranquility and heritage of St. Marys and were wary of exposing their place and lifestyle to a flood of tourists.

Those who wanted to market St. Marys, two dozen members of the local Lions Club, were primarily amateurs. They decided to sell the town as a tourist attraction based on the beauty and history of St. Marys. At the turn of the century, St. Marys was the site of a stone quarry and the town had built some unusual stone buildings, including an opera house. The buildings had fallen into disrepair over the years.

The enthusiastic but inexperienced marketers of St. Marys set out to change this.

The club faced immediate problems. The first challenge was to convince townspeople to buy into an investment in becoming a tourist attraction. They held meetings that were sometimes unsettling but in the end, townspeople who were against drawing tourists accepted that it was a better fate than the continued economic deterioration of the downtown area.

The Lions Club raised most of the money through fund-raisers, door-to-door solicitations, and large donations from the older town members who wished to see the city returned to its original condition. Approximately 10 percent of the funds came from two small grants allocated by the province of Ontario.

St. Marys's marketers also had to communicate and package St. Marys tourism experience for their target consumers in Stratford. The association realized that St. Marys attractions were worth at best a half-day trip, unlike a week's activity at Stratford. They needed, therefore, to design and finance walking tours, restaurants, exhibitions, landmarks, stories of the town's history, and a renovated town hall. Needless to say, St. Marys marketers are experiencing a mixed response to their efforts. They remain enthusiastic, however, and are beginning to see the results of their endeavors.[8]

This case illustrates that not all place marketers are professionals with training and experience in marketing, economic development, and communications. Many find themselves needing to acquire rudimentary selling and marketing skills from the ground up.

ST. PETERSBURG—A GRAND RAIDER. We now move to an example of superpower place warfare in which the city of St. Petersburg, Florida, engaged a huge arsenal of human and financial resources to attract the Chicago White Sox to relocate in St. Petersburg. St. Petersburg wanted a professional baseball team in the worst way. The reasons were simple. From an image point of view, St. Petersburg was perceived as sunny and pleasant, and at the same time dull and boring. The large and growing senior population of St. Petersburg epitomized its image. The notion of moving to or even visiting St. Petersburg was limited to the over-65 crowd of golfers and shuffleboard players.

St. Petersburg's objective was obvious—find an attraction that was so overwhelming that it would, in one grand stroke, change the image perception of St. Petersburg. The solution—build a state-of-the-art baseball stadium and attract a major league baseball team. This would provide St. Petersburg with big-city status, a vital and youthful image, and a tremendous vehicle for economic development.

Backing this strategy were numerous real estate officials, local government officials, and Florida Governor Bob Martinez. Their first task was to raise money from local citizens and private industry to build a domed stadium even before acquiring a baseball team. Their second task was to attract a major league baseball team. The neighboring city of Tampa, Florida, had tried two years earlier to attract a major league baseball team and failed. The St. Petersburg marketers clearly faced a tough sell.

When the Chicago White Sox appeared to be drifting away from Chicago and looking for a new location, St. Petersburg saw an opportunity to make a deal. The St. Petersburg marketers quickly contacted White Sox owners Jerry Reinsdorf and Eddie Einhorn and began their big sales pitch for relocating the team to sunny Florida.

A Florida company agreed to provide airplanes, financing, temporary housing, and other inducements to help close the deal. Governor Martinez spearheaded drives for the Florida legislature to provide public funds for the White Sox. St. Petersburg presented a benefit package to the team's owners that included interest-free loans, attractive concession and parking revenues, forgiveness on property taxes, and extravagant media coverage.

St. Petersburg also marketed the intangible benefits of moving the team to the Florida city. They invited Chicago White Sox management to join in the planning process for the new indoor stadium. The White Sox owners would participate in discussions on the architecture, landscaping, seat placement, concession decisions, and other key strategies. Involving the potential buyers in the stadium development process helped demonstrate St. Petersburg's enthusiasm and commitment to the White Sox.

By this time, the city of Chicago and the state of Illinois started its counterattack. Baseball is a sport wrapped in nostalgia and place pride. It is a powerful image-generator machine and an important economic anchor for a city. And in Chicago, especially, baseball can be very political. The sellers of St. Petersburg had to do more than present the White Sox owners with a generous plan and an enthusiastic city of baseball fans. They had to out-compete the state of Illinois and the city of Chicago for the chance to have the White Sox. This proved to be an impossible task.

Former Governor Jim Thompson decided that Illinois could not afford to lose the prestige of a major league baseball team in Chicago. The media in Chicago blanketed the city with news of the internal battles over the future of the White Sox. Neighborhood coalitions and baseball fans became involved in the fight to keep the White Sox in Chicago. Governor Thompson became the point man in the fight to retain the Chicago White Sox. His efforts involved considerable political arm twisting and countless concessions to legislators all over the state whose support he needed.

In the end, all the competing lobbyists came together during the last meeting of the Illinois legislature before its recess. The odds for a White Sox saving package seemed remote. The citizens of St. Petersburg watched the final deliberations on live television in this superpower place war. At 12:03 A.M., the Illinois House voted 60–55 for acceptance of the plan to keep the White Sox in Chicago. The people of St. Petersburg sank into depression while their marketers began to search the ball clubs for a new prospect.

CONCLUSION

St. Petersburg illustrates the magnitude of the place marketer's challenge. The challenge is one not only of money but also of people, culture, history, image, and pride. The selling component of the strategic place marketing process is often the most crucial and yet the least understood part of a place marketing plan. The job of selling a place to target visitors, industries, or export consumers is more dynamic, political, and risky than ever. The challenge for place marketers is to understand better the needs, perceptions, preferences, and resources of target buyers before developing their strategic market plan. To this task we now turn.

3

How Target Markets
Make Their Choices

A business firm preparing to build a manufacturing plant, a trade association planning for a convention, or a family deciding on a vacation destination are all examples of place buyers. Each faces a complex buying decision as they try to choose which place offers the most benefits.

Place buying equals place selling in its complexity. By more fully understanding the place buying process, the place seller is in a better position to compete for the buyer's choice.

This chapter addresses three questions:

1. What are the main steps and factors influencing the place buying process?
2. What additional factors influence place decision making?
3. How influential are published ratings of places in the place buying process?

A MODEL OF THE PLACE BUYING PROCESS

Place buyers examine a variety of factors in choosing a place. In addition, place buying factors vary with the type of place selection decision: The choice of a two-week vacation destination involves different factors than the choice of a city to move to, or a business firm's choice of a new factory site.

Regardless of the particular type of selection decision, there are common elements to all place selection decisions. Buyers tend to pass

46

through five buying stages: problem recognition, information search, evaluating alternatives, purchase decision, and postpurchase behavior. We now examine these stages in detail.

Problem Recognition

The buying process starts when someone recognizes a problem, need, or opportunity. An employee may lose his job and consider moving to another city; a company may need to relocate to lower wage costs; an executive may feel stressed out and contemplate a vacation.

The person who recognizes a problem, need, or opportunity is not necessarily the one who makes the buying decision. Marketers distinguish among six *buyer roles:*

Initiator.   A person who first recognizes a problem, need, or opportunity and takes some action, such as gathering information or mentioning it to others.

Influencer.   A person who gets involved at some stage in the decision-making process and exerts some influence on the decision.

Decision maker.   A person who has the authority to make the final decision or some decision along the way.

Approver.   A person who can approve or reverse the final decision.

Buyer.   A person who implements the final decision.

User.   A person who consumes or uses the final product or service.

To illustrate, a meetings planner working for the American Hospital Association (AHA) needs to choose a convention site for the next annual meeting (role: *initiator*). The planner proceeds to gather data on feasible convention sites and favors Denver, Seattle, and Portland, in that order (role: *influencer*). The planner presents recommendations to the manager who decides on Denver (role: *decision maker*). The Denver site, however, will cost more than the other sites because it features a new convention center. So the manager phones AHA's financial vice-president who okays the less economical decision (role: *approver*). He then calls in AHA's site selection supervisor to negotiate and finalize the plan to locate next year's convention in Denver (role: *buyer*). The AHA members who ultimately attend the Denver convention the following year find the conference satisfying (role: *users*).

In this situation, different persons played different buyer roles. In simpler situations, one person can play all six roles, as when a bachelor decides that he needs a vacation (*initiator*), gathers data (*influencer*), decides on Club Mediterranean in Cancun Mexico (*decider*), looks at his bank account to be sure that he can finance this trip (*approver*), orders tickets and accommodations (*buyer*), and implements the decision (*user*). At the other extreme, as when Honda Motor Company searches for a location for a new manufacturing plant, hundreds of persons play various roles in a decision that could stretch over months, if not years.

For the place marketer, the implications are clear. To effectively promote a place, the place marketer must consider:

1. Which persons are involved in the place buying decision and what are their buyer roles?
2. What criteria are used by the various decision makers?
3. What are typical patterns of initiation, influence, and decision making for the particular place selection decision?

The answers to these questions help place marketers choose effective messages and media, and direct them to the right parties at the right time.

Information Search

An interested buyer may not engage in an extensive information search. This may happen if the buyer is well informed, if the buyer has a strong initial place preference, or if the buyer must make the decision quickly.

If the buyer undertakes some search, we can distinguish between two levels: The milder search state is *heightened attention*. For example, the AHA meetings planner starts noticing related ads and news. The planner may begin an *active information search*, examining published information and contacting informed individuals. How much search the planner undertakes depends on the amount of initial information, the ease of obtaining additional information, and the value placed on additional information. Normally, the amount of buyer search activity increases as the buyer moves from decision situations of *limited problem solving* to *extensive problem solving*.

Of key interest to the place marketer are the major sources of information that the buyer consults, and the relative influence each has on the subsequent place decision. Buyer information sources fall into four categories:

- *Personal sources:* family, friends, neighbors, acquaintances
- *Commercial sources:* advertising, salespersons, travel planners
- *Public sources:* mass media, place-rating organizations, experts (see exhibit 3-1)
- *Experiential sources:* visiting the place

The relative influence of these information sources varies with the type of place decision and the buyer's personal preferences. Typically, the buyer receives the most information about places from commercial sources. On the other hand, the most trusted information comes from personal sources. Each source plays a different role in influencing the buying decision. Commercial information normally performs an informing role, and public and personal sources perform a legitimizing role. Experiential sources, that is, physically going to and examining alternative sites, plays an evaluative role. Thus, the AHA convention planner may learn about Denver's new convention center from a Denver salesperson, interview past users for more objective information, and then visit Denver to reach a final decision.

Often, the place buyer starts the search with published place ratings. Examples include: *Best Cities to Live In*; *Best Cities to Retire In*; *Best Cities to Visit as a Tourist*; and *Best Places to Locate a Factory*. These rating studies are discussed later in this chapter. Keep in mind that buyers treat published ratings only as a starting point. A particular buyer has his or her own views of the criteria used by the publications to rate the places. Published ratings only create initial impressions and do not determine the final decisions.

The box at the far left of figure 3-1 shows the *total set* of conventions sites that are potentially available to the AHA convention planner. The planner is aware of only a subset of these convention sites, which we call the *awareness set*. Only some of these places satisfy the planner's initial buying criteria and make up the *consideration set*. As information is gathered about these places, only a few remain as strong contenders and make up the *choice set*. The final choice is made from the choice set, based on the buyer's evaluation criteria.

The practical implication is that the place seller must get the place's name into the buyer's awareness set, consideration set, and choice set, or else lose the opportunity to sell to the customer. The place seller must learn which other places are likely to remain in the buyer's choice set so that the competition is identified and appeals can be planned. The place seller should ask place buyers how they first heard about the chosen place,

EXHIBIT 3-1

New High-Tech Tools for Place Location

Geographic Information Systems (GIS) and the U.S. Census Bureau's TIGER files for states and localities provide new, valuable tools for buyers, sellers, and a host of intermediaries (consultants, real estate developers, and other economic development professionals) involved in attracting, retaining, or creating businesses. GIS may be likened to spatial spreadsheets on which successive overlays of information—site locations, transportation networks, and economic/demographic characteristics—can be produced through software on a microcomputer. These computerized maps range from a general area to a specific site location, and can produce a wealth of geographic/demographic data from market size to labor availability.[1]

The Census Bureau's TIGER files, available for the first time with 1990 census data for the entire United States, provide economic/demographic data for metro regions, metro fringes, and states, down to the detail of a census track and even block level. With such data and analytical tools, one can better calculate distance and location reducing travel time and costs, better target specific consumer markets, and refine various cost calculations for locating or expanding businesses in specific areas. As Donald Cooke, president of Geographic Data Technology, notes, "The demographic data industry is a $100 million a year business. Moving objects and people is a $600 billion a year industry."[2]

[1]Robert H. Pittman, "Geographic Information Systems: An Important New Tool for Economic Development Professionals," *Economic Development Review,* Fall 1990, p. 4.
[2]Joe Schwartz, "Donald Cooke Discusses the New Business Opportunities TIGER Will Create," *American Demographics,* June 1990, p. 19.

FIGURE 3-1

Successive Sets Involved in Buyer Decision Making

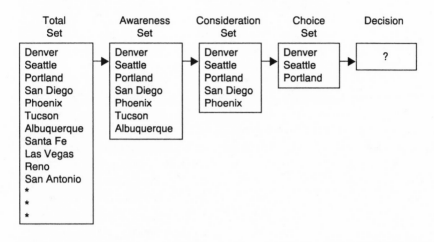

what information later influenced the buyers, and the relative influence of the different information sources. With this information, the place seller can more effectively prepare and distribute information to the target market in the future.

Evaluation of Alternatives

We have seen how information narrows the choice set. The question is, how does the buyer organize the information and arrive at a final choice? The fact is, there is no simple and single evaluation process used by all buyers, or even by one buyer, in all buying situations. Most models of the buyer evaluation process see the buyer as forming product judgments on a conscious and rational basis; this is not a perfectly reliable assumption (see exhibit 3-2). However, certain basic concepts help us understand buyer evaluation processes.

First, the buyer sees a given place as a bundle of particular attributes. Some attributes of interest for different place decisions are:

Vacation sites: Climate, recreation, attractions, cost
Places to live: Job opportunities, educational system, transportation, cost of living, quality of life
Factory site: Land costs, labor skills, energy costs, taxes
Convention cities: Facilities, capacity, accessibility, service, cost

EXHIBIT 3-2
Buyers Beware

An old adage in sales states "There is a buyer for every product." Unfortunately the product is sometimes land under water, factories with environmental hazards, or hotels with sinking foundations. Under pressure from a smooth-talking salesperson, the place buyer is capable of making seemingly irrational decisions.

In the 1960s, newspaper advertisements described Tres Piedras Estates and Rio Ranchero Estates as "a place away from the crowd." Located in the untamed Southwest, these affordable plots of land were so cheap that buying seemed low risk. In exchange for a down payment of $500 and a mere $99 a month, the buyer was promised a king-sized estate of austere beauty, clean air, and solitude. So much solitude, in fact, that when buyers finally saw their land, they discovered no roads, water, or neighbors. The deal was a mirage.

The target market was older buyers who couldn't afford to buy real retirement property. The price was so low that the risks seemed worth taking. A person living in Kansas City would have a tough time imagining that such a massive plot of land was not worth at least $2,000. In the end, the land returned to the natural elements, and the buyers returned to the snow belt.[1]

The decades change, but irrational buyer behavior remains. In the 1970s, the time-share industry was in full stride and many buyers found themselves with a two-week condo that was rapidly declining in value. In the 1980s, condo developers offered buyers a case of wine and a free week's stay in Arkansas in exchange for their attendance at a high-pressure seminar on planned communities. That decade also found bank and pension buyers purchasing office buildings with no tenants, or shopping malls surrounded by few customers and blazing competition. The rational approach to buying isn't always in fashion.

[1] T. Arbrister, "Land Frauds—Look Before You Buy," *Saturday Evening Post,* April 27, 1963, pp. 18–22.

Second, buyers vary in which place attributes they find salient and important. Some attributes are salient because the buyer has just been exposed to a commercial message mentioning them, making these attributes "top-of-the-mind." The buyer then decides which attributes are really important and attaches *importance weights* to the relevant attributes.

Third, the buyer is likely to develop a set of *beliefs* about where each place stands on each attribute. The set of beliefs the buyer holds about a particular place is the place's *image*. The buyer's beliefs may be at variance with the true attributes owing to his or her particular experience and the effect of selective perception, distortion, and retention.

Fourth, the buyer is assumed to have a *utility function* for each attribute. The utility function describes how the buyer expects value or satisfaction to vary with different levels of each attribute. For example, the AHA meetings planner may expect that the attendees' satisfaction with a convention center will increase with its facilities, capacity, accessibility, and service. If we combine the attribute levels where the utilities are highest, they make up the planner's ideal place. The expected utility from actual convention centers is below the maximum utility that would be derived from an ideal convention center.

Fifth, the buyer arrives at attitudes (judgments, preferences) toward the place alternatives through some *evaluation procedure*. Buyers have been found to apply different evaluation procedures to make a choice among alternatives. Assume the AHA convention planner has narrowed the choice set to Denver, Seattle, and Portland. Assume that the planner is primarily interested in four attributes: facilities, capacity, accessibility, and service. Table 3–1 shows researched beliefs about how each convention city rates on the four attributes. The planner rated Denver on a ten-point scale as follows: facilities, ten; capacity, eight; accessibility, six; and service, four. Similarly, the planner has beliefs about how the other two cities rate on these attributes. Which convention site is the planner most likely to favor?

Clearly, if one city dominates the others on all criteria, we would predict that the planner would choose it. But the choice set consists of cities that vary in their appeal. If the planner rates facilities above everything, the preference is Denver; if the planner wants the most capacity, the preference is Denver or Seattle; if the planner wants the best accessibility, the preference is Seattle; if the planner wants the best service, the preference is Portland. For buyers who care about only one attribute, we can easily predict their choices.

TABLE 3-1
Buyer's Beliefs About Three Convention Sites

	Attributes			
	Facilities	*Capacity*	*Accessibility*	*Services*
Denver	10	8	6	4
Seattle	6	8	10	5
Portland	4	3	7	8

Note: Each attribute is rated from 0 to 10, with 10 representing the highest level for that attribute. Thus, Denver is rated as having the best facilities. The consumer is assumed typically to want more of each desirable attribute.

   Most buyers consider several attributes but assign different weights to them. If we knew the importance weights that the AHA planner assigned to the four attributes, we could more reliably predict the preferred city.

   Suppose the planner assigned 40 percent of the importance to facilities, 30 percent to capacity, 20 percent to accessibility, and 10 percent to service. To find the planner's preference for each city, the weights are multiplied by beliefs about each city. This leads to the following perceived values:

Denver   = 0.4(10) + 0.3(8) + 0.2(6) + 0.1(4) = 8.0
Seattle = 0.4(6) + 0.3(8) + 0.2(10) + 0.1(5) = 7.3
Portland = 0.4(4) + 0.3(3) + 0.2(7) + 0.1(8) = 4.7

We would predict that the planner, given the weights, will favor Denver.

   This model, called the *expectancy value model* of buyer choice, is one of several possible models describing how buyers go about evaluating alternatives. Place marketers, of course, should interview meetings planners to find out how they actually evaluate convention site alternatives.

   Suppose most convention decision makers say that they form their preferences using this evaluation model. Knowing this, a convention site marketer can do a number of things to influence meetings planners. The Portland marketer, for example, could apply the following strategies to increase the convention planner's relative preference for Portland:

- *Alter the real attributes:* The place marketer could improve the convention facilities or capacity in Portland. This will take time. This is called *real repositioning.*
- *Alter beliefs about the attributes:* The place marketer could try to alter buyers' beliefs of where Portland stands on key attributes. This is especially recommended if buyers underestimate Portland's true standing. It is not recommended if buyers are accurately evaluating Portland. Exaggerated claims would lead to buyer dissatisfaction and bad word of mouth. Attempting to alter beliefs about a place is called *psychological repositioning.*
- *Alter beliefs about the competitive places:* The place marketer could try to change buyers' beliefs about where the other cities stand on each attribute. This may make sense where buyers mistakenly believe a competitive place has more quality than it actually has. This is called *competitive depositioning* and is often carried out through sending out comparison information.
- *Alter the importance weights:* The place marketer could try to persuade buyers to attach more importance to the attributes in which the place excels. Portland can tout the many benefits of choosing a convention center with great service because Portland is superior in this attribute.
- *Call attention to neglected attributes:* The place marketer could draw the buyer's attention to neglected attributes. If Portland has some special visitor attractions that outshine those of competitive cities, the Portland marketer could introduce attractions as another attribute to be rated.
- *Shift the buyer's ideals:* The place marketer could try to persuade buyers to change their ideal levels for one or more attributes. Portland's marketer can suggest that if a convention center's capacity gets too large, the convention center seems cold and impersonal.

Purchase Decision

In the evaluation stage, the buyer forms preferences among the places in the choice set, and begins to lean toward choosing a particular place. However, two factors can intervene between the purchase intention and the purchase decision.

The first factor is the *attitudes of others.* Suppose the AHA planner talks to a close friend who works for another trade association and who handles convention site selection. The friend tells the planner that Denver's new convention center still has some bugs: service personnel are poorly trained and food quality is only average. As a result, the planner's *purchase probability* for the Denver site is reduced.

The extent to which another person's criticism can taint one's preferred choice depends on two things: (1) the intensity of the other person's negative attitude toward the buyer's preferred choice and (2) the buyer's perception of the other person's credibility. The more intense the other person's negative attitude, and the closer the other person is to the buyer, the more the buyer adjusts her purchase intention. The converse is also true. A buyer's preference for a place increases if someone he likes or respects favors the same place. The influence of others becomes complex when several people close to the buyer hold contradictory opinions and the buyer respects all of them.

The buyer forms a purchase intention on the basis of expected benefits and costs. When the buyer is about to act, *unanticipated situational factors* can erupt to alter the purchase intention. The AHA planner might hear about an imminent water shortage in Denver, or Seattle may suddenly offer a lower convention rate. Thus, buyers' purchase intentions are not always carried out.

A buyer's decision to modify, postpone, or avoid a purchase decision is heavily influenced by *perceived risk*. Purchases, especially costly ones, involve *risk taking*. Buyers cannot be certain about the purchase outcome. This produces anxiety. The amount of perceived risk varies with the amount of money at stake, the amount of choice ambivalence, and the amount of buyer self-confidence. A buyer develops certain routines for reducing risk, such as decision postponement, further information gathering, and preference for safe situations. The marketer must understand the factors that provoke a feeling of risk in buyers and provide information and support to reduce the perceived risk. A buyer might be worried that a football game in Dallas might tie up traffic for a software convention. The marketer could anticipate this objection with plans for alternative traffic routes and special buses. Exhibit 3–3 defines the five types of buyers marketers encounter.

Postpurchase Behavior

After purchasing and experiencing the chosen place, the buyer experiences some level of satisfaction or dissatisfaction. The buyer also engages in postpurchase actions of interest to the marketer. The

EXHIBIT 3-3

Spotting the Buyer

Place buyers appear in many guises. The challenge is to understand types of buyers and their varying needs and decision processes. Here are five types of buyers:

The Shopper. A buyer who is usually at the very beginning of the selection process. The buyer asks general questions in an attempt to narrow the options and learn more about the product. A vacationer might want to find a pleasant, sunny location to play golf for a week at a reasonable cost. The buyer might be interested in the public courses in Missouri or a round-robin tournament in Ireland. The shopper is impressionable and the place seller is in a position to structure the buyer's search.

The Detailer. A buyer who usually has a checklist of requirements that must be fulfilled. The seller must be prepared with specific data to address these specific needs. If the factory requires a railroad siding, the seller either builds one or proposes another site.

The Pawn. A buyer who is not the decision maker. The decision will be made by someone else and the pawn is simply keeping all options open. The seller should try to bypass this buyer and deal directly with the real authority.

The Grinder. A buyer interested only in price and a bargain-basement deal. This buyer wants a six-day vacation in Las Vegas for $199.00 including airfare, meals, hotels, and ground transportation. The grinder is often switched to another place and needs to be convinced it is just as good.

The Browser. A buyer more interested in shopping than in making a decision. A seller can spend a lot of time with the browser and later find out that the decision is years away or has been delayed a number of times.

In the place selling business, qualifying the buyer with a number of questions is a good idea.

marketer's job does not end when the product is bought but continues into the postpurchase period.

POSTPURCHASE SATISFACTION.   Choosing a place almost always involves some postpurchase dissonance:

> When a person chooses between two or more alternatives, discomfort or dissonance will almost inevitably arise because of the person's knowledge that while the decision he has made has certain advantages, it also has some disadvantages. That dissonance arises after almost every decision, and further, the individual will invariably take steps to reduce this dissonance.[1]

What determines whether the buyer is highly satisfied, somewhat satisfied, or dissatisfied with a purchase? The buyer's satisfaction is based on the closeness between the buyer's *expectations* and the place's *perceived performance*. If the Denver convention center falls short of expectations, the customer is disappointed; if it meets expectations, the customer is satisfied; if it exceeds expectations, the customer is delighted. These feelings make a difference in whether the buyer chooses the same place again and talks favorably or unfavorably about the place to others.

Buyers form their expectations on the basis of information received from sellers, friends, and other sources. If the seller exaggerates the benefits, buyers experience *disconfirmed expectations,* leading to dissatisfaction. The larger the gap between expectations and performance, the greater the buyer's dissatisfaction. Here the buyer's coping style comes into play. Some buyers magnify the gap in performance, and they are highly dissatisfied. Other buyers minimize the gap and are less dissatisfied.

This suggests that the seller must make claims that faithfully represent the place's likely performance so that buyers experience satisfaction. Some sellers might even understate performance levels so that buyers experience higher-than-expected satisfaction with the place.

POSTPURCHASE ACTIONS.   The buyer's satisfaction or dissatisfaction with a place influences subsequent behavior. A satisfied buyer has a higher probability of choosing the place again. The satisfied customer also tends to say good things about the place to others. According to marketers: "Our best advertisement is a satisfied customer."

A dissatisfied customer responds differently. Dissonant buyers resort to one or two course of action: They may try to reduce the dissonance by asking for a refund or damages. Or they may do the opposite and seek information that might *confirm* the place's high value in spite of their experience. Our convention planner might reduce the association's payment to the Denver convention center or poll attendees to see if they are, in fact, more satisfied than first thought.

Marketers should be cognizant of the ways in which buyers handle dissatisfaction. Buyers have a choice between taking and not taking any action. If the former, they can take public action or private action. Public actions include complaining to the seller; going to a lawyer; or complaining to business, private, or government agencies. In all these cases, the seller loses something in having done a poor job in satisfying the customer.

Marketers can take steps to minimize the amount of buyer postpurchase dissatisfaction. They need to provide convenient channels for customer complaining. They need to respond quickly and positively in redressing customer grievances. Smart organizations welcome customer feedback as a way to continually improve their performance.

Understanding buyer needs and buying processes is essential to building effective marketing strategies. By understanding how buyers go through need recognition, information search, evaluation of alternatives, the purchase decision, and postpurchase behavior, marketers can pick up clues as to how to better satisfy buyer needs. By understanding the various players and roles in the buying process, and the major influences on their buying behavior, marketers can design effective marketing programs for their target markets.

OTHER FACTORS IN PLACE DECISION MAKING

The model outlined in the preceding section helps organize our understanding of what many place buyers go through in making a place decision. If it suffers from any weakness, it is that the model provides an overly rational explanation of how place decisions are made. Many place buyers shortcut the decision-making process for a variety of reasons. In this section we present two cases that illustrate how other factors influence place decisions.

Rust-Oleum's Move to Pleasant Prairie, Wisconsin

Rust-Oleum Corporation is a major specialty paint supplier whose original manufacturing facilities were located in Evanston, Illinois. In the mid-1980s, Rust-Oleum needed to expand production but there was no suitable space left in Evanston. Thus, the stage was set; new needs led Rust-Oleum into considering relocation, possibly to Tennessee.

At about the same time, the residents of Kenosha, Wisconsin, were having an attack of high anxiety because of the closing of Chrysler Corporation's automotive plant. Kenosha's leaders, in cooperation with Wisconsin Electric Power, decided that they needed to develop a large industrial park in nearby Pleasant Prairie and attract some new companies to replace the lost Chrysler jobs. They recognized, also, the importance of attracting a major company to this new industrial park to entice other companies to follow.

The park developers, hearing through the grapevine about Rust-Oleum's situation and its negotiating with Tennessee, went to work. They contacted Rust-Oleum's chairman and made a presentation to him and its officers. They invited the company's executives to visit the new industrial park and to choose a prime location. The state, county, and electric company put together an incentive package, including a tax exemption, free electricity during the early years of operation, and a $1 million research grant. The deal's centerpiece was 25 acres of land at bargain rates, with an elaborate highway building program for easier access to the facilities.[2] In addition, Wisconsin's congressional representative, Les Aspin, who happened to head the House of Representatives Armed Services Committee, promised that Rust-Oleum would be highly recommended as a supplier when it came to choosing paint for U.S. Army bases around the world. The company officials were given special treatment including banquets, political visits, and a welcoming parade.

When Illinois officials finally became aware of Wisconsin's courting of Rust-Oleum, it was too late. They asked Governor James Thompson of Illinois to intervene and counterpropose. The governor arrived at Rust-Oleum in a helicopter and with a full entourage dashed into the headquarters and offered to match Kenosha's offer. But Rust-Oleum had been so wined and dined and committed to Kenosha that no counteroffer prevailed. Shortly thereafter, Rust-Oleum Corporation closed its operations in Evanston and opened them in Pleasant Prairie, Wisconsin.

Figgie International Moves to Richmond, Virginia

Figgie is a Fortune 500 company manufacturing sporting goods, firefighting equipment, aerospace technology, and a wide variety of service industries. Its longtime location was Cleveland, Ohio. In the early

1980s, Harry E. Figgie, Jr., the founder and chief executive officer (CEO), was becoming increasingly upset with Cleveland's deteriorating quality of life. He saw the city going downhill, and property and business taxes continuously rising. He was considering moving his headquarters to another location.

About that time, the CEO mentioned his concerns to civic leaders in Richmond, Virginia. When Richmond's economic development office learned of the opportunity, they immediately started laying plans to attract Figgie to Richmond. They studied the CEO's personal hobbies and activities. Recognizing that he liked fishing and enjoyed a good country club, they contacted him and invited him to come to Richmond. All the leaders in Richmond were coached to be enthusiastic in their meetings with Figgie's CEO. Soon the CEO was convinced about the advantages of relocating his headquarters to Richmond, which he proceeded to do.

Clearly Richmond's officials successfully conducted the *presale process*. But they forgot to manage the *postsales process*. Harry Figgie built a fine home in Richmond and moved in. Soon various fundraisers for Richmond causes solicited him for donations but he resisted, since he was tied to his other charities. His warm welcome was replaced with increasing indifference. He could not break into the tight Southern social circles at the Country Club of Virginia. Partly, the fault was his in that his temperament as an entrepreneur did not mesh with Southern style. He felt they liked his money but not his independent character. The payback was swift:

> Just six years after buying 1,200 acres and moving his company headquarters to Richmond, Virginia, Harry Figgie, 64, in an apparent snit, is moving it all back to his hometown of Cleveland. . . . Word is that Figgie is pouting because the staid Richmond circles never accepted him with what he considered respect. So he's taking his billion-dollar business and going home.[3]

He gave the reason that Cleveland had begun to turn around and he missed the city. Another factor is that Cleveland's economic development group continued to visit him and appeal for his return.[4]

Thus, we see that personal benefits and emotional commitments can play a strong role in place decision making. We have all heard of cases where a company president moved his headquarters to be near his home town, or a particular lake, and so on. Or the company president may owe favors to certain friends, acquaintances, or politicians, and this sways the decision making. In extreme cases, the place buyer may respond to outright favors or bribes. All this means is that the place seller must be good at identifying the "hot buttons" of key place buyers.

THE ROLE OF PLACE RATING SERVICES

All the buyers of places are looking for guidance to make their decision-making process more productive. The various place-rating systems provide a glimpse into a place and its position relative to other places. The ratings have grown in importance as the buyers grow more demanding and the competition intensifies.

Consider the following examples of place rating success stories in the past decade:

Rand McNally's *Places Rated Almanac* declared Pittsburgh the best place to live in the United States.
The National League of Cities anointed Baltimore as the nation's most successful city in economic development.
Inc. magazine cited Austin, Texas, as the best city for starting or growing a company.
A *New York Times* survey crowned Atlanta as the top choice of American business executives for a business location, although New York City continued to attract the most new office space.
Seattle was heralded the "City of the Future" by a SUNY-Buffalo group.
North Dakota was rated as the state with the best "business climate" by Grant Thornton.

This is only a small sample of ratings results that different organizations and media vehicles publish periodically. Table 3–2 lists the major published ratings on life quality and business quality. Because these lists can have some influence, we need to ask three questions: How are place ratings compiled? How reliable are place ratings? How useful are place ratings to buyers and sellers?

How Are Place Ratings Compiled?

To understand how the ratings are compiled, let's consider Rand McNally's method of determining America's most livable cities. Rand McNally's *Places Rated Almanac* uses the following nine criteria to rate

TABLE 3–2
Some Leading Place Ratings Organizations and Sources

LIFE QUALITY RATINGS
1. *Rand McNally*. Private, nonprofit research group that rates the growth, population, and poverty levels in U.S. metropolitan cities.
2. *Money* magazine. Annually publishes *The Best Places to Live*.
3. G. Scott Thomas. Publishes *The Ratings Guide to Life in America's Small Cities*.
4. *Savvy* magazine. Rates the best places to raise children.
5. *Zero Population Growth*. Rates the most/least stressful cities.
6. *Population Crisis Committee*. Rates the status of women and how their treatment compares with men in ninety-nine countries.
7. *National Center for Health Statistics*. Rates the odds of living to 100 in different states.
8. *Psychology Today* magazine. Rates the best places for psychological well-being.
9. *Forbes* magazine. Rates which cities are good for marriage.
10. *Federal Bureau of Investigation*. Rates the metropolitan areas with the highest crime rates.

BUSINESS QUALITY RATINGS
1. *Louis Harris & Associates*. Rates the best places to locate businesses.
2. *Grant Thornton*. Rates the manufacturing climate in the continental United States annually.
3. *Corporation for Enterprise Development*. Major competitor of Grant Thornton; rates business climates.
4. *Fortune* magazine. Rates the ten best urban areas for business.
5. *Metropolitan Consulting Group of New York*. Rates the costs of operating businesses in ten major cities.
6. *Corporate Travel* magazine. Publishes *The Most Expensive Cities for Business Travel*.
7. *Council on Competitiveness*. Ranks America's ability to compete with other countries.

cities: cost of living, jobs, crime, health care, transportation, education, the arts, recreation, and climate (see table 3–3). The cities rated as the most livable do not necessarily score at the top of all criteria. Pittsburgh, the 1985 top-rated city, earned seventh place in education as its highest criteria score. It won top ranking because it had no extremely low scores out of 329 metro regions ranked. Rand McNally said of its choice: "Pittsburgh is like the Steelers' front line ... not incredibly strong in any one area, but consistently good overall."[5]

TABLE 3–3
Places Rated Almanac Criteria

1. The *cost of living* looks at household incomes and taxes, and it also measures the costs of important items such as housing, food, health care, and college tuition.
2. *Jobs* evaluates prospects for local employment growth in nine basic areas, including manufacturing, trade, services, finance, and government.
3. A metro area's *crime* rating is measured by the average annual number of violent and property crimes per 100,000 people over the past five years.
4. The supply of general health care facilities and practitioners, plus available special options, forms the basis for a metro area's *health care* rating.
5. *Transportation* is rated by local commuting time, public transit, and the diverse intercity travel options of air, rail, and interstate highway.
6. Each metro area's public school system and private school alternatives, as well as their local colleges and universities, produce an *education* rating.
7. The *arts* compares cultural assets, among them museums and public libraries, opera companies, and symphony orchestras.
8. *Recreation* also rates assets, from good restaurants to public golf courses, zoos, professional sports, inland lakes, and national park acreage.
9. *Climate* is rated on mildness; that is, how close temperatures remain to 65 degrees Fahrenheit throughout the year.

Source: Richard Boyer and David Savageau, Places Rated Almanac, p. 15. © 1989 Prentice Hall, Englewood Cliffs, NJ. Reprinted by permission of the publisher, Prentice Hall Travel/A division of Simon & Schuster, New York.

The raters at Rand McNally use hard data wherever possible and then apply importance weights to the various measures to come up with a rating score. Any change in the criteria or weights would alter the city rankings. Clearly, a place buyer needs to use the ratings carefully. Thus, Pittsburgh's high ranking would not have much meaning to a vacation seeker, but it would have high appeal to a family seeking to move to a city with a good quality of life.

Other ratings systems include a mix of subjective and objective measures. For example, the U.S. Conference of Mayors in 1987 cited San Antonio as one of the most livable cities in America. The major criteria used in this rating was a subjective assessment of mayoral leadership. The judges cited San Antonio's Mayor Henry Cisneros as exceptional for creating the city's Arts and Cultural Advisory Committee and for adopting the Historic Landmarks' District Ordinance. Cisneros is no longer mayor and a study of this nature is only as good as the leader's reelection campaign.

Clearly, formal rating systems don't tell the whole story of a place. Philadelphia is rated as one of the worst American cities for crime, pollution, traffic, and jobs, but many people would live nowhere else. Their reasons vary. Perhaps the hockey team, or the historic district, or Philly's cheese steak sandwiches draw a person to Philadelphia—these soft characteristics cannot be measured by a rating system. Soft characteristics contribute to the image of a place. Our attitude toward Dallas is partly shaped by the news coverage of John F. Kennedy's assassination in that city and then modified by the film *JFK*. Our image of Cuba is influenced by their Olympic boxing team, clips of Castro's speeches, and filmic portrayals such as *Havana*. Our understanding of the antebellum South is influenced by the book and film, *Gone with the Wind*.

These soft characteristics, as well as hard facts, provide place marketers with palettes from which they can paint their cities in the most favorable light. If a particular city stands high on certain hard facts, such as climate or housing, the city touts these facts in its self-promotion. Lacking a good standing on any hard characteristics, the city marketers hunt for marketable soft characteristics.

How Reliable Are Place Ratings?

Place ratings have two questionable characteristics.[6] First, different ratings services often produce inconsistent rankings for the same city.

Laura Van Tuyl posed the dilemma of a person trying to decide on the merits of Columbus, Ohio. Three different rating services came up with widely divergent opinions of the city. *Newsweek* magazine enthusiastically labeled Columbus one of the top ten most livable cities; Rand McNally liked Columbus well enough to place it 61 out of 333 metropolitan areas; but *Money* magazine considered Columbus mediocre, and ranked it a lowly 185 out of 300.[7] A person considering a possible move to Columbus might be better off driving to Columbus, renting a motel room, and spending a few days.

Or, suppose a company wanted to choose a top business location. Tom Walker compared *Fortune's* 1990 list with Cushman & Wakefield's survey of the same year conducted by Lou Harris & Associates. Salt Lake City ranked first in the *Fortune* poll, but doesn't even appear in the top ten of Cushman & Wakefield. To further complicate comparisons, Minneapolis-St. Paul is second in the *Fortune* poll and drops to ninth in Cushman & Wakefield. *Fortune* also ranks Austin, Phoenix, Jacksonville, and Oklahoma City in their top ten and none of them appear in Cushman & Wakefield's top ten list.[8] The bad news is the lack of consistency may confuse and stall companies interested in relocating, and the good news is that more cities can claim top ten ratings.

The second problem with rating systems is that a place's rank often fluctuates from survey to survey within the same rating vehicle. The *Places Rated Almanac* ranked Atlanta; Washington, D.C.; and Greensboro/Winston-Salem/High Point, North Carolina, as their top three choices of 1981. The three cities found themselves excluded from the top five in 1985. Greensboro's fall is particularly harsh as the 1989 poll finds it resting in sixty-second place. Some terrible events must be striking North Carolina as Raleigh/Durham finished an impressive third in 1985 and fell to twenty-third in 1989. The upward and downward movements of these cities make the rankings difficult to use or believe.

It's not surprising that fluctuations in the ratings are pervasive in business rankings. In the Cushman & Wakefield survey for 1988, 1989, and 1990, the rankings change dramatically over a small amount of time. Chicago, after ranking fourth in both 1988 and 1989, suddenly drops to fourteenth in 1990. The city had no change in leadership, no acute financial situations, and it didn't burn down. Norfolk, Virginia, in contrast, after holding eleventh place in 1988 and nineteenth place in 1989 moved up to a surprising fourth place. What has happened in Norfolk in that short period of time? The answer is not much, as most places evolve significantly over longer periods of time.

One problem of basing a decision about where to move on the ratings is that the contradictions are hard to rationalize. A company deciding to move to Atlanta on the basis of Cushman & Wakefield's study naming it the top city from 1986 to 1989 and a strong sixth in 1990 might be puzzled by other rankings. For example, Atlanta in recent years was ranked number one in FBI crime ratings, number six in EPA ozone tests for smog, the fourth worst city in the South in infant mortality, and the 259th out of 261 cities in stress according to *Psychology Today*.[9] Clearly, these ratings do not commend Atlanta as a good place to live or work.

How Useful Are Place Ratings to Buyers and Sellers

Why are ratings so popular, given the arbitrary criteria and often inconsistent and fluctuating results? Published ratings apparently offer a quick and convenient picture. They require little effort to use, relay important information, and often eliminate the need for further research. J. D. Reed of *Time* comments: "Whether the subject is the beefiest burger or the biggest corporation, Americans have a penchant for making lists of the best and the worst, then arguing about the results."[10] Bearing this out, exhibit 3–4 lists the most and least stressful cities.

Those places that score high in the rating game normally tout it for all it's worth. Pittsburgh's citizens and officials were thrilled in 1985 with being named America's most livable city. According to several commentators, the rating helped Pittsburgh attract high-tech companies and persuaded young people to move back after finishing college. The rating dispelled the twenty-five-year-old image of Pittsburgh as a steel-based smoky city. Pittsburgh proceeded to broadcast its "livability" to the whole world, using the rating in all of its literature and public relations campaigns. Pittsburgh defends the methodology and brilliance of the rating scheme. Why not?

By the same token, those places that draw a low rating attack the statistical methodology and decry the study's validity. Glens Falls, New York, placed 290th in Rand McNally's list. Mayor Edward Bartholomew commented: "We're going to have a public burning of [Rand McNally's] almanac and all their maps."[11] The citizens of Flint, Michigan, in 1988, were so angry with their low rank in *Money* magazine's ratings that they publicly burned copies of that month's issue. The

EXHIBIT 3-4

What's Stress?

The rating systems become more specific each year. The Zero Population Growth Organization (ZPG) rates the 192 most stressful cities.

In the ZPG poll, Gary, Chicago, Houston, Baltimore, and Jersey City were the top five stressful cities, and the least were less populated places such as Cedar Rapids, Iowa; Madison, Wisconsin; Ann Arbor, Michigan; Lincoln, Nebraska; and Fargo, North Dakota. Factors that are weighed include violent crime, education, water, sewage, hazardous waste, individual economics, community economics, population change, crowding, air control, and births.

Yet all polls and rankings should be used carefully. If you're interested in the arts or big-league baseball or football, Los Angeles may well be a more serene city than any of the least stressful cities. A resident of Cedar Rapids might find the relatively art-free environment highly stressful.

Source: See Philip Franchine, "Chicago Near the Top of 'Most Stressful' List," *Chicago Sun Times,* October 20, 1988, p. 16.

mayor of Wheeling, West Virginia, whose city fell from third in 1987 to 45th in *Money* magazine's 1988 list, said that his economy "isn't any weaker than when we were named number three. I don't know how they came up with these figures."[12] Unfortunately, this kind of negative media image is unlikely to succeed. Some mayors of low-rated cities take their lickings more quietly and instruct their agencies to figure out quickly how to improve the city's rankings on the rater's criteria.

Extremely low ratings can have a negative impact on a place's economy. According to *Money* magazine in 1989, Benton Harbor, Michigan, was considered the worst place to live out of 300 cities. The city had already lost a major Whirlpool Corporation plant and was trying to find new companies to replace job losses. Benton Harbor desperately needs jobs, and the bad image now highlighted by ratings is one more obstacle to overcome in trying to revitalize the city.

Ironically, strong positive ratings sometimes produce negative outcomes. Thousands of people were attracted to cities such as Seattle, Santa Fe, and San Diego after surveys rated them as wonderful places to live. The cities tried to control congestion and development and even to discourage more newcomers. To be the most livable city may be an honor but it may also bring waves of immigrants, traffic congestion, rising costs, and all sorts of other problems. The Grant Thornton study claiming North Dakota as the best place to do business only brought the state ridicule. Both the methodology and basic assumptions were assailed by critics and North Dakota saw little in the way of new business.

As for place buyers, they would be foolish if they placed too high a reliance on the ratings. Generally, the places high on the list are all pretty good and the places low on the list are pretty deficient (even here there are exceptions). The place buyer would be wise to look at the individual criteria ratings that make up the total ratings of the higher-rated places, and put personal weights on these attributes. The place buyer should read more about these places, talk to trusted people, and visit the top places to gather a firsthand impression.

CONCLUSION

The buyers of a place have much to consider. When moving a business, families are uprooted, old clients are inconvenienced, and new relationships need to be formed. The convention and tourist buyers, while not making such momentous decisions, still are allocating valuable time to work or pleasure. Because of the stakes, buyers are trying to become more systematic and rational about a process that has historically been hit and miss. In chapters 8, 9, 10, and 11, we address specific buyer strategies in tourism, business development, exports, and residential choice.

4

The Place Auditing and Strategic Market Planning Process

Today's headlines dramatize the growing plight of many cities, states, and regions. A sampling of recent headlines includes:

Woes Many Cities Face Are Starkly Etched in Nashville Today
New York City Nears "Drop-Dead" Date
Philadelphia: Former Showpiece Now a Source of Shame
The City of the Future Is a Troubling Prospect if It's to Be Los Angeles
Washington's Crime Gives Visitors Jitters
West Virginia, Mired in Poverty, Corruption, Battles a Deep Gloom
Tough Times in the Northeast Signal Budget Woes Nationwide

Why the plight of these places? Are they victims of powerful global forces and sea changes that no amount of planning could have averted? Or are these places partly the cause in failing to plan their futures better?

The truth is that most troubled places are both victim and cause. Seismic changes are occurring in the location of the world's major industries. When the economics of automobile production starts favoring Tennessee, Kentucky, or Mexico over Detroit, Detroit can do little to prevent the out-migration of auto factories. At the same time, if Detroit fails to attract replacement industries, it is also partly to blame.

Most places fail to anticipate changes, and many simply resist

70

change. They drift until shaken by some great crisis that makes them lose companies, residents, and tourists. Only then do concerned public officials and business leaders hastily form commissions charging them with the mandate to save their place.

Consider the case of Akron, Ohio:

Akron, Ohio, stood for many years as the Rubber Capital of the United States. Its massive factories and blue-collar workers churned out millions of tires annually. Today, Akron's rubber industry has all but disappeared. Goodyear, Goodrich, General Tire, and Firestone have moved their plants elsewhere. Blue-collar jobs fell from 46 percent of all Akron jobs in 1964 to 23 percent in 1990. Today, downtown Akron is filled with empty factories and closed stores.

As all of this was happening, local business people pressed public officials to cut taxes, while public officials resented interference from business. Finally, the crisis forced both parties to come to a truce and they formed the Akron Regional Development Board. It was too late to re-attract the tire makers; but presently the Akron Regional Development Board is working hard to stimulate growth among small and midsize companies, where the most expansion is taking place. In addition, Akron's planners have their eye on building another major industry, polymers. If Akron succeeds, it must not make the same mistake of overdepending on a single industry on which to base its future. Most large cities are learning the merits of diversification.

What is puzzling is that communities such as Akron usually have an apparatus in place that should identify and respond to these problems—a planning commission, an economic development agency, a chamber of commerce, or all of these groups—but judging from the plight of so many places, either these organizations are not doing their jobs or they are not communicating effectively with the city leaders concerning what can be done. Clearly, something is needed.

Can places do a better job of forecasting and planning their future? This chapter addresses two questions:

1. What planning approaches are places using today to guide their development?

2. How can *strategic market planning* help places improve their planning results?

FIVE APPROACHES TO PLACE DEVELOPMENT

There are five time-honored approaches to place development, namely community development, urban design, urban planning, economic development, and strategic market planning. Each approach uses a different philosophy and approach to the problem of creating and maintaining viable communities. We can understand these approaches better if we consider them in the context of a troubled city like Detroit. What solution would each framework offer to solve Detroit's problems?

Community Development

The basic idea behind community development is to create a quality environment for the people currently living and working in the community. Community development experts support good schools, strong neighborhoods, increased public safety, and adequate health facilities, basically emphasizing the role of strong community-based institutions in affecting the quality of a place. Much community development philosophy originated with the idea of community participation and citizen empowerment within neighborhoods rather than in whole cities, but later developed into a guiding concept applied to overall urban development.

Proponents of this approach would suggest that Detroit must develop stronger neighborhood organizations and invest its limited resource in improving basic services for its citizens.[1] Its major infrastructural elements—education, health, public safety, housing, transportation—must be improved so that citizens are satisfied with their neighborhoods and city. If Detroit succeeds in developing more livability and a better quality of life, it will be easier to attract new businesses and retain existing businesses. Clearly community quality of life is a growing factor in place location.

On the other hand, community development cannot serve as a complete solution for improving a place's viability and attractiveness. First, the place may lack the required resources to make the levels of investment. Second, there will be turf wars between neighborhoods and organizations as to which are more deserving of community redevelopment funding. Third, the community development approach suffers from *inside-out thinking* instead of *outside-in thinking.* It amounts to planning a community's future without paying attention to the turbulence reshaping the world economy. No systematic attempt is made to figure out how to fit the community competitively into its metropolitan, regional, national, or even global setting. It assumes that if a place is a "good product," people will want to live there. It commits what marketers call "the better mouse-trap fallacy," in assuming that if someone builds a better mousetrap, people will rush to buy it.

Urban Design

Urban design professionals share the assumption of community development professionals that a place must be pleasant to live in. They differ in placing more emphasis on the design qualities of a place—its architecture, open spaces and land use, street layout and traffic flow, cleanliness, and environmental quality—than on its community institutions and people. Urban designers assume that people's attitudes and behavior are strongly influenced by the quality of their physical environment, and changing that, in turn, will improve attitudes and behavior.

Urban designers have been especially active in smaller towns and communities whose streets and buildings have fallen into neglect. These "dowager" towns need a face-lifting and they invite urban designers to propose a broad scheme to put a prettier face on the town. Some urban designers go beyond simply refurbishing the town's appearance. They propose a visual theme to guide the town's reformatting. Among the popular town formats are the Swiss chalet town (Vail, Colorado), the frontier cowboy town (Aspen, Colorado) and small town U.S.A. (St. Charles, Illinois).

More recently, urban designers have incorporated ecological/environmental considerations in their thinking and planning. For example, they might assess the ecological consequences of greater density and high-rise living on traffic congestion and parking, air pollution, city space, and so on. Emphasizing aesthetics and quality of life is a natural and positive development.

Urban designers did play a role in Detroit's attempt in the 1970s to revive its downtown area. A grand plan centered on building Renaissance Plaza, a project largely funded by Henry Ford. The project lost $140 million in the first four years and by 1983 needed refinancing.[2] The project never met expectations, as lack of political leadership, severe budget cuts, and a continually unattractive surrounding area discouraged visitors and new businesses.

While urban design can improve a place's physical environment, it suffers from many of the same limitations as the community development approach. The community may lack sufficient resources for a thorough face-lift. The community may be sharply divided over what constitutes good design and where the money should be spent. And urban designers tend to take an inside-outside perspective on place development. They seek to make a place more habitable and attractive without addressing the larger issues of how to make the place economically viable.

Urban Planning

Most cities have an urban planning unit within the government, often called the urban planning commission, steeped in land use, zoning, density concerns, and traffic control. This commission's task is to evaluate the many projects proposed by developers and various government agencies. Suppose Detroit at a given time faces proposals for modernizing its airport, adding a domed stadium, widening a major highway, and building a new city hall. Furthermore, suppose Detroit's budget cannot fund all these projects. The urban planning commission would evaluate the benefit/cost impact of these competing proposals and recommend the best investments, given the budget constraints.

Many urban planning commissions go beyond reviewing submitted proposals, and instead initiate projects and proposals on their own. They may take responsibility for evaluating the community's economic base and proposing new industries to attract to the community. They may propose a long-term plan for improving the city's infrastructure and attractiveness, but typically most of the urban planning commission's time is consumed in analyzing a never-ending flow of proposals and protecting the "public interest."

Economic Development

Growth and development often are used interchangeably. Economic growth refers to more output which means more jobs, people, and related impacts such as congestion and pollution. Economic development, in contrast, suggests not only more output but also different kinds of output than produced before—new industries, more productive use of resources, and greater innovation. Houston illustrates the distinction. It experienced considerable growth in the energy industry boom years of the 1970s, but more development in the 1980s due to industry diversification and new business growth.

Economic development professionals focus largely on helping a place enhance its competitiveness. They analyze a place's strengths and weaknesses, opportunities and threats as they are affected by external forces. Their task is to determine how the local economy best fits a changing regional, national, and global context, mindful that places must export to survive. Places need a business core and related support industries to earn the money to pay for the goods and services they import.

Many cities have established *economic development agencies,* separate from *urban or community planning agencies,* with the latter's focus on infrastructure. As examples, there are the San Antonio Economic Development Commission, the Philadelphia Industrial Development Corporation, and the St. Louis Planned Industrial Expansion Authority. These commissions often work with outside consultants who specialize in urban economic development. Thus, Mesa, Arizona, hired PHH Fantus to help plan its economic development strategy. The Gadsden–Etowah County Industrial Development Authority in Alabama hired the Battelle Memorial Institute; Wichita, Kansas, hired Stanford Research Institute; Miami hired Arthur Andersen & Company; and Cleveland, Ohio, hired McKinsey & Company.[3]

The leading economic development consulting firms also may take different approaches to economic development. PHH Fantus and Battelle typically help a city determine the best industries to target, recommend improvements in the city's infrastructure and zoning, and help plan specific marketing programs to attract the target industries.

SRI takes a broader view of economic development which they define as follows: "Economic development is the process by which our community will improve its capacity to grow and develop—economically, educationally, socially and culturally."[4] Their view incorporates community development thinking along with economic development thinking. They assume that a place's attractiveness depends on four community factors (quality of life, positive image and marketing, economic development capacity, and physical infrastructure) and three economic infrastructure factors (accessible technology; skilled, adaptable, and motivated human resources; and available financial capital).[5]

When Arthur Andersen & Company worked for Miami, it used a

more grass-roots approach. They guided a steering committee of 50 Miamians and eight task forces (involving some 450 people) to develop their own strategic plan, thereby insuring strong community support.

Finally, in their Cleveland study McKinsey emphasized how Cleveland could improve its competitive position *vis-à-vis* four competitor cities and develop a strong national image marketing program.

The point is that several approaches can be applied to urban development and improvement; they differ in *scope, approach, balance,* and *responsiveness.* Furthermore, we argue that a comprehensive approach is sufficiently inclusive to incorporate perspectives from community development, urban design, and urban planning, along with that of urban economic development.

Underlying all these approaches is the idea that places, if they are to succeed, must use the tools of businesses, because they are competing for resources. They must recognize dynamic global forces that impact their local industries. They must understand that they compete with other places for tourists, conventions, educated residents, factories, corporate headquarters, and start-up firms. They must be excellent or superior in some special ways. They must be market-conscious and market-driven. The infrastructure, industries, attractions, and people skills that they build today will affect their market position tomorrow. If they choose the wrong industries, if they make the wrong bets, they are in the same position as companies that produce the wrong products: namely, they will nosedive into obscurity.

To think like a business, places must develop and operate a planning methodology. They must not turn to planning as a result of hard times but must adopt planning to avoid hard times.

Strategic Marketing Planning

Strategic market planning, in the context of places, has passed through three stages (see table 4–1). The first stage consisted largely of smokestack chasing. It had its origins in the 1930s with aggressive efforts by southern states to lure businesses, plants, and investment from the North by promoting their "better business climates." They exploited the advantages of least-cost production—cheap labor and land, low taxes, and public financing—to attract new business and investment.

Over the next four decades, place competition aimed at business attraction changed little in goals, methods, rationale, and marketing messages. Places assumed that it was a buyers' market, largely unaffected

TABLE 4–1
Three Generations of Economic Development Marketing

	Objectives	Methodology	Underlying Marketing Rationale
First Generation (Smokestack Chasing)	Manufacturing jobs	Luring facilities from other locations	Low operating costs Government subsidies
Second Generation Target Marketing	Manufacturing and service jobs in target industries now enjoying profitable growth	Luring facilities from other locations Retention and expansion of existing firms Improving physical infrastructure Improving vocational training Public/private partnerships	Competitive operating costs Suitability of community for target industries Good quality of life (emphasis on recreation and climate)
Third Generation (Product Development)	Preparing the community for the jobs of the 1990s and beyond Manufacturing and high-quality service jobs in target industries expected to enjoy continuing growth into the future	Retention and expansion of existing firms Spurring local entrepreneurship and investment Selective recruiting of facilities from other locations More intense public-private partnerships Developing technology resources Improving general and technical education	Prepared for growth in the contemporary worldwide economy Competitive operating costs Human and intellectual resources adaptable to future change Good quality of life (emphasis added on cultural and intellectual development)

Source: John T. Bailey, *Marketing Cities in the 1980s and Beyond* (Chicago, American Economic Development Council, 1989), p. 42. Used with permission of American Economic Development Council.

by changes occurring outside of the United States. Their task was to reach buyers, discover their needs, package various incentives into a competitive deal, and make the sale. Little wonder, then, that incentive bidding among competing places escalated into an unchecked arms race in the 1970s, when the U.S. economy slowed and unemployment rose.

In the 1970s and 1980s, places moved to a second stage, that of *target marketing*. Instead of pursuing a single goal, business attraction, they moved to a multiplicity of goals—retention, start-ups, tourism, export promotion, and foreign investment. As the U.S. economy changed and competition intensified, places changed from a hit-or-miss approach to more refined strategies based on competitive analysis and market positioning. Places learned to segment markets and buyers, and to target their products and services to specific customers based on research and analysis. Place sellers moved from *mass marketing* of diffuse products (incentives) to *specialized marketing*, emphasizing specific products tailored to specific customer wants and needs. Places also put more emphasis on maintaining and supporting internal markets and resources: the place's own businesses, industries, entrepreneurs, new products, and collective resources (universities, research firms, financial institutions, etc.).

In the new decade of the 1990s, places are moving to the third stage of *product development* and *competitive niche* thinking. They are seeking to define themselves as distinctive places with specific competitive advantages for target industries. They are developing those niche products and services that create value for target customers. They are investing in a diversified portfolio of industries while pursuing some clusters of related businesses. They are educating human resources so that their citizens can function effectively in a high-tech, information society. And they are investing in a well-functioning infrastructure to support a good quality of life.

While these development stages are not mutually exclusive, they reflect the growth, development, and sophistication of place competition in a changing world economy. Places have become more businesslike and market-oriented in their economic development activities as a result of external competition and internal political pressures. In an era of scarce fiscal resources and widespread resistance to taxes, the tax-paying public has turned against large tax-inducement packages to retain and attract a single firm. The public has grown more skeptical about public officials assertions that incentive benefits always exceed incentive costs, and that governments can alter economic forces to stop businesses from moving.

Public resistance has been joined by market resistance. Conventional business recruitment programs built on financial incentives were not enough to replace the jobs and businesses in the 1970s. In some cases, business retention strategies generated their own dynamics of incentive bidding to retain older, mature, and, in many cases, less competitive firms. This often unproductive strategy came at the expense of alternative investments with possible larger public benefits and greater contributions to a place's longer-term competitive position.

Furthermore, economic development as a state and local responsibility came into its own in the 1970s. No longer would place development be viewed as a policy enclave reserved for the national government nor even an activity limited to the public sector. It has become everyone's business—all governmental levels, all sectors, and inclusive of all organizational forms from national-international to local-neighborhood levels. As responsibility shifted from national to state-local governments, and resources to support place development activities shifted from public to private, places designed their own decentralized programs to meet their needs. As federal resources shrank and program responsibilities moved downward in our governmental system, places refocused internally for resources, institutions, and leadership to build competitive capabilities.

In this dynamic process, place marketing emerged as a promising integrating process linking a place's potential competitive advantages to overall economic development goals.

THE STRATEGIC MARKET PLANNING PROCESS

Places must begin to do what business organizations have been doing for years, namely *strategic market planning*. We do not mean *budgeting*, as when a community estimates annually its expected revenues and costs to achieve an approximate balance. Nor do we mean *project planning* as when a place decides to build a stadium, a new highway, or a water sewage treatment plant. We do not mean *short-range planning* as when a place makes some decisions about finances, taxes, and investments over the next year or two. Nor do we mean *long-range planning*, which consists of extrapolating the place's future population and resources and developing suitable infrastructure expansion, as may be found in capital budgets.

Strategic market planning starts from the assumption that the future is largely uncertain. The community's challenge is to design itself as a functioning system that can absorb shocks and adapt quickly and effectively to new developments and opportunities. The community must establish *information, planning,* and *control systems* that allow it to monitor the changing environment and respond constructively to changing opportunities and threats. The aim is to prepare plans and actions that integrate the place's *objectives* and *resources* with its *changing opportunities.* Through the strategic planning process, a place decides which industries, services, and markets should be encouraged; which should be maintained; and which should be deemphasized or even abandoned.

We acknowledge at the outset that managing strategic market planning is more difficult for communities than for individual companies. Companies typically have a clear line of authority and hierarchy, as well as a balance sheet and a profit-and-loss statement to measure yearly progress. Communities, on the other hand, are chronic battlegrounds where interest groups vie for power and push their competing agendas and strategies. Whereas the private sector operates on the unifying goal of profit, community economic development runs the risk of being diluted by multiple interest groups, periodic elections, and the vagaries of the ballot box. Where institutional arrangements fail to reconcile conflict, and leadership is unable to emerge, communities fail or stagnate. Strategic market planning is highly unlikely to succeed in sharply divided communities where consensual building mechanisms fail to work. We believe, however, that the strategic planning process can work in most communities where institutions and procedures exist to make decisions about a place's future.

Strategic planning can be carried on in various ways: A single government department can conduct strategic planning functions. Several government agencies might join forces, pool resources, divide tasks, and form a joint strategic plan. Public/private commissions and committees might be formed to carry out the planning task. And, increasingly, authority and responsibility for strategic planning under public oversight are delegated to private organizations.

Whatever organizational structure is established, the strategic market planning process moves through five stages to answer the following questions:

1. *Place audit.* What is the community like today? What are the community's major strengths/weaknesses, opportunities/ threats, major issues?
2. *Vision and goals.* What do residents want the community to be or become?
3. *Strategy formulation.* What broad strategies will help the community reach its goals?
4. *Action plan.* What specific actions must the community undertake to carry out its strategies?
5. *Implementation and control.* What must the community do to insure successful implementation?

The following discussion describes major concepts and tools used at each stage of the strategic planning process.

CONDUCTING THE PLACE AUDIT

The first task facing a group responsible for charting a community's future course is to understand accurately what the community is like and why. The tool for doing this is called a *place audit,* a systematic examination of a place's economic/demographic characteristics, followed by an attempt to sort them into competitive strengths and weaknesses, followed by an effort to relate them to opportunities and threat, thus providing the basis for constructing a potentially attractive future for the place.

Establishing the Place's Economic/Demographic Characteristics

A place audit must start with good information about the place's economic/ demographic features, such as its population size and composition by sex, age, income, race, and education; housing market characteristics; industry structure and labor market characteristics; community health characteristics; natural resources; transportation facilities; public safety and crime statistics; education and research institutions; and recreation and cultural resources. This information goes into a community fact book or some other promotional piece from which various community marketers can prepare their cases as they attempt to attract different target markets. The information helps answer such questions as: What is the place's "livability" when it comes to attracting new residents? What is the place's "visitability" when it comes to attracting tourists? What is the place's "investibility" when it comes to attracting business and investment?

Identifying the Place's Main Competitors

Establishing a place's competitive advantages cannot be restricted to what constitutes a "good fit" or what makes it a good place to operate a particular business. Every place needs to identify other places with which it has a close rivalry. The twin cities of Minneapolis and St. Paul frequently compete for the same businesses; New York City competes with nearby New Jersey and Connecticut for company location; Florida and California compete for tourists and residents seeking a warmer climate.

A place needs to identify its main competitors in each specific competitive arena. In attracting large business conventions, Chicago competes with traditional rivals New York and Las Vegas and newer ones such as Orlando, Atlanta, and Denver. In attracting European tourists, the main competitors are New York City, Los Angeles, Las Vegas, Miami, New Orleans, and San Francisco. In attracting large regional offices, it competes with its own suburbs, Columbus, Minneapolis, Kansas City, and Indianapolis.

We can define three levels of competitors: A superior competitor is one who, when competing with the specific community, wins most of the time; a peer competitor is one who wins approximately half of the time; and a weak competitor is one who loses to the community most of the time. The community's key problem is to figure out how to improve its odds over its peer competitors and in the long run catch up with its superior competitors.

The challenge is to learn how the particular target buyers make their decisions. A community needs to know which criteria buyers are using, the importance weights they assign to the different criteria, and their perceptions of how the competitors rank on the criteria. Knowing this, the place marketer can try to influence the criteria set, the importance weights, or the perceptions the buyers have of the place and its competitors.

Identifying the Major Trends and Developments

Preparing for the future involves anticipating the main trends and developments likely to affect places. Communities must pay special attention to the following trends:

- Places will receive less direct funding from national and state sources and have to rely more on generating their own funds to support basic services.
- Places will need to be more attentive to environmental forces and regulations in planning their future, which will require getting the most out of existing facilities, making public facilities and investments fit better into the natural environment, and meeting needs more creatively.
- Places will be influenced more than ever before by global developments and changes, and therefore must actively monitor and anticipate their impact on the place.
- Places caught between business-as-usual tax increases to support more public services and service decline due to tax-resistant voter will simply have to do more with less, which means different and more productive approaches to service delivery.

These and other macrodevelopments not only must be identified, but the community must assess their impact and take steps to respond to these developments.

Analyzing the Place's Strengths and Weaknesses

It is one thing to catalog a place's characteristics and another to identify its major *strengths* and *weaknesses*, as well as its *opportunities* and *threats* (called a *SWOT analysis*). The challenge is to move from a *place profile* to a *place analysis*. Thus when the city of Cincinnati hired consultant Sherry Kafka Wagner to help them plan, she concluded her marketing audit with "You [Cincinnati] have holes. A pretty girl missing teeth isn't quite complete."

A place needs to identify which of its characteristics represent a major strength, minor strength, neutral factor, minor weakness, or major weakness in terms of what specific place buyers are seeking. A place's competitive position reflects two sets of conditions: those outside forces that are generally beyond local influence, and locational characteristics that specific location action might be able to influence. The resulting analysis forces places to be more realistic about their prospects:

A survey conducted to assess U.S. visitors' perceptions about India as a vacation destination revealed that poverty, low cleanliness standards, political instability, and quality of transportation were reported weaknesses. On the other hand, respondents were impressed with India's culture, history, and exoticism—all aspects attracting visitors to that country. In the short run, India can only tout its strengths. In the long run, it must try to correct its weaknesses.[6]

Consider Detroit. Table 4–2 lists nine criteria used in the 1989 edition of Rand McNally's *Places Rated Almanac,* along with Detroit's rated position on each attribute. Two major weaknesses of Detroit are revealed: high crime and high cost of living. Detroit also has some minor weaknesses, such as poor climate and transportation. According to the almanac, Detroit's educational system is a major strength. As for minor strengths, Detroit could list the arts and recreation.

Note that this analysis constitutes a *macroassessment* of Detroit's strengths and weaknesses. A *microassessment* would reveal specific strengths and weaknesses within the larger categories. Thus, within the

TABLE 4–2
Detroit's Strengths and Weaknesses

	Major Strength	Minor Strength	Neutral	Minor Weakness	Major Weakness
Climate				X	
Cost of living					X
Health care and environment			X		
Crime					X
Transportation				X	
Education	X				
Arts		X			
Recreation		X			
Jobs			X		

Source: Inferred by the authors from Richard Boyer and David Savageau, Places Rated Almanac (Englewood Cliffs, N.J.: Prentice Hall, 1989).

arts, Detroit has a world-class art museum, an excellent opera company, and a first-rate professional theater. The larger Detroit area contains some excellent recreational resources such as Dearborn Park, two major zoos, and a large coastline. As for specific weaknesses, Detroit has a staggering number of unemployed black youth and a lack of new energetic business development in the central core.

Of course, not all attributes are equally meaningful to different target groups that Detroit might want to attract. It is necessary to choose the attributes of importance to each target group and assign importance weights to these individual attributes. When combining performance ratings and importance levels, four possibilities emerge (see table 4-3). In cell A are important attributes where the place unfortunately rates poorly and, therefore, where critical improvements are needed; hence, "concentrate here." In cell B fall important attributes where the place is already strong; hence, "keep up the good work." In cell C fall unimportant attributes where the place is performing poorly; these attributes consequently are of "low priority." In cell D fall unimportant attributes, where the place is performing strongly; perhaps, it is overinvesting in these attributes, that is "overkill."

Even the concept of a strength must be carefully interpreted. Although a place may have a major strength (i.e., a *distinctive competence*), that strength does not necessarily constitute a *competitive advantage*. First, it may not be an attribute of any importance to the target market. Second, even if it is, competitors may have the same strength level on that attribute. What become important, then, is for the place to have *greater relative strength* on an attribute important to a target

TABLE 4-3
Performance-Importance Matrix

		Performance	
		Low	*High*
Importance	*High*	A. Concentrate Here	B. Keep Up the Good Work
	Low	C. Low Priority	D. Possible Overkill

group. Thus, two competing cities may both enjoy low manufacturing costs; but the one with the lower manufacturing cost has a net competitive advantage.

Clearly, a place does not have to correct all its weaknesses nor push all its strengths, because some attributes are unimportant. Instead, a place must probe deeper into those strengths and weaknesses most affecting the perceptions and behavior of target markets. The resultant analysis becomes a major basis for laying future plan. Exhibit 4–1 describes how Chemainus, Canada, executed a plan to change its image.

Identifying the Place's Opportunities and Threats

The next step is to identify the opportunities and threats facing the particular place. Whereas strengths and weaknesses are internal to the place, opportunities and threats are external. We define a place opportunity as follows:

> A place opportunity is an arena for action in which a place has a fairly good chance to achieve a competitive advantage.

Let's look at the example of Hollywood, California, in the 1980s. Few places are more depressing than Hollywood. A place with a magic name, and yet, a walk down Hollywood Boulevard dispels any lingering romance. The famous walk of fame is unsightly and many stores are abandoned or sell cheap souvenirs. The surrounding areas are crime-ridden and the homeless are everywhere.

For five years the Hollywood Community Redevelopment Agency has been pushing forward a $1 billion rehabilitation plan. The object is to make famous Hollywood Boulevard a showpiece once again. The project is intended to rebuild theaters, launch museums, provide new housing, and support medical and relocation plans for senior citizens, the homeless, and AIDS patients. It all sounds terrific.

The plan has faced a series of legal battles since its inception. Local groups have sued because they fear rising homeowner costs and a loss of historic buildings. Even more troubling is their fear that large real estate interests are going to ravage Hollywood, leaving the rich in high-rises and forcing the poor and middle-class to move elsewhere.[7]

This planning paradox has been repeated in practically every city in the world. The Hollywood planners needed to consult the opinion leaders and community organizations early in the process. The concerns of the displaced should be carefully evaluated and considered. The large

EXHIBIT 4-1

Chemainus, Canada Finds a Solution

The town of Chemainus is located on the east side of Vancouver Island, British Columbia, Canada. Most of its income comes from those working in the surrounding forest industry. As this industry sputtered into decline, and a new highway skirting the town by one mile drew traffic away, Chemainus fell on hard times: shops were closed, income tax was difficult to collect, and basic service began to deteriorate. The citizens began to feel a sense of loss and inevitable decline.

In this crisis, a bold plan was conceived: It was decided to renovate Chemainus as a tourist town, using grants and loans from the province of British Columbia. The plan required the cooperation of the business people who would have to invest in new sidewalks, cleaning up the streets, and other improvement to make the town attractive. The bold idea was to employ artists to paint five giant murals based on actual photographs on the town buildings depicting lumber industry history. They called the attraction the Chemainus Festival of Murals. The festival was a stunning success and led to the addition of twenty-five murals, making thirty in all. Since the advertisement of the murals, hundreds of thousands of tourists have visited Chemainus and seventy new businesses have opened. The town became solvent. In addition to tourism, the revitalization encouraged the building of a $21 million sawmill, the making of a film, *The Little Town that Did*, and the building of a replica of the 1924 ship, *The Spirit of Chemainus*, as a goodwill ambassador to the Expo in Vancouver. All together, the scheme and partnership worked well for this town, and other towns request information to attempt similar projects.

Source: Karl Schutz, "Changing Chemainus' Image," *Public Management*, June 1986, pp. 9–11. Interview with Marcia Robinson, office manager of the Art and Business Council of Chemainus on January, 13, 1992.

EXHIBIT 4-2

San Francisco SWOT Analysis— Housing Threat

Consider San Francisco's SWOT Analysis, a strategic plan prepared by Arthur Andersen & Co. for the city's Chamber of Commerce in the early 1980s called "Making a Great City Greater." In the strategic planning process, city officials and business representatives identified four strategic issues from its place audit: housing, transportation, city finances, and jobs and business opportunities. These, in turn, were subjected to analysis regarding a forecast of key external factors in the city's broader environment that it could not control, but that would have a major impact on these issues and the city's future. Next, San Francisco's internal strengths and weaknesses were assessed related to each issue, with particular attention given to comparing the city to its competitors.

The high cost of California housing generally and San Francisco housing specifically are major strategic issues in business attraction, retention, and expansion. Unfavorable trends outside the city's control included higher interest rates and housing costs

projects such as the renovation of the El Capitan Theater and the New Galaxy Theater and shopping center needed to be balanced with small projects that cleared up streets and re-opened small shops. Hollywood has a good plan to rescue itself. Residents need, however, a more expansive vision of what their place needs to do.

All opportunities—whether it is building a theater complex or a festival market waterfront, must be assessed according to their *attractiveness* and *success probability*. Each opportunity ends up as one of three types: The best opportunities are those that are intrinsically attractive and have a high success probability. Management needs to develop plans to exploit these opportunities. The worst opportunities are those with low attractiveness and low success probability, and they should be disregarded. Moderate opportunities, those with either high attractiveness or success probability, but not both, should be monitored.

as well as strong demand, offset in part by trends that suggested growing consumer acceptance of smaller, denser housing with few amenities. Switching to internal analysis, those forces that the city can control and actions it might take to make housing more affordable included the following six actions as being most important to future housing production: rent control, zoning, housing permit process, land costs, utilization of secondary units (within existing housing stock), and mobilization of a pro-housing constituency.

Actions aimed to increase the supply of the city's affordable housing stock clearly would encounter sizable political constraints in this high-participation, neighborhood-focused city. In addition, rent control on existing housing constituted a major deterrent to new rental housing; it was feared that new construction also would be brought under controls, severely limiting investor returns. San Francisco's zoning, land use, rent control, and development fees already had discouraged investment in the city, promoting economic decentralization in the Bay area and causing some corporate relocation to the Los Angeles and Seattle areas. The city needed to modify its strategy to enable new builders to turn a profit.

Source: Arthur Andersen & Co., *Making a Great City Greater* (San Francisco: Arthur Andersen & Co., 1983), p. 9.

In addition to opportunities, every place faces threats, a challenge posed by a unfavorable trend or development in the environment that would lead, in the absence of purposeful action, to the erosion of the place's condition. Planning groups need to identify various threats. These threats can be classified according to their *seriousness* and *probability of occurrence.* Major threats are those that can seriously hurt the place and have a high probability of occurring. The place needs to prepare a contingency plan that spells out what steps to take before or during a major threat's occurrence. Minor threats are those with a low probability of occurring that would not hurt the place badly; they can be ignored. Moderate threats are those with either high potential harm or high occurrence probability but not both; they must be watched. (See San Francisco SWOT Analysis—Housing Threat, in exhibit 4–2.)

By assembling a picture of the major threats and opportunities facing a specific place, it is possible to characterize the place's overall attractiveness. An *ideal place* is one that is high in major opportunities and low in major threats. A *speculative place* is high in both major opportunities and threats. A *mature place* is low in major opportunities and threats. Finally, a *troubled place* is low in opportunities and high in threats.

Establishing the Main Issues

The SWOT analysis permits strategic planners to carry out *issue identification and management.* They need to identify the main issues facing the community. For example, Chicago currently faces the following major issues:

- Should Chicago attempt to reinvigorate its shrinking manufacturing base or market itself decisively as a service center? If the latter, how fast should it move and what service industries should it emphasize?
- Should Chicago expand its convention facilities to remain number one or can it coast safely on its present superior facilities?
- Should Chicago build a legal gambling complex and where should it be located?
- Can Chicago provide jobs for its minority population and prevent increased gang wars and illegal drug sales?
- Can Chicago substantially improve the quality of its primary and secondary public school system?

Having identified these issues, all of which involve sizable investments and long-term commitments, place planners should appoint committees to research each issue and report its findings and recommendations. This information can be publicly debated, to allow for community participation and hearings, as well as media scrutiny, and afterward to allow the strategic planners to work on the resulting recommendations.

SETTING THE VISION AND OBJECTIVES

As a result of carrying out a SWOT and issue analysis, strategic planners arrive at a comprehensive picture of the community's situation. The planners need to prioritize these projects and invest in those that fall within the place's resource constraints. However, the danger is that the miscellaneous projects will not add up to a coherent development plan and vision. In fact, without a coherent vision, it is difficult to prioritize the various projects except in limited criteria such as the number of tourists or businesses attracted, jobs created, and the like.

Vision development calls for the planners to solicit input from the citizens as to what they want their community to be like ten or twenty years from now. It is important that two or more broad alternative visions (i.e., scenarios) be developed and debated. Each vision should carry some promise as well as risk.

Consider, for example, the city of San Diego, the nation's sixth largest city, which is currently attracting many new residents. What are the possible scenarios for San Diego twenty years down the road? At least three scenarios can be distinguished:

1. *Uncurbed growth.* San Diego continues to permit and encourage free and open growth. It grows in power and wealth but suffers urban sprawl, traffic snarl, and inadequate public services. It becomes another Los Angeles.
2. *Managed growth.* San Diego establishes growth guidelines so that there is a healthy balance between population growth and infrastructure growth. San Diego continues to grow in size but along a disciplined growth trajectory.
3. *Zero growth.* San Diego decides to limit further growth to protect its current character and amenities. San Diego takes steps to demarket certain groups and industries from migrating in to preserve its "good life."

Actually San Diego has four choices, not three. The fourth choice is to drift along rather than to adopt any vision. Most cities cannot agree on a single vision, or simply refuse to adopt one because they believe it limits their freedom to maneuver. However, to be without a vision is to be without direction and motivation (see Finding a Vision for the Great Plains in exhibit 4–3).

Developing alternative visions goes further than simply distinguishing among potential growth paths. A vision should take a stand on such issues as:

1. Which mix of industries make sense for the community? Should a community base its future on one or two industries or develop a diversified industrial base? Should a community focus on manufacturing or service industries? If manufacturing industries, should the community attract heavy industry or light industry?

EXHIBIT 4-3

Finding a Vision for the Great Plains

A vision is not always developed from strength as in the San Diego example. Many places find themselves under siege and must create a vision under the pressure of decline. In the late eighties, Frank Popper and Deborah Epstein-Popper, researchers at Rutgers University, proposed that the states of the Great Plains (most of the Dakotas, Nebraska, much of Kansas, Oklahoma, Texas, Montana, Wyoming, Colorado, and New Mexico) might be better off going out of business. They noted that the region doesn't have the climate, rainfall, or soil type to be agriculturally productive without government subsidies. In fact, these states are noted as extreme weather climates with burning summers, frigid winter, and habitual floods, droughts, and tornadoes.

Popper and Epstein-Popper suggested that the Great Plains states ("America's steppes") should be downscaled to what they termed a giant "buffalo commons," which basically would be a large game reserve. In addition, they proposed that Indian tribes who have claims on portions of the Great Plains be given back much of this land. The researchers suggested that the region was ultimately hopeless and large portions of the Great Plains would be deserted in the next thirty years.

The Great Plains communities were stunned. William Patrie, North Dakota's director of development, boldly claimed that the researcher were greatly underestimating the will and determination of people in North Dakota. "He [Popper] is assuming the future will be like the past. Well, we've seen the past and know it doesn't work,"

2. What land use and housing patterns make sense for the community? Should industry be concentrated in industrial parks? Should the community encourage high-rise construction or home ownership?

3. Which public services should be provided by local government and which should be let out to private contract?

Patrie said. Arlen Leholm, an agricultural economist at North Dakota State University Center for Rural Revitalization, was also upbeat about the future of the Great Plains states. "He [Popper] assumes we have no entrepreneurial spirit at all. This theory assumes we will lie down and die, and we're not going to do that." Leholm further noted that North Dakota is very productive in spring wheat and as long as this market remains internationally competitive, North Dakota will earn an income.

However, the Popper and Epstein-Popper forecast has some credibility. The Great Plains suffered through the drought of the late eighties far worse than any other section of the country, according to former United States Agricultural Secretary Richard Ling.

The question is what vision should the Great Plains states adopt? The Popper and Epstein-Popper vision is that the Great Plains should decline gracefully and the land should be turned back to its original state. They argue that no amount of federal aid or private industry could help these states compete with the more fertile and productive areas of the country. Vision two, suggested by state officials, is to do what these states are doing now, but better. Keep improving agricultural productivity and win out over the drought. Vision three would be to develop new industries in those states that can gain a competitive edge.

The choice is not a simple one. Each vision affects various interest groups differently. The region also lacks a strong regional planning mechanism. Therefore, it is likely that the future of the Great Plains states will be determined more by drift than resolve.

Source: Rogers Worthington, "Grim Forecast Just Riles Up Those Plainsmen," *Chicago Tribune,* August 2, 1988, p. 6.

4. How should public services by financed? How much financing should come from general taxes versus user taxes?

Given that a community can prepare different visions, how might it choose among them? Normally, the mayor and city council debate and decide. Various interest groups and citizens may present their views at public hearings. Less frequently, a place might survey the citizenry for its views. Several years ago, the Dallas city council sent questionnaires to citizens to probe what they wanted their city to be like in ten years. The survey results were published and influenced the course of the debate in the city council. In still rarer cases, the alternative visions for a city may be put to a public referendum.

The choice of a vision is greatly influenced by the *values* that citizens and government officials hold. If they highly value immediate jobs and profits, they favor high growth. If they highly value preserving a way of life, they lean toward managed or restrained growth.

Once the members of a community agree on a vision, they need to set specific *objectives* and *goals*. Objectives are statements about what a place wants to achieve; goals add specific magnitudes and timing to these objectives. For example, San Diego might adopt the "managed growth" vision and decide on the following objectives:

1. To attract high-tech industry while discouraging heavy industry.
2. To discourage the immigration of low-income residents by ceasing the construction of low-cost housing.
3. To improve business zoning standards and enforcement to prevent unsightly commercial strips from developing.

Objectives are directional only. They must be turned into goals to make them measurable and motivating to those who are responsible. For example, the first objective can be turned into the following goal statement:

Attract four or more high-tech companies to move their headquarters to San Diego with the aim of creating 300 new jobs by December 1994.

This statement provides clear direction to those in San Diego's economic development office as to the expected achievement. It also becomes the basis of allocating the resources needed to accomplish this goal. If only an objective had been stated, there would be no way to know whether it was accomplished because the magnitude and time frame had not been specified.

FORMULATING THE STRATEGY

Once the planning group has defined the vision, goals, and objectives, they can move into identifying and choosing strategies for accomplishing the goals. We saw, for example, that San Diego wants to attract four or more high-tech companies to move their headquarters to San Diego by December 1994. A large number of possible strategies include:

1. Establishing a high-tech industrial park that offers low-cost facilities and substantial tax advantages to prospective tenants and promoting this industrial park through feature articles, ads, and direct mail.
2. Attracting Nobel Prize physicists to the University of California at San Diego and promoting their presence to attract high-tech companies to locate in San Diego (There are 38 colleges and universities in San Diego County).
3. Targeting a specific set of high-tech companies located in Silicon Valley and inducing them to move their headquarters to San Diego.
4. Identifying some European high-tech companies and inducing them to move their headquarters to San Diego.

For each potential strategy, the planning group must ask the following two questions: *What advantages do we possess that suggest that we can succeed with that strategy? Do we have the resources required for a successful implementation of that strategy?*

Even communities without major strengths of resources can sometimes figure out a creative strategy, as shown in the examples of Paisley, Oregon, and International Falls, Minnesota, (see exhibit 4–4).

DEVELOPING THE ACTION PLAN

The place marketers must put together a specific action plan for carrying out the strategies. The plan lists actions that specific people must take at specific times of the year. For example, San Diego's plan may call for three city officials attending the June Electronics Show at Chicago's McCormick Place to search for the names of promising high-tech entrepreneurs who have set up booths at the show. The action plan must list each action, and next to it four additional components: who is responsible, how the action is to be implemented, how much the action will cost, and the expected completion date.

This level of detail provides several advantages: First, everyone involved in the action plan knows what they must accomplish. Second, the place marketer can easily discern whether the various actions are being satisfactorily implemented. Third, the action detail permits can-

EXHIBIT 4-4

How Paisley, Oregon, and International Falls, Minnesota, Turned Their Negatives into Positives

What happens when a community lacks any advantages on which to build a strategy? The community has *no* pretty scenery, *no* historical events, *no* attractions. The answer may be in turning a negative into a positive.

Take the dilemma of the residents of Paisley, Oregon, a town of 345 mosquito-bitten residents. This little corner of Oregon has the worst mosquito infestation in America. The town can't even muster the resources for a spraying truck. Some towns might lock up and move to higher ground during the invasion. The solution for Paisley was to launch a Mosquito Festival and transform the insect into a celebrity. In fact, since the mid-eighties, the festival has drawn thousands of bite-lovers. The festival includes a Ms. Quito contest and parades.

How about the remote town of International Falls, Minnesota? Stuck on the Minnesota–Canada border, the land is unfarmable and the weather is extremely cold. The answer: Promote the town as The Ice Box of the Nation. Each year, companies test their products in the cold environs of the "Falls." In fact, the town bought the exclusive rights to the coldest place slogan from a Colorado competitor.

These places may not have the attributes of Paris or London. Lacking the advantages of such places, they showed even more imagination than would be expected from the typical place marketer.

celing specific actions and their subsequent costs if the budget is being exceeded toward the end of the period.

One of the major planning challenges is to allocate the budget equitably to the various areas within the place's boundaries. Over half the population of Minnesota, for example, is concentrated in the Minneapolis/St. Paul area. The Twin Cities have been very successful in high-tech development, in addition to being an educational and cultural center. The southern and central sections of the state are tied to a declining agricultural base and some areas are severely depressed. Tourism is an emerging industry in northern Minnesota, but it is not as developed as in some other states. The plan should set goals and targets for each region rather than describing only broad initiatives for the entire state.

Abraham Shama makes a similar point about New Mexico's five-year plan.[8] Albuquerque accounts for almost half of New Mexico's population and has "a stable and growing economy, higher per capita income, higher degree of education, and has more professionals, managers, and administrators." The rest of the state is primarily mining, agricultural, and rural, and has large pockets of troubled industries and worrisome degrees of unemployment. Clearly, any effective state planning document needs to make distinctions—which the New Mexico five-year plan did not—about the have-not portions of the state. In contrast, South Dakota's development plan carefully divided the state into six regions with a comprehensive profile, market analysis, and marketing plan for each region. The same principle applies to plans for nations and cities with co-existing areas of opportunity and poverty, often adjacent to each other.

IMPLEMENTING AND CONTROLLING THE MARKETING PLAN

Plans are not worth anything until they are effectively implemented. The planning group needs to convene at regular intervals to review the community's progress toward its goals. For example, if the year passes and the San Diego economic development group has not managed to attract one new high-tech company, the goal, strategy, or actions have to be reconsidered.

Every community should issue an annual report, much like companies do, to highlight their accomplishments for the year as well as discuss their failures to achieve certain goals. The report should contain various statistical indicators describing where the community stands on jobs, income, housing, health, crime, and public transportation in relation to where it planned to be. The community's annual report should receive broad public distribution; it can be included as an insert in the major newspapers. Ideally, various citizen and business groups discuss the results and pressure the officials to sustain the drive to achieve the community's long-run objectives.

CONCLUSION

The underlying argument here is that places can and must do better jobs of managing their future. Too many places fail to recognize threats before they become overwhelming, if not irreversible. They react, rather than proact.

Yet this passivity is not inevitable. Some places have responded with approaches such as community development, urban design, urban planning, and economic development. Strategic market planning represents an approach by which a place can design a better future. It calls for profiling the place's situation; identifying the place's strengths/ weaknesses, opportunities/threats, and main issues; setting a vision, objectives, and goals; defining effective strategies for accomplishing these goals; developing appropriate actions; and implementing and controlling the plan.

Although this version of strategic planning oversimplifies many of the problems of managing complex entities such as cities, states, and nations, it represents a more promising approach than any of its alternatives, such as a trial and error approach with its risk of haphazard changes. Some cities have already put into practice important elements of strategic planning thinking with some success. We mention in other parts of this book the turnarounds of cities such as Baltimore, Indianapolis, and St. Paul. Each of these cities engaged in some form of strategic planning to create a better future.

5

Strategies for Place Improvement

Too many place improvers believe that *marketing a place* means *promoting a place*. They view marketing as an image-building exercise, confusing it with one of its subactivities, namely promotion. Promotion is, ironically, one of the least important marketing tasks. Promotion alone does not help a troubled city. In fact, it only helps place buyers to discover early how troubled the city really is.

Suppose East St. Louis, Illinois, produces a campaign to attract tourists to "Beautiful and Historic East St. Louis." However, arriving tourists immediately encounter piles of uncollected trash, scores of homeless people, x-rated movie theaters, and open drug sales on the main streets. Fearing for their personal safety, the tourists cut short their visit, return home, and tell friends to avoid East St. Louis at all costs. Consequently, East St. Louis's promotion campaign serves only to accelerate the rate at which people learn how undesirable the place is as a tourist attraction.

Place marketing means designing a place to satisfy the needs of its target markets. It succeeds when citizens and businesses are pleased with their communities, and meet the expectations of visitors and investors.

In this chapter, we examine various investments a place can make to improve livability, investibility, and visitability. We see this as a process made up of four components. First, a place needs a sound design that enhances its attractiveness and more fully develops its aesthetic qualities and values (Place as *character*). Places need to develop and maintain a basic infrastructure that moves people and goods in ways compatible with the natural environment (Place as a fixed *environment*). Third, a place must provide basic services of quality that meet business and public needs (Place as *service provider*). Finally, places need a range of attractions for their own people and visitors (Place as *entertainment and recreation*). As we shall demonstrate, these components are not mutually exclusive.

While we cover more generic strategies for place improvement in later chapters, these place improvement strategies— design, infrastructure, services, and attractions—can be viewed as the building blocks for specific competitive strategies. Whether or not a place adopts a strategic market planning approach for place competition, careful attention to these features and attributes can create the foundations of a place strategy.

These components are far too often assumed as "givens" in place competition. For the most part, attention to them is well within the range of a place's collective endeavors. They are preconditions that set the stage for often riskier and more opportunistic efforts to compete for economic advantages.

I. URBAN DESIGN

Urban design tells us a great deal about the character of a place and redefines how that character is transmitted from one generation to the next. Interweaving a diverse array of physical structures into an overall place fabric is an art. Urban design makes a statement about a place because it reflects how values and decision-making combine on issues that affect development.

Historically, places have formed next to natural harbors, near river connections, and along canals, followed by railroads, which often paralleled water routes. Dirt paths turned to horse and wagon routes, which later accommodated streetcars and automobiles. Transportation patterns shaped the contours of place development, connecting commercial, industrial, and patterned residential growth internally and markets for raw materials and finished goods externally.

Older U.S. cities followed a concentric form of expansion, pushing outward from a hub business district along the nexus of key transportation routes, which separated worker, middle-class, and more affluent residents. As manufacturing situated itself along transportation grids, concentricity gave way to more sectoral forms of development, in which industrial, commercial, and residential areas took on more random patterns pushing out from the central city to the urban fringe and beyond. Within this patterned development, some cities formed a gridlike geometric patterns of streets with rectangular blocks, as in Chicago, New York, or London. Others, like Paris or Washington, D.C., followed a wheel-and-spoke pattern, where diagonal roads radiated from the center. A third, more random pattern combined several design formats, specifically in places of irregular terrain and village annexation.

Still other places, often great cities like Paris, Venice, and Florence, followed master plans in which visionary leadership emerged at the right time for designs to make an indelible imprint on people and places.

The redevelopment of Paris began in 1853, when Napoleon III selected Georges-Eugène Haussmann to conceive and implement a plan to renew completely the central section of Paris. Baron Haussmann worked for seventeen years to implement a plan that blended order, variety, convenience, and grandeur. Haussmann fathered many monuments, the wide boulevards of Paris, the famous Opéra of Paris and les Halles—the central marketplace of Paris.

Chicago's beautiful lakefront and park system was the brainchild of Daniel H. Burnham, Sr., who sought to protect Chicago's valuable scenic assets from private development. During Chicago's intense growth period in the early 1900s, Burnham laid out a plan to preserve Chicago's space for citizens and visitors. Burnham's plan gave Chicago a focus for the cultural and civic activity of the city. A trip on Lakeshore Drive now features the art and science museums, Soldier's Field, Shedd Aquarium, and the expansive Grant Park, highlighted by Buckingham Fountain. The plan, which also tied together highways and freight and passenger rail lines, and created forest preserves, encouraged other American cities to plan their future.[1]

As a result of vision, some cities emerged as works of art:

"Imperial Paris and London . . . were deliberate artistic creations intended not merely to give pleasure, but to contain ideas, inculcate

values, and serve as tangible expressions of thought and moral-
ity."[2]

Most cities never had the benefit of visionary leaders' plans, in
which aesthetics and physical principles applied discipline to growth.
Their development simply responded to new technologies, economic
changes, and outward growth. Streetcars and trolleys were superseded
by rapid transit rail and car, with the further enhancement of bridges,
tunnels, and expressways. For most cities, the fixed environment simply evolved sequentially and over time.

Inevitably, growth and place maturity produced generic problems—
central city deterioration, crime, loss of manufacturing employment,
and traffic congestion—which could not be ignored. Such postwar solutions as urban renewal and public housing proved extremely short-
sighted for many. Cities reclaimed blighted homes and obsolete factories by constructing more roads and by destroying ethnic
neighborhoods, replacing them with high-rise public housing and impersonal skyscrapers.

In *The Death and Life of American Cities,* the social critic Jane Jacobs attacked this urban bulldozer approach to city planning and re-
building, arguing passionately against what she considered to be a com-
puter-driven, nonhumanistic approach to urban revitalization.[3] Her call
for a return to a street culture with mixed housing, irregular streets,
and small shops proved to be shock therapy for those who had neglected the human, social, and aesthetic sides of urban planning.

Years later, places would rediscover their heritage, in which a city
divided by class, ethnic, and historical lines allows for celebration of its
rich diversity in neighborhoods. For example, St. Louis's rebirth stems
largely from its efforts to restore old areas—the southside Italian neighborhood known as "The Hill"; the German neighborhood of Baden
North; the old Irish neighborhood of Montgomery–Hyde Park; the
Central West End area of parks, upscale shops, and restaurants; and
the old riverfront, with a stadium and Gateway Arch.

Observing the results of badly managed urban growth, several
schools of urban planning emerged, each with its own vision of what
the modern city should look like. One of the most influential urban
planners, Franco-Swiss architect Le Corbusier, proposed a rigid separation of the city's residential, commercial, and industrial sections. Citizens would live in clusters of high-rise buildings, each cluster served by
common amenities such as schools, shopping, and playgrounds. There

would be lots of space between clusters, and roads would be designed for heavy traffic.[4]

The 1950s marked the construction of many "new towns," such as Reston, Virginia, and Brasilia, Brazil, as well as several new towns surrounding Paris. Urban planners could test their new theories on what constituted highly livable and attractive cities. They thought of new towns as design challenges, where the aim would be to create and blend livable streets and neighborhoods (clean, safe, and secure); minimum density to support city life; linking of activities (working, shopping, meeting, worshiping, and recreating); a human environment; and different buildings, space arrangements, and relationships.[5]

Not all new towns drew the critics' raves. James Holston sees modern Brasilia, the new capital of Brazil, as the ultimate embodiment of Le Corbusier's ideal city, composed of identical multistory buildings, uninterrupted highways, clear separation of residential and industrial areas, unused spaces among the clustered groups of industrial areas, and unused spaces among the clustered groups of buildings. He points out that Brasilia alienates and disorients many residents because life there is so different from the life they lived in São Paulo or Rio de Janeiro: "In planned Brasilia, there are no urban crowds, no street corner societies, and no sidewalk sociality, largely because there are no squares, no streets, no street corners."[6]

Today, old and new communities alike seek guidance from consultants on urban development. Among the more prominent organizations are the Urban Land Institute, American Institute of Architects, American Society of Landscape Architects, Institute for Urban Design, International Downtown Association, National Main Street Center, Partners for Livable Places, Project for Public Spaces, and Waterfront Center.[7] Professionals responsible for planning redevelopment projects use public hearings to solicit ideas from outside experts and the public on how best to improve urban living. Local design boards have learned through experience the importance of incorporating aesthetic and/or humanistic values into project evaluations; those values include historic preservation, the natural environment, and what is loosely termed "good design."[8]

One area of focus is small town renewal, specifically main street renewal. Main streets reflect the living history of many American towns. In an effort to rebuild main streets, the American Institute of Architects' Regional/Urban Design Assistant Teams send consultants

---

EXHIBIT 5-1

Design Michigan

Frankfort, Michigan, is a small city of 1,600 residents located on the eastern shore of Lake Michigan. In the mid-1980s, town leaders and business owners took a growing interest in finding ways to draw automobile and pleasure-boat tourists to the city's commercial district. Past development projects and renovation efforts had been poorly coordinated, hence, ineffective.

In 1987 Design Michigan was called to assist this struggling community. Design Michigan is a nonprofit design program operated by the state and the Cranbrook Academy of Art. Defined as "a creative planning and management process which optimizes a community's function and image," Design Michigan utilizes various methods to change a city's design effectively.

In Frankfort's case, the Design Michigan team first visited the town for a daylong audit. It took slides, sketched maps, and made videotapes of Frankfort's entry points, public corridors and

---

(for just expenses) to interested towns. Rome, Georgia, and Heraldsburg, California, have benefited from the expertise and assistance provided by the National Main Street Center.[9] Exhibit 5-1 describes how a similar group, Design Michigan, helped renovate Frankfort, Michigan.

One place-improvement strategy is to educate public officials on the principles of good urban design. This task is being handled by the Design Arts Program of the National Endowment for Arts, which organized the Mayors Institute for Civic Design. The institute focuses on combining the efforts of expert design specialists and public officials to overcome design problems. A network of informal workshops tutors mayors and other officials in design strategy. The institute has concentrated on smaller cities with diverse populations that can benefit from superior urban design.[10]

With the assistance of these agencies, several U.S. cities have moved ahead with major urban redesign plans:

spaces, buildings, interiors, and signs. One month later the team returned to present its findings.

Because community involvement is heavily emphasized in Design Michigan programs, the results were disclosed at a town meeting presentation. The design team displayed hundreds of panels featuring photos of buildings and entryways, along with a data sheet listing weaknesses and recommended changes. In addition, the team conducted a walk-in design clinic, where property owners could speak directly to designers in an individualized counseling session. The new look was a facelift to give Frankfort a historically accurate style.

The response to Design Michigan's suggestions was mixed. Sixty percent of businesses purchased the design changes. While business is still not as prosperous as Frankfort would like, the mood is upbeat. The renovation is proving to be a catalyst for change, and the city receives accolades from visitors and free publicity such as a photo in *Midwest Living* magazine. The city business leaders now hope the remaining merchants will renovate and have no doubt that the city has improved its chances for place success.

Source: Jack Williamson, "Design Michigan Creates a Community Design Advisory Program," *Small Town,* September–October 1987, p. 5. Interview with Peter Sandman, Downtown Frankfort Association on December 27, 1991.

In 1988 Portland, Oregon, approved a twenty-year plan to revitalize the downtown area and seven other districts. The comprehensive plan included recommendations for rehabilitating the city's human services, parks, entertainment areas, and riverfront.[11]

One of the most attractive sections of Chicago is River North, which occupies one hundred blocks of prime northside real estate. The city planning committee carefully inventoried important historical buildings and interesting features and created a community that reflects old and new strengths of the section. In 1988 the American Planning Association cited the River North Urban Plan as an outstanding project.[12]

Other places have actively developed urban revitalization plans. Arlington, Texas, won the 1989 American Planning Award for its plan. North Philadelphia developed an all-inclusive comprehensive physical and economic development plan. The San Francisco Neighborhood Commercial Rezoning Study was developed to retain the ambience and integrity of the city. Forsyth County, North Carolina's Vision 2005 Plan, is considered different from traditional plans and has earned a cutting-edge reputation. The focus in Oakland County, Michigan, is on graphic audits of natural resources and guidelines for streetscape design.[13]

For a variety of reasons, places have returned to thinking more broadly about the importance of urban design in place competition. Scarce resources and environmental or legal constraints on old-fashioned bulldozing have compelled places to embrace adaptive reuse. Current approaches to urban design emphasize what is environmentally compatible with existing physical and national features, along with ways to resurrect the older character and history of places. Such thinking also requires vision, blending old with new, and an appreciation that place character is a valuable asset in retaining firms and people as well as in attracting new investment and businesses.

II. INFRASTRUCTURE IMPROVEMENT

Where urban design provides a framework or skeleton for a place, infrastructure makes the design possible. What benefits would Paris's spacious boulevards provide if they were riddled with potholes? How long can New York remain the world's financial capital without adequate subways, ferries, and bridges to move people on or off Manhattan Island? How great would Rio de Janeiro's beaches be if its waters were dangerously polluted? What value would Los Angeles's mountainside homes be without flood control works? How much development can the Southwestern United States sustain without adequate water and energy supplies? Countless examples illustrate the basic fact that much place advantage stems from the infrastructure that either supports or detracts from its attractions.

While excellent and well-maintained infrastructure cannot guarantee a community's growth, its absence is a serious liability. To sustain quality of life and to support economic productivity, a place—no less than a nation—requires that infrastructure be developed and maintained. This challenge is exemplified by Russia and Eastern Europe, which seek the transition to market economies with vastly underdeveloped infrastructure that inhibits the movement of people, goods, and information. These countries' prior underinvestment now requires government or business to invest heavily in order to induce future growth.

Far too often, residents take infrastructure for granted on the principle that "out of sight is out of mind." What one generation put in place may be lost to the next, when it assumes that water and sewer systems, bridges and tunnels, roads, and waterways promise perpetual use. For older, more developed places, their in-place infrastructure can confer unique advantages in competition with new places, which have to build from scratch, at great expense, entirely new systems to accommodate growth. However, as many older places have allowed their capital plants to deteriorate, have engaged in deferred maintenance to cut spending, or otherwise have neglected the repair of these valuable assets, they face an ever growing liability of replacing and renewing their capital stock.

Throughout the United States, places gradually have awakened to the infrastructure problem, which has assumed national proportions. Dating from the mid-1960s, infrastructure spending as a portion of our gross domestic product has declined. The specific causes are many: reduced federal funding, the high interest rates of the 1970s and early 1980s, taxpayer resistance, environmental constraints, and more pressing public expenditures. The sky may not be falling, but the obvious consequences of neglect and capital underinvestment grow more visible each day as the media report falling bridges, water shortages, polluted streams, unusable roads, decaying ports, and failing transit systems.

Every community must provide some basic standard of services to enable attracting and retaining people, businesses, and visitors. Admittedly, no uniform standards exist except where set by law and by health and safety regulations. While the issues of who pays, who administers, and who delivers services are vastly blurred by a federal system of national, state, and local governments, all places are subject to varying degrees of responsibility for roads and transportation, water and energy supply, and meeting environmental standards.

Needs Assessment

All places require a needs assessment of their capital facilities by age, condition, and scheduled repairs as well as related 5-to-20-year plans for rehabilitation and replacement. Years ago city engineers and architects possessed a good inventory of the relative condition, costs, and schedules for maintenance of a place's infrastructure. In many cases that institutional knowledge and capacity have been lost because of shifting intergovernmental responsibility, the growth of separate authorities, and systematic neglect. In other cases, places have been so committed to growth or development that they have underestimated or simply failed to anticipate the related infrastructure requirements and costs that accompany growth.

In 1987 Fairfax County, Virginia, was delighted to become the new home of Mobil Corporation. Additional Fortune 500 companies were expected to move into the area. As a result, the county found itself with embarrassing foul-ups in traffic despite considerable outlays of funds. The problem had to be attacked by approving a bond issue to finance new road projects and by rescinding the limits that the state had placed on local highway spending.[14]

Plastic refuse and litter float in Hong Kong's Victoria Harbor. Rubbish dumped by boats or carried to the sea by sewers pollutes Hong Kong's beaches. A large percentage of Hong Kong's chemical waste is simply deposited into the sea. In some parts of Hong Kong more than 90 percent of the storm sewer connections are illegal. The entire matter is out of control, because the government is too overwhelmed to prosecute large numbers of waste-related factory violations. Asia's most dynamic economies have all struggled with the conflict between rapid economic growth and environmental issues.[15]

While the exact costs of neglect can only be estimated, various studies have documented losses to governments, businesses, and people that stem from infrastructure underinvestment. Poor road condition adds considerably to the costs for operating motor vehicles. Deficient water and sewer supplies impede residential development and detract from business investment. Traffic congestion that adds to commuting time contributes to loss of employee productivity. Lack of energy availability and unreliability of services constitute a greater competitive disadvantage in the information age than high energy costs. When housing stock is allowed to deteriorate beyond a certain point, replacement costs greatly exceed the expenses of rehabilitation. Places learn the hard way that maintenance, repair, and rehabilitation pay for themselves.

Infrastructure Management

A good infrastructure-needs assessment, periodically updated and systematically tracked, is essential for *performance management*—a new approach to infrastructure required by resource and environmental constraints. The mobility of jobs and people from cities to suburbs to exurbia has created its own paradoxes. Cities have built costly new infrastructure on the expanding urban fringe while abandoning the already built, fixed urban environment in central cities and places. Simply building more and better roads to accommodate an expanding demand for auto transportation in many cases increases traffic congestion. The old idea of adding greater capacity to roads to handle more vehicles gradually has given way to the notion of moving more people with less fuel to generate less air pollution.

Thus, needs assessment and the management of infrastructure are linked by a new emphasis on performance—not simply construction. Places cannot replace everything. Formerly capital budgeting and planning took on the character of wish lists, that is, everything a place would like to build, rehabilitate, or replace should unlimited resources be available. However, resource constraints have compelled places and infrastructure authorities to think through various options that improve systemwide performance, provide the greatest return on investment, and balance multiple needs. Bruce McDowell has noted that "the future is more likely to focus on maintaining and getting the most out of existing facilities, keeping costs down, making public facilities fit more comfortably into the natural environment, and being more ingenious in meeting needs in the most efficient ways that science can devise."[16]

Each stage of the infrastructure management process introduces new opportunities for doing things differently. Design now involves better materials, technologies, and design techniques. Construction is enhanced through improved materials, quality control, and scheduling methods. Operations and maintenance draw on new materials, techniques, and management tools. Monitoring incorporates newer needs assessment methods, better management systems, and improved ways of estimating demand. Finally, in this integrated and multistage process, planning and programming use better forecasting, budgeting, and project development techniques.

Intergovernmental Planning

In the best traditions of architecture and engineering, "everything is connected to everything else" when it comes to infrastructure planning. Whether for historical reasons or owing to financing requirements, infrastructure systems and responsibilities are dispersed horizontally across separate governmental or private authorities and agencies, and are vertically regulated, funded, or operated by several higher governmental levels. For example, while the federal government funds nearly 30 percent of the nation's 4 million miles of roads and sets the policy for their construction and maintenance, states and localities are responsible for the majority of the roadways. Intergovernmental gridlock between and among adjacent jurisdictions thus augments traffic congestion. In bygone eras, when each community was responsible for its own city or village dump, places did not have to think about cooperating on nonpolluting landfills, building expensive solid waste incinerators, disposing of hazardous waste materials, or developing waste reduction recycling programs. They do now. Not cooperating with their neighbors puts them at great peril.

Separate public policies once governed environmental, transportation, and energy conservation programs. Gradually these programs are being linked in novel ways. Increasingly they affect everything that places do in the name of place development, including housing, zoning, land use, public health, and education. Consequently, places may find themselves suffering from system overload—contrary and contradictory regulations imposed by higher government levels that can result in operating paralysis. Regulators and consumers now require utilities to scale back new construction and embrace conservation. NIMBYs (not-in-my-backyarders) and environmental groups have stymied the siting of new landfills and expansion of existing ones. Antinoise citizen groups and environmentalists have organized to block new airport construction and expansion of existing facilities. All of this has contributed to urban sprawl by forcing the outward push of development. As both populations and economic activity disperse throughout metropolitan areas, public transit systems experience declining ridership and taxpayer resistance to subsidizing transit at the expense of personal auto use and more roads. Water shortages in the West and

Northwest have created growing conflicts between states and among industrial, agricultural, and residential water users.

Thinking across systems and intergovernmentally requires that places learn from one another through new technologies, innovations, and experiments. Germany, for example, leads European nations with its mandatory recycling programs. Oregon and Washington have gained national recognition for recycling inducements for consumers and businesses, while Portland and Seattle are urban leaders in waste management. Houston and Dallas are constructing a high-speed bullet train that may alter intermodal and intercity transportation. Virginia and California are innovators in privately owned new highways. The Northeast leads the nation in energy conservation techniques and methods. As the world becomes more interdependent, vast opportunities exist for infrastructure strategies that cross geopolitical boundaries and involve intergovernmental cooperation.

The Environmental Imperative

"Think environmentally" is not simply a good maxim but an operating imperative. In the past twenty years, from the National Environment Policy Act of 1970 through the Clean Air Act Amendments of 1990, public works projects have had to meet an endless list of new regulations and approvals to comply with federal, state, and local funding requirements. The resulting approval process from design to construction completion not only lengthens projects but may stop construction altogether.

Most large cities and their immediate suburbs suffer from major traffic congestion. Transportation choices and travel times affect people's decisions on where to live relative to work and schools, where they shop and dine, and where vacationers visit and stay. Millions of hours a year are lost as commuters find travel times—suburb-to-city or suburb-to-suburb—increasing because of constantly clogged roads. Congestion costs—in time, fuel, and insurance—have been measured for all metro areas and by costs per individual vehicle operation. Since 1980 the number of highway miles Americans travel annually has increased for all age groups, accelerated by the number of women who have joined the labor force as commuters.[17] Obviously this growing problem detracts from worker productivity and quality of life, and cannot be ignored.

Places experiencing this phenomenon have employed different solutions to ease the problem. New technologies known as Intelligent Vehicle Highway Systems (IVHS)—radar, sensors, smart cars, and satellite-linked electronic navigation systems—offer prospects for moving urban traffic more efficiently and safely. Los Angeles and Tokyo have installed sensors—electromagnetic devices embedded in roadways—to enable traffic control officials to identify trouble spots quickly and expedite traffic flows by adjusting traffic lights. New York City is considering a $100 million investment in a traffic-tracking network using sensors and "smart traffic lights" technology.[18] New technologies in air traffic control and airplane design are likely to reduce air congestion and improve air passenger flow. However, while new technologies may improve the flow of people and goods, they alone are unlikely to solve the people-moving problem.

A second line of defense that many places employ is to discourage auto use by limiting parking options and by increasing the costs of auto use. Places may raise fees for motor vehicle registration and licenses, increase parking meter fees and fines, and stiffen penalties for traffic scofflaws. The war on the automobile extends to special permits for neighborhood residents and various restrictions on downtown parking. Most countries use gasoline taxes as a means of discouraging auto use and for developing viable mass transit alternatives. Americans are still working through environment and energy use when it comes to gasoline taxes, car pooling, and other conservation actions. Florence, Italy, like several other European cities, has built large parking facilities at the city's rim and has banned private cars from driving to the city's center. Athens, Greece, admits cars into the city based on the number of their license plates, which means only half of the region's cars can enter the city on a particular day.

When places seek to demarket automobile use in central cities, a corresponding pressure builds for them to improve their mass transit systems. Metro areas experiencing no growth or even modest growth in population, however, face ridership losses with little adjustment in the supply of transit services. To operate effectively, mass transit requires certain population densities and demand levels, which are undermined by continuing population sprawl, making transit service less efficient to provide. Still, public demand for intersuburban van service has increased, with the result that both public and private providers now offer this service.

While new, heavily subsidized mass transit systems in Washington, D.C., Pittsburgh, Miami, and San Francisco are widely acclaimed, older systems suffer from deterioration and neglect. From the provider's vantage point, mass transit can be less costly than expanding and maintaining road systems; it also produces environmental benefits through cleaner air, more trees, and open spaces, and less concrete. However, at a time when automobile operating costs are at record lows and consumers continue to place a high value on auto convenience, mass transit faces an uphill battle unless changes in cost, convenience, and improved service accompany it. Many older fixed systems are outdated, unable to meet the demand of suburbanites, on the one hand, and inner-city dwellers seeking access to suburban job locations, on the other.

A fourth option is to make owning an automobile more expensive. This strategy can reduce auto pollution and can help gain public acceptance for mass transit. Already numerous states and regions place a larger fee on higher-octane automobiles to discourage the purchase of larger cars; enforce auto emission standards through annual auto inspections; and encourage large employers to use car pools or vans for employees. The 1990 Clean Air Act Amendments will impose far harsher standards on air quality nonattainment areas through employee trip reduction standards, which are scheduled to be phased in over the 1992–96 period. Cities experiencing the worst ozone pollution will have to comply with cleaner fuels. California and several Eastern states have imposed stringent deadlines for the introduction of electric vehicles and additional antipollution equipment for gasoline-powered cars and trucks.[19]

The leader in reducing automobile pollution, California, discourages out-of-state automobile transfers by charging a hefty $300 smog import fee, and subjects out-of-state cars to higher state standards governing pollution control equipment. The state is developing guidelines to give companies pollution credits for such actions as buying up and scrapping old cars. Japan imposes an annual inspection fee on autos at a rate which increases progressively with an automobile's age, thereby promoting better air quality and auto sales. The Netherlands' major cities no longer can bear the increased traffic loads. Congested roadways are the cause of 50 percent of the environmental pollution. One solution from the Department of Road Transportation is a plan to mandate a car pool arrangement on the major highway between Amsterdam and Hilversum. Another approach is a union contract that requires all workers at Schiphol Airport to commute by public transportation.[20] In short, places are employing multiple strategies for balancing their needs to move people and to maintain environmental quality.

Thinking environmentally about mass transit may be easier with implementation of the 1991 Intermodal Surface Transportation Efficiency Act, which is the first post-Interstate reauthorization of the federal highway and transit programs. Among major changes in intergovernmental relations that this legislation envisages are a new emphasis on mass transit, the allocation of funds to major urbanized areas for multimodal use, and the requirement that transportation plans be consistent with the plans of state and regional air quality agencies. While this multipurpose transit program remains to be fully funded, and regulations to be written, future transportation funding is likely to be conditioned on places' performance in meeting environmental policies and practices. Places, in turn, will have considerable latitude to experiment and to adapt their particular needs and conditions to the new environmental era.

Synchronizing Place Development Needs with Infrastructure Development

Finally, infrastructure planning and spending must meet multiple needs, but none more important than adjusting to overall place development priorities. Just as waging war may be too important to leave to generals, so infrastructure is too important to be left simply to engineers, architects, and the narrow confines of single-purpose infrastructure authorities (e.g., a tollway authority). Various constituencies—contractors, politicians, and authority boards—may be advocates of building new systems, replacing the old, or large single-function bond issues to benefit a single piece of the infrastructure puzzle. That situation should not discourage those who see the need for synchronizing public works with broader place development goals.

A classic example of how planners are rethinking the interconnections of infrastructure systems, environmental imperatives, and multipurpose uses involves multimodal terminals—improved links between rail and bus, ground and air transport, and moving local and long-distance travelers. "Planners of multi-modal terminals have been encouraged by Washington's Union Station, now a bustling center for trains, subways, tour buses, restaurants, movie theaters and shops."[21] The renovated terminal reopened in 1988, becoming a major focus for travelers, tourists, and office development. Dozens of U.S. cities are following similar forms of intermodal transport connections to ease congestion and spur downtown redevelopment.

In many cases, infrastructure investments, whether in getting more out of existing facilities or in making new investments that meet multiple needs and priorities, may be the most critical decision that places make in improving their competitive position. Indications nationally are that a generation of infrastructure neglect may be reversing itself, as indicated by recent financings in the capital markets and growing public demand for greater federal assistance. The question, however, is whether places will be prepared to take advantage of new spending and will develop the capacity to think and act creatively about what must be done.

Together, the environmental quality and physical condition of a place affect residents, businesses, visitors, and tourists. Industry seeks environmentally attractive sites where places have made or are making investments that will avoid higher costs and taxes later. Businesses are concerned about attracting and retaining employees; they want to avoid higher costs and liabilities for the overall safety and health of workers in places with low or lax environmental standards. Better ecological understanding, improved procedures for making public works investments, and a broader appreciation of the benefits of intergovernmental cooperation involve a shifting balance of interests. In many cases, innovation begins with few resources and a small but expanding pool of risk-taking leaders and citizen activists.

The city of Curitiba, Brazil, under the leadership of Mayor Jaime Lerner, has answered the environmental challenge with an innovative, small, but attractive campaign. Lerner has emphasized citizen participation programs— exchanging garbage bags for food, converting old buses into classrooms, designing a glass-tubed bus loader for quick entry and departure, and encouraging the planting of more than a million trees on a citizen–government co-pay agreement. While this city of 1.5 million still has problems, the progress is obvious, and the city is lively. Campaigns like Curitiba's demonstrate how small-cost programs can break the downward cycle of cities and also protect the environment.

III. BASIC SERVICES: POLICE, FIRE, AND EDUCATION

Like place design and infrastructure, good public services are assumed to be a "given" in place competition. The fact is that poor public services, especially education, can be a rather substantial place liability, while quality public services can be marketed as a place's primary attraction and product.

Consider the following questions for your place. Can you walk through the downtown at night without fear of crime? Do tourists or visitors worry for their personal safety when coming to your community? How far from work must employees and executives live to obtain either the public services or the environment they desire? Would you send your children to the local schools?

A place's ability to attract and to retain business activity is vastly diminished when its reputation for high crime and/or poor schools sticks in people's minds. In a bygone era, business often gravitated to places that had low taxes and few services. Now, with offshore locations providing such advantages, business is drawn to places that offer high-quality services and where the "value added" contributes to improved productivity and improve quality. Tourists and visitors increasingly factor security and safety considerations into their travel decisions. Parents' decisions on where to live and work often turn on the location of the best educational opportunities for their children. Public services make a difference.

Having earlier dealt with infrastructure and the environment, our point here is that all places should be concerned about their core public services: *protection of people and property*, and *education*. These basic, visible, and high-citizen-contact services are locally financed, administered, and controlled. Police and fire services take up more than half of most local governments' operating budgets and, together with independent school districts, account for 75 percent or more of most localities' annual property tax bills. Thus, these big-ticket services most affect people who use the services and those who pay for them.

In dealing with service adequacy, places face two issues: resources and remedies. Resources are restrained by a place's fiscal capacity, tax limits, and public willingness to spend. In terms of remedies, spending interventions—more employees, better training and equipment, more facilities—may have little impact on outcomes such as crime statistics, reading scores, and loss of or damage to property. Whether in education or police, much public debate surrounds the relation between spending and outcomes or inputs and outputs. Thus, in enhancing the quality and level of a place's public services, whether by some objective measurement or by more subjective public satisfaction scores, changes may not require more resources. Instead, places should think about a different mix of resources and about how these services are performed.

In the case of fire services, emphasis on prevention and better use of new technologies can have a major impact on the frequency of fires and damage related to fires. Better public education, more frequent inspections, and stronger building codes and enforcement may be more cost-beneficial than adding more personnel and equipment. Sprinkler systems, home fire detectors, communications systems, and home or business fire alarm cable systems can significantly reduce fire damage. In contrast to fire remedies, the causes of crime are more complex, associated with family and broader social-economic forces. However, more effective policing can help reduce public fear of crime and improve public satisfaction with police service.

In both police and fire protection, places are adjusting to the needs of customers in service delivery. In applying Total Quality Management practices to the Madison, Wisconsin, police department in the mid-1980s, Mayor Joseph Sensenbrenner surveyed citizens on their contacts with police—as victim, witness, complainant, and perpetrator— inviting them to rate how the police performed and to suggest how the police involved might have handled the situation better. Customer surveys were extended to individual neighborhoods to determine just what kinds of crime they wanted the police to concentrate on. So if a neighborhood considers graffiti or noise more of a problem than, say, prostitution at a local bar, they can make the former their priority. Moving away from the top-down model for police concentration on types of crime they consider most important, Madison police now offer a more customized rather than standardized service.[22]

Various forms of community policing now exist in most large cities, predicated on the proven advantages of getting more public and community resources to support greater citizen control over the people's immediate environments. Moving from a bureaucratic top-down or command-and-control approach in public services to greater customer orientation can deter certain types of criminal activity and behavior. This change can have a positive impact on how the public perceives police services. Greater customer orientation applies to more than police. The entire gamut of public services can benefit from the use of quality management techniques used so successfully in private industry.

Finally, regarding tourist and visitor concerns about a place's relative safety, both the quantity and the quality of protection can be enhanced through saturated patrolling, improved coordination of police and private protection services, and better use of new technologies.

A closed-circuit television system, originally set up in 1976 to help traffic control, helps Paris with security. In 1988 the French National Police had personnel on duty around the clock in a control room, where observers could watch all the action with 140 cameras. Troublesome situations were quickly noted on a comprehensive map, and police were sent to the problem areas. The system's positive impact on crime control, civil defense, and traffic control was certainly important in preserving Paris's mystique, which attracts millions of tourists every year.[23]

Programs for Improving Education

Every day, places are bombarded with statements from national commissions, governmental agencies, and business and civic leaders regarding deficiencies in our schools and in our labor force, which contribute to the loss of competitive advantage in the global market place. This new competition has changed the world of work. Unskilled jobs are vanishing, demand for skilled labor is increasing, and new workers must have the skills and attitudes necessary to meet this challenge. Business now spends $50 billion annually in formally educating and training employees, while informal training runs three or four times that amount. Businesses search for those places which can best meet their changing labor force needs, currently and into the future. Place improvers, in turn, increasingly recognize that programs that help to maintain or enhance their economic base—education and training—can be far more important than those aimed simply at persuading firms to relocate.

While many places subscribe to the notion that education investment contributes to growth, those involved in education—teachers, parents, administrators, employers, and taxpayers—may differ fundamentally on how to, and even who should, improve education performance. With 16,000 public school systems in the United States, each with its own board and tax levy, great debates surround such issues as choice and competition, efficiency and equity, standards and performance.

Educators and researchers engage in an endless search for programs, interventions, and methods to improve the educational performance of youth. Cognizant that turning around an educational system can be a decade-long or even a generation-long effort, we apply three tests to gauge a place's response to the need for giving people better preparation to succeed in productive employment or in higher education. They can be applied as well to states, which are already ranked by various education measures, and which determine the funding of and standards for local school districts.

- Broad-based public support of the schools
- Multiyear action plans for improvement
- Integrated approaches to education and training

Whether an individual decision to move into a city neighborhood or a business decision to relocate in a community, the question is usually the same: Do people support the local schools, whether public or private?

Public support of local schools also goes beyond how parents and others rate the quality of their schools, or even whether they favor spending more money on them. Rather, we are addressing the degree to which parents, civic leaders, businesses, unions, and other organized interests are openly and actively involved in a place's educational system. Although American business has a long tradition of educational involvement, increasingly places separate themselves by the degree to which business and their employees are involved, which, since the mid-1980s, has fallen into three categories:[24]

- Adopt-A-School, from involving guest speakers to providing various goods and services, estimated to exist in 40 percent of the public elementary schools
- Project-driven, where business seeks to change a school or program by means of teacher quality circles, curriculum development, or leadership training
- Reform-oriented efforts led by a company or consortium, as in Rochester, New York; Chicago; and Cincinnati, where it seeks changes in systemwide practices in governance, management, and curriculum (These reforms range from school choice through school-based management systems to third party contracts to run the schools.)

While many innovative and exciting changes can occur in a place's educational system without organized business involvement, business participation serves as a significant litmus test of local commitment to the overall educational goal of imparting skills and attributes that enable students to succeed in productive employment. Business has emerged as a significant ally of education in many places by helping define what schools can do, and also by targeting what must be done by other public or private institutions, from drug treatment and day care to job counseling and training.[25]

For BMW, the first European car maker to build cars in the U.S. since Volkswagon shut its Pennsylvania factory in 1988, the decision to build a new factory outside Germany turned on locating a qualified work force. According to PHH Fantus, a leading international business location consulting firm, which conducted the worldwide search, it looked at 250 sites, narrowed the list to 10, and chose one—Spartanburg, South Carolina. Why? Because that place met the requirements that Fantus-BMW set, particularly South Carolina's intense preemployment worker training program. Modified and tailored for BMW, South Carolina's high quality training programs and flexible educational structure could meet BMW's demand both for service and industrial workers. Production starts in 1995.[26]

Beyond commitment and various partnerships, places may be differentiated by the extent to which they formulate and pursue multiyear plans and goals for their educational systems. President George Bush worked with state governors in 1989 on national educational goals and later on developing an education strategy, "America 2000." Many places already have their own plans and strategies for decreasing illiteracy and school dropouts, meeting skill and competency levels, and better preparing students for the world of work.

Viewing education in place development, it increasingly is being defined and redefined more broadly to include human resources from prenatal care and early child development through formal education to job training and retraining.[27] Such an approach spans governmental levels and responsibilities and includes public, private, and nonprofit institutions. From community colleges to state universities, from research parks to small business assistance efforts, a variety of educational resources have become vital linkages for fostering local economic improvement. Community colleges, for example, can be instrumental in providing worker training programs, while local private industry councils can work with schools and technical assistance providers in fostering job training programs that meet local business employment needs.

Accordingly, providing a quality education involves more than increasing SAT scores and graduation rates. From a place development standpoint, improvement includes the degree to which broad supportive coalitions are dedicated to enhancing performance; education should be broadly defined, and a variety of services and resources for human development integrated into and linked to place development strategies.

IV. ATTRACTIONS

There is a difference between saying that a certain place works and saying that it is attractive. We use the term *attractions* to cover physical features and events that appeal to citizens, new residents, visitors, various businesses, and investors.

Places can be graded according to whether they have *no attractions,* a *single attraction,* a *few attractions,* or *many attractions.* Most small towns fall into the first group; they lack any attractions that might draw new residents, visitors, or businesses. Driving through the Midwest, one encounters town after town "look-alikes"—a shopping street stretching a few blocks, a few churches, a fire station, a school, and modest homes. The residents may love their town, but to the traveler there is nothing noteworthy. As these towns evolve, they increasingly resemble each other in featuring many of the same fast-food outlets, motel chains, and national merchandisers. They take on a quality of "placelessness"; travelers feel they have been there before, even though they have never been there. The visitor's reaction is concisely expressed in Gertrude Stein's remark about Oakland: "There is no *there* there."

Even though a small town may lack tourist attractions, it may prove attractive to small companies seeking a location combining modest wages and a good labor force, with lower land costs and taxes. But being attractive does not mean that the place has attractions.

Some cities feature a few attractions, enough to entice visitors from reasonable distances to visit them, but not enough to keep them beyond a day. Thus, one can visit Springfield, Illinois, to see the state capitol and Lincoln's home and tomb, or Mitchell, South Dakota, to see the ornate and bizarre corn palace. But after a few hours, little remains to hold a visitor's attention.

A handful of cities—Paris, Vienna, New York, San Francisco— possess abundant attractions. These places need not invent new attractions to add place appeal. Their basic problem is maintaining the infrastructure and services to support the huge numbers of tourists and business visitors who continuously descend on them to enjoy their treasures.

Laying aside these world-class cities, let us focus on those places that need to create more attractions. A place cannot alter its climate or natural terrain, but it can add new attractions.

San Antonio, once a sleepy south Texas town, has become the nation's tenth-largest city and Texas's top vacation spot, attracting nearly 11 million visitors annually. Dating from its 1968 HemisFair, San Antonio has added sequentially to its attraction portfolio: a convention center, a riverfront development and mall, Sea World, and an Alamodome scheduled for opening in 1993[28]

Many places have built domed sports stadiums for local teams, conventions, and other events; have developed festival marketplaces and waterfront restaurants; have promoted new hotels; and have constructed golf courses and recreational facilities, some of which have been highly successful while others have turned out to be white elephants. The city of Wichita Falls, Texas, having lost its waterfalls in a flood in the 1890s, replaced them almost a hundred years later to stimulate tourism. The artificial falls have reignited city pride and have given residents a place to take friends and visitors, but the tidal wave of tourists has yet to appear.

Under what circumstances does a particular type of attraction work? We shall assess here the major types of attractions that cities consider: natural beauty and features; history and famous personages; market places; cultural and ethnic attractions; recreation and entertainment; sports arenas; events and occasions; buildings, monuments, and sculptures; and other attractions.

Natural Beauty and Features

Natural beauty, in the minds of most people, consists of mountains, valleys, lakes, oceans, and forests. A place with a spectacular sight or world-class wonder such as the Grand Canyon has no problem attracting tourists. Beautiful beaches, such as those found in Jamaica, along the New England and Pacific Coasts, and many lakes, have no trouble advertising themselves. Towns and cities resting on picturesque terrain and enjoying splendid vistas can easily capitalize on these features, if they conscientiously protect them.

Older places have opportunities to make their towns and cities more environmentally, physically, and aesthetically pleasing. Congested roadways, alleys and abandoned lots, and concrete sidewalks can be improved through "greening"— planting trees, and floral displays, installing water fountains, and making better use of open spaces. Public and private efforts by civic groups, retailers, developers, and businesses can enhance a city's physical and economic environment.

History and Famous Personages

Places that were the scene of historic events or retain the flavor of bygone periods act as a magnet for tourists. Vicksburg, Savannah, and Charleston sponsor walking tours to visit their spectacular antebellum mansions. The birthplaces and residences of famous people serve as perennial tourist attractions. In Memphis, where Elvis Presley recorded his first songs, tourists visit his home, Graceland. The small town of Strasburg, North Dakota, is restoring the boyhood home of the bandleader Lawrence Welk and is already hosting large numbers of the "champagne king's" fans. In Hartford, visitors tour the adjacent homes of Mark Twain and Harriet Beecher Stowe.

Places lose much when they neglect or destroy their historical landmarks. City officials, erroneously thinking that the cost of maintaining these places exceeds their value, may bulldoze mansions and historical structures to make room for faceless new buildings. Consider the following situation:

Los Angeles, the home of the legendary Hollywood stars, boasted the famous Schwab's Pharmacy. It was at Schwab's that the movie star Lana Turner was allegedly discovered, and Schwab's was the hangout for such stars as Clark Gable, Marilyn Monroe, and Judy Garland. In the early 1980s Schwab's drugstore was closed, and much of the memorabilia was sold at an auction. The construction company Condor Westcorp bought the Schwab property and constructed a $40 million shopping complex on the

site. The new owners decided to reintroduce a glamorized version
of the old drugstore. The new Schwab's would recreate the old
one. Shoppers in this massive new mall could imagine Humphrey
Bogart ordering a chocolate soda or the gossip columnist Louella
Parsons interviewing a youthful James Dean. But the new
Schwab's has never been built, and the space remains empty. The
original owners are now in their eighties and unlikely to reopen
the drugstore.[29] A new Schwab's could represent a new wave of
restorations, wherein after the place has destroyed the landmark,
it builds a newer and fresher replica.

Marketplaces

Every community has one or more shopping area where people buy
their food, clothing, appliances, furnishings, and hundreds of other ob-
jects. Downtown areas like Fifth Avenue in New York, Michigan Avenue in Chicago, Rodeo Drive in Beverly Hills, and Montenapoleon
Street in Milan attract tourists from all over the world in search of the
best goods money can buy.

Today, many street-oriented shopping areas, whether main street or
neighborhood retailers, are fighting for survival against the growing appeal of regional and local shopping centers. Large shopping centers
contain major department stores, dozens of franchised stores, medical
and health services, and often movie theaters and other entertainment.
They offer easy parking, concentrated and easily accessible stores, and,
when enclosed, air-conditioning and protection against bad weather.
Indeed, while these centers once flourished, many now suffer from
overbuilding and competition with one another, leading to various
adaptive reuses of once prosperous malls.

Increasingly, more comprehensive downtown development is being
managed by a quasi-public body to provide services that local governments cannot or will not. For the past decade, special improvement or
economic improvement districts—often special assessment districts
that impose their own taxes—are being used. Typical of this approach
would be the Louisville, Kentucky, Management District in the heart
of that city's downtown areas, where a new trolleybus runs down tree-
lined Fourth Street, now upgraded with cleaner and better sidewalks,
attractive landscaping, and more security.[30]

Many larger street-oriented shopping areas have turned to another solution: creating a mall or walking area. Copenhagen's famous walking street always bustles with tourists. Venice itself is one giant walking area, since auto traffic is banned. Santa Monica recently closed Third Street to automobiles, renaming the area the Third Street Promenade. Older cities such as Washington and St. Louis have taken advantage of obsolete warehouses, public buildings, and train stations, converting them to specialty shops, colorful kiosks, markets, restaurants, theaters, and nightclubs.

A special version of the mall is the *festival marketplace* made famous by James Rouse and his associates.[31] Rouse put the first one together, the Faneuil Hall Marketplace, in Boston in the early 1970s. Boston intended to bulldoze three old warehouses. A group of historic preservationists stopped the city from doing so. Developers, however, showed no interest in the property until Rouse came along with a hunch that people yearned for a new life in the center of the city. His idea was to redevelop the area with old-town quaintness; to attract small stores with unusual goods that would appeal to recreational shoppers; and to add pushcarts, restaurants, and small entertainments, along with ethnic food. After raising money from the city and banks, Rouse finished the first phase, and the festival marketplace opened on August 26, 1976. To everyone's surprise, almost 100,000 people showed up on the first day, and 10 million visited the first year. Each year thereafter sales grew, and Faneuil Hall was a triumphant success.

Subsequently, Baltimore invited Rouse to develop its inner harbor into a festival marketplace. Baltimore, particularly the harbor waterfront, with its rotting warehouses, was saddled with a deteriorating downtown and outflow of population. Under the leadership of Mayor William Schaefer and the Baltimore Economic Development Corporation, and after a long political fight between factions for and against this development, the Harbor Place development was approved. Rouse opened Harbor Place on July 2, 1980, with more than 500,000 people attending on opening day, and more than 14 million in the first year. Harbor Place injected new life into Baltimore's downtown, a place people had stopped visiting except to work. Harbor Place stimulated the construction of new hotels, a major convention center, and a new aquarium, turning Baltimore into an important tourist city. Harbor Place was followed by Seattle's Westlake Center. Then, in August 1992 the $650 million, 2.5-million-square-foot and 78-acre Mall of America opened in Bloomington, Minnesota. The largest shopping mall in the United States, it is within a day's drive of 27 million people.

Rouse continued to develop new festival marketplaces for other, often smaller, cities, but not always with the same success. Many of the country's 250 festival malls aren't doing that well: the Water Street Pavilion in Flint, Michigan, and Toledo's Portside Festival Marketplace went bankrupt, and Richmond's Sixth Street Marketplace is in trouble. Waterfront renewal projects such as Bayside in Miami are now attracting more attention than festival malls. Many malls have failed—Eugene, Oregon; Galveston, Texas; Freeport, New York; Miami Beach, Florida; and Grand Rapids, Michigan, to name a few. While some malls have done well—Denver, Boulder, Portland, Oregon, and Burlington, Vermont—more places are "demalling" at a great cost and reopening their streets to traffic. Oak Park, Illinois, has found that restoration of auto traffic (re-streeting) proved vital to restoring retail health to the hundred merchants along the city's former pedestrian mall.[32] Eugene, Oregon has done the same.

Many downtowns, which experienced rapid growth during the first half of the century, began to decline in the 1950s, reaching a low point in the 1960s. To fight the growth of suburban shopping, these downtowns adopted a number of strategies, the single most important being skyscraper office space to maintain employment in the downtown area. To make downtowns more pedestrian- and shopper-friendly, some places have built labyrinthine skywalls and underground passageways to connect buildings, hotels, and convention centers, as well as retail and commercial locations, such as those in Minneapolis, Houston, Cincinnati, and Cedar Rapids, Iowa.

Each decade saw the building of more downtown office space than the previous decade, in turn supporting downtown retailing. Soon new high-rise shopping centers (galleria) were opened, such as the Water Tower in Chicago and the Carew Tower in Cincinnati, featuring well-known stores and restaurants on several floors of an attractive sky-scrapper. Although these high-rise shopping centers compete with established downtown department stores, the overall effect is positive in attracting traffic.

Downtown office and retail facilities draw traffic during the day but not necessarily in the evening. Fundamental to making downtown retail activities work is a strong residential sector in or near the downtown shopping areas. Some cities encourage the building of high-rise residential condominiums in the downtown area to attract permanent residents, whether suburbanties or empty-nesters who seek downtown entertainment and cultural amenities. Minneapolis and Chicago adopted this strategy early and stabilized their downtowns with attractive city apartment buildings, townhouses, and single-family residences. It is estimated that some 10,000 residents now walk to work in Chicago's central business district, helping stabilize what had been declining retail activity.

Cities also encourage the development of such downtown entertainment facilities as concert halls, stadiums, and multiplex movie theaters to keep people in the area at night. Some facilities flourish; many simply fail. When central city areas are unable to attract a critical mass of evening street traffic, they are often taken back by the homeless, addicts, and criminal elements. Frequently places respond by building out new enclaves for theaters, restaurants, high-rises, and entertainment, seeking to expand these through conventions and tourist promotions.[33]

Cultural Attractions

New York, San Francisco, Chicago, Boston, Philadelphia, and a few others stand out as cultural meccas. They feature great universities, museums, orchestras, ballet companies, theater groups, and libraries. Not only do these cultural institutions delight the residents, they also attract tourists and business people. Cities that hope to attract newer industries and professionals must make a special effort to build and promote their cultural assets.

In the meantime, some smaller cities contain a surprising number of museums. Indianapolis, a city of 710,300, has nineteen museums, including the Children's Museum, Eiteljorg Museum, Indiana Medical History Museum, Indiana Transportation Museum, and U.S. Army Finance Corps Museum. Sometimes a small town features one nationally or world renowned museum. Such is the case with the Bergstrom-Mahler Museum in Neenah, Wisconsin, a town of 22,500 people, whose closest big city neighbor is Green Bay. The museum is a mecca for glass paperweight collectors, who come from all over the world to view the world's best collection of glass paperweights. In this case, it took only a specialist museum to imprint a place on the minds of many people.

Recreation and Entertainment

Every place needs to provide its citizens with areas for recreation and amusement. The traditional institutions serving this function are the local bars, cafés, dance clubs, disco parlors, parks, community centers, performing arts companies, zoos, miniature and regular golf courses, and sports arenas. As efforts to serve locals will potentially attract outsiders, hotels, theme parks, and the amusement industry may be enticed to invest and build to accommodate the potential of expanded visitor traffic.

One increasingly popular attraction is the giant theme park, of which the Walt Disney Company properties are the prototype. Walt Disney World put Orlando on the world's map, and the whole area has grown at an unbelievable pace (see Exhibit 5–2). Since then, other cities have successfully bid for Disney properties, including Tokyo and Paris, where they met varying success. Los Angeles, the original home of Disneyland, boasts several other major theme parks, including Knott's Berry Farm, Japanese Deer Park, Busch Gardens, Lion Safari Country, Marineland of the Pacific, and Magic Mountain. Various smaller cities have added theme parks as tourist attractions.

Some places have made entertainment their main industry. Seaside, Oregon, serves as a recreational town for vacationers from Portland, Salem, and other nearby locations. Monte Carlo, is a world-famous attraction for those who want to experience high-stakes gambling.

Las Vegas and Atlantic City are the U.S. gambling capitals. although they are facing competition from other places seeking revenue. Since the late 1980s, land-based casino gambling (including native American reservations) has spread rapidly to nine states, while riverboat gambling, already in four states, is under consideration by every state with a major waterway, lake, or bay. Once, confined to off-shore islands, European capitals, and tourist enclaves, the gambling industry experienced an explosive growth over the past decade. Rapid proliferation of casino-hotel-entertainment complexes will result in more losers than winners. In the meantime, many places think they will be the surviving winners as casinos have become the "smokestacks of the 1990s."

Sports Arenas

Although a species of recreation and entertainment, sports arenas need to be singled out, because they represent a large investment fraught with major risks. Good professional teams confer several advantages on a city: A winning team builds civic pride and enthusiasm (witness the huge celebration in Atlanta when the Braves won the National League pennant). A major sports team can put a city's name on the map: Green

EXHIBIT 5-2
The City That Mickey Mouse Built

Orlando seemingly made a pact with the devil. To obtain Walt Disney World in 1967, it allowed the establishment of a separate county. The new town of Buena Vista has powers to establish zoning and building regulations and self-finance through municipal bonds. However, many of the benefits and costs have remained with Orlando.

This once sleepy city has become the center of a massive entertainment complex. In 1989 both Universal Studios Florida and Disney's MGM Studios opened to large crowds. The studios are hiring and attracting writers, directors, and other film and television talent to work in their new facilities. Orlando is currently the United States' fifth-largest job producer and has the third most motel rooms behind only New York and Los Angeles. In chapter 1 we noted Orlando's problems with air pollution, traffic congestion, and spiraling crime. Orlando also has new convention facilities, an enlarged airport, and a thriving business and financial services center, all because of the decision to accommodate Disney. The city now needs to create a plan for a large city that is as good a place to *live* as Walt Disney World is a place to *play*.

Bay, Wisconsin, would be just another city were it not for having a major-league football team franchise. A major sports team draws tourists and residents to its locality's restaurants and hotels. Night games are followed by eating out, and tourists stay overnight at hotels. Even corporations think well of the major league city as a place to locate or remain.

No wonder, then, that many cities lacking a major-league baseball team have made an all-out effort to obtain a baseball franchise. Denver and Miami recently won franchises, while St. Petersburg, Buffalo, Orlando, and Washington were passed over. The Adolph Coors Company was instrumental in financing the franchise cost for Denver, where the new stadium will have an estimated economic impact of $100 million on the city.

Yet the results of attracting a team and stadium may not always be favorable. Sports franchises and stadiums often require public subsidy, and the real cost can exceed the alleged economic benefits. As an incentive to remain in New York City, Yankee owner George Steinbrenner in 1987 got a cut-rate thirty-year stadium lease plus concessions, luxury boxes, new parking garage, and restaurant. To retain the Pittsburgh Pirates, local corporations came up with $2 million each to buy the team in partnership with the city in 1988. The Baltimore Orioles agreed in 1988 to keep the team there in return for local business-guaranteed sales of $1 million in tickets for ten years. In 1992, the fiercest battle waged in the nation's capitol is as much where to house the Washington Redskins' championship football team as who will be the next resident of the White House. The Redskins want a new stadium and are the most recent of professional teams threatening to move unless they get one. And so it goes, as cities go all out to retain or attract major sports teams.[34] When the cheering stops, the loss of a sports franchise can be as damaging to a place's image as the initial acquisition of the franchise was enhancing. Neither the risks nor the opportunity costs from such ventures are usually fully assessed.

Events and Occasions

Most places sponsor public events to celebrate occasions and anniversaries. Perhaps the prototype of these events is the annual parade, where several local organizations sponsor floats and marching bands while citizens line the streets to witness the spectacle.

Some well-known parades attract distant visitors. The twelve-day New Orleans Mardi Gras celebration draws people from all over the world. On Thanksgiving Day, thousands of people line the streets of New York and millions more watch on television to view the annual Macy's parade. Milwaukee, Montreal, and Stephenville, Newfoundland, feature midwinter festivals that capture much regional attention during the long winter months.

Places actively compete to be the site of special events like the Olympics. Seoul, Korea, successfully bid for and sponsored the Olympics in 1988. Barcelona won the Olympic bid for 1992, and Atlanta prevailed over several competitors as the chosen site for the 1996 Olympics (see Exhibit 5–3). St. Louis is still remembered as the 1904 site not only for the World's Fair, which is memorialized in song and by the invention of

EXHIBIT 5-3
So Much for Zeus

Several cities competed vigorously to be the site of the 1996 Olympics, among them Athens, Atlanta, and Minneapolis. Athens marketed itself to the Olympics Committee for more than a three-year period, arguing that 1996 marked the 100th anniversary of the modern Olympics and that both the ancient and modern Olympics began in Greece. Athens was the bookmaker's favorite by 7–2 odds. The Olympics Committee's decision, announced in September 1990, surprised everyone: Athens was turned down in favor of Atlanta. Why was Athens denied this honor? One possibility is that Athens and Greece are less stable politically and more subject to possible terrorism. In their disappointment and rage, however, the Athenians claimed that the Olympic Committee sold out to the Coca-Cola company and CNN (both based in Atlanta), believing that the Olympics would earn more money in Atlanta than in Athens. The truth is that Athens is correct on all counts and more. Atlanta had a clearer focus in its marketing plans for the Olympics. It was a comprehensive and coordinated effort involving both the political and business communities. The Olympics was now a major economic place event, and the quaint, amateur style of a century ago had given way to modern stadiums, traffic control, television rights, and lobbying.

the hot dog and ice cream cone, but also for the Summer Olympics, which left behind Forest Park.

Places also vie to be the site of music festivals and concerts. Although the actual site was Whitelake, Woodstock, New York, has gone down in history as the site of the famous outdoor concert that drew 300,000 young people in 1969. Jeff Krueger, a veteran of Woodstock, runs a three-day annual concert near the remote location of Detroit Lakes, Minnesota, which nevertheless draws nearly 40,000 campers from as far away as Texas, Canada, and California. Places must think creatively about developing and sponsoring events that, on a one-time or permanent basis, can bring higher visibility to a community.

Buildings, Monuments, and Sculptures

Another pathway to place distinction is to add or preserve interesting local buildings, monuments, and sculptures. People travel far to view interesting sights. The Parthenon has been producing income for Athens, Greece, for more than 2,500 years—not a bad investment. New York City didn't need an Empire State Building to rate as a world-class city, but many people remember New York City as having the world's tallest building. Chicago took the title away when the Sears Company built Sears Tower, the world's tallest building. And Sears Tower is the least of Chicago's architectural treasures, in that the Chicago area contains some of the world's finest skyscrapers created by Louis Sullivan, Mies van der Rohe, and Helmut Jahn, as well as other architectural treasures, including many Frank Lloyd Wright homes. A small town or city can creatively distinguish itself by sponsoring a dramatic building program:

Columbus, Indiana, a city of 31,000, invited some of the world's leading architects—such luminaries as Eliel and Eero Saarinen, I. M. Pei, Alexander Girard, Robert Trent Jones, and Harry Weese—to design its new schools, library, churches, and various public buildings. It ranks fourth, after New York, Chicago, and Los Angeles, as having the most distinguished buildings designed by contemporary architects. Much of the money to cover the architectural gems came from a foundation set up by the Cummins Engine Company, the city's largest employer. Thousands of Midwestern people drive hundreds of miles to spend a day in this architecturally endowed town.

As for monuments, consider the countless millions who over thousands of years have visited the Sphinx, the Pyramids, or the Colosseum. Parisians, at first appalled by the Eiffel Tower, now will defend it vociferously. Washington, D.C., leads this country in the number of distinguished monuments, including the Lincoln Memorial, the Jefferson Memorial, the Washington Monument, and the Vietnam Memorial. The small town of Blue Earth, Minnesota, has erected a three-story Green Giant sculpture as a symbol of the principal industry in the area. Not long ago, an investor transported the famous London Bridge to Lake Havasu City, Arizona, to add as an attraction.

Some cities have commissioned celebrated public sculptures: West Berlin to celebrate its 750th anniversary converted its best-known street, Kurfurstendamm, into a dramatic open-air gallery featuring ten Berlin sculptors. Seattle has become a national center for public art, with an eclectic collection ranging from a giant troll squashing a car to Northwest Native American totem poles.

Small towns with insufficient funds to develop distinguished buildings, monuments, and sculptures may have a hidden treasure—namely, their old-fashioned look. They appear to function in a time warp, and people might visit these towns as a nostalgic reminder of the past—Victorian homes, antique shops, summer theater, bed and breakfasts, specialty foods, or simply an escape from urban living.

Although buildings, monuments, and sculptures can add immeasurably to the charm of a place, they do not guarantee success. Clearly, place improvement involves imagining the kinds of attractions a place can realistically add over time. Many attractions are proposed by local boosters, such as real estate developers, financial institutions, and sports enthusiasts whose interests may not comport with civic values. These proposals may be too expensive, too risky, or simply inappropriate, which underscores the importance of public evaluation and debate.

The key is to choose attractions that fit into an overall plan for the place's development. Rarely do single attractions save a town. Cashing in on a fad may confer short-term advantages, but they incur longer-term costs. Yet a grand plan may also produce a high return. Consider Denver's voters, who in March 1991 approved billions of dollars in municipal bond issues to finance the construction of a new international airport, a convention center, a public library, street improvements, a stock-show arena, and a new sports stadium.[35] Such huge capital investments may well pay off over the next several decades. In contrast, Montreal's huge building spree in the 1960s for a World's Fair and sports complex saddled the city with enormous debt for decades and had only a short-term effect on tourism.

Other Attractions

New attractions do not necessarily require a lot of money. Ocean City, Maryland, lures tourists to its beaches each year by hiring six professional sand sculptors to build a sand replica of King Arthur's Camelot.[36] The tiny town of Darwin, Minnesota, prides itself on possessing the world's largest ball of string, the work of Francis Johnson who wrapped strips of baling

---

EXHIBIT 5-4

Americus, Kansas, Saves Its Café and Its Soul

Some place attractions are subtle. The town of Americus, Kansas, is a small farm community of 1,200 people. The town recently lost its only café. The City Café closed it doors, leaving the citizens with no place to congregate and discuss the day's events.

At first glance, this closing hardly seems noteworthy. Yet the old café had served as the center of the town's culture. According to one local citizen, "It is more than a place to eat. When one of the older men doesn't show up, people start to wonder why, and soon somebody's out checking on him." The café was the town's psychological center, a place to reaffirm values, family, and culture.

The town took action and formed a corporation with sixty stockholders. With the help of a $45,000 Small Business Administration loan, the café reopened as the Breckinridge Country Café.

In essence, the town needs a place where the citizens can gather, eat, and talk about the concerns of the day. The Café is the town's main attraction.

Source: William Robbins, "Town Goes Public to Resurrect Café," *New York Times*, October 11, 1988, p.8.

---

twine for years until it stood 11 feet high. It was rolled to downtown Darwin, where it is prominently displayed in a glass-enclosed gazebo as a source of community pride. Little and big things can serve as attractions, and no place can complain that it lacks ways to distinguish itself. For instance, exhibit 5-4 describes the effect of a café on one Kansas community.

PEOPLE

A place can possess a fine infrastructure and many attractions and yet be unsuccessful because of the way visitors perceive its people. The hospitality of a place's residents can affect the place's attractiveness in a number of ways.

Outsiders often carry an image of the people who live in a particular place. These images have a strong effect on whether outsiders want to deal with the community. Here are some widely shared images of the people living in certain places:

- Sicily—dangerous, criminal inhabitants
- Deep South—slow-moving and friendly people
- Maine—controlled, taciturn, and conservative inhabitants

Some place inherit an unfortunate and often undeserved image that is hard to shake. A Hollywood film entitled *The Big Easy* created the impression that New Orleans is a dangerous place to live. On his radio program, Garrison Keillor created a lasting impression of a rural Minnesota jam-packed with small-town storytellers and slow-going people.

Communities whose inhabitants are unfriendly to visitors spoil what might otherwise be a happy experience:

Many tourists who visited Paris in the 1950s and 1960s admired the marvelous character of this city but left complaining about the shopkeepers. The shopkeepers were haughty, especially to Americans. In the mid-1970s the French government started a campaign to recultivate French attitudes toward foreigners. Eventually the attitude and demeanor of French shopkeepers and citizens improved considerably.

The point is that a place's citizens are an important part of the product. Visitors to Tokyo complain about the aggressiveness of the motorists and the difficulty of getting help on the street when lost or looking for an address. Contrast this big-city phenomenon to smaller towns, where visitors often comment on how facilitative the people are. Places seeking to expand their tourist and attraction markets must invest in customer services from points of entry at air or transit facilities to points of delivery at hotels, restaurants, and attractions. To the extent that communities seek tourist and hospitality business, they must promote public understanding regarding the multiple job, spending, and related opportunities that flow from tourism. Probably no country invests more than England in training—from cabs, to hotels, to Trust tours and attractions. Many places are finding an invaluable resource in using retired older citizens as paid service agents and unpaid volunteers in place promotion.

TABLE 5-1
Audit Instrument for Infrastructure, Attractions, and People

	Current Status			
	Poor	Fair	Good	Excellent
INFRASTRUCTURE				
Housing				
Roads and transportation				
Water supply				
Power supply				
Environmental quality				
Police and fire protection				
Education				
Lodging and restaurant facilities				
Convention facilities				
Visitor services				
ATTRACTIONS				
Natural beauty and features				
History and famous persons				
Marketplaces				
Cultural attractions				
Recreation and entertainment				
Sports arenas				
Events and occasions				
Buildings, monuments, and sculptures				
PEOPLE				
Friendly and helpful				
Skilled				
Civic				

CONCLUSION

Few places have or even can have it all—character, infrastructure, services, and attractions. Great character in design and history may support tourism and visitors but may lose other vital or new businesses unconcerned with nostalgia and aesthetics. A city with top-flight at-

Improvement Potential

None	Modest	Major

Impact Potential

None	Modest	Major

tractions may be inundated with crime, pollution, and poor public services. Great infrastructure without much business does not buy much. Clean air, friendly people, and an attractive environmental setting may not help a place that lacks transportation, access to major markets, and key attractions.

In focusing on four aspects of place development—design, infrastructure, basic services, and attractions—we have presented readers with a series of options, namely a practical appraisal concerning what improvements may be necessary and how such improvements can respond to more than one need (e.g., infrastructure and the environment). We have offered illustrations and examples to emphasize the range of possibilities and opportunities. An audit instrument can be designed for each, which can be objective and quantifiable or more subjective and qualitative. Table 5-1 reflects the latter in assessing infrastructure, attractions, and people. They may warrant immediate attention because of their visibility and major importance.

6

Designing the Place's Image

What comes to mind when you hear the name Galveston, Texas? A gulfport city that lies forty miles south of Houston, Galveston bubbles with contradictions. Drive to the west end of its beach, and high-rise condos and hotels confront you—a fast moving, upwardly mobile, trendy environment. In this area, the buildings are modern brown cement and wood, and the cars in the driveways are Saabs and Oldsmobiles. Turn around and head south along the beachfront boulevard and you see large, unruly crowds and tacky tourist hangouts. There are weekend traffic jams as youthful groups wander the fast-food outlets making more conservative or conventional visitors anxious. Drive north to downtown and witness the revitalization of old Galveston, a seaport trading city. A combination of shops and galleries line the old Strand. A few blocks away are rundown bars and slum housing. Is Galveston the Hamptons or Coney Island? Is it a new-wave city of the future or another tourist trap trying superficially to redefine itself?

What comes to mind when you hear of the country of Turkey? For those who have seen the film *Midnight Express*, Turkey's image is of a country that violates human rights, is vehemently antidrugs, and is poor and dirty. While many Americans have this negative image of Turkey as a result of its portrayal in the film industry, most people have little or no image of Turkey as a travel or investment site. Few travelers

EXHIBIT 6-1

Selling Subarus in the Plains

A sleek Subaru sports car flashes over the bleak prairie roads in the opening shots of the commercial. The young driver pulls up before a farm and shows his father the new car. The father, the proud owner of a Subaru station wagon barks, "I thought I told you to get a Subaru!" "I did," answers the son. Subaru liked that ad and ran it over and over again.

Why did it work? The ad's message was that the new generation— even in Iowa—is buying upscale Subarus. And, that the conservative farmer and the dependable Subaru wagon can still live and flourish together. The pulling power of the ad is the contrast between new and sleek urban technology and the utilitarian farm life. In a thirty second commercial, the farmer's son bought a little bit of California. However, when the backwoods turn to deep snow in January, that low- slung coupe might need some towing.

think of Turkey as a potential vacation destination because it rarely appears in the mix of potential choices. A traveler looking for sun and antiquities is much more likely to think first of Greece, which is similar to Turkey and a great rival. The Turkish consulate general, underscoring the rivalry between Greece and Turkey, says, "Our coasts are longer, our water is unpolluted. The fish are all on our side. When our hotels and motels are built, we will take over. Why go to Greece?"[1] Still, Greece outdraws Turkey for tourists at an overwhelming rate and the image of this Islamic country remains clouded at best.

What comes to mind when you hear of the state of Iowa? On the positive side, Iowa evokes warmth, friendliness, and neighborliness. It has all the virtues of stereotypical midwestern life; hardworking, earnest people, who till the land and drink large amounts of cherry Kool-Aid. That same image, however, can be negative when seeking tourists who are reluctant to spend vacations in cornfield-laden flatlands or industries that have a conception of Iowa as a "god-forsaken" land. Compounding the problem is the image of Iowans as dull and conservative; all the hip, with-it, trendsetters live on the coasts. Exhibit 6–1 illustrates this contrast.

Like Galveston and Turkey, Iowa has begun to reposition its image—trying to attract new industry, finding ways to attract tourists and keep them spending money in their state, and even more telling, trying to keep the best of their educated students living in Iowa.

A place's image is a critical determinant of the way citizens and businesses respond to the place. Therefore, a place must try to manage its image. Strategic image management requires examining the following five issues:

1. What determines a place's image?
2. How can a place's image be measured?
3. What guidelines are there for designing a place's image?
4. What tools are available for communicating an image?
5. How can a place correct a negative image?

WHAT DETERMINES A PLACE'S IMAGE?

We define a place's image as the sum of beliefs, ideas, and impressions that a people have of a place.[2] Images represent a simplification of a large number of associations and pieces of information connected with the place. They are a product of the mind trying to process and "essentialize" huge amounts of data about a place.

An image is more than a simple belief. The belief that Sicily is an island of Mafia gangsters would be only one element of a larger image of Sicily; other elements would include that it is a picturesque island, it is warm most of the year, and it has many fine beaches. An image is a whole set of beliefs about a place.

On the other hand, people's images of a place do not necessarily reveal their attitudes toward that place. Two persons may hold the same image of Sicily's warm climate and yet have different attitudes toward it because they have different attitudes toward warm climates.

How does an image differ from a stereotype? A stereotype suggests a widely held image that is highly distorted and simplistic and that carries a favorable or unfavorable attitude toward the place. An image, on the other hand, is a more personal perception of a place that can vary from person to person.

Different people can hold quite different images of the same place. One person may see a particular city as a childhood hometown while others may see it as a bustling city, an urban jungle, or a great weekend

EXHIBIT 6-2

Nova Scotia is not Necessarily Canada

A survey of the U.S. travel market commissioned in 1985 by the federal government of Canada uncovered a surprising result: 80 percent of Americans surveyed had no intention of visiting Canada. In response, the province of Nova Scotia launched a creative strategy to overcome this problem. They basically concealed their Canadian union and promoted an image of Nova Scotia as a free-standing entity. They executed the redefinition, according to Dan Brennan of the Board of Tourism, because Americans hold an image of Canada as a cold climate. The results of the redefinition of Nova Scotia were a 90 percent increase in U.S. visitors and a 66 percent increase in inquiries. No published information exists on American visitors' reactions when they discovered they were in Canada and not Hawaii in February.

Sources: Jerry M. Dybka, "A Look at the American Traveler: The U.S. Pleasure Travel Market," *Journal of Travel Research,* Winter 1987, pp. 2–4; and Paul Dunphy, "Travel & Tourism: Nova Scotia's Strategy Maps Increase in Visitors," *Advertising Age,* July 14, 1986, pp. 519–521.

getaway destination. New York City comes to mind as a place that evokes all these images depending on who you ask.

Image has always been of great interest and concern to marketers. What is our brand image? How do consumers perceive our product relative to the competition's product? How can we identify, measure, and control our product's image to attract consumers to our product and build market share?

All these questions must also be of concern to the strategic place marketer. Today's place marketer must consider image as a major influence on a buyer's choice. A vacation place buyer will more likely choose Greece instead of Turkey if the image of Greece is more familiar and positive. Exhibit 6-2 describes Nova Scotia's image making efforts.

We define strategic image management as follows:

Strategic image management (SIM) is the ongoing process of researching a place's image among its audiences, segmenting and targeting its specific image and its demographic audiences, positioning the place's benefits to support an existing image or create a new image, and communicating those benefits to the target audiences.

The underlying premise of SIM is that because place images are identifiable and change over time, the place marketer must be able to track and influence the image held by different target audiences. Normally, an image sticks in the public's mind for a long time, even after it loses its validity. Some people still think of Pittsburgh as a smoke- belching, steel-making city even though today's Pittsburgh is very different. At other times, a place's image may change more rapidly as the media and word of mouth spread vital news stories about place. Iraq is seen one day as an ancient exotic Middle Eastern nation and the next day, thanks to Saddam Hussein, as a villainous country. Image management is an ongoing process of researching image changes and trying to understand their dynamics.

HOW CAN A PLACE'S IMAGE BE MEASURED?

Planners follow a two-step process to assess a place image: First they select a target audience. The target audience must be easily characterized by common traits, interests, or perceptions. The second step requires planners to measure the target audience's perceptions along relevant attributes. We now examine these two steps.

Selecting an Audience

The first step in assessing a place's image is to select the audience segment whose perceptions are of interest. Seven broad audiences might be interested in living, visiting, or working in a place and they may hold different images of it. They are:

1. *Resident.*   Places may want to attract new residents. Today, Australia and Canada are offering citizenship to immigrants from the Far East who can bring in $200,000 or more.
2. *Visitors.*   Places may want to increase the number of tourist and business visitors, and therefore need to know the images the visitors have of this destination.
3. *Factories.*   Places may want to attract factories and need to

know what the prospective management knows and thinks about the place.

4. *Corporate headquarters and offices.* Places may want to attract corporate headquarters and divisional offices of major companies, so they need to know what opinions location specialists and company leaders currently hold.

5. *Entrepreneurs.* Places may want to attract entrepreneurs and small businesses and need to know how the prospects view the place as a community to live and work.

6. *Investors.* Places may want to attract investors such as real estate developers and other financiers who show confidence in the place's future by making generous loans and investments.

7. *Foreign purchasers.* Places may want to convince foreign buyers that the place's products and services are of high quality.

Even within each broad audience, a large variance in the image of the place often exists. Tourist perceptions differ depending on whether the tourists are "sunlusters" or "wanderlusters"; the perceptions of manufacturers differ depending on whether the manufacturers are heavy-duty industrial or software developers.

Targeting specific audience groups is required to avoid the problem of unstable or inconsistent images. For instance, South Africa's racial problems did not prevent South Africa from attracting thousands of wealthy foreign tourists for sightseeing and hunting. Mala Mala, Sabi Sabi, and Landozi private game parks in South Africa continue to attract affluent tourists who pay thousands of dollars to join a hunting safari. The parks claim an excellent customer satisfaction rate with approximately 80 percent making return visits. Although South Africa suffers from an unfavorable overall image, the place carries an attractive image for a target group wishing to hunt.[3]

There are numerous ways of splitting a market into smaller groups as Portugal has done; see exhibit 6–3. Researchers should identify characteristics that maximize discrimination among groups holding different images. The characteristics include simple objective measures (demographics, geographical), complex objective measures (social class, family life cycle, life-style), behavioral measures (buying occasion, usage rate), or inferred measures (personality, needs, sought benefits).

The segments are most useful when they have six characteristics:

1. *Mutually exclusive.* The various identified segments should not overlap.

EXHIBIT 6-3
April in Portugal

Within Europe, Portugal's image is one of low industrial potential, heavy bureaucracy, and social backwardness. Along with Portugal's weak influence within the European Community, this image kept Portugal out of the running for major manufacturing projects. The combination of a huge economic crisis followed by the political turmoil of Portugal's 1974 revolution stalled attempts to reposition Portugal's image. Only by the middle 1980s did the country start to overcome its problems and to attract foreign investments.

Since then, Portugal's officials have assessed their specific strengths and the opportunities they offer. One of Portugal's greatest strengths is its natural beauty. It boasts of as many hours of sunshine as California, stable weather, and a good inventory of beaches, deserts, forests, and mountains within a radius of 120 miles. When they added their low wages to the picture, Portugal quickly realized they had a chance to become the film capital of Europe. Since then, Portuguese officials have descended on Hollywood and secured agreements from the major studios to send delegations to Portugal to help them become the Hollywood of Europe.

Has Portugal selected the right target? The film industry requires a strong infrastructure of reliable transportation, specialized production equipment, and a skilled labor force. In addition, the competition for film production has intensified with low-cost countries such as Hungary and Czechoslovakia now competing. The lure of the high-profile Hollywood film industry may be obscuring more prosaic, yet more obtainable targets for Portugal to develop.

2. *Exhaustive.* Every potential target member should be included in some segment.
3. *Measurable.* The degree to which the size, purchasing power, and profile of the resulting segments can be readily measured.
4. *Accessible.* The degree to which the resulting segments can be effectively reached and served.

5. *Substantial.* The degree to which the resulting segments are large enough to be worth pursuing.
6. *Differentially responsive.* The segment is useful only if it responds differently from the other segments to various amounts, types, and timing of marketing strategy.[4]

To illustrate these criteria, suppose a South African gaming park wants to send direct mail advertising their park to high-potential prospects for a hunting safari. They would need to characterize the people who would be interested in hunting safaris, know that they have the discretionary income to respond positively, access their addresses, ascertain that a sufficient number of them exist, and project that a sufficient number of them will open their mail and respond positively.

Once the overall audience is segmented by relevant criteria, and groups of interest selected, the key task is to identify the attributes a particular target audience uses to profile the place. For example, a study of tourists who returned repeatedly to a small resort area in Michigan revealed five attributes: (1) availability of facilities for water sports, (2) scenic beauty, (3) opportunity for rest and relaxation, (4) suitable accommodations, and (5) pleasant attitudes of the people.[5]

Measuring the Audience's Image

Many methods have been proposed for measuring images. We describe three approaches.[6]

FAMILIARITY-FAVORABILITY MEASUREMENT. The first step is to establish how familiar the target audience is with the place and how favorable members feel toward it. To establish familiarity respondents are asked to check one of the following:

Never heard of	Heard of	Know a little bit	Know a fair amount	Know very well

The results indicate the audience's awareness of the place. If most of the respondents check the first two or three categories, the place has an awareness problem

Those respondents who have some familiarity with the place are then asked to describe how favorable they feel toward it by checking one of the following:

Very unfavorable	Somewhat unfavorable	Indifferent	Somewhat favorable	Very favorable

If most of the respondents check the first two or three categories, the organization has a serious image problem.

SEMANTIC DIFFERENTIAL.   The place marketers must go further and research the content of the place's image. One of the most popular tools is the semantic differential,[7] involving the following steps:

1. *Developing a set of relevant dimensions.* The researcher asks people to identify the dimensions they would use in thinking about the place. People could be asked: What things do you think of when you consider a vacation? They might reply weather, recreational opportunities, historical interest, cost, and so on. Each of these would be turned into a bipolar scale, with adjectival extremes at each end. The scales can be rendered as five or seven-point scales.

2. *Reducing the set of relevant dimensions.* The number of dimensions should be kept small to avoid respondent fatigue in having to rate several vacation sites. The researchers should remove redundant scales that add little information.

3. *Administering the instrument to a sample of respondents.* The respondents are asked to rate one place at a time. The bipolar adjectives should be arranged so as not to load all of the negative adjectives on one side. After the results are in, the scales can be rearranged to display all the positive adjectives on one side for convenience of interpretation.

4. *Averaging the results.* The respondents' perceptions are averaged on each scale. When the averages are connected, they represent the average image that the audience has of the place.

5. *Checking on the image variance.* Because each image profile is a line of means, it does not reveal how variable the image actually is. If the variance is high, the image doesn't mean much and further audience segmentation is necessary.

Table 6-1 shows a set of bipolar scales used to measure the image of New Orleans. The line connecting the means shows the image that a particular group of respondents had of New Orleans.

EVALUATIVE MAPS.   One measure of how citizens view a place is to inventory their visual impressions. Jack Nasar and his associates used a technique whereby they interviewed a city's residents and collected

TABLE 6-1
The Image of New Orleans

	1	2	3	4	5	6	7	
Innocent						X		Sinful
Feminine		X						Masculine
Friendly		X						Cold
Romantic	X							Boring
Old	X							New
Safe				X				Unsafe
Interesting		X						Uninteresting
Vibrant			X					Stagnant
Pretty			X					Ugly
Sophisticated		X						Simple
Natural		X						Artificial
Harmonious			X					Conflictual

their impressions and feelings about different areas of the city. Figure 6-1 shows the evaluative map reflecting how Knoxville, Tennessee, residents view their city. The labels represent words that came up when residents were asked about the different parts of the city. The shadings show how the residents evaluated different areas from most liked to least liked. Nasar concluded:

> residents and visitors disliked the appearance of chaotic and run-down districts, paths, and edges—that is, the CBD [Central Business District], the streets feeding it, and the inner-city neighborhoods—and that they liked the looks of new, spacious landmark centers, vegetated districts, and paths with views of the river and Smokeys.[8]

WHAT ARE THE GUIDELINES FOR DESIGNING A PLACE'S IMAGE?

Once planners understand the place's current image, they can deliberate on what image they can properly build of the place. Fresno, California, illustrates the task of defining a desired image. In an image survey

FIGURE 6-1

The evaluative image of Knoxville from verbal description by residents.

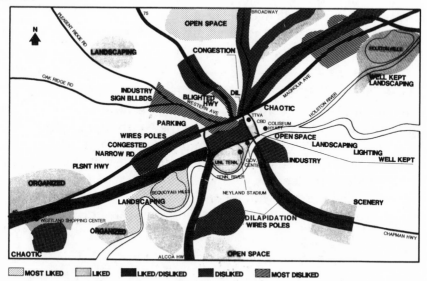

Reprinted by permission of the *Journal of the American Planning Association*, 56.1, Winter, 1990.

of the city, the following words came up repeatedly: boring, raisins, housewives, fictional, car rest stop, oranges, Carol Burnett special. Each response has some justification in fact. Fresno does produce fruit, is a rest stop between San Francisco and Los Angeles, and has been the subject of a television series. While the responses reflect some aspect of reality, they seem haphazard and unfocused.

The problem for Fresno and most places is to create an effective image for each target group. For an image to be effective, it must meet the following criteria:

1. *It must be valid.* If a place promotes an image too far from reality, the chance of success is minimal. For example, Indianapolis's Convention and Visitors Bureau adopted the campaign theme: "Move over, New York; apple is our middle name." The image stretch was far too great and the theme failed.

2. *It must be believable.* Even if the proposed image is valid, it may not be readily believable. If the Hawaiian island of Kauai claims that it is twice as beautiful as Maui, while this may be true, people may not be

ready to believe it. It may make more sense for Kauai to first claim that it is as beautiful as Maui and later increase the claim. (Yet the contrary view holds that a shocking statement may be more effective because it grabs attention and challenges beliefs.)

3. *It must be simple.* If the place disseminates too many images of itself, it leads to confusion.

The residents of Huntsville, Alabama, may see their city as a space center with legitimate aspirations to become a technological hub of the new South. A newcomer from the North may see the city as dominated by rednecks with Ford pickups and gunracks. An outsider who never stepped foot into Huntsville may see the city as a cauldron of race riots and Ku Klux Klan activity. A foreign investor may see only nonunion labor, cheap farmland, and a young work force. Getting across a central idea about Huntsville is the challenge.

---

4. *It must have appeal.* The image must suggest why people would want to live there, visit, invest, and so forth. The state of Michigan conducts a campaign with the catch words "Yes Michigan." By itself, this lacks any argument for paying attention to Michigan; it is an empty statement. This campaign endures because an upbeat group sings a song that suggests that Michigan is a forward-looking, happy place. The infectious beat of the jingle is repeated often on inexpensive radio ads and, like a popular song, embeds itself in the consciousness of the listener. On the other hand, New York's trademark, "I Love New York" has even more positive content in suggesting that there are things to love about New York.

5. *It must be distinctive.* The image works best when it is different from other common themes. There is an overuse of the words "a friendly place," and "a place that works." Indiana invented "Wander Indiana" suggesting that there is much to see and discover in Indiana. Indiana later dropped this campaign. People visualize Indiana as basically farm fields and don't think of it as a place to wander. Moreover, the juxtaposition of "Wander" and "Indiana" is awkward and lacks a positive feeling.

Sometimes, a quirk in a place's history becomes the basis not so much for its overall image but a handle for creating interest. (See Canton, Ohio: A Bomb Target? in exhibit 6–4.)

EXHIBIT 6-4

Canton, Ohio: A Bomb Target?

A former resident of Canton, Ohio, was trying to describe her image of the city to her classmates. She found that most of the students had no image of this mid-sized city. She described Canton as a city with major manufacturing facilities, the Pro Football Hall of Fame, and the New Market downtown revitalization program for theater and the arts. Her explanation moved the city from the position of no image to that of a negative image. The class concluded that Canton is a typical, boring, industrialized midwestern city.

Then she suddenly recalled an experience: "I remember sitting in my fourth-grade class and hearing from the teacher that during World War II Canton was a major U.S. target of the Germans." Imagine, right after the cities of Chicago, New York, and Los Angeles, appears the name of Canton. That fact suddenly crystallized the concept of Canton. If Canton is destroyed, the nation might fall. That's an image that the former resident never forgot and it gave meaning and fullness to what it meant to live in Canton.

WHAT TOOLS ARE AVAILABLE FOR COMMUNICATING AN IMAGE?

Place image makers can draw on three tools to implement an effective image of a place: (1) slogans, themes, and positions;[9] (2) visual symbols; and (3) events and deeds. Each medium has its own rules and possibilities.

Slogans, Themes, and Positions

Typically, image makers develop a slogan to unify a specific campaign and the slogan, if successful, is carried over many campaigns. A slogan is a short catchall phrase that embodies an overall vision of the place. Table 6–2 lists several place slogans. The slogans are useful in generating enthusiasm, momentum, and fresh ideas.

A good slogan provides a platform from which the place's image can be further amplified. Thus, a slogan such as the Atlanta Advantage not

TABLE 6–2
Place Campaign Slogans

Spain	Everything Under the Sun
Pennsylvania	America Starts Here
Hershey, Pennsylvania	The Sweetest Place on Earth
Detroit, Michigan	The Renaissance City
Boston, Massachusetts	The Bicentennial City
Quebec	It Feels So Different
Aruba	Our Only Business Is You

only teases the public as to what the Atlanta Advantage is but also can be used to disseminate specific advantages that Atlanta possesses.

Consider the case of New Brunswick, Canada:

New Brunswick wanted to establish an umbrella image to market everything: tourism, new business, and exports. The province was clearly underexposed, in spite of its strong assets such as natural resources, dramatic scenery, low-cost energy and labor, and proximity to major population centers. After much analysis, the slogan emerged: "This is New Brunswick." Certainly, not earthshaking or incredibly clever. The potential, however, is significant. The planners envision that slogan stamped on all of New Brunswick's products—every food can, foot of lumber, and piece of mail. The slogan has the advantages of simplicity, directness, and brevity. It fits on all the products and is easily understood.[10]

A variation from using a catchall slogan is to spell out themes to drive specific marketing programs addressed to specific audiences. The most effective themes are versatile and flexible, yet grounded in reality. New Zealand calls itself "The Environmental Destination of the 1990s," recognizing that tourists now feel guilty about spoiling the beautiful scenery they cherish. The country now promotes ecotourism, a form of seeing and not disturbing.

However clever, the message must also be backed by real performance. As one person observed, "It doesn't matter how pretty a picture, say Houston, paints of itself, if once you get there, you can't drive through the streets because of traffic."

Another tool is *image positioning* where the place positions itself in regional, national, and international terms as the place for a certain type of activity or as a viable alternative location/attraction to another place that may have a stronger or more well-established position. The challenge of image positioning is to develop an image that communicates benefits and unique attributes that make the place stand out among other places. Several examples of image positioning are shown in Table 6-3. Again, image positioning must be supported by reality. For example, Thailand's tourist image positioning can be increasingly questioned. Thailand has neglected its tourist infrastructure—roads, hotels, waste treatment—with the result that its massive tourist expansion efforts are producing declining returns due to polluted beaches, traffic congestion, poor hotel quality, and poor services. The *message* is there, but not the *product*.

Visual Symbols

Visual symbols have figured prominently in place marketing. Many landmark sites of places are permanently etched in the public's minds: Eiffel Tower (Paris), Big Ben (London), Red Square (Moscow), the Great Wall

TABLE 6-3
Image Positioning Statements

Denver—Economic, business, transportation, and financial center of the Rocky Mountain Region
Seattle—Leading center of Pacific Northwest—the alternative to California
Atlanta—Center of the New South
Miami—Financial capital of South America
Fairfax County—Nation's second most important address
Berlin—Capital of the new Europe
Spain—Rising star of the European Community
Costa Rica—Latin America's most stable democracy
New Hampshire—The alternative to Massachusetts
Mitchell Field (Milwaukee)—The Northern Illinois alternative to O'Hare congestion
Thailand—Tourism haven of the Far East
Palma, Majorca—Sunny alternative to the British Isles

(China), and the Astrodome (Houston). When used well, these visual symbols appear on official stationery, brochures, billboards, and dozens of other places.

A visual image, to be successful, *needs to reinforce* an image argument. If the visual is inconsistent with the slogan, themes, or positions, it undermines the place's credibility. Northern Ireland made this mistake in trying to represent the country as only bucolic, rural wonderland. The tourist brochures featured a seemingly never ending collage of hills, streams, and thatched cottages. To a large audience, Northern Ireland is urban, brutal, and dangerous. The news media endlessly announce the killings and scare tactics of the conflict between the British and Irish Republican armies. Clearly, Northern Ireland needs a more believable visual image strategy than pastoral greenery, and might emphasize its surprising low crime rate, its remarkable collection of Victorian buildings, and a wide array of constructed and natural attractions.

Here are four commonly used visual image strategies:

1. *The diverse visual.* In the diverse strategy, viewers are treated to a wide range of visual images about the place. The aim is to dispel the notion that the place has a single character. Singapore, in its *Economic Development Board Yearbook 1988–1989*, presented itself with an overwhelming array of photographs of global business endeavors. Throughout the book, however, are photographs of tourist attractions, abstract paintings, landmarks, and a page devoted to local artists. The overall visual effect is one of versatility and completeness.

2. *The humorous visual.* In the humorous strategy, the visual treats the place in a witty style. This is especially useful when dealing with a negative aspect of the place. When Bradford, England, was trying to combat its negative image as a sooty, industrialized relic, the city introduced its first-tourist-to-Bradford campaign. After touting the city's newly revived central city, cleaning of buildings, historical and literary stars, they produced a memorable shot. They filmed "the first tourist" alighting from the train amidst bands, hoopla, and political proclamations. It worked! The visual told the entire story: Bradford is redeveloping, it is a short-trip destination, and it is a city that trusts itself enough to parody itself.

3. *The denying visual.* Another way to handle a negative image about a place is to overwhelm the target audience with positive images, some of which subtly deny the negative aspects. There are places where ignoring the obvious is risky. For example, many tourists would not visit South Africa because of apartheid. To counter the image, the South

African Tourism Board gives each prospective visitor a twenty-minute video. The opening shot shows spinning newspaper headlines attacking South Africa's apartheid stand. The visual shocks the viewers and also reminds them of the 1940s film style of spinning newspapers. The style implies the attempted problem is in the past. The video then shows blacks and whites mixing together in various settings, with everyone smiling and on the move. Then it adds shots of some of South Africa's most beautiful scenery.

4. *The consistent visual.* When a place possesses a positive image, it is easier to assemble strong visuals. Consider Williamsburg, Virginia, the historic state capital and home of the College of William and Mary. Williamsburg has developed the image and attractions of a first-rate historic town. The visual images of colonial craftspersons, traditional American dress, and hot apple pie come easily to mind. The problem occurs when Williamsburg addresses business expansion. A visual image of high-tech parks spoil the deeply rooted and carefully developed historic image. A far better strategy is to pursue an education image, or an art and culture image that would bring in researchers, artists, theater companies, students, and new residents. The accompanying visuals would work well together.

Events and Deeds

Most image campaigns take the form of catchy slogans, advertisements, and videos. But images can also be communicated through events and deeds. The events can be bold, or they can be on the quiet side, subtly influencing an audience over time. For years, the former Soviet Union has been exporting its ballet and gymnasts to the United States for performances. The aim was to reach the intellectual public and the opinion leaders, improving their knowledge of the country so that Americans would feel more comfortable in visiting and doing business in the former Soviet Union.

Japan is particularly creative in its attempts to win over Americans. Much use is made of events and deeds, as is shown in exhibit 6–5.

HOW CAN A PLACE CORRECT A NEGATIVE IMAGE?

Many external forces beyond the place's control shape a place's image. When Los Angeles suffers an earthquake, or Alaska experiences an oil spill, or New York has another subway murder, there can be a tremen-

EXHIBIT 6–5

Nobody Does it Better: Japan's Image Campaign in America

An excellent example of event marketing is the campaign the general consulate of Japan launched in the late 1980s. Americans had turned increasingly critical toward Japan, their feelings moved from surprise to envy to dislike to anger toward the Japanese. Anti-Japanese feelings surfaced over Japan's trade barriers, unfair dumping practices, seemingly insensitive comments by Japanese political leaders, the high cost of doing business in Japan, and a general feeling that the Japanese were not playing fairly.

The Japanese responded with an image campaign using American talent and touting American values. For example, Honda hired actor Burgess Meredith to talk about Honda cars on television commercials. Meredith's voice, very warm and familiar to Americans, implied that the car was as American as apple pie. A more long-term effort was the orchestration of the Japan Festival held in Chicago in 1988. That summer the Chicago papers announced a number of events Japan was sponsoring in Chicago to celebrate this festival. The Japanese government officially stated that Japan was repaying Chicago for the visit of the Chicago Symphony Orchestra—a world-class organization—to Japan and also wishing to recognize the efforts of Illinois Governor James Thompson, who had visited the country on a number of occasions.

The festival events included a Grand Kabuki performance, a Japanese film series, a three-act modern jazz dance version of Japanese history, students from Japan performing impromptu compositions, woodblock prints of Kabuki theater scenes, contemporary Japanese prints, Japanese technological exhibits, a Nishijin fabrics exhibit, calligraphy by contemporary Japanese masters, carved wood and ivory toggles, additional Japanese crafts, two days of comic storytelling in a Japanese style, and many other events.

These activities were aimed at a wide range of audiences: theater-goers, college students, elementary and junior high students, popular culture and high culture lovers, and parents who could take their children to puppet performances. It was an encyclopedic festival demonstrating and dramatizing the Japanese contribution to culture.

The sponsors list included the general consulate of Japan, the Japanese Chamber of Commerce and Industry of Chicago, the Japan-American Society of Chicago, the state of Illinois, and the city of Chicago. The primary source of funding for the festival, however, was the Japanese government, as well as some Japanese companies. A coordinated festival has the advantage of exchanging information, deepening an understanding of a country, and, more importantly, demonstrating a certain generosity and concern for the citizens of Illinois. And this phenomenon operates on several levels. The first level is in the media. In covering the various events, newspapers, television, and radio clarify and enrich understanding of Japanese culture. Second, many of the performances were aimed at the influential. The art exhibits, the Kabuki presentations, the fashion displays, were held in downtown Chicago and in locales likely to attract the opinion leaders of the city: those intellectuals, professionals, and merchants who influence others and in some cases visit or do business in Japan.

The strategy of using indirect communication strategies—of using the culture and the less strident forms of presentations—contains some risks for the image maker. The advantages of such a plan may not come to fruition for several years and some of the benefits may be so indirect that accurate measurements is impossible. Furthermore, there is always the possibility that the audience will not see the connection between Japanese culture and their highly criticized business behavior. Appreciation of Grand Kabuki may not translate to a softening of American attitudes toward Japanese dumping and protectionism.

Source: See the newsletter of the Japan Information Center, April–May 1988.

dous wave of negative publicity. Or when a place has a chronically poor economy, humid climate, or repressive leadership, it has to address the problem of its negative image.

Making a Positive Out of a Negative

One option is to admit to the problem and turn the negative into a positive. For years, Minnesota lived with the reputation of being a cold-weather state from which one should flee. When asked about the most negative aspect of their state, citizens always brought up the frigid winter that begins in early November and persists until sometime in April. As evidence of the winter problem, there was significant migration of Minnesotans into states such as Arizona and California.

How did Minnesota deal with this problem? Minnesota, in the last decade, has aggressively promoted its winters. Not only does the state promote tourist attractions and winter events but Minneapolis also features downtown walkways that shield citizens from the winter, and St. Paul sponsors its famous winter carnival, an old institution that has taken on new life. Minneapolis' ads read: "We Like it Here." The promo copy reads: "In Minneapolis, we have something more. An Attitude. It's friendly, it's proud, and it's reasonable."

The city of Johnstown, Pennsylvania, provides another example of turning a negative into a positive and, in fact, celebrating their problem. Johnstown's image has always been tarnished by the Great Flood of 1889. In this flood, a large earthen dam collapsed and 20 million tons of water flooded the Conemaugh River Valley destroying the city and killing more than 2,000 people. The town suffered further great floods in 1936 and 1977, earning the reputation of being waterlogged.

What did Johnstown do? The city decided to market itself as a short-trip destination by hosting a yearlong hundredth anniversary celebration of the great flood. During the Memorial Day, Fourth of July, and Labor Day weekends of 1989, activities included a laser light sculpture, a Bon Jovi rock concert, and the screening of an Academy Award–winning short documentary film about the flood. An estimated 1 million people flooded into Johnstown for the events, and interest in the region has been maintained to the present.[11]

Should a place base an image making campaign on a negative circumstance? John Trutter, president of the Chicago Tourism Council, said, "I am not strong for celebrating tragedies. I don't like image-building on something negative."[12] Therefore, he explains, he disagreed with the yearlong celebration of the Great Chicago Fire of 1871 and would resist leveraging the Al Capone gangster era into a tourist promotion.

But for a place like Johnstown, what are the alternatives? If the town does nothing, they will not attract tourists and will continue to lose population. The town applied to the federal government for $4 million for a downtown museum restoration, but this was rejected. Then the town applied for federal funds to build a new National Park Services Visitors Center at the dam site and managed to restore the downtown museum with funds from that project. The Johnstown leaders had the foresight to hire a New York consulting firm to design museum displays and a Boston firm to plan traffic patterns. Given this window of opportunity, Johnstown acted with vigor to capitalize on its long-standing image problem. Today, Johnstown is busy transforming another of its negatives, its old steel mill, into an attraction based on the industrial heritage of the region.[13]

Marketing Icons

Another strategy for correcting a negative image is icon marketing. Consider the image of the former Soviet Union which, until recently, struck people as a vast, closed country—a prison. The image evoked pictures of Siberian forced-labor camps; grim shortages of food and products; citizens living in stark apartments, repression of Jewish citizens; clunky Russian cars based on a thirty-five-year-old design; and taciturn, secretive Soviet leaders. The overall impression was one of darkness and control—a place that few people wanted to visit.

Enter Mikhail Gorbachev, then Soviet premier and new-style international icon. In a winning demonstration of impression management, Gorbachev used his own "warm personality" to help reshape the public's image of his country. When visiting Washington to discuss the arms reduction agreement with President Ronald Reagan, he demonstrated how a single person, well positioned in understanding the demands of the marketplace, can influence and reshape a public's perception of a place. During his visit, Gorbachev consented to a personal interview with NBC anchor Tom Brokaw, toasted with great humor his new American friends, and even leapt out of a car to greet American citizens on a city street. These impressions gave American citizens a new window through which to view what was then the Soviet Union. Gorbachev and his friendly, informed, witty wife Raisa, expressed the new openness, *glasnost,* of the Soviet Union. Slowly, the fabled iron curtain lifted, revealing a new cooperative partner.

The icon strategy has a downside. The unrelenting problems in the former Soviet Union continued to erode the impression- making strategies of Gorbachev. In addition, some internal audiences were uncomfortable with his personal style of openness, lighthearted kidding, and easy familiarity. The strategy works best when the issues are less dramatic and the audience is not troubled by political or economic problems. Even under those circumstances an icon can help (see Exhibit 6–6).

Removing the Negative

Image improvement is too often used as a panacea or a quick-fix for a place's problems. Place leaders besieged by failing businesses or a drop in tourism are usually quick to demand a new image. Yet in most instances, it does not work if the place has not started to correct its deep-seated problems.

Consider the case of Glasgow, Scotland. When Europeans prepared a list of deeply troubled urban cities, the city of Glasgow would inevitably be included. A place with an unemployment rate more than 21 percent, high crime rates, and buildings blackened by coal dust, Glasgow had earned its reputation. One of Glasgow's own politicians described the city as "A hellish mixture of poverty, drink, and violence."[14]

Yet today, Glasgow, while not without problems, is an improving city that is considered an arts capital of Europe. What steps did it take? First, the city attracted government grants from London, Edinburgh, and its own city council to rehabilitate tenements and rebuild public places. One project was to repair the Burrell Museum, now considered Britain's most magnificent art gallery. Various political forces cooperated for the first time to improve the city's condition. One city official saw the starting point as "a change of attitude in the people that ran the city."[15] When Glasgow citizens began to witness the cleaning up of their city, and the new jobs created, their attitude started to improve. They began to police themselves; encourage innovation and change; and monitor their own political, economic, and educational institutions.

Second, the city image makers began to tie together the changing reality of Glasgow. They adopted the slogan, "Glasgow Miles Better." They produced glossy brochures demonstrating the city's transformation visually and in words. Articles began appearing in newspapers and magazines heralding the arrival of a new giant in the arts. Image met reality in Glasgow. A visitor to the city saw the changes and experienced the arts revival. Glasgow is "Miles Better."

EXHIBIT 6-6

Your Majesty: Jordan's Queen as Icon

The kingdom of Jordan was in deep trouble during the Persian Gulf War. The country found itself trying to please Iraq on the one hand and trying not to permanently alienate Western powers on the other. Luckily, the fourth wife of Jordan's King Hussein is American-born and Western in style, glamour, and deportment. After the king had made a disastrous trip to Washington, D.C., to present the Jordanian side, she appeared.

The setting was a prime-time television interview with Barbara Walters. The queen, whom Walters repeatedly called "Your Majesty," looked straight into the camera and explained how the American media misjudged Jordan's intentions. Queen Noor, a graduate of Princeton, further argued that Jordan is a modern country and treats women with dignity.

The evidence for all this? The icon. The queen offered no photographs, statistics, or expert testimony. The only argument was the queen herself as an illustrative example of the real Jordan.

CONCLUSION

The creation of a powerful image is part of the entire marketing process. It demands a good strategic marketing audit, determined improvement of the product, and creative invention of the symbols. Once the place has taken these steps, its next task is to disseminate its new image to its target. The next chapter examines how place messages and images can be efficiently distributed.

7

Distributing the Place's Image and Messages

Every place needs to develop a story about itself and to tell it consistently and well (see Wisconsin: A Master Promoter in exhibit 7–1). Yet, the sheer number of markets and media channels creates a high risk of contrary and confusing messages. If the tourist commission at Fort Myers, Florida, decides to promote Fort Myers as a peaceful place to retire and the chamber of commerce promotes it as a commercial center, confusion could easily arise. If the Irish Investment Board promotes Ireland as an attractive site for heavy industry and the Irish Tourist Board advertises Ireland as an unspoiled land of leprechauns and magic, the two pictures collide.

This chapter examines the challenges involved in distributing a strong and coherent image of a place. Those in charge of distributing the place's image must address the following questions:

1. Who is the target audience?
2. What broad influence tools are available?
3. What major advertising media channels are available and what are their respective characteristics?
4. What criteria should be used in choosing specific advertising media vehicles?
5. How should the advertising messages be timed?

EXHIBIT 7-1

Wisconsin: A Master Promoter

The state of Wisconsin is a master promoter of its image and products. Its image evokes a picture of many lakes, good skiing, a healthy dairy industry, and a strong beer industry. Fairly early, Wisconsin entered the place marketing game. In the 1920s, Wisconsin attracted many Chicagoans to its lakeside cabins, fishing, and other inexpensive activities. Today, Wisconsin continues to draw tourists and businesses, even though its place marketing expenditures are one seventh of Illinois's and one fifth of Michigan's. Why is Wisconsin so successful given its relatively low place marketing budget?

Wisconsin operates a very efficient place marketing machine. The state's place promoters include the State Tourist Commission; various cities and regions, hotels, motels, and restaurants; tourist attractions; universities/colleges; industries (cheese, wine, beer); sports teams; and cultural attractions (painters, musicians, filmmakers).

Wisconsin, calling itself the Badger State, uses a well-known slogan, "Wisconsin You're Among Friends." It advertises a high-profile phone number, 1-800-432-TRIP, that reaches a large number of potential visitors. It operates clean attractive tourist centers along its highways providing information, state maps, hotels/motels, and advice on where to find the best fishing.

Various Wisconsin cities support the state's efforts and also develop their own place marketing plans. Milwaukee, Green Bay, Appleton, and La Crosse have their own chambers of commerce, tourist bureaus, and business attraction efforts. Each city invests in tourist advertising, especially to promote summer vacations. Milwaukee promotes its lavish Summerfest along its lake shore. Green Bay capitalizes on having a National Football League franchise (the Green Bay Packers) and operates a Packer Hall of Fame.

(continued)

EXHIBIT 7–1
Wisconsin: A Master Promoter (continued)

Wisconsin's regions have also developed promotional plans. Various regions publish and distribute newspapers and brochures describing their attractions and accommodations. Some regions promote fishing and water shows; others promote summer camps; some promote county fairs; and still others promote local products, such as raspberries or cherries.

Wisconsin's resorts and hotels actively promote their properties, as well as the state. The Abbey Hotel in Fontana runs ads in Chicago and many other locations seeking to attract tourists. The Door County condo complexes promote the virtues of living in Wisconsin. Big hotel chains, such as Sheraton and Best Western, run regional ads for summertime vacations in Wisconsin. Restaurants, while they rarely advertise nationally, often acquire a regional reputation like Karl Ratzsch's in Milwaukee, Al Johnson's in Door County, or the Hoffman House in Madison. Visitors crisscrossing the state travel out of their way to frequent these restaurants.

Wisconsin industries also create favorable impressions of the state through their products. Wisconsin discovered wine-making, and local regions now feature fruity local wines. The beer industry promotes the pure waters and natural beauty of Wisconsin. The water industry sells Wisconsin with La Croix reminding consumers of Wisconsin's springs. Any discussion of beer in America includes Miller and Pabst of Milwaukee, and Old Style of La Crosse.

The state of Wisconsin is the champion producer of cheese, with a 35 percent market share. The term "Wisconsin Cheese" is now a brand name. Each year, the Wisconsin Cheesemakers Association stages a World's Natural Cheese Championship Contest. As of 1988, nine of the seventeen world champions have emerged from Wisconsin's own state. Wisconsin also promoted its cheese reputation with the "Cheese–Mobile"—an especially designed, freon-cooled trailer truck—which measured twenty feet long and six feet high and carted around a block of Wisconsin cheddar cheese weighing 40,000 pounds! Jim Tillison, director of the Wisconsin Cheesemakers Association, claimed: "By the time it's done, it will have been viewed by 20 million people and we estimate an additional 50 million will read or hear about it." The cheese was on the road for two years imprinting in the minds of consumers the overwhelming dominance of Wisconsin as the leader in the manufacture of cheddar, gouda, edam, swiss, and a variety of other cheeses.

Wisconsin publishes and distributes an article by Helen Killingstad entitled "Packaging Wisconsin for Tourists," in which the author advises restaurant owners to become friendly "know-it-alls" about their towns. Wisconsinites are urged to advise tourists where to go for entertainment and how to keep the kids distracted on a rainy day. Wisconsin not only encourages the support of its boosters but also wants them all distributing the same image. All said, Wisconsin has achieved a virtual integration of its image distribution system.

Source: For information about the Wisconsin cheese–mobile see Rogers Worthington, "Regional Dispute over Who's the Big Cheese," *Chicago Tribune,* October 9, 1988, sec. 1, p. 5.

6. How can the mix be developed?
7. How can the communication results be evaluated?
8. How can conflicting media sources and messages be handled?

CLARIFYING THE TARGET AUDIENCE AND DESIRED BEHAVIOR

The first step before choosing messages and media is to clarify the target audience. For example, does the tourist office in Cancun, Mexico, want to attract young singles, young marrieds, families, or retirees? Each potential target market calls for different messages and media. Should the tourist office rely on ads or feature articles? Should it place messages in *Rolling Stone* magazine or the *New Yorker?*

A second step calls for visualizing the target behavior that the place marketers want to elicit from the target audience. That behavior may be to spend four days on a beach, to buy a condo, or to visit in the summer rather than in the winter.

Beyond these steps, it is necessary to determine the *target buyer's stage of readiness to undertake the target behavior.* A tourist seeking a winter sun vacation may hold one of several mind-sets regarding Cancun as a destination: *knows nothing* about Cancun, *has some awareness* of Cancun, *knows a lot* about Cancun, *would like to go* to Cancun, *intends to go* to Cancun. A media strategy for those who *know nothing* might utilize a barrage of 15-second television spots. A media strategy for those who *want to go* might be to mail them discount coupons to provide an incentive to act now.

The same issue of the buyer's readiness arises with business targets. In marketing a factory site, place sellers need to distinguish between suspects, prospects, hot prospects, and customers. Each buyer group warrants a different media mix strategy. Ads in trade journals offering a free booklet describing the factory site and its advantages might ferret out suspects. Prospects might receive phone calls followed by sales calls. Hot prospects might be driven to the site; introduced to government, business, and labor leaders; and treated to the best that the city can offer.

CHOOSING THE BROAD INFLUENCE TOOLS

Place markers can use several broad influence tools to promote their place to target markets. The major influence tools are advertising, direct marketing, sales promotion, public relations, and personal selling. Descriptions of their characteristics, effectiveness, use, and costs follow.

Advertising

Advertising is the use of any paid form of nonpersonal presentation and promotion of ideas, goods, or services by an identified sponsor. Thus, the purchase by an identified city or state of printed space (magazines, newspapers, billboards) or broadcast time (television, radio) constitutes advertising.

Because of the many forms and uses of advertising, it is difficult to generalize about its distinctive qualities as a component of the promotional mix. Yet the following qualities can be noted:

Public. Advertising is a highly public mode of communication. Its public nature confers a kind of legitimacy on the place and its products and also suggests a standardized offering. Because many persons receive the same message, buyers know that their motives for purchasing the product will be publicly understood. Thus if a person vacations in Bali, he or she will expect others to interpret Bali in the same romantic way that the travel ads present it.

Pervasive. Advertising is a pervasive medium that permits the seller multiple repetitions of a message. It also allows the buyer to receive and compare the messages of various competitors. A seller's large-scale advertising suggests something positive about the seller's popularity and success.

Dramatic. Advertising provides opportunities for dramatizing the place and its products through the artful use of print, sound, and color. However, sometimes the tool's very success at expressiveness may dilute or distract from the message.

Impersonal. Advertising is often less compelling than personal presentation. The audience feels no obligation to pay attention or respond. Advertising is able to carry on only a monologue, not a dialogue, with the audience.[1]

Advertising can be used to build up a long-term image for a place and, on the other hand, to trigger quick sales such as an ad offering a special low-price airfare to Bali limited to the month of March. Advertising is an efficient way to reach numerous geographically dispersed buyers at a low cost per exposure. Certain forms of advertising, such as television, require a large budget, while other forms, such as newspapers, can be done on a small budget. Advertising might have an effect on sales simply through its presence. Consumers might believe that a heavily advertised place must offer good value; otherwise, why would place marketers spend so much money touting the place?

Direct Marketing

Direct marketing encompasses the use of communication media whose effect on individual members of the audience is measurable. The two traditional tools of direct marketing are direct mail and the telephone. Thus, the Bermuda Department of Tourism can mail or phone to a defined group such as newly marrieds and offer them a special travel rate. Those who receive the offer can ignore it, write or telephone for more information, or place an order. The direct marketer can immediately measure the response percentage of inquiries, intenders, and buyers. This feature contrasts with advertising, which usually does not contain any response mechanism such as a mail-back coupon or a sponsor telephone number. Although direct marketing advertising costs more per person reached, its superior targeting and response features often more than make up for the extra cost.

Direct marketing media have taken more forms in recent years, including direct-response radio and television where a product is offered and the customer can immediately call an 800 number to place an order using a credit-card number. Logically, the personal sales call also is an example of direct marketing since the salesperson knows the response at the end of the visit. However, we treat personal selling later as a separate influence channel.

Direct marketing has a number of distinctive characteristics:

1. *Targeting efficiency.* The marketer can be selective as to who should receive the message.
2. *Message customization.* The marketer can customize the message for each prospect, based on what is known about each prospect.
3. *Interactive quality.* The person receiving the message can interact and communicate with the marketer as to questions, suggestions, and orders.
4. *Response measurement.* The marketer can measure response rate to determine the success of the marketing program.
5. *Relationship building.* The marketer can build and enhance the relationship with a particular prospect through sending thoughtful messages on special occasions (e.g., birthdays and anniversaries) or giving patronage awards.

These characteristics of direct marketing place it high on the list of preferred influence channels by place marketers. Direct marketing is an efficient way to acquire leads on prospective vacation seekers, job hunters, headquarters or factory relocations, and so on. Once the leads are collected, direct marketing can further present offers, test interest, and measure readiness to buy. For these reasons, we expect direct marketing to occupy a growing part of the place marketer's budgets in the coming years.

Sales Promotion

Sales promotion encompasses the use of short-term incentives to encourage buyers to purchase a product or service. Whereas advertising offers a *reason* to buy, sales promotion offers an *incentive* to buy. Not surprisingly, sales promotion yields faster purchase response than does advertising.

Sales promotion includes such devices as free samples, coupons, cash rebates, discounts, premiums, prizes, patronage rewards, free trials, warranties, demonstrations, and contests. Place marketers have worked up a whole set of such tools in their bidding wars for corporate and factory relocation: inducements include tax concessions and deferrals, subsidized housing and job retraining, special financing, infrastructure improvements, and cheap land (for a complete list, see chapter 9, page 233).

Although sales promotion tools—coupons, contests, premiums, and the like—are highly diverse, they have three distinctive characteristics:

Communication. They gain attention and usually provide information that may lead the target audience to show more interest in the place.

Incentive. They incorporate some concession, inducement, or contribution that gives value to the target audience.

Invitation. They include a distinct invitation to engage in an immediate transaction.

Sales promotion tools create a stronger and quicker response than any other influence channel. Sales promotion can dramatize product offers and boost sagging sales. Promotion effects, however, are usually short term, and do not build lasting place preferences.

Public Relations

Public relations is the effort to build good relations with the organization's publics by obtaining favorable publicity; building up a good public image; and handling or heading off unfavorable rumors, stories, and events. Major public relations tools include press relations, event publicity, and lobbying. The appeal of public relations is based on its three distinctive qualities:

Highly credible. News stories and features seem more authentic and credible than ads do.

Indirect. Public relations can reach many prospects who might avoid salespeople and advertisements. The message gets to the buyers as news rather than as a sales-directed communication.

Dramatic. Public relations has, like advertising, a potential for dramatizing a place. Marketers tend to underuse public relations or use it

as an afterthought. Yet a well-thought-out public relations program coordinated with other promotion-mix elements can be extremely effective.

The craft of public relations is segmented and specialized. There are
financial public relations, employee public relations, government public relations, and so on. The branch we are interested in is called *marketing public relations (MPR)*.[2] In the hands of a place marketer, MPR
can contribute to the following tasks:

Assist in the launch of new products. Each time Walt Disney Company adds a new theme park in the Orlando area, such as EPCOT
Center or MGM Studios, it launches a public relations campaign
with press interviews, press releases, and special events to moti-
vate people to revisit Orlando and see the new marvels.

Assist in repositioning a mature product. New York City had an extremely bad press in the seventies until the "I Love New York"
campaign began, bringing millions of additional tourists to the
city.

Build up interest in a product category. As a dairy state, Wisconsin
is hurting as consumers switch away from milk, cheese, and other
dairy products. Wisconsin is helping the American Dairy Association use PR to rebuild interest and purchase of dairy products.

Influence specific target groups. Greece, in its efforts to build up
more tourism, implements special campaigns directed toward
Greek communities in the United States to go back and visit
Greece.

Defend places that have encountered public problems. When parts
of the Miami area were devastated by hurricane Andrew in 1992,
the tourist industry feared cancellations by tourists. The public
relations departments of southeastern Florida overnight sent out
thousands of faxes, newsreleases, and videotaped interviews assur-
ing that the damage was limited. The quick response is credited
with helping restore business and clarifying misconceptions of the
storm's impact.

Build the place image in a way that projects favorably on its products.
Atlantic City has a largely negative image as the spectacular gambling centers contrast with shabby boardwalk shops and slum housing. Donald Trump, owner of Trump's Plaza, has launched a public
relations campaign to reposition the city as the boxing center of the
United States. The strategy, which includes weekly bouts on ESPN

and championship fights on HBO, is meant to capture overnight visitors and big spenders. The boxing events provide story material for every sports section in America and build word of mouth about the appeal of Atlantic City.

As the power of mass advertising weakens due to rising media costs, increasing clutter, and smaller audiences, marketing managers are turning more to public relations. Often PR can create a memorable impact on public awareness at a fraction of the cost of advertising. The place does not pay for the space or time obtained in the media. It pays for a staff to develop and circulate stories and manage certain events. If the place develops an interesting story, it could be picked up by all the news media and be worth millions of dollars in equivalent advertising. Furthermore, it would have more credibility than advertising. Some experts say that an audience is five times more likely to be influenced by editorial copy than by advertising.

Personal Selling

Personal selling is the use of oral presentation in a conversation with one or more prospects for the purpose of making a sale. Personal selling is the most effective tool at certain stages of the buying process, particularly in building up buyers' preference, conviction, and action. The reason is that personal selling, when compared with advertising, has three distinctive advantages:

Personal confrontation. Personal selling involves an alive, immediate, and interactive relationship between two or more persons. Each party is able to observe each other's needs and characteristics at close hand and make immediate adjustments.

Cultivation. Personal selling permits all kinds of relationships to spring up, ranging from a matter of fact selling relationship to a deep personal friendship. Effective sales representatives normally keep their customers' interests at heart if they want long-term relationships.

Response. Personal selling makes the buyer feel under some obligation to respond after having listened to the sales talk. The buyer has a greater need to be attentive and respond, albeit it with a polite thank you.

These advantages come at a cost. A sales force represents a firm cost commitment. Advertising can be turned on and off, but the size of a

---

EXHIBIT 7-2

Getting on Board in Smyrna

When Tennessee Governor Lamar Alexander decided to get into the bidding for a major Nissan factory, he needed the cooperation and support of all the important groups in Rutherford County where the site would be offered. He needed to forestall dissent and facilitate his bid. To accomplish this, he invited all the leaders of Rutherford County to a private meeting in his mansion. A group of eighty people heard him speak confidentially, but off the record, about his plans to lure Nissan Motor Corporation. He ultimately asked, "Do you want it?" They gave him their consent. His ability to sell this group on cooperation prevented the fighting and conflict that usually result when interested parties are left out of decision making.

Source: See David Gelsanliter, *Jump Start* (Toronto: Harper & Collins, 1990), pp. 49–50.

---

sales force is more difficult to alter. Former Governor Lamar Alexander did some personal selling in Tennessee; see exhibit 7–2.

Other Tools

Additional image and promotion tools—not all under the place's control—can help or hurt a place. Included are film, television, shows, popular music, team sports, bowl games, and related T-shirts, caps, and posters. Here are some examples:

TELEVISION.   In the early 1980s when "Miami Vice" first appeared on television, the city leaders were leery. A dramatized version of drug activity hardly seems desirable. To everyone's surprise, "Miami Vice" became a catalyst for Miami to improve its buildings and self-image.

The show needed brightly colored visuals and energetic Latin music to crystallize the image of Miami. For shooting purposes, many Miami Beach faded art deco buildings were repainted in pinks and oranges. The citizens began to take renewed pride in the edifices and began to repaint their own buildings, attracting attention to Miami's fabled architectural heritage.

Similarly, Dallas began to redefine its stodgy image as a result of the long-running television program "Dallas." The crucial element is for the place to take advantage of these unplanned occurrences. Place film offices are already using grants to encourage writers to base script plots on their cities.

SONG.   Every place would like a song that has the emotional power of "I Left My Heart in San Francisco," "A Foggy Day in London Town," or "I Love Paris." When Richard Rodgers and Oscar Hammerstein wrote "Oklahoma!" they were not working for the Oklahoma Department of Tourism and Recreation, yet the state benefited. Every state university has a football fight song that is played many times over; Michigan's "Hail to the Victor," heard frequently on national television, instills state pride and promotes its educational reputation. Places can run song contests and encourage musical theater productions to leverage a place's identity.

SPORTS.   A championship season is often the catalyst to launch effective place distribution campaigns. When the Minnesota Twins won the World Series in 1987, they cooperated with General Mills and produced a Wheaties box cover with the team's picture. They also produced a Minnesota Hankie to serve as a good luck charm and bedevil the opposition. After their second victory in 1991, the Twins flooded the region with sweatshirts, T-shirts, posters, and caps. In each case they marketed the place with the cooperation of manufacturers, city bureaus, and media support. The campaigns contributed to the perception of Minneapolis and Saint Paul as enthusiastic and coordinated centers for major sports events.

SITES.   The media occasionally shine a sudden spotlight on an obscure place and tourists become determined to visit it. The television reruns of "Route 66" that featured two young men driving a Corvette up and down that now faded highway draw thousands of foreign tourists who wish to experience the thoroughfare. The problem becomes developing hotel and tourist packages that enable travelers to visit the highway. Dyersville, Iowa, the home of the baseball field in the film *Field of Dreams*, now serves as a magnet for 50,000 tourists a year wishing to connect to the mystical place. The task of the county is to make sure they have housing, food, and enough spin-off attractions.

SELECTING THE ADVERTISING MEDIA CHANNELS

Selecting effective media channels and vehicles is a formidable task. There are, in the United States, 11,238 magazines, 482 newspapers, 9,871 radio stations, and 1,220 television stations.[3]

The first step in selection calls for allocating the advertising budget to the major advertising media channels. These channels must be examined for their capacity to deliver reach, frequency, and impact. The major media channels include television, radio, magazines, newspapers, billboards, direct mail, and telephone. In addition, there are new alternative media appearing. Table 7–1 summarizes the advantages and disadvantages of the major media. They are discussed next.

Television

Television is the most effective medium for dramatizing the look and sound of a place. The television placement can range from 15-second network commercials to 30-minute narrow-cast cable shows. In many cases, televised commercials for places are paid for by corporate sponsors.

El Al Airlines, responding to an upsurge in travelers' concerns about Israel during the intifada problems of 1990, ran a series of television commercials extolling the founding of Israel. The commercial certainly created interest and awareness, but may not yield leads and customers. The airline is probably satisfied, given the situation, with that outcome. Other channels such as group sales and public presentations can follow the campaign.

If a commercial fails to incorporate reality, the campaign can backfire. The gap between image and reality is nowhere more obvious than in television (see exhibit 7–3).

A continuing trend in television is the pursuit of narrow targets through low-cost cable. Guntersville, Alabama, seeks retirees through commercials during ESPN's cable sports coverage of fishing tournaments. The travel channel reaches specific markets, and the local cable programs promote new businesses at low cost.

Radio

Radio can be used in a number of ways to promote a place. Spot radio ads can advertise vacations, land availability, or job availability. Different radio stations deliver different audiences and, therefore, must be selected carefully.

TABLE 7-1
Profiles of Major Media Types

Medium	Advantages	Limitations
Newspapers	Flexibility; timeliness; good local market coverage; broad acceptance; high believability	Short life; poor reproduction quality; small "pass along"audience
Television	Combines sight, sound, and motion; appealing to the senses; high attention; high reach	High absolute cost; high clutter; fleeting exposure; less audience selectivity
Direct mail	Audience selectivity; flexibility; no ad competition within the same medium; personalization	Relatively high cost: "junk mail" image
Radio	Mass use; high geographic and demographic selectivity; low cost	Audio presentation only; lower attention than television; nonstandardized rate structures; fleeting exposure
Magazines	High geographic and demographic selectivity; credibility and prestige; high- quality reproduction; long life; good pass-along readership	Long ad purchase lead time; some waste circulation; no guarantee of position
Outdoor	Flexibility; high repeat exposure; low cost; low competition	No audience selectivity; creative limitations

In many markets, radio programs have sprung up that specifically address tourist needs and provide travel information. Because these programs have a continuous need for guests, place tourist and convention promoters can find ready access to these markets. In addition, most markets have radio stations that actively promote social and cultural events. KMOX in St. Louis, WCCO in Minneapolis, and WGN in Chicago, regularly feature their respective cities.

EXHIBIT 7-3

Morning in Spring Hill

When the television advertising campaign for the Saturn automobile was unveiled, it featured the down-home charm of its plant site in Spring Hill, Tennessee. The idyllic ads demonstrated the basically country values of a rural community. A country music track, soft nostalgic photography, and a slow pace made Spring Hill the capital of "having it all." The people seemed content with the factory; the cracker-barrel charm of Spring Hill appeared intact.

A downturn in perception occurred when residents were interviewed about their feelings. Many natives resented the outsiders who came for jobs and brought big-city values and prices. Some were upset with housing developments that despoiled natural scenery and caused pollution problems. Others lamented the overcrowded schools that forced classes into trailers. It was now morning in Spring Hill, and some residents wondered if their coffee would ever smell that good again.

Magazines

The virtue of magazines is that so many are available the advertiser can reach almost any target group by knowing their reading habits. Public relations people often attempt to place long favorable stories about a place in magazines such as *Atlantic, Harpers,* or *Esquire.* Tourist bureaus can buy ads in *Travel* or other magazines likely to be read by the target group. States often buy full-page ads in widely read business magazines such as *Business Week, Fortune,* and *Forbes,* to promote their states as attractive places for investments, factories, corporate offices, and sales branches. And places that produce highly exportable products can buy promotional ads in the appropriate magazines of foreign countries to promote their products.

A place ad must have some believability if it is to be effective. The state of Mississippi aggressively pursued the Supercollider project with an ad aimed at conveying a scientific image. Although the ad claims that Mississippi is "the perfect location for America's new high-tech quantum leap," the evidence for Mississippi is meager and vaguely expressed.

WE'RE ON A COLLISION COURSE WITH HISTORY. MISSISSIPPI. . . MORE THAN A RIVER.

One of nature's oldest assets makes Mississippi the perfect location for America's newest high-tech quantum leap.

The Superconducting Super Collider will be the world's most powerful atom smasher, a surgically precise tool for unlocking the most intimate secrets of matter itself.

Mississippi is a prime site for the SSC. For good reason. Our Selma chalk formation exceeds all geological requirements for construction of the super collider. But, while the right foundation is essential, what we've built here in Mississippi is equally important.

We're talking about a tradition of technological leadership.

Mississippi is home to NASA's National Space Technology Laboratory, the National Center for Physical Acoustics and the Institute for Technology Development, as well as our own Technology Transfer Center. Our universities are leading the way in biomedical research, polymer sciences and microelectronics design.

Our commitment to technology and education makes Mississippi an obvious choice for the historic SSC program. Our significant geological superiority makes the choice a natural.

We're in the right place. With the right stuff.

We'd like to tell you more about our past, our future, and what we can do for you now.

Because Mississippi has a reputation for having the lowest educational achievement rates in the United States, the image stretch is too great and the copy's hyperbole fails to convince. The accompanying picture showed a space-age graphic coupled with a baldheaded, seemingly naked 21st-century astronaut; it reinforced the lack of a convincing image.

On the other hand, the Alabama ad is convincing (see Figure 7–1). The slogan "It isn't where you think it is" acknowledges that audiences have mixed images of Alabama. The detailed text specifically discusses achievements in the medical field. The concrete picture pairs a sports

FIGURE 7–1

Alabama attracts people notorious for their handwriting, and the Medical Center of the University of Alabama at Birmingham (UAB) is just one of many reasons. Fortunately, the names of our physicians and researchers are more often seen in print, for their work in areas from cancer research to sports medicine. Alabama is a state dedicated to attracting innovative talent to improve our quality of life.

While some states follow national trends, Alabamians lead advancements in a number of areas. Medicine is just one. UAB is recognized for several innovations. One UAB researcher has been chosen to go on a NASA space shuttle mission. He will perform experiments growing protein crystals in space, which may lead to the development of treatments for cancer, diabetes and birth defects. Other UAB researchers are world-renowned for pioneering the use of genetically engineered antibodies to search out and destroy cancer cells.

Health care is Birmingham's primary industry, with 21 hospitals in the area, including Baptist Medical Centers, the nation's fourth largest not-for-profit health care system. About 100,000 medical professionals come to the area each year for continuing education. And, as Bo knows, one of the world's recognized leaders in sports medicine has a thriving practice at Alabama Sports Medicine and Orthopaedic Center on the HealthSouth campus. Other well-known

Dr. Jim Andrews with patient Bo Jackson at the Alabama Sports Medicine and Orthopaedic Center.

athletes who come to the Center for treatment include Jack Nicklaus, Charles Barkley, Jerry Pate, and Bruce Smith.

The Medical Forum, another innovation in the medical field, will offer an unprecedented opportunity for physicians, educators, and research and development companies from around the world to exchange the latest advancements. Opening in Birmingham in 1992, it will provide state-of-the-art continuing education facilities for physicians and others who come to the area for further study. Several international medical companies will make the Forum their headquarters in the U.S. market.

Alabama's dedication to attracting and nurturing talent in all fields will continue, because we've never been content to follow national trends. We're more interested in setting them.

When Your Medical Facilities Are Among the Top In the Nation, You Just Seem to Attract Them.

UAB's Medical Center has been twice named to the top three medical centers in the country by The Best In Medicine, a survey of 300 prominent physicians.

It isn't where you think it is.

Reprinted with permission of Lewis Advertising, Birmingham, Alabama, and Economic Development Partnership of Alabama.

physician with Bo Jackson, a celebrity superstar. The state of Alabama's ad is more focused and uses an argument that has a chance to succeed because it is credible.

Newspapers

Newspapers offer a quick way to communicate messages about a place, such as news about festivals and art exhibits. The weekly travel section of newspapers provides an opportunity to promote both editorial material as well as advertisements of a place's vacation attributes. Stories and ads about business opportunities can be placed in the business sections of newspapers. Newspapers do not provide the same quality of artwork as magazines can provide, but represent a lower cost way to reach selective geographical audiences.

A major advantage of newspapers over magazines is to reach audiences in a timely manner. The advertisement for Myrtle Beach, South Carolina, in Figure 7-2, attempts to rescue the fall tourist season. A humorous opening featuring Elvis Presley and Mark Twain takes edge off the copy. After the ad states the facts on the hurricane damage, it then sells the virtues of the area. A weakness is the number of confusing and conflicting 800 numbers.

Billboards

Billboards represent a geographically fixed medium seen only by those who drive past them. They can advertise nearby attractions to highway travelers: Visit the Great Car Museum in Walla Walla. Airlines use them to promote travel destinations and land owners to point to land development opportunities.

At their borders many states now feature billboards that urge out-of-state motorists to return as residents or to relocate their businesses for reasons of clean air, low taxes, or sheer fun. Some billboards announce new state initiatives or business acquisitions.

Direct Mail

Direct Mail has the capacity to reach a highly focused target audience. The message can be standard or, on the other hand, completely customized for each recipient. The mail piece can describe an offer, serve as a reminder, make a suggestion, or issue a request. It can consist of a long letter with personal greetings, or it can include four-color

FIGURE 7–2

"I SAW ELVIS LAND A FLYING SAUCER IN DOWNTOWN MYRTLE BEACH."

Sounds like something you'd read at the checkout counter of your local supermarket, doesn't it? So do some of the reports we've been hearing about the condition of our area. It reminds us of when Mark Twain said, "The reports of my death have been greatly exaggerated."

These kinds of rumors would be humorous to us here in Myrtle Beach except for the fact that they're keeping some people from coming and enjoying all the good times that are here and now.

The truth is that almost all of the damage that occurred in Myrtle Beach and North Myrtle Beach during the hurricane was minimal and confined to some pools, decks, and the ground floors of a few hotels directly on the beachfront. And during the recent high tides the only damages reported on our beaches were sunburns.

If you want golf, call now while tee times last. The courses are as great as ever with more than sixty courses going strong.

Over 1,000 restaurants await you, along with our famous Grand Strand shopping. All of our campgrounds are open, and a navy of fishermen are ready to take you on a chase after the big ones. Plus, Brookgreen Gardens and the historic riverfront of Georgetown were virtually untouched.

So, if you're one of the ones who's still wondering what's really going on here at the beach, come and join the thousands of visitors since Hugo who've discovered that Myrtle Beach is up and running and ready for fun. Call today and select from more than 30,000 available rooms and villas.

THE MYRTLE BEACH AREA

For Reservations and Information Call Toll-Free:
Myrtle Beach Area Chamber of Commerce 1-800-356-3016
Georgetown County Chamber of Commerce 1-800-777-7705
Myrtle Beach Hotel & Motel Association 1-800-626-7477
Myrtle Beach Golf Holiday 1-800-845-4653

South Carolina
Smiling faces. Beautiful places. ⊕

Reprinted with permission of DuRant Ryann DuRant, Ltd., Advertising & Design.

graphics to jump start interest in a place. Direct mail, in contrast to mass advertising, is a measurable response medium. The medium permits experimentation with different headlines, copy, envelopes, offers, or prices to arrive at the most effective ad.

Telephone

Telemarketing is one of the fastest growing sales tools. It has all the virtues of direct mail plus the ability to add a personal touch. The telephone can be used to gather leads, qualify them, sell to the leads, and arrange personal calls.

A major problem for many communities is coordinating the rapid proliferation of their 800 numbers. Chicago has ten different 800 numbers. Consumers must dial to request information or service, or to file complaints. Ohio is implementing a voice-mail program that will combine all its current numbers. In addition, Ohio's 800 number operators now go beyond offering information; they can also make reservations for tourists.

Places are finding new and inventive strategies for increasing their telephone effectiveness. Idaho uses prisoners to answer incoming tourist calls. New Orleans targets frequent travelers from Dallas and Birmingham with an invitation to call an 800 number for coupon books or chances at free trips. Las Vegas, with an inventory of thirty-eight wedding chapels, now has an appropriate phone number: 1-800-322-VOWS.

Brochures

The advantages of brochures are their low cost, flexibility, and portability. The place marketer can use brochures to tell the place's story in a complete and sometimes dramatic manner.

The small town of Red Oak, Iowa, uses a business attraction brochure aimed at low-tech companies and distributes it at conventions whose activity is dominated by major cities. It is surprising to see the Red Oak marketers among the giants, and their brochure serves as a focal point of their presentation.

The English Tourist Board (ETB) faced problems in using travel agencies as a channel to distribute their brochures promoting domestic holidays. Travel agencies argued that rack space was not available for noncommission paying material. The English Tourist Board used six different channels to overcome this problem: (1) *Good Housekeeping* magazine, (2) *TV Times*, (3) tourist information centers, (4) door-to-door deliveries, (5) addresses on the ETB's data base list, and (6) brochures distributed in response to small-scale advertising campaigns run in the national press.[4]

Alternative Media

The media planner needs to consider an additional range of less conventional media channels, such as audiotapes, videotapes, faxes, interactive videos, trade missions, travel writers' conventions, welcome centers, and consulates. Each has its own set of advantages and disadvantages, as shown in exhibit 7-4.

Here are examples of how less conventional media channels have been used to promote a place:

- In an effort to attract Japanese tourists, Newport, Rhode Island, promoted a festival celebrating Newport native Commodore Perry's opening trade with Japan.[5]
- The Hong Kong Tourist Association (HKTA) promoted tourism by duplicating and distributing hundreds of videotapes, most of which ended up on the shelves of broadcast libraries. HKTA then decided to use satellite transmission as an alternative. For a cost of $18,000, they were able to air on major TV networks a videotape of the Dragon Boat Race, which millions of television viewers saw around the world.[6]
- The Sonoma County (California) Convention and Visitors Bureau had a limited promotion budget. Under the circumstances, they organized monthly luncheons of groups within the meeting industry, distributed inexpensive press kits, and ran photo contests to generate new photographs for advertising purposes.[7]
- A trio of small cities in New South Wales, Australia, wanted to attract industry from Sydney. Instead of spending money on a 30-second TV commercial, with limited impact, the cities prepared a tongue-in-cheek videotape depicting the typical day of a distraught Sydney factory worker facing traffic snarls, crowded conditions, and an upset boss. The videotape, widely shown in Sydney, then depicted life in the small cities as easier, less expensive, and less stressed.

EXHIBIT 7-4

Call the Consul to Learn about the Place?

Consuls in Chicago were called to see how they handled inquiries. The following observations were made:

- *Iceland.* The consul general of Iceland offered little information about his country. He attempted to be helpful, but there were few activities to report. He spoke in a dull monotone that dissuaded any further interest in the country.
- *Austria.* The vice-consul of Austria offered interesting information. He explained that Austria operates five offices: in Washington, Chicago, New York, Los Angeles, and Houston. They promote cultural exchanges, handle public relations, and answer a variety of questions.
- *Finland.* The Finnish office concentrates on promoting and supporting Finnish-American business activities. The office treats tourist information as of secondary importance.
- *Hungary.* The Hungarian representatives in the Washington, D.C., New York, and Chicago offices were all on long vacations. A lone staff member suggested that Hungarian trade information could best be obtained by calling the Library of Congress.

If we needed country information, we would call Austria.

Choosing Among the Advertising Media Categories

Marketers choose among these major media channels by considering the following variables:

1. *Target audience media habits.* For example, direct mail and telemarketing are among the most effective media for reaching location decision makers.
2. *Product or service.* Media categories have different potentials for demonstration, visualization, explanation, believability, and color. Television, for example, is the most effective me-

dium for describing a place or for creating an emotional effect, while magazines are ideal for presenting a single four-color image of a place.

3. *Message.* A message containing a great deal of technical data might require specialized magazines or direct mailings.

4. *Cost.* Television is very expensive, newspaper advertising is inexpensive. What often counts, of course, is the cost per thousand exposures rather than the total cost.

Many place marketers employ a variety of media because they recognize that audiences might pay attention only to certain media. Using several media extends the message's reach and reemphasizes the content, but avoids repeating the message to the same audience.

On the basis of media characteristics, the place marketer allocates the given budget to the various media channels. For example, the Jamaican Tourist Bureau might decide to allocate $14 million to evening television spots, $4 million to singles magazines, and $2 million to daily newspapers.

SELECTING THE SPECIFIC MEDIA VEHICLES

The planner's second step is to choose the specific media vehicles within each media category that would produce the desired response in the most cost-effective way. Suppose the Colorado Tourism Board wants to advertise skiing adventures targeted to young male adults. They consider the category of male-oriented magazines, which includes *Playboy, Home Mechanix, Esquire,* and *Motorcycle.* The media planner examines data published by *Standard Rate and Data* that provides circulation and cost information for different ad sizes, color options, ad positions, and quantities of insertions. Beyond this, the media planner evaluates the different magazines on qualitative characteristics such as credibility, prestige, availability of geographical or occupational editions, reproduction quality, editorial climate, lead time, and psychological impact.

The media planner makes a final judgement as to which specific vehicles will deliver the best reach, frequency, and impact for the money. The first variable, *reach,* is a measure of how many people are normally exposed to a single message carried by that medium. When the objective is to deliver the message to a large audience, mass media— particularly national television—are recommended.

EXHIBIT 7–5

Devils Tower, Wyoming: A Forgotten Landmark

How many people have been to Devils Tower, Wyoming? For a brief period in the 1970s, the informal impression–making machinery of Hollywood made it a household name. Devils Tower was the central prop in the highly successful Columbia Picture *Close Encounters of the Third Kind*. In the film, actor Richard Dreyfuss, plays an ordinary Joe looking for the magical place where the meeting between earthlings and outer space visitors will occur. In a memorable scene in the film, on Thanksgiving Day, Dreyfuss unwittingly sculpts his mashed potatoes into a model of this four-sided large hill. Later, the entire U.S. space elite descends on Devils Tower to greet the space people. During the film's run, Wyoming's natural wonder enjoyed a tremendous increase in visitors. Today, however, the mountain is no longer a tourist mecca. Its isolated location and lack of local support let the memory of the place fade away. A one-time impression is the beginning, not the end, of a place promotion.

Some messages are effective only if they result in multiple exposures to the same individuals: this second variable is *frequency*. Some frequency of exposure is necessary if places are to avoid passing into oblivion as Devils Tower did; see exhibit 7–5.

The third variable, *impact,* describes how effective a particular medium is with the target audience and type of message. Thus *Vogue* magazine would have more impact carrying a Bali vacation ad than would *Popular Mechanics*; the latter reaches the wrong audience. Usually, media that customize the message (such as direct mail) or allow personal contact (such as conventions, exhibits, missions, and personal selling) achieve higher impact levels.

Media planners normally calculate the cost per thousand persons a particular vehicle reaches. Suppose the Colorado Tourism Board wants to target the Los Angeles area and is considering advertising in either the Los Angeles regional edition of *Time* magazine or *Los Angeles* magazine. In 1992, a one-page four-color ad in *Time* magazine cost $16,436 and in *Los Angeles*, $9,020. While *Los Angeles* is less expensive, it has a circulation of only 172,000 while *Time* reaches 271,000. On a cost-per-thousand basis, *Los Angeles* is the better buy at $52.44 per thousand compared to $60.35 for *Time*. Costs for other potential vehicles, including television and radio, can be calculated in the same way.

Communication objectives and costs guide what planners want to do, but budget determines what they can do. The budget heavily shapes media choices. Many methods have been proposed for setting communication budgets. The budget can be set by arbitrarily allocating a certain amount of money or percentage of sales to be spent, deciding what the place can afford, basing the decision on previous experience, establishing a percentage of the financial return expected as a result of the campaign, observing what competitors have done, or by other methods.

The budget is also influenced by how much information and persuasion must be created to sell the particular place. How much should a place spend to attract visitors? Paris and Montreal are internationally known destinations and attract visitors with little promotion. Moreover, they are well- connected with tour planners and are automatically included in tourist itineraries. However, if South Dakota wants to attract tourists, it needs to launch a wide range of promotional tools to persuade prospects. A budget for South Dakota has to be large enough to overcome its off-the-beaten-path image.

Finally, planners should know that communication investments and returns are not necessarily linear. To invest too little money can be worse than investing no money. A certain minimum level of investment is required to create initial interest in a place. Higher levels of investment produce a higher level of audience response. However, above a certain level, still further investment may not yield response at the same rate. In fact, if the message is seen too frequently, most people stop noticing it and others become irritated.

DECIDING ON MEDIA TIMING

The third step in media selection is timing. It breaks down into a macroproblem and a microproblem. The macroproblem is that of cyclical or seasonal timing. Audience size and interest in a place vary at different times of the year. Most marketers do not advertise when there is little interest, but spend the bulk of their advertising budgets when natural interest in a place increases and peaks. Counterseasonal or countercyclical advertising is rare.

The other problem is more of a microproblem, that of the short-run timing of advertising. How should advertising be spaced during a short period of, say, one week? Consider three possible patterns: The first is *burst advertising* and consists of concentrating all the exposures in a very short period of time, such as all in one day. Presumably, this burst will attract maximum attention and interest and if recall is good, the effect lasts for a while. The second pattern is *continuous advertising*, in which the exposures appear evenly throughout the period. This pattern may be most effective when the audience buys or uses the product frequently and needs to be continuously reminded. The third pattern is *intermittent advertising*, in which intermittent small bursts of advertising appear with no advertising in between. While this pattern creates somewhat more attention than continuous advertising, it has some of the reminder advantage of continuous advertising.

Timing decisions should take three factors into consideration: Audience turnover is the rate at which the target audience changes between two periods. The greater the turnover, the more continuous the advertising should be. Behavior frequency is the number of times during the year the target audience takes the action one is trying to influence. The more frequent the behavior, the more advertising should be continuous. The forgetting rate is the rate at which a given message is forgotten or a given behavior change extinguished. Again, the shorter the audience's memory, the more continuous the advertising should be.

EVALUATING THE MEDIA RESULTS

Measuring the results media campaigns produce is not an easy task. For instance, after Zechman & Associates created the award-winning campaign "Illinois: We put you in a happy state," the state claimed to have received $57 in increased tourist spending for every dollar invested in tourism marketing.[8] Was the campaign that productive or were other factors at work? Perhaps the economy improved at the same time, or other tourist destinations became less desirable that year. It is difficult to isolate the effects of advertising from other factors operating in the marketplace.

Nevertheless, evaluation research helps media planners locate possible weak points in the communication implementation process. Did the message reach the right people? Did they understand the message and find it credible and persuasive? Did it reach them frequently enough or at the right times? Should more have been spent? The advertising program should regularly evaluate the communication effects and sales effects of advertising.

Measuring the communication effect tells whether an ad is communicating well. Called *copy testing,* it can be done before or after an ad is printed or broadcast. There are three major methods of advertising pretesting: The first is through direct rating, in which the advertiser exposes a consumer panel to alternative ads and asks them to rate the ads. These direct ratings indicate how well the ads get attention and how they affect consumers. Although an imperfect measure of an ad's actual impact, a high rating indicates a potentially more effective ad. In portfolio tests, consumers view or listen to a portfolio of advertisements, taking as much time as they need. They then are asked to recall all the ads and their content, aided or unaided by the interviewer. Their recall level indicates the ability of an ad to stand out and its message to be understood and remembered. Laboratory tests use equipment to measure consumers' physiological reactions to an ad— heartbeat, blood pressure, pupil dilation, and perspiration. These tests measure an ad's attention-getting power but reveal little about its impact on beliefs, attitudes, or intentions.

There are three popular methods of post-testing ads: Using recall tests, the advertiser asks people who have been exposed to magazines or television programs to recall everything they can about the advertising message. Recall scores indicate the ad's power to be noticed and retained. In recognition tests, the researcher asks readers of a given issue of a magazine to point out what they recognize as having seen before. Recognition scores can be used to assess the ad's impact in different market segments and to compare the company's ads with competitors' ads. In persuasion tests, persons are asked whether the ad has caused them to be more favorably disposed toward a place and by how much. The sales effect of advertising is often harder to measure than the communication effect. Many factors besides advertising affect sales—such as place features, price, and availability.

One way to measure the sales effect of advertising is to compare past sales with past advertising expenditures. Another way is through experiments where similar territories receive different advertising intensities to see whether this leads to different sales levels.

Advertising's communication impact is most easily measured where direct response measurements can be obtained. Mail or phone orders, requests for catalogs, or salescalls all help the marketeer measure response. They allow the place marketer to determine how many inquiries the mail pieces generated and how many purchases came from the inquiries.

In general, measurement efforts are designed to answer three basic questions: (1) what response was obtained; (2) were the objectives met; and (3) what changes are recommended. A well-designed set of evaluation procedures enables the message and the media to be constantly improved.

MANAGING CONFLICTING MEDIA SOURCES AND MESSAGES

A place can spend millions of dollars advertising for tourists, residents, or factories only to find uncontrolled communications overwhelming the formal messages. For example, in Buenos Aires, Argentina, Bruce Springsteen appeared in his worldwide $18 million rock concert tour which Amnesty International arranged to promote human rights. The concert drew 60,000 Argentines to what was described as a highly emotional, eight-hour rock and roll concert. News coverage of the concert noted that Springsteen dedicated one of his two Argentine concerts to the 9,000 citizens who disappeared during the military administration that ruled from 1976 to 1983. Subsequently, British rock star Sting danced on stage with members of the Mothers of the Plaza del Mayo, a human rights group made up of mothers of kidnapped persons. The concerts threw an immediate spotlight on Argentina as a country with a history of human rights violations. And while the country can counter these informal impressions with tourist brochures, paid media commercials, speakers' tours, and VIP information sessions, the informal impressions can overwhelm even the best-laid plans.[9]

A similar circumstance occurred when Miriam Makeba, a black folk singer who is popular in her native South Africa, returned to the United States in 1987 as a performer in Paul Simon's Graceland tour. A world-renowned artist, she was a South African exile whose songs had been banned for years. Her appearance in highly visible media centers reminded citizens all over the world that South Africa continues to have problems. These types of informal impressions tend to offset and negate the more formally controlled impressions.

Place planners themselves often reinforce planned impressions with less formal ones and staged events. During the two-week Walt Disney film festival in Moscow and Leningrad, Disney arranged for Mickey Mouse to stroll on Moscow's Red Square with his Russian counterpart, Misha the Bear. The photographs of the two animated figures standing in front of Red Square was a public relations bonanza for the Soviets and for Disney.

The best of all possible worlds occurs when informal and formal impressions merge to reinforce the image. Such good fortune occurred when entertainer Johnny Carson returned to his boyhood home of Norfolk, Nebraska, to dedicate a regional cancer center in honor of his parents. Carson felt that he should give his home area a regional radiation center because of the area's hard times due to the drought of the late 1980s. He announced, "If you're lucky enough in life to accumulate enough funds to live better than you have any right to, then you have a moral obligation to pay back the community, or to the country or to the place that brought you up."[10] This kind of event does more for publicizing Norfolk, Nebraska, than any public relations budget can normally accomplish.

Ideally, a place would like to showcase only its positive features. It would like to hide from view the slums, homeless people, indelicate treatment of minorities, and other unflattering impressions. However, this degree of media control is unavailable. More typically, a place finds itself driven by unplanned and often unwelcomed events. Jamaica's problems are detailed in exhibit 7-6.

What should places do about negative impressions? There are three possibilities: The first is to *ignore them*. The thinking is, "Act as if it doesn't exist and it will go away." The second is to *counter-attack* by swiftly sending out a countermessage. The third is to *solve the problem* that gives rise to the negative impressions.

None of these responses is the best under all circumstances. Much depends on how serious is the negative impression, how widespread it is, and how remedial it is. If the damage is not serious, if public knowledge is very limited, and if it is easily remedied, it is best to ignore the negative impression. If the damage is not serious but is widely known, and easily remedied, it may pay to counterattack. If the situation is very serious and widely known and not easily remedied, it is best to work toward a long-term response rather than ignore the situation or coun-

EXHIBIT 7–6

Jamaica Blues

In the swirl of real events, unplanned events can hurt or destroy entire economies overnight. Consider the experience of Jamaica. Jamaica's tourist strategy has been to convince U.S. tourists that Jamaica is a haven where Jamaican citizens welcome visitors. Jamaica presented a series of commercials and advertisements stressing safety and friendliness, strongly highlighting programs where tourists spend time in the homes of native Jamaicans.

The paid campaign, however, was consistently overwhelmed by media reports of tourist robberies and beatings. Many tourists returned dissatisfied because when they wandered off the traditional tourist paths, they encountered threatening situations and neighborhoods that seemed less than safe.

Jamaica suffered a further cruel blow when it was hit by a devastating hurricane in 1989. Many tourists found their treatment by the government during that calamity less than satisfactory and said so when reporters interviewed them on their return to the United States. As newspeople jammed mikes in the faces of upset tourists, millions heard, "I'll never go back to Jamaica—never again." These remarks and other negative impressions may linger indefinitely and ultimately undo all the good words and deeds built up meticulously over the years.

Jamaica, in the instance of the hurricane, needed to demonstrate compassion and efficiency. A spokesperson could easily have explained the problems and the relief work being undertaken. Instead, the story was one-sided and unanswered, and therein harmful to Jamaica's interests.

EXHIBIT 7–7
Mississippi Burning

The events leading to the release of the film *Mississippi Burning* illustrate the challenge of managing a negative development. The governor of Mississippi approved the request to have the film *Mississippi Burning* shot on location in Philadelphia, Mississippi, a small town of 6,800, which had gained notoriety in the 1960s when three civil rights workers were murdered by the Ku Klux Klan. Mississippi's governor believed that the state had turned the corner on race relations and this filming was an opportunity to demonstrate openness and transformation.

When the film was released, many of the town's residents were incensed while others were unrepentant. The town's mayor summed up their feelings: "I think most people know what happened here. Why don't you all just let us alone?" Special agent Joseph Sullivan, who led the FBI investigation of the murder, said of the county, "Neshoba was an incredibly closed and racist county . . . almost every adult white male in the county had connections with the Ku Klux Klan." The city of Philadelphia tried to communicate how much the city had changed in the last twenty years. The mayor argued that Neshoba County now had an integrated school system, and a black policeman, fireman, and alderman. While evidence indicated that times had changed, the overall image was of a place still back in 1964.

terattack. Exhibit 7–7 describes how Philadelphia, Mississippi, officials responded to a negative development.

CONCLUSION

The number of places that compete for the attention of buyers is overwhelming. A casual reading of the *New York Times* travel section reveals ads for every place on the globe. The trade journals for business

What should Philadelphia, Mississippi, have done after the film was released? There were two possibilities: One course would be to ignore the film, which would soon be forgotten as economic and cultural events shifted audiences' attention to other issues.

The second course is to use the event as a catalyst for redevelopment and further improving of race relations. A coordinated media and public relations campaign needed to support the strategy to tell the new Philadelphia story. But that did not happen. Rather, the media news coming out of Philadelphia showed a certain haplessness. The mayor was defensive and didn't know all the facts. At one point he said, "It was just a coincidence that the murders happened here. The people who were killed were outsiders and the people who did it were, too." In fact, that was not true: nine of the eighteen killers were from Neshoba County and the area was certainly infested with racial problems.

The film could have served as an opportunity for Philadelphia to plan the town's redefinition. Because the film took several years to produce, the town had fair warning. As one strategy, the mayor, city council, leading business people, and residents could have taken a media training course in which they became proficient at extolling the virtues of the city. Philadelphia missed an opportunity to distribute an improved image of itself.

Source: Strat Douthat, "Town's Residents Weary of 'Mississippi Burning,'" *Chicago Sun-Times*, January 12, 1989, p. 47.

sites are full of promises of cooperation and offers of brochures and videotapes.

Place promotion has the best chance for success when the message is matched to the media, all the players are pushing in the same direction, and informal impressions reinforce the paid efforts.

In the next three chapters we apply marketing thinking to the four major sources of place enrichment: tourism and business hospitality, business attraction and development, export promotion, and new residents.

8

Attracting the Tourism and Hospitality Business Markets

In 1990, Cunard Lines celebrated the 150th anniversary of its first passenger ship service across the Atlantic. Cunard's transatlantic line was the first such service offered in 1840; virtually hundreds of competitors existed by 1920 and, by 1990, Cunard was the last Atlantic passenger ship service left. In the interim, the world of travel and tourism had been revolutionized. The world had become a global community for travelers opening up places unimaginable decades earlier: the wonders of Antarctica, the secrets of the Himalayas, the rain forests of the Amazon, the beauty of Tahiti, the Great Wall of China, the dramatic Victoria Falls, the origin of the Nile, and the wilds of Scottish islands. Tourism has become a global business whose expanding market now leaves no place untouched.

According to the World Tourism Organization (WTO) of the United Nations, more than 415 million tourists traveled internationally in 1989, spending over $230 billion (excluding transportation). Tourism accounts for 7 percent of total world exports, more than 25 percent of international trade in services, and more than 100 million jobs worldwide. It employs more people than any single industrial sector, and has an infrastructure (lodging, transportation, and restaurants) investment conservatively estimated to exceed $3 trillion.[1]

Travel and tourism now affect every continent, country, and city.

The basic reason people travel—to visit family and friends—means that everyone's economy is impacted either by their people traveling elsewhere (import-spending in other places) or travel service exports (expenditures by nonresidents in that place). Places must decide how much travel service they want to capture because travel service is today's fastest-growing business and is expected to be the world's largest industry in the next century. Yet as an industry, it is subject to cycles, fashions, and intense competition.

This chapter is divided into two sections: tourism, and the hospitality business (conventions, trade shows, and business meetings). Although the two overlap somewhat, they are distinctive enough in markets, needs, facilities, and competition to warrant separate treatment.

THE TOURISM MARKET

In discussing tourism, we need to address the following questions:

- How important can tourism be to a place's economy?
- How can the tourist market be segmented and monitored for shifting trends, life-styles, needs and preferences?
- What kinds of strategies and investments must places and businesses make to be competitive in the tourist industry?
- How can a place gain access to or establish a niche in the tourist business, and what are the risks and opportunities of such a venture?
- What kinds if messages and media are effective in tourist attraction and retention?
- How should a place's tourism be organized and managed?

How Important Is Tourism?

Due to location, climate, limited resources, size and cultural heritage, some regions have no real choice but to engage in tourism to grow, develop, and improve their living standards (see exhibit 8–1). Other places engage in tourism with mixed emotions, and at times, ambivalence. For instance, Bali is concerned that tourism is destroying its culture as farmland becomes resorts and new jobs unravel family values. "Bali and tourism is not a marriage of love," observed a Bali tourism official, clearly focusing on the dilemma of a cultural breakdown and an economy booming from 500,000 tourists a year.[2] Londoners need, but are not enthusiastic about, the Arab influx to their hotels, and recreational,

EXHIBIT 8-1

Some Facts About Tourism

Places differ in their dependence on, or interest in, attracting tourists. Of the 178 nations represented in the United Nations, tourism is the first or second largest business of more than half. France has a commanding lead as the world's largest tourist market, followed by the United States, Spain, Italy, Austria, Hungary, Britain, Germany, Canada, and Switzerland. For Caribbean nations, tourism accounts for more than 70 percent of jobs and income. In several Caribbean nations, such as Jamaica, the relative standard of living and borrowing capacity with international creditors fluctuates with tourism trade. In many countries, the ministry of tourism and travel is one of their larger and more strategic governmental agencies.

Tourism and travel is the United States's second largest service industry and is expected to be its largest by the year 2000.[1] In 1988, it employed 6 million people, involved $330 billion in retail sales and constituted 6 percent of GNP. In 1988, the government established a U.S. Travel and Tourism Administration within the U.S. Department of Commerce, allocating to it a $16 million annual budget (an amount lower than that spent by at least four U.S. states and half of what most European countries spend separately). In contrast, United Airlines had an advertising budget of $100 million alone, while all U.S. domestic carriers spent nearly $500 million to promote air travel in 1990.

cultural, and transportation facilities. Many European capitals experience a mass summer exodus of residents to avoid summer tourists.

Places may not uniformly welcome tourists. Some people and businesses benefit, others may not. While a place's economy may be better off from tourism, place residents may feel that the costs and losses—quality of life, convenience, cultural or social values—are not worth the benefits. Exhibit 8-2 describes the debate about tourism in San Francisco.

Not all places and people are enthusiastic about tourist-generated jobs. Curacao, a tourist island off the Venezuelan coast, sought to ex-

The U.S. Travel Data Center estimates that for each day 100 visitors tour the average U.S. community they create 67 new jobs, produce $2.8 million in new retail and service industry sales, and add $189,000 worth of state and local sales taxes.[2] Federal, state, and local governments receive more than $40 billion per year from tourism-generated tax revenues. Indeed, most places have their own estimates of visitor-per-day expenditures, tax benefits, and multiplier effects on their economies from visitor spending. Hawaii, our largest tourism state, realized $800 million in taxes, 23,000 jobs, and nearly $5 billion in household income in 1988 from 6 million visitors who spend more than $9 billion.[3] New York City estimated 25 million tourists in 1989 spent about $9 billion with an economic impact of about $12 billion.[4]

State governments now spend more than $300 million annually in travel office budgets. New York leads the other states by spending $24 million (1988), followed by Illinois ($23 million), Texas ($18 million), and Hawaii ($16 million). States spend more than twenty times as much as the federal government on tourist promotion, a significant departure from other nations in which tourist promotion is a major national government responsibility.

Sources: [1] Rockwell Schnabel, "Inbound Tourist Could Double by the Year 2000," *Network Magazine,* November 1990, p. 6.
[2] U.S. Travel Data Center, preliminary figures for 1990.
[3] *1988 Annual Research Report* (Revised), Hawaii Visitors Bureau, Market Research Department, 1989.
[4] Sara Bartlett, "Lag in U.S. Tourists Hurt New York," *New York Times,* June 5, 1991, p. A16.

pand tourism when its once thriving oil processing business declined. Unemployed oil workers felt betrayed by the prospect of $4 an hour jobs replacing $14 an hour oil jobs. Jamaica confronted the same dilemma when its major export, bauxite, collapsed, and unemployed workers faced the prospect of employment in much lower-paying tourist jobs.

Tourism's primary benefit is jobs through hotels, restaurants, retail establishments, and transportation. These direct jobs can be calculated on a per diem or per trip spending basis. Indirect jobs are those created by tourism employees' expenditures in a place's economy that, in turn, create more jobs. The second benefit of tourism is its multiplier effect

EXHIBIT 8-2
Lifting the Fog

Can a city place too much emphasis on tourism and hospitality industries? Are there risks? That's the question being debated in San Francisco these days, a city in which one of eight dollars in its economy comes from visitors' spending and where tourism employs more city residents than any other business.

Among the issues of public concern are how much the visitor industry actually generates for the city's economy. California's Department of Commerce estimates that San Francisco had 32,500 visitor-derived workers earning $47 million in 1986, and $78 million in visitor-generated local tax revenues, while the city's Convention Bureau estimates are double that. For the city's 3,000 eating establishments and 25,000 hotel rooms, worries abound about the growth of low paying, nonunion wages and workers. As important as the tourism and convention business is to San Francisco's economy, critics are equally concerned about the city's loss of financial services, corporate relocation to the suburbs, and the relative decline of shipping and other industrial-era businesses.

San Francisco must decide among three broad alternatives: (1) pursue tourism even more aggressively because its physical and historical beauty provides it with a competitive advantage in this industry; (2) hold tourism to its present level and invest in building other industries more aggressively; and (3) build tourism and other industries in a balanced way. The decision is not easy because of the conflicting interests of different voting blocks.

Sources: Louis Trager, "Trouble in Touristland," San Francisco Examiner, July 30, 1989, p. D1; and Carla Marinucci, "What Becomes a Legend Most,"San Francisco Examiner, July 30, 1989, pp. D1–4.

as direct and indirect tourist expenditure is recycled through the local economy. The federal government, states, and localities use economic impact models to estimate overall employment gains in goods and services consumption resulting from tourism multipliers. Tourism's third benefit stems from state and local tax revenues that tourists provide.

Tourism helps a place shift its tax burden to nonresidents. For example, tourism accounts for more than half of Bermuda's foreign exchange which enables it to export well over half its tax burden. Bermuda's $20 per head embarkation fee is one of the highest in the world, as are its import taxes on durables from cars to refrigerators. In the meantime, it is one of the few developed countries without an income tax. New York's cumulative bed tax on hotel rooms raises more than $300 million in annual revenues. Dallas, Los Angeles, and Houston all have bed taxes in excess of 12 percent. Hawaii derives nearly 40 percent of its total state and county taxes from tourism. Taxation of travelers has become a popular, often hidden tax, jumping by an estimated $2.5 billion in the United States alone in 1991 due to airline ticket taxes, hotel taxes, and other user fees.[3]

Tourism also yields a fourth benefit: It stimulates exports of place-made products. Estimates of tourist and conventioneer spending on gifts, clothing, and souvenirs are in the range of 15 to 20 percent of total expenditures. The degree to which these products are made or assembled in a place affects its impact on a place's export economy.

Segmenting the Tourism Market

Places must decide on not only how many tourists they want and how to balance tourism with other industries or strategies but also *what kind* of tourists they want. The choices will be constrained, of course, by the place's climate, natural topography and resources, history, culture, and facilities. Like any other business, tourist marketers must know the actual and potential customers, their needs and wants, determine which target markets to serve, and decide on appropriate products, services, and programs to serve these markets.

Not every tourist is interested in a particular destination. A place would waste its money trying to attract everyone who travels. Instead of a shotgun approach, a place must take a rifle approach and sharply define its target markets. Exhibit 8–3 explains how modern technology helps tourists find the markets they seek.

A place can identify its natural target markets in two ways: One is to collect information about its current tourists: Where do they come from? Why do they come to this place? What are their demographic characteristics? How satisfied are they? How many are repeat tourists? How much do they spend? By examining these and other questions,

EXHIBIT 8-3
Electronic Buying

The experienced travel agents of yesterday are rapidly dying out. The new young travel agents have less firsthand knowledge of destinations; they face buyers who know little geography but have leisure time and money to spend. The solution is to equip travel agents with computer and video technologies to help them match clients with the right destinations.

The key is to ask the client about his or her objectives and preferences regarding a vacation. Included might be questions to which the client might answer "I don't like to pack and unpack," or "I don't like to move around and see many things." This information is fed into a computer that produces a list of suggested destinations and travel programs matched to the client's preferences. The client then views video programs describing those destinations that seem most appealing. The video programs are stored on CD rom laser discs. In this way, travel agencies use modern technology and software prepared by experts to compensate for the inexperience of many of their agents.

the place can determine which tourists are easiest to attract and which are worth attracting.

The second approach is to audit the place's attractions and conjecture about the types of tourists who would have a natural interest in them. The aim is to identify new sources of tourists. One cannot assume that the current tourists reflect all the potentially interested groups. For example, if Kenya has been promoting only safaris, it has missed other groups interested in its native culture or cuisines.

Different tourists are attracted by different place features. The local tourist board or council must ask questions keyed to the segmentation variables in table 8-1. These variables—attractions sought, market areas or locations, customer characteristics, and/or benefits sought—can help to define the best tourist prospects to attract.

After a place identifies its natural target market, the tourist board

TABLE 8-1
Segmentation Variables for the Tourist Market

Attractions Sought	Market Areas/ Locations	Customer Characteristics	Benefits
Sun, sea, ski	Foreign	Age	Price
Natural beauty/ wilderness	National	Income	Convenience
Recreation	Regional— 500 miles	Family	Quality
Gaming	Local—100 miles	Singles	Food
Culture/history/ people	Seasonal/ year round	Professionals	Service
		Life-styles	Quantity/diversity
Events/sports		Ethnic/religious	Facilities
Theme parks			
Exclusiveness			
Facilities/ports/ hotels			
Unique products —liquor, perfume, clothes, watches			

must research where these tourists are found. Which countries contain a large number of citizens who have the means and motivation to enjoy the particular place? For example, Aruba attracts mainly sun and fun tourists. The best sources for these tourists are the United States, Canada, and certain European countries. Eastern Europeans are ruled out because they lack the purchasing power; Australians are ruled out because they have their own nearby sun and fun destinations.

This analysis can uncover too many or too few natural target markets. If too many are identified, the tourist board must calculate the potential profit from attracting each segment. The potential profit of a target tourist segment is the difference between the amount that the tourist segment would spend and the cost of attracting and serving this segment. The attraction cost depends on the marketing plan. The serving cost depends on the infrastructure requirements. Ultimately, the

tourist board ranks the potential tourist segments in order of their profitability and concentrates on attracting those segments highest on its
list (see exhibit 8–4).

If the analysis identifies too few natural tourist segments, the tourist
board must undertake *investment marketing*. A natural market is attracted by existing features of the place; an investment market is attracted by new features that might be added to a place. Investment
marketing consists of allocating money toward infrastructure improvements (hotels, transportation, etc.) and attractions that can potentially
attract new types of tourists. The payoff from investment marketing
comes only some years later but this lag is necessary if the place cannot
identify a sufficient number of natural tourist segments.

Consider Ireland, which continues to attract many tourists, not only
ethnic Irish from North America, but also many Europeans. The Irish
Tourist Board recently observed that although an increasing number
of young European tourists were visiting the Emerald Isle to enjoy its
natural, unspoiled beauty, as backpackers and campers they spent little. A serious question for Ireland was whether the Tourist Board's
tourism scorecard should be based on the number of tourists attracted
(the prevailing standard) or the spending quality of the tourists. A consensus emerged that Ireland was better off attracting fewer but higher-
income tourists who stay longer and spend more.

Toward this end, the Irish Tourist Board now touts not only
Ireland's mountains, water, and ancient buildings but also its literary
giants—Oscar Wilde, John Synge, Sean O'Casey, George Bernard Shaw,
Brendan Behan, Samuel Beckett, W.B. Yeats, and James Joyce. They
want to attract high-income culture-seeking tourists to visit Dublin where
the Irish sparkling speech and wit of old can be experienced today. The Irish
also are ready to improve Dublin's hotel and restaurant facilities as an act of
investment marketing.

Whatever tourist segment a place aims at, it needs to be very specific. True, a ski area attracts skiers; swimming and natural reefs attract
snorkelers and divers; arts and crafts attract the art crowd; gambling
attracts gaming tourists. Yet, even with such givens, places must segment tourists by additional characteristics. Sun Valley, Aspen, Vail,
and Alta appeal to upper income/professional skiing market; Keystone,
Winter Park, Copper Mountain, and Telluride to the family market;
Tahoe and Squaw Valley to the skiing-gaming markets. Monte Carlo
appeals to an international gaming segment while Deauville, in France,
markets to a more regional gaming market near Paris. In the United

EXHIBIT 8-4

Israel Develops and Sustains Its Natural Market, Overseas Jews

The government of Israel has maintained and sustained one of the most effective tourist marketing operations in the world. Tourism is Israel's dominant industry with an estimated 500,000 Israelis dependent on it for their livelihood. They understand that their primary market is Jewish-Americans who for sentimental, historical, and religious reasons are drawn to Israel.

The Israeli government and American Jewish groups have created a deep infrastructure of educational, social, and political groups that are likely to visit Israel regularly. The kibbutz system of socialized farms, for example, offers yearly and summer work-study vacations for young Jewish students who can cut their expenses by spending time on collectives. Tours sponsored by Hillel, the B'nai B'rith, the American Jewish Congress, Hadassah, and other Jewish groups continuously visit Israel because of various interests. Local synagogues often feature trips with their rabbis who lead groups to Israel to study artifacts and religious questions; these tours are often done on a yearly basis. Some American Jews visit Israel as many as ten or fifteen times during their lifetimes. And they receive a deep experience rather than a superficial one. Depending on their special interests, they meet leaders, study with scholars, or farm with orchard growers. In so doing, they bond with Israel and through word of mouth encourage others to visit Israel.

Israel has recently begun marketing to a broader audience by launching a campaign with Egypt and Greece that features a combined visit. Another campaign intended to attract Holy Land visitors was promoted on the Christian Broadcast Network. The task for Israel is to build these new markets and not allow erosion of their successful primary target.

EXHIBIT 8-5

Stratford, Canada: Growing Theater Market

Everyone knows Stratford, England, as the home of Shakespearean theater. But what about Stratford, Canada? Stratford, Canada, currently has one of the most successful Shakespearean festivals in the world. In the summer season, thousands of tourists come to Stratford, attend the three theaters showcasing up to six plays daily, eat in Stratford's restaurants, buy its gas, and sleep in its hotels. In fact, Stratford has become synonymous with the Shakespearean festival, and people come from around the world to participate in and enjoy the experience.

But who picked Stratford? Was it ordained that Stratford was to be a mine of Shakespearean talent? Did the town have a rich heritage of Shakespearean memorabilia? Was Stratford a logical choice for such a monument to Shakespeare? The answer in all cases is no. The town of Stratford was originally a blue-collar factory town with as little to do with Shakespeare as one can imagine. There was a river running through the town called Avon that suggests the bard's origins but there was little there other than the city's name to suggest any kind of developing relationship and festival. When local industry began to decline, one man, Tom Patterson, became determined to investigate the possibility of turning it into a Shakespearean festival city. He alone made numerous contacts to market the concept; after a number of failed attempts to

States, Iowa's new riverboat gambling tours attract a much broader, family-oriented market than Atlantic City's casinos do.

These places seek to expand from a single season—summer or fall—to year-around business: Aspen, Colorado from winter skiing to summer recreational, educational, and cultural attractions; Quebec from summer-fall tourism to winter carnival attraction; West Virginia from the summer-fall season to include Appalachia's spring season.

Markets and attractions change over time. Stratford, Canada's Shakespeare Festival which began as a small regional attraction, grew

put together a package for launching a theater, he finally combined Canadian government funding and city leadership to begin a season. He used the strategy of icon marketing by employing Sir Tyrone Guthrie, a famous English director, to form the initial repertory season. Because Patterson had an original proposition, and Toronto, Detroit, New York, and Chicago were driving distances from Stratford, the festival began to develop an audience. Moreover, the city citizens and the newcomers began to create a tourist environment compatible with the innovative proposition. A number of local businesses supported the festival as English country inns opened, beds and breakfasts were offered in local homes, and a variety of restaurants began catering to the tourists. Stratford now has three four-star restaurants, probably the highest percentage of four-star restaurants of any city its size in North America.

It is an incorrect notion that anyone can save a declining heavy-industry city by putting together a Shakespearean festival. Five ingredients made Stratford work. First, its name was directly related to Shakespeare's hometown. Second, the city is just over the Canadian border, giving it that British ambience that lent it a great deal of credibility. Third, the marketplace was ready for a full summer season Shakespearean festival. In the middle section of the country, no summer festivals would compete with the high-quality production standards that the founders of Stratford had envisioned. Fourth, the Canadian government financed the initial theater building and funded the first season. Fifth, the burgeoning support system of merchants interested in creating the theatrical environment reinforced the festival itself. So when people entered the city of Stratford, the bookstores, the pubs, and the gardens all interrelated to present a coherent picture for the visitor.

national in scope in the United States and Canada, and today is international (see exhibit 8–5). Most musical and cultural festivals in Europe followed the same pattern such as Salzburg, Edinburgh, and Spoleto. Europe's 1991 Festival of Arts provides a selection among 50 musical festivals from Norway to Spain, several dozen dance competitions, major summer art exhibits, and theater from London's West End to

Berlin's Festival Weeks. The entire European continent, including Eastern Europe, has exploded in summer place competition for tourists.

Competition results in hot and cold tourist attractions, ups and downs, or ins and outs (see table 8–2). A place's attractiveness can be diminished by violence, political instability, natural catastrophe, adverse environmental factors, and overcrowding. Greece and Thailand, two nations highly dependent on tourism, are classic examples where infrastructure investments have lagged tourist development. The result is tourist falloff due to high pollution, inadequate sanitation, and major traffic congestion. Greece's national treasure, the formerly white marble Parthenon in Athens stands as a pollution-stained symbol of environmental neglect. Thailand's beautiful beach resorts and temples have been severely damaged by pollution and poor sanitation.[4] The Indian government's plans to make 1991 "Visit India Year" were undermined not only by sectarian and caste violence but also plane crashes. Western countries, including the United States and Japan, declared India to be an unsafe destination.

Places that fail to maintain the necessary infrastructure run significant risks. Italy's Adriatic Sea coast has been devastated by the adverse

TABLE 8–2
In versus Out Places: U.S. Tourists

In	Out
Spain: 1992 Olympics/ World Fair	*California:* Earthquakes, fires, freeways, drought
Costa Rica: Two oceans, peace	*India:* Worst violence since 1947, plane crashes
Australia/New Zealand: Outdoors, hospitality	*Colombia:* Drugs, violence
Banff/Lake Louise, British Columbia: Hiking, natural beauty	*Yugoslavia:* Violence, factions
Cancun, Mexico: Rebuilt, cultural diversity	*Thailand:* Pollution, congestion, poor facilities
Santa Fe, New Mexico: Desert country, art community	*Grand Canyon:* Polluted, crowded, inadequate facilities
Eastern Europe: Bargains, old culture	*Haiti:* Boat people, poverty, violence
Indonesia: Cultural diversity	*Russia:* Unrest, hunger, long lines

publicity associated with growth of brown algae that made bathing nearly impossible. Growing pollution levels at the Grand Canyon and overcrowding in Yosemite Valley have significantly diminished the attractiveness of these great national parks. Some of East Africa's renowned game parks are being turned into dust bowls by tourists ferried around in four-wheel-drive vehicles.

Places must be ready to respond to changing demographics and lifestyles. The growing percentage of retired Americans has vastly expanded the tourism business. An increasing percentage of two career couples has resulted in the trend toward shorter, more frequent vacations. Longer vacations (ten or more nights) have been declining for years, while shorter vacations (3 nights including weekends) rose 28 percent from 1984 to 1989.[5] Overall, the U.S. Travel Data Center estimated that vacation length rose from 5.2 nights to 5.8 nights from 1980 to 1984, then steadily declined to 4.1 nights by 1990.[6] Hotels and airlines have accommodated these trends with low-cost weekend excursion packages. Business travel now includes mixed business and leisure. To capture the trend toward shorter vacations, within driving distance of home, new local and regional tourist attractions have been growing as have family oriented resorts.

Foreign visitor travel has become an increasingly important segment of the U.S. travel industry. Since the dollar's decline in 1985, foreign tourism in the United States has grown each year, climbing from 25.4 million foreign visitors in 1985 to an estimated 44 million in 1991. European tourist interests in the United States vary. British Isles visitors seek out New York and Florida, while Continental visitors have a strong fascination for the U.S. West, particularly California. Hawaii's tourist market consists of 66 percent from the mainland and 20 percent from Japan. Hawaii targets Japan because of its high GNP and spending, and because 50 percent of all Japanese visitors to the U.S. mainland spend part of the trip in Hawaii. The Japanese repeat market is higher than any other market. In 1987, Japanese visitors outspent U.S. mainland visitors by a 4:1 margin, $586 per day versus $119 per day.[7]

Places, in general, need to determine their best tourism targets; Florida has identified four targets, as exhibit 8–6 explains.

Accommodating changing life-styles and needs is a dynamic challenge for the tourism industry in light of demographic trends and income shifts. The high-living baby boomers of yesterday are today's older baby boomers. Where baby boomers once opted for status destinations and elaborate accommodations, older baby boomers now opt

EXHIBIT 8–6

Florida's Multiple Tourist Target Markets

Older citizens accounted for a high percentage of Florida's 35 percent population growth between 1980 and 1990. Retirees drive the state's economy: high income, high consumption, and low-service demand levels. Retirees take to Florida their pensions, social security checks, securities, and often proceeds of home sales. Thus, older citizens are much more than a tourist market; their visits often lead to permanent residency.

Florida also markets to families. Walt Disney World alone attracted 28.5 million visitors in 1990, making it the fourth largest destination after France, the United States, and Spain. Sea World of Florida attracted nearly 4 million visitors, mostly families.

Florida also markets to college students. Approximately 300,000 to 400,000 students trek to Daytona Beach, Fort Lauderdale, and other Florida beach areas in late March and early April.

Florida also markets to foreign visitors who stay longer than U. S. visitors (fourteen days versus four to five days), and spend an estimated 50 percent more per diem.

One of Florida's attractions, Miami Beach, is reviving following a thirty-year decline. Once the garden spot for tourism and fashion in the 1920s, Miami Beach declined precipitously in the 1960s, bypassed by air travel, competition, and Walt Disney World's 1972 opening. With its fading glamour attracting only the fixed-income elderly, Miami Beach gained the dubious distinction of having the oldest population in the nation.

Could the city's former glamour be restored sufficiently to attract tourists seeking the nostalgia of yesteryears? Florida officials thought so and invested $250 million initially in upgrading public facilities, services, and infrastructure. Miami Beach created a 700-acre Art Deco Architectural District that contains 800 historically significant buildings and renovated hotels, and brought back entertainment, bars, and restaurants. Crowning this boom to bust revival, Ocean Drive celebrated its grand opening in January 1990, and Miami Beach once again had become a prized tourist attraction.

Source: For Miami Beach, see Kent O. Bonde and Stuart L. Rogel, "Ocean Drive," *Economic Development Commentary,* Winter 1991, pp. 4–6.

for all-inclusive resorts and package tours that promise comfort, consistency, and cost-effectiveness. Indeed, some see travelers in the 90s returning to the 50s style vacation that their parents enjoyed. These "new traditionalists" look for bargains, up-front costs, flexibility, and convenience.[8]

Tourism Strategies and Investments

Tourist competition is fierce amidst a growing and constantly changing tourist market. Besides new places, competition expands when declining places upgrade and make new investments in place development. A major trend in place revival is *heritage development*, the task of preserving the history of places, their buildings, their people and customs, the machinery, and other artifacts that portray history. Leavenworth, Washington, an old logging and mining town, experienced revival when it transformed itself into a Bavarian village. Kemmerer, Wyoming, an abandoned coal town, capitalized on being the home of the original J. C. Penney store which it restored as a tourist attraction. Winterset, Iowa, actor John Wayne's birthplace, is now visited by more than 30,000 tourists annually. Chicopee, Massachusetts, an old textile town, turned an aging plant into a $25 million Amazon rain forest. Seymour, Wisconsin, lays claim to being home of the first hamburger, hosting August Hamburger Days; in 1989, Seymour organizers cooked the world's largest hamburger, weighing 5,520 pounds.[9]

Countless examples exist of places rediscovering their past, capitalizing on the birthplace of a famous person, and event, a battle, or other "hidden gems." Places rely on various monikers for identification: Sheboygan, Wisconsin, as City of Cheese, Choirs, Children, and Churches; Crystal City, Texas, as the Spinach Capital of the World; Lexington, Kentucky, as the Athens of the West; New Haven, Connecticut, as the City of Elms. Many places still bear nicknames of their economic heritage: Hartford, Connecticut, as Insurance City; Holyoke, Massachusetts, as Paper City; Westfield, New York, as Buggy Whip City; and Patterson, New Jersey, as Silk City. With the current U.S. trend toward shorter but more frequent vacations, many places within 200 miles or so of major metropolitan areas have found new opportunities to access the tourist market. The renewed growth of the family vacation market also has redirected some places toward a "family friendly" appeal market. Orlando, San Diego, San Francisco, and Milwaukee are examples of places whose family vacation appeal has been particularly successful.

In light of the 1990–91 Persian Gulf War and threats of terrorism, overseas air travel fell 50 percent, devastating the travel business. However, local tourism and convention bureaus marketed such a change to their advantage with the '91 theme, "Stay Close to Home." The Louisiana Office of Tourism spent $6 million to market a summer travel bargain program to a 500-mile market. St. Louis and Atlanta did much the same, while Hawaii targeted the West Coast. One place's adversity is often another place's opportunity.

The 1970s ushered in an era of theme parks led by Disneyland (Anaheim, 1961) and Walt Disney World (Orlando, 1972). More than 100 theme parks have since opened in the United States, some in cities, but most near major interstate highways accessible to several markets. Many have failed, did not meet expectations, or priced themselves out of family budgets. Given Walt Disney Company's success, many places seek to replicate it on a smaller scale. Tokyo's Disneyland has been a success, and a $4.4 billion Disneyland opened 20 miles outside of Paris in 1992. This new Euro Disneyland spreads over 5,000 acres and is one-fifth the size of Paris. Some French critics have complained that Disney characters will pollute the nation's cultural ambiance, but most anticipate eventual success and look forward to a future European EPCOT Center.[10]

The environmental movement has compelled the travel industry to adapt earth-friendly approaches, and places are seeking to develop "green" images. Developers and architects have accommodated changing tastes in designing hotels—low rise, more green space, native architecture, and energy efficient.[11] Tourist places have become more sensitive to zoning, density, land use, and the problems of overbuilding. Government tourist agencies, airlines, hotel chains, and tourist organizations are all talking about green issues, and how best to accommodate growth while respecting environmental values.

Event-based tourism has become a vital component of tourist attraction programs. Small or rural places typically begin with a festival or event to establish their identity. All urban newspapers and suburban weeklies publish a listing of events, festivals, and celebrations occurring within a day's driving distance. State and local tourism offices do the same, making sure that travel agents, restaurants, hotels, airports, train and bus stations have event-based calendars for posting. Nearly every European country now has a 900 number one can call in the United States to get a listing of forthcoming events. Every major U.S. city has a summer program of scheduled events and some, such as Milwaukee, have well-established year-round events. Milwaukee's June–September lakefront festivals (e.g., Fest Italiana, German Fest, Afro Fest, Polish Fest, etc.) attract tourists regionally and nationally, and are considered to be the best of their type in the country.

Tourism investment ranges from relatively low-cost market entry for festivals or events to multimillion dollar infrastructure costs of stadiums, transit systems, airports, and convention centers. Regardless of the cost, urban renewal planners seek to build tourism into the heart of their city's revitalization. Boston's Quincy Market, New York's Lincoln Center, and San Francisco's Fisherman's Wharf are recent examples. The ability to concentrate attractions, facilities, and services in a convenient, accessible location is essential to creating a strong destination pull.

In more centrally planned economies (Eastern Europe and developing countries), their governments control, plan, and direct tourist development. Tourism is necessary to earn hard currencies for trade and development and serves national purposes. Tourist expansion is highly dependent on public investments, which have proven to be woefully inadequate without private investment and market mechanisms to respond to changing consumer needs and wants. These nations now promote private investment through joint ventures, foreign ownership, and time sharing for individual investors. The new Mexican Riviera—Puerto Vallarta, Cancun, Ixtapa—are examples of new public-private combinations of successful tourism investments where state investment in infrastructure works with private investment in tourist amenities from hotels, restaurants, and golf courses to shopping areas.

Place specific tourism in the United States increasingly builds on public-private partnerships or joint development in planning, financing, and implementation. Public authority is required to clear, develop, and write down land costs and make infrastructure investments. The place often must subsidize or provide tax incentives for private investment in hotels, convention centers, transit, and parking. Restoration is often carried out by nonprofit development corporations from the National Historic Trust to the U.S. Park Service, with private investment promoted through various tax incentives. From airlines to hotels, the tourist industry provides dedicated tax revenues from fuel, leases, bed taxes, and sales taxes to support long-term bonds for capital construction of tourist-related infrastructure and other public improvements. Such steps made it possible for New York City recently to add the Southport Sea Museum, Javits Convention Center, and Ellis Island Immigration Museum to its tourist attraction portfolio, which now stands as the top United States attraction in the number of annual visitors.

Much more than financial capital or hospitality investments is required for tourism promotion. Places find that they must expand public services, specifically public safety, traffic and crowd control, emergency health, sanitation, and street cleaning. They also must promote tourism internally to their own citizens and businesses—retailers, travel agencies, restaurants, financial institutions, public and private transit, lodging, police, and public servants. They must invest in recruiting training, licensing, and monitoring tourist-related businesses and employees. Singapore's cab drivers are known for their professional training and service, which include English language exams, safety programs, and location skills. Some places invest little in that area, even though airport cabs and public transit may be the first encounter visitors have with a place and such impressions can be critical to tourist satisfaction.

Positioning and Niching in the Tourist Market

To attract tourists, places must respond to the travel basics of *cost, convenience,* and *timeliness.* Tourists, like other consumers, weigh the costs against the benefits of specific destinations—and investment of time, effort, and resources against a reasonable return in education, experience, fun, relaxation, and prospective memories. Convenience takes on various meanings in travel decisions: time involved in travel, airport to lodging, language barriers, cleanliness and sanitary concerns, access to interests (e.g., beaches, attractions, amenities), and special needs (elderly, disabled, children, dietary, medical care, fax and communication, auto rental). Timeliness embraces those factors that introduce risk to travel: wars, terrorism, civil disturbances and political instability, currency fluctuations and convertibility, airline and transit safety, and sanitary conditions.

As a general rule, all places and tourist businesses seek to be competitive in costs, minimize risks, and maximize conveniences and amenities. Tourist packages range from total planning of hour-by-hour detail to multiple options and choices. To accommodate multiple tourist needs, packages range from destination-to-destination no-frills only, to site-and-event-based full-frills luxury. Beyond basics, travelers make comparisons about the relative advantages and disadvantages of competing destinations: geographically (local, regional, national, international), special interests (hiking, snorkeling, recreation), and amenities (music, art, entertainment, etc.). Should I ski in Europe or in the United States? Should I take a chance on Arizona or Florida winters, or take a sure bet on the Caribbean? Tourists, like other consumers, constantly make trade-offs between cost and convenience, quality and reliability, service and beauty, and so on. With the U.S. dollar's decline in the late 1980s, nearly half of Vail and Aspen lodgings were then booked by foreign ski enthusiasts who have found it to be less expensive to ski in Colorado than in Europe, especially when its skiing conditions are more predictable than Europe's. With 80 percent of the world's 60 million skiers living overseas and our aging baby boom a factor in flattened skier demand, U.S. ski resorts are now aggressively marketing overseas.[12]

Places must market not only their *destination* but also their specific *attractions*. Places must provide easy access to their attractions by bus, boats, carriages, and planes. They can distribute brochures, audiotapes, and videotapes to travel agents and individual prospects. All major hotels now provide in-home video packages to assist visitors in planning local tours, booking events, or in seeing various sites. City bus companies prepare half-day, full-day, and evening tours to highlight the place's major attractions. Concentrating attractions, services, and facilities in a small area creates excitement, adventure, and crowds. Too many places try to scatter their attractions to avoid overcrowding but this may be self-defeating. Exhibit 8–7 describes how Niagara Falls uses concept integration to package romance.

A place may promote one, a few, or many of its attractions. Chicago's marketing theme—"Chicago's Got It"— featured pictures of its famous architecture, lakefront, symphony, world's tallest building, financial exchanges, Wrigley Field (home of the Chicago Cubs) to suggest that the city had everything: business, culture, entertainment, recreation, and sports. In contrast, San Francisco's ad played off its well-developed image as seductive and mysterious: a photo of a foggy, softly lit Golden Gate Bridge with the copy, "In the beginning, God Created Heaven and Earth. San Francisco Took A Little Longer."[13]

Places need to monitor closely the relative popularity of their various attractions by determining the number and type of tourists attracted to each location. The popularity of the Metropolitan Museum of Art, Arch of Triumph, Big Ben, or the Colosseum, can suddenly or gradually change. Places should seek to deepen their attractions' quality. Virginia builds on "Birthplace of Presidents," Mississippi on "The

EXHIBIT 8-7

Niagara Falls: Packaging Romance

A major strategy for tourist attraction is concept integration—tying all the diverse elements into one central theme. Niagara Falls, Ontario, provides a good example. The first view of Niagara Falls is of spectacular cascading water. And yet, the perceived image is of a honeymooner's paradise. According to Gordon Paul, president of the Niagara Falls Tourism Council, "The mating of this spectacular waterfall to honeymoons began as early as 50 years ago." By associating honeymoons with Niagara Fall's natural beauty, Niagara Falls managed to extend its tourist season into the winter. It appeals to newly marrieds who are within driving distance and have a limited budget. More than fifty hotels on the Ontario side offer honeymooners a choice of heart-shaped bathtubs, Jacuzzis, canopy beds, and waterbeds. The entire romantic aura of champagne waiting in your room, mirrors on the ceilings, and quiet and discreet quarters, encourage the honeymoon market. In addition, the support structure of wax museums, a wide variety of restaurants, and taffy shops create the aura of a fantasyland that is partly tacky and partly romantic. The atmosphere of Niagara Falls is such that honeymooners are in the majority; it is unlikely that they'll stand out from the crowd. And since the honeymooners ultimately want to be alone, their affection goes unnoticed. The large number of honeymooners find a complete package—dramatic beauty and a catering business community—resulting in a satisfying tourist experience.

Source: Michael Giuliano researched Niagara Falls at Northwestern University in May 1988, and interviewed Gordon Paul, April 26–27, 1988.

Heart of Dixie," Greece on "The Birthplace of Democracy," and Florence on "The Center of the Renaissance." Such appeals transcend specific attractions and become a platform for building a place's appeal.

However, features and sites alone do not attract visitors. Most places seek to deepen the travel experience by providing greater value and making the experience more significant and rewarding. Such appeals are couched in history, culture, and people. New York City is a case in point. About one in four of the city's visitors is a foreign tourist. The city already draws a high percentage of Europeans visiting the United States—about 50 percent of Italians and Spaniards. Consequently, city officials must make New York more "foreign friendly," by creating tours that emphasize nationality interests, designing brochures in a variety of languages, and providing hassle-free currency exchanges.[14] To provide that value-added dimension and friendship, these tour packagers try to deepen cultural bonds and ties between the United States and the foreign visitors.

Competition for place advantage in tourism extends to restaurants, facilities, sports, cultural amenities, and entertainment. Which place has the most four-star hotels; best culinary fare; most museums and theaters; top-ranked athletic teams; the best wine and drink; best chefs; or best native, cultural, or ethnic flair? Place campaigns are carried out in specialty publications: *Gourmet; National Geographic Traveler; Food and Leisure; Traveler; Michelin Guides; New York Times Sophisticated Traveler;* and *The Economist.* These testimonials and rankings are found in travel brochures, place advertising, and in travel guides. In addition to specific sites and attractions, amenities are critical to the travel business, vital to tourism and hospitality business, and are part of the comparative advantages one place enjoys over another.[15] Exhibit 8–8 describes how Bradford, England, created a new, competitive product.

Communicating with the Tourist Market

Tourist competition, like business attraction and retention, involves image-making. Place images are heavily influenced by pictorial creations of the place, often in movies and on television, and sometimes by music, and in other cases by popular entertainers and celebrities. Decades later, these place images still persist. Ireland exploits the John Wayne-Maureen O'Hara *Quiet Man* as a successful image of the Irish, while Austria still relies on *The Sound of Music* image of its country's beauty and people.[16] India experienced a 50 percent increase in tourism following the box office smash, *Gandhi.* Burned to the ground by Civil War General William Sherman's army, Atlanta has revived its *Gone with the Wind* image by its selection as the site for the 1996 Olympics. The coming Olympics is being billed as the city's sec-

EXHIBIT 8-8

Bradford: Creating a New Product

The city of Bradford, England, at first glance seems a bad bet as a tourist attraction. For decades it suffered from a poor image and a declining industrial base, especially in its staple industry, wool textiles. The city council, finally recognizing the problem, allocated a one-time grant of £100,000 to explore new tourist markets.

The audit of potential attractions was promising —millshops, home of the Brontë sisters, television and film themes (*Wuthering Heights, Emmerdale Farm, Last of the Summer Wine*), an industrial heritage tour, and the National Museum of Photography, Film, and Television. A good inventory, but the crucial decision was yet to be made.

Bradford's marketing department decided to reinvent their place as a short-break holiday market. The reasoning was insightful:

1. They had excess capacity in July and August, the short-break months.
2. The city would never become a destination for long-term visits. They lacked the primary attractions.
3. The primary market was visitors from surrounding cities.

The city then turned to promoting the city as a weekend package to wholesalers. Discovering that without wholesalers offering the Bradford option there was no channel to reach their customers, they followed up with print ads in publications that were strong in reaching the mainstream tourists in England. They reinforced their campaign with a steady stream of rehab projects and new events.

The result was a sharp pickup in holiday packages. The local citizens began to take pride in the new attention and saw visual evidence of the upturn in new clubs, wine bars, and shops. The general air of confidence in Bradford was derived from a confluence of cooperation—city council, marketing department, wholesalers, merchants, and citizens.

ond renaissance, the other being 1864 after its wartime destruction.[17] Australia's booming tourist business used actor Paul Hogan of the hit film *Crocodile Dundee,* to dramatize the country's humor, adventure, and ruggedness. Australia also used Olivia Newton-John and Mel Gibson in ad campaigns. British Air employed actor Robert Morley; Mexico featured Linda Ronstadt; Manchester featured the Beatles; Wales utilized Richard Burton, and Chicago touts Michael Jordan. These places take advantage of news events, sports and entertainment stars, movies, and whatever else they can to stimulate tourist interest and convey a place image.

Television also affects relative place attractiveness. The pub site for the television hit "Cheers" became an overnight tourist bonanza in Boston, while Public Broadcasting System serialization of English dramas has opened up Britain to American audiences. Late in 1990, the PBS eleven-hour series "The Civil War," also sparked record sales of Civil War reading material and sales of memorabilia. The benefit for Virginia, where more than 60 percent of the war was fought over four years—more than 1,000 battles—was a record-breaking surge in tourism.

Changing an image, however, is more difficult. Las Vegas, for example, is seen as a vice capital known for sex and gambling. Gambling still accounts for a sizable 60 percent of the local economy, but consider these facts: Las Vegas is (1) a family-oriented tourist mecca for sports, entertainment, recreation, and performing arts; (2) a university town with one of the fastest growing, most prestigious universities in the West with emerging graduate schools and a bittersweet memory of a controversial national champion basketball team led by Coach Jerry Tarkanian; (3) a high-tech regional service center that attracted ninety new companies in 1989–90, including Lockheed Engineering and Sciences Company and office complexes. Greater Las Vegas has become the fastest-growing region in the country. The valley's population has nearly doubled between 1980 and 1990, from 463,000 to 768,000. Its population grows by a rate of 1,000 newcomers per week.[18]

Can Las Vegas accommodate the valley's population boom? A well-managed city and can-do attitude faces the reality of unbridled growth, mounting infrastructure and education needs, water limitations, environmental constraints, and prospects for an eroding quality of life. Can Las Vegas make the transition in repositioning itself as a place for gambling chips to silicon chips, conventions to families? Is it a unique city capable of building on success and diversification or just another growth town that traded quality of life for big-city troubles? Will it run the gauntlet of image cycles—poor, improving, excellent, tarnished star, and decline? The choices Las Vegas makes in selecting a mix of communication messages and channels will largely determine its emerging identity.

State media investment on attracting tourists has grown rapidly in recent years. Between 1987 and 1989, states such as Texas, Colorado, and Alaska more than quadrupled their tourism media budgets, although more recent state financial difficulties have caused a cutback.[19] Nations and states invade and advertise in each other's markets. For instance, Illinois targets New York, California, Texas, and Japan. It produces multilanguage travel guides, videotapes, radio segments, and selected segments for golfers, fishers, bicyclists, and conventions.

Places have increasingly formed partnerships with travel, recreational, and communication businesses on joint marketing efforts. They advertise in national magazines and travel publications, and do vertical marketing with business-travel promotions to link the growing business-leisure segment of the traveling public. They target their own travel agencies and agents; which, according to the International Association of Travel Agency Networks (IATAN), number 40,000 agencies and 200,000 agents. Many states have located welcome centers along major interstate highways that include unstaffed two-way video systems to answer questions from a central location or otherwise assist travelers. States also target tourism to their own residents, regionalizing attractions with brochures, maps, and calendars of events targeted for subregions.

Places constantly discover hidden assets that have vast tourist potential. Illinois, for example, has more public and semipublic golf courses per population than any other state except Florida. It now markets abroad golf tours to its top-rated public golf courses. One successful buyer has been Japanese tourist agencies that have packaged a golf and Chicago shopping tour for Japanese visitors. Pennsylvania has reclaimed old coal mining areas with championship golf courses, expanding its recreational facilities to promote tourism. Places are learning to advertise a product to a particular target.

Finally, effective place imaging requires a congruence between advertising and the place. Glossy photographs of sunsets, beaches, buildings, and events need to have some relationship to what tourists actually experience; otherwise places run the risk of losing tourist goodwill and generating bad word of mouth. Travel agents are extremely responsive to place feedback from customers, while tourists can provide the best or worst promotion of a place depending on their experiences.

Organizing and Managing Tourism Marketing

Making a place tourist friendly is the task of a central tourist agency which may be public, quasi-public, nonprofit, or private. Outside the United States, this agency is run by the central government, state, or province, together with local government officials. The European Travel Commission, a twenty-four-nation group bent on luring U.S. visitors to Europe, coordinates promotional activity here in the United States.

Some cities divide responsibilities for promoting tourist and hospitality business: the former largely public supported and the latter supported by the travel-tourist business. In smaller communities, tourist-travel activities generally fall under a local chamber of commerce and private support. Local chambers of commerce have become aggressive promoters of bed-and-breakfast lodgings in private homes which began in New England and now flourish on the West Coast.

Tourist organizations differ significantly in their budget, revenue sources, and marketing programs. In general, chambers of commerce are critical for tourist boosterism; cooperating with the tourist-travel industry in developing products; and directing bookings, marketing, and total place promotion. They are tourist industry advocates, negotiators, and key connection makers with public officials and agencies. In nearly all cases, these agencies believe they are underfunded relative to their tasks and the competition.

Table 8–3 shows the tourism and convention agency operations in four major cities. Las Vegas clearly is the largest, best financed, and most aggressive in this group.

THE BUSINESS HOSPITALITY MARKET

There are five groups that define the meetings market: trade shows, conventions, assemblies, conferences, and consumer shows. The key revenue factors are the size of the group, its length of the stay, and its service demands. Ten thousand convention delegates who buy food, hotel accommodations, equipment, and retail products spend $7.5 million during their stay.[20] Not surprisingly, meeting space requirements have been growing at 5 percent per year throughout the 1980s, and, in

TABLE 8-3
Tourist and Convention Agency Operations in Four Cities

City	Las Vegas	San Francisco	Atlanta	San Diego
SIZE OF BUDGET	$81M $2M Chicago Office	$9M	$8M	$6M
PUBLIC/ PRIVATE	Room tax, Gambling tax, Convention facilities and operations	53% Hotel tax 47% Private	Hotel/motel tax	80% Transit/ occupancy 20% Private
SOURCE OF PRIVATE SUPPORT	No private money	Membership fees, Advertising, Cooperative Ventures	Members, Sale of merchandise	Membership, Cooperative advertising in 4 publications
MARKETING	Major advertising offices: Washington, D.C., Chicago, Tokyo, Taiwan; Promoting 4 new hotels, Water Park, new Disneyland West	Local/national ads, Trade shows, Cooperative publications	Advertising in magazine, papers, PSA's; Cooperate w/USTTA, Full scale push for Olympics	Market for 2 + nights, Concentrate on SW & NE, Travel/Trade shows, Cooperative advertising
RELATIONSHIP TO CITY	Quasi-governmental authority Las Vegas Authority	Nonprofit corporation SF Convention and Visitors Bureau	Nonprofit organization Atlanta Convention Bureau	Quasi-public/nonprofit organization San Diego Convention & Visitors Bureau

Source: Chicago Office of Tourism, 1991.

spite of the 1990–1992 recession slowdown, are expected to grow by this rate through the 1990s.

Developing Competitive Convention Facilities

As the meetings market has grown, so have the number of places and facilities competing for the business. An estimated 255 cities in the United States and abroad compete for convention business, spending $250 million annually for destination market advertising and promotion. Spending can range from less than $100,000 in small markets to as much as $16 million annually for the large Hong Kong market.[21]

The race to build, renovate, and modernize convention facilities vastly accelerated in the 1970s and 1980s. Two hundred and fifty facilities alone were built or renovated between 1975 and 1985, while sixty cities vastly expanded existing or built new convention centers. An example of that competition occurred on the West Coast: San Diego opened in early 1990 as the largest West Coast facility. Anaheim then expanded, while San Francisco's new facility opened in late 1990. That prompted Los Angeles to enlarge its center which, in turn, got San Diego to initiate a study of doubling the size of its new facility that had opened only 18 months before.[22]

Chicago remains the nation's leading convention site. With 1.6 million gross square feet, McCormick Place is the largest U. S. exhibition complex, and the seventh largest in the world, a position that planners argue it would have to relinquish to Las Vegas and others without further expansion. In 1991, Chicago gained financing for McCormick Place expansion, to be started in 1993 and completed in 1996. It will add 75 percent more exhibition space and other improvements necessary to meet competition from Las Vegas and other convention centers. Exhibit 8–9 describes how the Chicago car show lost prestige to Detroit.

The meetings market is further segmented by convention and trade show size. Chicago captures slightly less than 25 percent of the major U. S. meetings market followed by New York with 21 percent, and Las Vegas, San Francisco, and Atlanta with 12 to 15 percent each. While Chicago captures a leading share of large shows (12,500 +) and small shows (fewer than 7,500), New York City and Anaheim, California, have larger shares of medium-size shows (7,500 to 12,499). Chicago hosts more shows, but New York accommodates more delegates and participants overall.[23]

The hospitality business increasingly requires attractive exhibition facilities combined with ample meeting space. More than 50 percent of conventions include exhibits and displays, and combine exhibitions with meetings. The Jacob Javits Convention Center in New York opened in 1986: architect I. M. Pei's "crystal palace" covers 1.8 million square feet with 900,000 square feet of exhibition space. The modern state-of-the-art center can seat up to 10,000 for a banquet, accommodate more than 100 concurrent meetings, and has three prime halls, one of which is 410,000 square feet—one of the largest in the Western Hemisphere.[24]

The competition for hospitality business begets a certain spiraling space race among competing cities. There is both an internal and external dynamic. The internal dynamic stems largely from hotel and hospitality business expansion which builds or overbuilds to meet prospec-

EXHIBIT 8-9
Car Wars

A tradition among car manufacturers is to cosponsor an auto show with the local dealers. The show features the latest models of the forthcoming year and is expected to ignite the spring selling season. The largest auto show was traditionally the Chicago Auto Show held in February. The upstart was the Detroit Auto Show which is held in January, but it attracted lower attendance and fewer new models than Chicago. The Detroit organizers convinced the big three to favor them with more cars. GM, Ford, and Chrysler agreed and the Detroit Auto Show became the nationally recognized North American International Auto Show, which now overshadows its Chicago counterpart. Meanwhile, in Los Angeles, auto show organizers began to lobby the Japanese manufacturers for more new cars. The Japanese agreed in principle, but Los Angeles has failed to establish a strong niche in the auto show marketplace.

The moral of the story is that nothing is sacred in attracting consumer shows. Detroit listened to the manufacturers and emphasized the new car's technical qualities. It now gets the premium cars. The Chicago show continues to be dominated by the dealers who emphasize selling. It is now a second-tier venue. Los Angeles flounders because it refused to change the date of its show from the same week as Detroit's. Chicago could have anticipated and prevented the Detroit attack by increasing the manufacturers' input and downplaying the selling activity. Los Angeles simply needed to move around some dates.

Sources: Jim Mateja, "Chicago Auto Show under Fire," *Chicago Tribune*, July 11, 1989, p. 9; and an interview with Jim Mateja, June 25, 1992.

tive demand from conventions and trade shows. When hotel occupancy falls below profitability—roughly 60 percent occupancy—pressure mounts to expand exhibition and meeting space as a method to increase hotel occupancy rates.

The external dynamic comes from competitors' space expansion plans. Chicago's hospitality planners estimate the city needs 1 million square feet of new exhibition space and 300,000 square feet of meeting facilities to maintain its market share. Miami, San Francisco, Los Angeles, and New Orleans all have plans to double their exhibition space, while Atlanta will increase its space by 50 percent. Smaller communities increasingly demand a share of local or regional hospitality business: they offer to exchange regional meetings facilities in return for operating subsidies for their own local facilities.

International convention competition has greatly expanded in recent years. With the European Community's move toward a single market, numerous trade associations held European-based meetings in the 1990s to educate members about market opportunities for their products. Japan, Hong Kong, and Korea have also become aggressive competitors in the international business hospitality market.

Strategies for Winning in the Business Hospitality Market

In contrast to a tourist attraction, convention and trade show business involves dealing with dedicated specialists such as trade association directors, site selection committees, and convention specialists who make site selection recommendations based on price, facilities, and various amenities. Facilities are critical to accommodating association needs—which often means the capacity to run multiple shows concurrently—and providing Class A space at reasonable rates. Discounted hotel, restaurant, theater, airline, auto rental, transit, and other amenities are all part of competitive packaging. Operating costs per square foot range from $12.50 in Las Vegas to nearly $50 in New York in 1988 among the top ten competitors in the U.S. convention business. Almost all convention centers operate with tax-supported subsidies for debt service and operations. Las Vegas, for example, subsidizes more than 50 percent of its $14 million convention center's operating budget. New York's high operating costs and 21 percent tax on hotel occupancy (bed tax) greatly disadvantages it in price competition with other major cities.[25]

Facilities also must be upgraded to meet aesthetic and convenience needs—restaurants, shops, people movers, restrooms, cleanliness, speed of set-ups, and take-downs, security, and proximity to central shopping areas and restaurants. Washington's, New Orleans's, and San Francisco's facilities are located centrally, within walking distance from the city's main attractions; Los Angeles's, Chicago's, Miami's, and

New York's are not. Chicago is considering a rail-based circulator to connect its shopping areas, hotels, and transit lines to its convention facilities.

Each convention center has its competitive advantages and disadvantages that convention site selectors debate. Chicago, for example, has excellent facilities and competitive hotel and restaurant rates, while its disadvantages include unpredictable weather, high costs, and negative perceptions about its labor force. Due to high labor costs and theft rates, New York City's Javits Center has incurred adverse publicity that can seriously damage a place's competitive position for shows. California competitors—San Francisco, Los Angeles, and Anaheim—are no match for Chicago's facilities, but rank highly on other scores, except geographic accessibility.

Major convention and trade shows may be booked up to five years in advance. Convention bureaus often set up booths at annual conventions held elsewhere (typically when the following year's convention is to be held in that city) to market their places and help future attendees plan their trips. Large convention bureaus such as Chicago may have professional staffs of twenty to forty people with budgets of $10 to $20 million, most of which is spent on marketing and advertising. Convention representatives follow closely the meeting plans of hundreds of associations, professional societies, exhibitors, consultants, and companies.

Hospitality locations know their target markets and respective niches. Chicago has an edge on the high end of the market, the largest shows that attract 100,000 or more attendees, but competition is intense in all markets. Markets erode, and competitors often engage in bidding wars over the larger, more prestigious gatherings. City competition to host the Democratic and Republican National Conventions elicits bids in the multimillion-dollar range. New York and Houston won the 1992 prizes, and competition is already fierce for 1996. Corporations often join with their convention centers in sponsoring events. Orlando, a second-tier convention site shocked convention planners when it was selected as the site of the 1990 American Bankers Association (ABA) Convention. Orlando offered the ABA nearly $200,000 to subsidize the costs of transportation and meeting rooms. Convention centers not only use direct payments as inducements but also sometimes rent domed stadiums for large events, or organize a variety of special events to entertain guests. New entrants to the large convention business, such as Denver, must be willing to sustain considerable losses in start-up stages to gain market share (see exhibit 8–10).

EXHIBIT 8-10

Denver: Getting Into the Convention Game

It would be hard to argue that Denver is not an interesting site for conventioneers. The largest city between Chicago and Los Angeles, it has outstanding dry weather, and beautiful natural scenery that includes some of the greatest mountain ranges and skiing in the world. A meetings market campaign would hardly seem to have a difficult time competing with the nation's other great convention centers. However, in the late 80s, Denver found itself between a rock and a hard place.

The problem is that Denver was unable to attract larger conventions and trade shows because Currigan Hall, built in 1969, holds only 100,00 square feet. This space compares unfavorably with McCormick Place in Chicago (1.5 million square feet), New York's Javits Convention Center (750,000 square feet), Cobo Hall in Detroit (720,000 square feet) and Atlanta's World Congress Center (650,000 square feet) and resulted in Denver being unable to compete for the large meetings market, a situation that no amount of marketing could overcome.

In response, the city of Denver launched a massive campaign to build a 300,000-square-foot center downtown. Even after a titanic struggle to raise the money from the state and other sources, delays caused the city to cancel eleven conventions worth a total of nearly $15 million in business to Denver. The city is also faced with large investments in a new airport, and services to support new hotels and ground transportation infrastructure.

Will it all pay off for Denver? Denver's Metro Convention and Visitors Bureau claims bookings for 1991 ran 300 percent above their projections. It probably helped that the first convention was the Christian Booksellers Association.

Source: Douglas Vaughan, "Focus Denver: Convention Center Coming," *New York Times,* July 17, 1988, p. RY1.Vaughan reports different footages for McCormick Place and Javits Center from those in previously cited sources. The numbers are difficult to prove, as the sellers do the measuring and the battle for customers insures hyperbole.

The hospitality business draws a growing universe of new and expanding players whose markets may be local, metropolitan, statewide, regional, national, and international. Most state capitals have built convention centers. Some corporations such as Du Pont and Southwestern Bell run their own hotels in headquarters cities, while others, such as Arthur Andersen & Company and IBM, have established their own conference and educational training centers. Companies and organizations have become increasingly cost-conscious in managing business travel. Some have their own travel managers who oversee all corporate travel arrangements and expense accounts, while others contract with travel agencies within organizational travel guidelines or rules.

When times are tough, organizations cut back on travel for professional development, trade shows, and even sales contact; some travel is being replaced by video conferences, teleconferences, and fax machines. Like tourism, the meetings market has experienced steady growth over the years, but still is subject to economic and business cycles.

Convention facility managers seek close relations with the American Society of Association Executives (ASAE), the professional society for those who manage trade associations and professional societies. Primarily involved in promoting association management, ASAE has more than 20,000 members who represent more than 6,000 associations. Located in Washington, D. C., together with nearly 3,000 trade associations that have made that city the association capital, ASAE runs training programs for convention managers of trade associations. When ASAE holds a meeting in your city, you treat the association royally.

In addition, convention leaders cultivate the goodwill of officers, staffs, convention planners, and committees of specific associations. Associations alternate their convention locations, and keep a close tab on convention/trade show feedback on member satisfaction with costs, facilities, and city amenities. Member attendance is the lifeblood of most associations so host cities work with convention planners in targeted direct-mail appeals to membership to help capture attendance. Because repeat business is vital to hospitality centers, postconvention follow-up is necessary to assure the association's satisfaction.

Convention bureaus provide hotels with videotapes and other information to inform business meeting attendees of various sites, events, and activities going on in a city during the meetings. Chicago estimates that if it could get business travelers to stay one extra day in the city, this would generate an additional $2 billion annually.[26]

CONCLUSION

Tourism and the business hospitality market have emerged as viable place development strategies on a footing equal to business retention, business attraction, grow your own businesses, and export-development/reverse investment. In a service-driven economy of aging population, these two businesses are generally expected to grow at rates ahead of the national economy.

Several tourism-travel related trends that places might benefit from are worth noting:

- The economic development plans of places will increasingly emphasize the contribution of the tourism and travel industry.
- Greater market segmentation will follow from better marketing information, and tourism strategic marketing and management will receive increased emphasis.
- Travelers will more often combine business and personal travel with emphasis on cultural and recreation activities requiring places to adapt to cross-marketing.
- Greater interest in sports and recreation will require places to invest more in open space and recreational facilities, and to capitalize on lower-key environmentally sensitive experiences.
- Foreign visitation to the United States will increase, as will the attractions dealing with cultural/heritage experiences.

In most cases, places can enter these businesses at the lower competitive end and at relatively little cost. However, as they seek access to broader markets, the cost for public and private investments rises rapidly. At the upper end of the scale, large capital investments are required for airports, convention centers, basic infrastructure, and public services. Private sector investment in hotels, shopping areas, theaters, and restaurants needs to be carefully coordinated and planned with public investments, lest one proceeds without the other. Physical assets must be continually upgraded, and new products developed. Table 8–4 contains a test of a place's visitor friendliness which is key to its development.

Competition in these businesses has become more fierce as development often runs ahead of demand which, coupled with cyclicality, can have devastating consequences on a tourist-dependent economy. The benefits from tourism and hospitality also are considerable in jobs, income, and economic growth for a local economy. Some places, due to

TABLE 8-4
A Visitor Friendly Test for Places

Caveat: While no exact test exists to measure how visitor friendly a place is, the following 10 questions provide a rough approximation. With 10 points for each favorable answer, a passing score is 60. Anything less probably spells trouble.

1. Are the central access points to your community/place (road, rail, plane) equipped with visitor information centers or do they provide instructions to easily accessible information?
2. Should an airport be the primary access point, does it provide a full range of visitor information services (e.g., accommodations, tourist booth, visuals on sites, listing of events and what to do, specialized information for elderly, foreigners, families, etc.)?
3. Do visitor facilitators—cabs, buses, airline personnel, security, airport operators, reservation personnel—receive any formal training, and does a system exist to monitor quality of visitor facilitator services?
4. Do hotels/motels offer in-house television access channels for visitors with information on events, attractions, restaurants, and things to do?
5. Is a single organization/agency responsible for visitor business, and are public funds provided for its activities?
6. Does that organization/agency have a marketing profile of visitors, and is this profile used in marketing activities?
7. Does the place's hospitality industry accommodate foreign visitors' needs (language, directions, special interest, do's and don'ts, etc.)?
8. Does a range of accommodations exist to meet actual or expected visitor needs (by price range, size, facilities, access to sites, etc.)?
9. Is access to sites, attractions, and amenities (events, recreational, central location) easily available at reasonable costs frequency?
10. Does the place welcome visitors and accommodate their needs (commercial hours, credit cards, language, signage, traffic, parking, public services, etc.)?

geography, history, or resources, have few other choices but to compete for tourist and business hospitality markets. Others have more strategic options or seek to balance tourism/hospitality strategies with other businesses as part of a total economic development plan.

From a marketing vantage point, tourism and convention bureaus seek to build a positive image of a place not unlike other place development strategies. They, too, must develop products that clearly target customer needs, and compete on price, quality, convenience, and other factors that enter into buyers' decisions. They, too, must sell their products directly to wholesalers (associations, tour packagers, etc.) and in retail fashion, use the best mix of marketing tools and strategies to reach buyers. As service sellers, they must respond to constant changes in buyers' needs and wants and follow shifts in life-styles and traveling trends.

Finally, the tourist and hospitality business parallels the promotion of other place development strategies. What began as a relatively unsophisticated business of mass marketing to a mass audience or simply promotional advertising touting the beauty or interest of a place, progressed to a well-developed business, built on strategies, competitive advantages, targeted markets, and mixed marketing techniques and appeals to reach actual or would-be buyers. However, in many places, tourism and hospitality agencies or bureaus operate separately and independently from other economic development activities and, indeed, at times competitively. In fact, it is not uncommon to find tourism under one agency and conventions or hospitality business under another. This harkens back to earlier chapters on place development strategies, images, and marketing where fragmentation and unplanned development is still the rule, rather than the exception.

To maximize its effectiveness, tourism and hospitality marketing must be integrated into and, at times, lead other place marketing strategies. Where development strategies are mixed—tourism and, say, business attraction—a coordinated marketing effort produces better results at less cost where vertical marketing is involved. Furthermore, a community may want to attract someone to visit the place on vacation and for business, and, simultaneously, sell them on locating a company or division there as well. Comparable examples can be found in trying to convert foreign visitors into investors. Each marketing strategy should begin fitting into others to establish a place's image and to convey the right messages.

9

Attracting, Retaining, and Expanding Businesses

Every place performs particular economic functions. Some place economies are diversified, while others are dominated by a single industry. Some are service centers, while others are agricultural communities. However, a place's economic activities are not necessarily constrained by their surrounding economic boundaries; that is, a small village in Kauai need not grow sugar cane, and a suburb of Detroit need not manufacture cars. By looking at a place through a broader regional lens, one can better understand how a place functions in a national or international context.

The capacity of a place to compete changes over time. At one moment, a place may be thriving, dynamic, well positioned for growth and further development, and at the next moment, losing jobs, businesses, and people. Size and location alone no longer guarantee economic vitality. Places, just like corporate giants and entire industries, may rise and fall with new technologies, new competitors, and shifting consumer preferences.

Over the last sixty years, a general pattern emerged in place strategies. From 1930 to 1975, business attraction dominated as the preferred approach for replacing lost jobs or for expanding employment. In the late 1970s, that strategy gave way to an emphasis on business retention and expansion, which has remained a top priority since. However, beginning in the early to mid-1980s, places also turned to promoting growth from within by encouraging new business start-ups and helping small businesses to grow as a distinctive strategy for growth. This progression follows from fundamental changes that swept the U.S. economy from 1970 to 1990.

Successful places survived these changes by understanding the three main factors that control whether businesses invest or disinvest in a place: (1) characteristics of the firm or industry, (2) characteristics of a place, and (3) outside forces influencing the economy of a place. When necessary, these places leaned on government assistance to help them turn their economies around.

There are six generic strategies that places use to improve their competitive positions:

1. Attracting tourist and business visitors.
2. Attracting businesses from elsewhere.
3. Retaining and expanding existing business.
4. Promoting small business and fostering new business start-ups.
5. Expanding exports and outside investments.
6. Expanding the population or changing the mix of residents.

We have already examined the first strategy, expanding tourism and hospitality business in chapter 8. We examine the last two strategies, expanding exports and investments, and altering the residential population base in chapters 10 and 11. In this chapter, we focus on place strategies for attracting, retaining, expanding, and starting new businesses.

ATTRACTING BUSINESSES FROM ELSEWHERE

Attracting businesses from elsewhere has a long history in the United States. To attract businesses, places must understand their strengths and weaknesses. One reason why places became dislocated in the 1970s is that many businesses suddenly changed their place rating criteria due to increased foreign competition. They needed either lower costs, higher-quality workers, more central location, better quality of life, or a more supportive environment.

How Businesses Select Locations

Places should begin their business attraction activities with an assessment of their economy and an audit of their locational characteristics. An accurate and frequent updating of operating conditions, cost factors, and quality-of-life features provide an understanding of how well one place compares to others. Table 9–1 offers a list of basic factors businesses consider important in site designation.

Once a firm decides to build a new facility or relocate, the selection process follows two stages: The first stage involves a search and eventual selection of a region that offers the desired economic advantages. The regional selection is based on overall economic criteria related to the factors of production: labor, transportation, markets, and materials. Roger Schmenner found that six concerns are involved in a major manufacturing firm's decision to build a new facility: labor costs; labor unionization; proximity to markets, proximity to supplies and resources, proximity to other companies, and quality of life.[1] The relative importance of these and other factors, of course, depends on the type of industry and a firm's specific needs.

The second stage involves choosing a site within the selected region; the selection process narrows to specific sites where other factors come into play. Usually the company, assisted by consultants and real estate experts, narrows a site selection choice down to two or three sites, at which point various incentives can be important or more subjective factors emerge, such as proximity to a favored golf course.

During the 1970–1990 period, industry needs changed which meant that place-competitive advantages, strengths, and weaknesses also changed. As table 9–2 indicates, new noneconomic factors became increasingly more important to location-expansion decisions. In the tran-

TABLE 9–1
Basic Information Sought by a Business Searching for a Location

1. Local labor market
2. Access to customer and supplier markets
3. Availability of development sites, facilities, and infrastructure
4. Transportation
5. Education and training opportunities
6. Quality of life
7. Business climate
8. Access to R&D facilities
9. Capital availability
10. Taxes and regulations

TABLE 9–2
Locational Characteristics: Old and New

Characteristics	Old	New
Labor	Low cost, unskilled	Quality, highly skilled
Tax climate	Low taxes, low services	Modest taxes, high services
Incentives	Least-cost production cheap land cheap labor	Value-added adaptable labor force professionals
Amenities	Housing transportation	Culture, recreation, museums, shopping, airport
Higher education	Not key	Quality schools and research facilities
Schools	Availability	Quality schools
Regulation	Minimum	Compatible quality of life and business flexibility
Energy	Costs/availability	Dependability reliability
Communication	Assumed	Technology access
Business	Aggressive chamber of commerce	Partnerships

sition from cost to noncost factors, quality factors gained prominence and assumed multiple forms: quality of public education, skilled labor force, political and fiscal stability, modern telecommunications, good infrastructure, recreational activities and sports teams, shopping facilities, cultural institutions, and general quality-of-life considerations.[2] Environmental considerations also grew in importance, not just clean air but also factors deemed essential in citing a new facility regarding compliance with stronger air, water, and chemical and waste disposal regulations.[3]

In a market characterized by many sellers and few buyers, the main thing that sellers can do is compete on place inducements. Place inducements are not possible for some players, and their competitive advantages shift to place and firm-specific factors, especially noncost factors. Places that have broad advantages such as universities, research facilities, and good quality-of-life factors can compete for a wider range of businesses than those places that have not invested in these types of institutions.

In competing for factories, the frequent objective, in addition to job creation, is to expand the tax base, increase the value of real estate, and to shift the real estate tax burden from homeowners to the commercial and industrial sectors. Fairfax County (Virginia) Economic Development Authority, for example, began its highly successful business attraction program in 1979 with the goal of increasing the proportion of nonresidential tax base from 12 to 21 percent. Between 1979 and 1985, the results proved to be impressive: a shift from 12 to 25 percent nonresidential tax base, a 10 percent reduction in the overall real estate tax rate, an expansion in public services, fiscal stability, and an AAA bond rating. In short, business attraction had worked extremely well for places such as Fairfax County, until the late 1980s when excessive growth and related costs became an issue.[4]

The Race for High-Tech Industries

Communities once focused solely on attracting basic manufacturing industries. Today "clean" factories (otherwise known as light industry due to its assemblage of products and chemicals produced elsewhere) are preferable to "dirty" factories that emit pollution, deal in toxic waste, or whose by-products require special handling. From 1975 to early 1980, high tech attraction had become a top priority of communities of all sizes and locations. Six states—North Carolina, Arizona, Illinois, Michigan, Massachusetts, and New York—put several hundred million dollars into efforts to develop Silicon Valleys. High-tech corridors sprouted: Colorado's Silicon Mountain Corridor, Silicon Gulch between Austin and San Antonio, Bionic Valley in Salt Lake City, Florida's Silicon Swamp, Arizona's Silicon Desert, Ann Arbor's National Center for Robotics, and Oregon's Sunset Corridor to name a few. In Scotland, the seventy mile stretch between Edinburgh and Glasgow was christened Silicon Glen, while the French pushed for "sunrise industries" in the Riviera. The world's most ambitious high-technology venture, Japan's Technopolis Concept, involves a plan to build nineteen high-tech cities and to link them to Tokyo by bullet trains.

Yet, the "high-tech hustle" was based on fundamental assumptions that proved to be wrong or misguided. The facts are:

- Not all places have an equal chance or opportunity to capture a share of the high-tech growth business.
- The number of potential high-tech companies and jobs, as a proportion of current manufacturing jobs, is greatly overestimated.
- It is difficult to identify which new technologies will have the highest growth potential, and which are more labor intensive than capital intensive.
- Location determinants for high-tech proved to be far different than for traditional manufacturing insofar as operating costs are rarely a consideration, while nontraditional factors such as quality research facilities at universities, physical environment, and community attractiveness to engineers and scientists became major variables in siting firms.[5]

Today, more than a decade later, many high-tech highways and silicon strips lie underdeveloped or become highly subsidized research parks, incubators, and technology centers yet to produce their promised benefits. The fact is that high-tech firms have followed rather basic location factors: urban areas, strong universities, access to air transport, concentration of defense and government research, high quality of life, and, perhaps most important, the availability of technicians and skilled labor. Forty percent of high-tech jobs are concentrated in four states, and 70 percent in ten states.[6] Mark Satterthwaite found that high-tech firms bunch together for intra-industry needs, namely their need for recruiting specialized, experienced, and skilled professionals who meet specific requirements.[7] Places that meet that need or were potentially attractive locations through an intra-industry labor market have a competitive advantage by reducing the costs and time necessary for firms to recruit, screen, and hire candidates. Every place may want high-tech jobs, but high-tech is not in every place's future. Places learned this lesson the hard way. Exhibit 9–1 underscores this point.

For the few places that are in a position to attract high-tech industries, the policy implication is to provide labor force information and exchanges with prospective businesses. The marketing implication is to target ads and appeals to skilled labor and high-tech professionals.

EXHIBIT 9-1
A Nuts and Bolts City

In the 1980s, there was probably not a sadder place in America than Rockford, Illinois. A city ninety miles to the west of Chicago, Rockford appeared lost in what was now becoming a high-tech and service America. The collapse of Rockford, a city of 138,000, was so complete that the unemployment rate reached close to 25 percent. The city's manufacturing base of screws, nuts, bolts, chairs, and hammers began to erode from foreign competition and aging plants and machinery. A symbol of Rockford's crushing decline was the elimination of all sports programs in its high schools. It is hard to imagine any city suddenly telling its parents and children that football, basketball, and baseball, many of the rites of youth, are eliminated. The damage to the image of Rockford was devastating as media all over the country recorded the sad plight of families who transferred their children to Catholic schools or found that park district programs were now the only alternative.

Since that embarrassing decline, Rockford has begun to reinvent itself. Unemployment dropped as low as 8 percent and the city rediscovered a sense of purpose. While the community has not totally recaptured the vigor of its post–World War II years, there are signs that a turnaround has begun.

How did Rockford do it? The city went through two specific stages in recovery. The first was marked by innovation and support. Rockford's leaders moved in the following areas:

1. Opened an economic development office in Chicago to position themselves for foreign markets and to sell their inexpensive real estate to Chicago's developers.

Attracting Service Industries, Corporate Headquarters, and Regional Offices

Since the 1960s, the number of U.S. workers employed in manufacturing has remained relatively constant, around 20 million, while service-sector employment has surged.[8] Consequently, few places registered a

2. Studied similar cities and decided that low-tech was their future.
3. Reinstituted the Rockford Local Development Corporation that provided consistent funding for new business ventures.
4. Targeted small business development by funding a technology center at Rock Valley College.

In the second stage, they began to refine their efforts:

1. Placed restrictions and demands on all inducements awarded to new business site expansions and move-ins.
2. Funded development of sophisticated computer program to look for low-tech companies that would match Rockford's needs.
3. Emphasized to all new business targets their location, strong industrial base, low wages, and cost of living.
4. Emphasized quality improvement by aiding small businesses with help in technology, efficiency, and human resources.

The payoff for Rockford has been considerable. The city has received more than $140 million in exports from 1985 to 1992. A long list of companies have invested in new plants and machinery in the city.

However, problems remain with persistent slums and a deteriorating downtown. Rockford is now a niche marketer featuring inexpensive housing, experienced and low-cost labor, and a strong support system for low-tech manufacturing. The long-term test will be Rockford's ability to continue to adapt to changes and refine their promising revival.

Sources: Steve Kerch, "Rockford Rebounding," *Chicago Tribune,* July 17, 1988, sec. 16, p. 1. Interview with Jim Jenkins, Council of 100, Rockford, April 23, 1992.

net growth in goods-producing jobs. Transition to a service-based economy proved troublesome. Conventional views about service-sector employment suggested that it is concentrated in large cities, provides low-paying, low-skill work, exports little, and has a low economic multiplier. While not fully accurate, such notions made service-sector attraction a less desirable target for many place improvers than manufacturing firms.

However, this was not the position of most older, larger industrial-based cities that sought to build their service sector to escape the often severe cyclicality of their manufacturing economies. Following the ravages of the 1973–75 recession when manufacturing to service sector layoffs approached a 10 to 1 ratio, these places encouraged service-sector growth as a form of industry diversification.[9]

Meanwhile, economists debated whether or not the service sector had become sufficiently independent of manufacturing to sustain its own growth. If manufacturing and service employment are interdependent, places had to protect and promote their declining manufacturing, while simultaneously seeking to expand their service sector. Should the two be increasingly independent of one another, then places may be advised to adopt policies to accelerate the transition from one to the other.[10] For some places—government and health care centers, new suburban office enclaves, rural agricultural communities—strategic choices were far less complex. Such places base their economies on the service sector.

Events and research again demonstrated the shortcomings of traditional assumptions. In metropolitan Seattle, William Beyers found that more than half of the area's service producers did more than 10 percent of their business outside the Seattle region. Some 1,100 companies accounted for 84,000 jobs, and more than half of them were involved in out-of-the-local-area sales. The key point is that "The number of jobs resulting from these exported services was *larger* than the number of export-tied manufacturing jobs in the central Puget Sound region."[11]

Service producers offered well-paying jobs and surprising export potential, and had a higher multiplier value than commonly believed. However, this discovery provided cold comfort to some places that embraced service-sector diversification as a protection against economic cycles. The service-sector downsizing of the late 1980s and early 1990s took a huge employment toll in New York City and elsewhere in the 1990–92 recession when national employment contracted by nearly 3 million jobs, and the manufacturing to service sector layoff ratio narrowed to 3 to 1 (versus 10 to 1 in the 1973–75 recession).

A primary target of larger places was to attract the headquarters of Fortune 500 companies. The factors that strongly influence the selection of corporate headquarters locations are:[12]

- How close are the current facilities and customers?

- Can we easily keep in touch with our facilities and customers through existing air transportation and communication systems?
- Is there a strong climate of business and professional support services?
- Is the general area of high quality? Business and taxes? Operating costs? Quality of life? Community image?[12]

Yet, it should be recognized that headquarters relocations are infrequent. Places cannot lure or entice a move if the company is not looking to move. Relocation is most likely to occur when the company is under pressure (e.g., takeovers, mergers, breakups, or reorganizations) or when the working conditions at a particular location become less desirable (e.g., higher operating costs, increased taxes, declining quality of life).

Headquarters and regional/divisional offices of major firms constituted a moving target for business attraction from 1970 to 1990. Their attractiveness was often based more on image than reality, namely that a corporate headquarters (1) provided a large, highly paid, professional employment base; (2) consumed large office space and new office buildings; (3) purchased a wide array of business and professional services locally; (4) offered large charitable support to and otherwise promoted community and cultural services in a community; and (5) enhanced a community's image, providing an impetus to attracting other businesses. While some companies conform to this image, most fall short on one or more counts. For example, from 1970 to 1990, Fortune 500 companies registered a net loss of nearly 4 million jobs. Following technology-driven decentralization and corporate downsizing, headquarters have become smaller, lower-profile operations, that purchase fewer local services and contribute less to a local community's civil and social fabric.

Regional cost differences, however, can influence headquarters and divisional moves. Soaring housing costs can lead to business flight, as occurred when United Parcel Services (UPS) fled from Manhattan for New York's suburbs in the 1970s only to announce in 1991 that it would leave its Greenwich Office Park in Connecticut for suburban Atlanta. Now that soaring Fairfield County, Connecticut, housing prices have adversely affected its culture, some argue that headquarters seem "more like a punishment than a reward."[13]

Regional housing markets are a key barometer of regional economic activity as is the cost of labor. When the median housing sales price is divided by the average annual wage, we get an *affordability ratio*. That ratio also can be an indicator when a boom period may have peaked. In the late 1980s, in seven major cities on both coasts, (Boston, New York, Providence, Hartford, Anaheim, San Francisco, and San Diego) median home prices soared to more than six times average annual income, causing considerable difficulty in attracting professionals and skilled labor.[14] With the average home sales price more than $95,000 in 1988, states such as Hawaii, Massachusetts, Connecticut, New Jersey, and California with home prices ranging from $150,000 to $214,000, gave below or average price states such as Texas, Oregon, Washington, Tennessee, and Nebraska a real recruitment opportunity to gain a foothold on regional sales and division offices.

A classic example of how low housing costs can be a tremendous boost to company relocation and expansion is Dallas. A vastly depressed real estate market caused Dallas's median home prices, $93,200 in 1986, to remain largely static through 1990. In the interim, the following companies added or relocated more than 500 jobs there: American Airlines, General Motors, UPS, FoxMeyer Corporation, and Cardinal Industries (1986); LTV Aerospace and J.C. Penney Company (1987); GTE, Texas Instruments, Fujitsu Ten Corporation of America, Children's Medical Center (1988); E-Systems, MCI Communications Corporation, GTE, J. B. Hunt Transport Services, and American Airlines (1989).[15]

Once places embraced a service-sector strategy, a notion developed that new office buildings somehow generated new jobs. That idea proved to be illusory. Admittedly, new structures may improve a place's appearance, project modernity and a city on the move, and provide indirect benefits by encouraging other investments, but as Carl Patton concluded, "The above rationale may be convincing, if cities did not put public funds into office development."[16] They did, and many paid a very dear price in seeking to create a market that did not exist in the first place. In the 1980s almost 45 percent of the office space ever built was constructed, and this huge office overload may hinder new building development into the next century.[17]

Attracting Shopping Malls and Retailers

Probably no single business location phenomena has more transformed a place's landscape and economy than changing retail forces. From horseback peddlers, to department stores, to large retailer-anchored suburban shopping malls, to anchorless malls and minimalls of specialty stores or factory outlet malls, to discount warehouses, retailing patterns have transformed place development.

Not so long ago, most Americans shopped at department stores that prospered in central cities as well as rural hamlets. When Gimbels closed its million-square-foot store in midtown Manhattan, an era ended in the dominance of downtown department stores in every American city, as Gimbels was soon joined by Detroit's fifty-acre J. L. Hudson; Philadelphia's Lit Brothers; Washington, D.C.'s Woodward and Lothrop; as well as the takeovers and mergers of Marshall Field's, Saks Fifth Avenue, Bloomingdales, Jordan Marsh Stores Corporation, Carter Hawley Hale Stores, and other former giants. As downtown department stores failed or moved to suburban locations, places experienced a ripple effect on public transportation, food and entertainment businesses, and other shopping patterns that reverberated through a community, driving down real estate values, and depressing job growth and tax revenues.[18]

In the 1960s and 1970s, suburban shopping malls proliferated, shifting tax structures and growth benefits within and between communities, and even states. Among the world's largest is Schaumburg, Illinois' Woodfield Shopping Mall with $550 million in retail sales, 4,000 to 6,000 jobs, and 100,000 weekend shoppers. This mall generates so much sales tax revenue that the municipality does not levy a property tax for municipal services.[19] Cities attempted to adjust to shifts in retail buying through closed pedestrian malls, multistoried parking, and other strategies to stem the loss of shoppers. Even some older suburbs have been overtaken by changing retail trends such as greater class- and age-conscious buying patterns. Smaller communities proved to be the real losers, as Wal-Mart Stores for example, the nation's largest retailer with a strong rural base, altered the condition of scores of communities by its location decisions. Retail competition produced winners and losers but, other than construction, rarely added net new jobs or benefits. It was a classic zero-sum game with high stakes.

No community proved invulnerable to such widespread changes. As retail competition intensified and giants fell to changing markets, more places used their place improvement tools—tax abatements, infrastructure improvements, special use districts, and property and sales tax increment financing—to capture benefits from their neighbors. Retail sales competition changed not only the economic condition of places but also altered their social and civic fabric. The demise of the department store, for example, has fundamentally altered the character and viability of many downtowns.

In New England, a region of small towns and cities tightly clustered together, each with its own traditional commercial center, malls have by and large adversely affected older communities. Since World War II, downtown decay occurred incrementally—propelled by fringe growth to highway strip malls to the emergence of the regional mall. In low-population, slow-income-growth areas, the mall represents a zero-sum game, a redirection of shoppers' purchases from one place to another. In high-population, high-income-growth areas, downtowns are better able to hold their own against urban sprawl and greater competition. However, the lessons are clear insofar as communities must anticipate these developments both in preparing their commercial areas for change, capturing whatever competitive advantage they can, and in negotiating with benefiting areas or communities outside that manage to capture malls. In this sense, downtown development follows a similar pattern of attraction, retention, and starting of new businesses.

A Critique of Incentives

The 1970–1990 period in place development is characterized by the conspicuous importance attributed to place incentives: the proliferation, escalating size, and common usage of government-sponsored incentives to get specific businesses and their economies to respond in a way that places and their officials desired: more jobs, more growth, and more output. That things did not work out this way raises several questions: Why did incentives dwarf all other aspects of what states and localities did to affect their economies? Why did business and government alike embrace their use? What role are incentives likely to play in place development in the 1990s?

The escalation and national scope of inducement wars dates from the mid-1970s, propelled by shifts in regional economies and competition in which the unchecked and, at times, indiscriminate use of incentive packages became common practice in a new era of smokestack chasing.[20] Between 1966 and 1980, virtually every state introduced at least one new financial incentive, tax exemption, or special service in an effort to attract or retain industry. The Council of State Governments, the National Governors Association, the National Association of State Development Officials documented the escalation of incentives and their use.[21]

Once Scranton, Pennsylvania, lured the first foreign auto producer, Volkswagen, to locate there in 1978 with a $78 million incentive package, the quest for attracting high-paying auto industry jobs would work its way through the entire U.S. economy with related impacts on other industries and sectors. From 1978 to 1988, Japanese car makers opened seven major assembly plants in the United States (and three in Canada) and more than 200 part suppliers followed. In the midst of the transplant phenomena, General Motors announced in 1985 that it would build a $5 billion manufacturing complex to produce up to 500,000 subcompacts called the Saturn by 1989. Some thirty-eight states made a public or private proposal; more than half of these states' governors embraced Saturn as both a personal and political campaign and marched to GM's Warren, Michigan, Technical Center armed with glowing brochures, videotapes, and bundles of goodies to offer the corporate giant. Reportedly, the winning state would get 6,000 plant jobs, 22,000 related jobs in the community, and a minimum $500 million boost to the economy.[22]

Little wonder, then, that in the industrial heartland of the Midwest—written off as the center of American manufacturing by some in the 1970s—the auto chase would spark an incentive feeding frenzy that, over time, began distorting the fundamental basics of business-location decisions. In 1985 alone there were, including Saturn, four major deals—Michigan landed Mazda Motor, which invested $550 million and hired 3,500 workers; Toyota Motor invested $800 million in Kentucky and employed 3,500 workers; and Diamond Star Motor pledged $600 million to Illinois and hired 2,500 workers.[23] The heated Midwest auto competition battle soon spread to other regions, other industries, and other sectors.

At a time of vast economic dislocation and business restructuring, one can understand why businesses expected places to bid for their services. Equally understandable is why places engaged in incentive bidding. On the one hand, places came to be blamed for selectively and unnecessarily increasing the profits of individual firms by subsidizing capital costs and/or lowering operating costs, while businesses, on the other hand, are accused of playing free agent, selling out to the highest bidder. Each side blamed the other.

In its infancy, incentives had a certain compelling logic, namely that incentives offered a temporary advantage, a competitive edge, a kind of early-bird-gets-the-worm reasoning. As more states and places joined the incentives contest, competitive advantages blurred. However, a negative-sum game (where all bidders lose) did not end the practice. Places are still willing to offer incentives to attract or retain a business.

From the vantage of elected public officials, inducements initially constituted a win-win game, irrespective of what economists and others may think. Should officials fail to grant a concession or play the bidding game, either the failure to attract a business or the loss of a business could cause them to lose the next election. Should they overpay or offer incentives that detract from other values (tax equity) and get a firm to come or to stay, greater short-term political risk still lies with the former rather than the latter.[24] For defensive reasons alone, incentives escalated. This entire period can be captured, perhaps, by an editorial from the *Chicago Tribune* boasting that Illinois would enjoy great benefits from the pursuit in 1985 of GM's Saturn automobile plant:

> It may not get the plant, but it has demonstrated that it understands the value of new industry and that it knows how to put together a package of inducements that can't be beat. That's an important message to send to business here, around the country—and overseas.[25]

What changed this political-economic calculus? What has deescalated the unchecked arms race of incentives and suggests that incentives will play a far less important position in place development in the 1990s? Several factors produced this change: (1) disappointed expectations; (2) the 1990–92 recession; and (3) a growing recognition of the economic importance of other place-development strategies. Let's look at each trend briefly.

Evidence mounted that various incentives fell well short of their touted benefits. It was clear from several of the most celebrated bidding wars that incentives had failed or, at best, not lived up to expectations. Scranton's VW plant closed in 1988; the billion-dollar Texas Supercollider failed to generate adequate federal funding; Chrysler sold its share of the Mitsubishi plant venture in Bloomington/Normal after Illinois had invested $88.8 million in the project. Bidding wars and bloated incentive packages began to draw negative media attention when it was pointed out that place buyers were paying in excess of $100,000 for each net new job. Furthermore, evidence emerged that footloose firms

EXHIBIT 9-2

Courting Mr. Clean

John Vlahakis, executive vice-president of Venus Laboratories, Inc., discovered that a small manufacturer could benefit from the incentive wars. He announced to the media that he was unhappy with Illinois's business climate and would entertain offers to move. A detergent manufacturer employing only 100 workers in normal times, he thought that his wanderlust would be ignored. On the contrary, in the new competitive environment he was overwhelmed with offers. The Seaway Port Authority of Duluth, Minnesota, offered him prime, free land at its airport. Ubiquitous Wisconsin offered $500,000 in training, 30 percent reduction in electricity rates, free water, and bargain land costs. Iowa flew him around the state in a LearJet searching for sites and promising a version of Monty Hall's "Let's Make A Deal." He decided he would meet with Missouri, but delayed offers of meeting with other states. Vlahakis had seen the holdups staged by Rust-Oleum, Subaru, and Penney's and decided a small company should benefit.

Sources: Interview with John Vlahakis, June 17, 1991. Also see Tom Androeli, "We Suspect This Gentleman's Phone Will Be Busy This Week," *Crain's Chicago Business,* July 15, 1991, p. 8.

that shopped for the best inducements also tended to move again when the firm-specific benefits were exhausted or cost advantages could be found elsewhere.

What helped sour the public on incentives was not simply failed deals, but that corporations and their negotiators were taking advantage of the public. Places were being played off against one another over jobs and being whipsawed on concessions (see exhibit 9-2). Louisville triumphed over Kansas City for the location of the national headquarters of the Presbyterian Church USA with a $30 million package. San Antonio outbid numerous suitors for expansion of Orlando's Sea World with a donated loan and a 100 percent property tax abatement.

A public reaction began to take place against politicians who offered excessive incentive packages. Indiana's lieutenant governor John Mutz, under whom economic development responsibilities had resided, lost his bid for governor when the public perceived the true costs of attracting the Japanese owned Subaru-Isuzu plant to Lafayette. That successful incentive packages could be used against incumbents in Indiana, Illinois, and elsewhere turned a political win-win game into a political uncertainty. Elected officials could stiffen their resistance to corporate blackmail. The game had changed and with it, the size and importance of incentive packages.

Public officials became better place bargainers. They developed more consistent policies on subsidies as opposed to ad-hoc, case-by-case actions. They developed the analytical capability to evaluate costs and benefits of subsidies, and learned in many cases to negotiate with businesses as equal partners. Finally, they learned how to protect themselves and public investments through legally binding contracts that included cancellation of agreements for nonperformance and recovery of subsidy expenditures, penalties, and adjustments for renegotiation of agreements and nonperformance.

The 1990–92 recession contributed temporarily to the de-escalation of bidding wars. In this period, states raised taxes and cut expenditures by nearly $50 billion. Several southern states found their economies in shambles once their low-cost firms could no longer compete with lower-cost foreign competition. Public officials were not about to run the risk of offering huge tax incentives to attract jobs during a period in which they were laying off employees, cutting public services, and raising taxes. The National Governors Association held several meetings on actions to stem the incentive war, while governors regionally warmed to the notion of treaties and agreements not to raid each other's businesses.

Finally, successful place development requires policies and strategies that transcend the narrow use of incentives. Place development also involves human capital development, education and training, physical infrastructure, business and environmental regulation, land use, natural resources, fiscal stability, quality of life, and other considerations. These other functions fall within state and local spheres of influence, and have far greater impact on place development than smokestack chasing or incentives. Once these other factors gained greater recognition and visibility on the place development scale of importance, incentives diminished in importance and use.

RETAINING AND EXPANDING EXISTING BUSINESSES

The principal cause producing a strategy shift from attraction to retention and business expansion was the mounting evidence that the vast majority of new jobs generated in the United States came from existing companies and new business start-ups. Local governments needed to retain existing businesses as the first line of defense. Otherwise, jobs would be lost and outside businesses might interpret this to mean that such places had troubled economies, a poor business climate, or that taxes would rise to compensate for revenues lost by move-outs.

Currently, retention and local business expansion have been the most widely embraced place development strategies and are likely to remain so for the foreseeable future.[26] Pennsylvania epitomized a state-led effort to make its industries more competitive, improve their business climate, and to invest in technologies and innovations to allow existing businesses to grow and new businesses to start. Pennsylvania lost more than one-quarter of its manufacturing jobs between 1979 and 1984, while its forty largest corporations lost one-half of their employment base. With four of the nation's top fifty graduate research institutions and as a leader in engineering training, Pennsylvania focused on making its economic base and businesses more competitive. In rejecting business attraction—a repudiation of its earlier VW plant acquisition—Pennsylvania's Ben Franklin Partnership between universities and the private sector became a national model for spurring innovation, commercializing new technologies, and assisting mature businesses to adapt to technology changes. The partnership also invested in job training and retraining of workers in new technologies and their applications.[27]

The shift to business retention is epitomized by two local government leaders, one which pioneered this strategy, and the other which recorded modest successes in implementing it. The Philadelphia Industrial Development Corporation (PIDC), organized in 1958 as a quasi-public partnership of the Greater Philadelphia Chamber of Commerce and the city of Philadelphia, became one of the—if not the first—city-based economic development agencies in the country with powers to incur debt, condemn land, and bank vacant land. Starting in the early 1970s, PIDC focused on business retention, reorienting its marketing strategies into intraorganizational marketing, namely how to get city agencies and personnel to better

EXHIBIT 9-3

Illinois Retains Sears and Loser Charlotte Celebrates

On October 31, 1988, Sears, Roebuck & Company, a much-mentioned takeover target, announced that it was putting its $1 billion plus, ninety-five-story Sears Tower up for sale, relocating its 6,000 member Merchandise Group from Chicago to "smaller, less costly facilities over the next several years, possibly in the Chicago suburbs or another state." Sears Chairman Edward A. Brennan stated at the time that, "Our desire is to stay in the Chicagoland area, but it is our responsibility to keep all of our options open." At this point, then Illinois Governor James Thompson publicly committed the "full resources" of his office to help Sears find a suitable Illinois location.

What followed was an eight-month drama in which Sears rejected a city of Chicago location, downsized its estimates of employee relocation, and narrowed its selection to Atlanta, Charlotte, Dallas, Denver, Houston, Kansas City, and Pittsburgh, besides Chicago's suburbs. Illinois' negotiation strategy was to find out what

serve existing business customers. PIDC developed a field service operation that contacted every substantial Philadelphia employer annually to determine how the city could better service existing business. It developed an early warning system on possible business move-outs as well as on businesses considering expansion. While Philadelphia would experience political and financial instability in later years, its example influenced countless others' approaches to place development.[28]

One constant that runs through place development activities is businesses' need for decisions about uses of public authority on land, site planning, construction schedules, infrastructure improvements, and approvals. Places that consolidate, economize, and expedite these tasks gain an advantage. PIDC also established a reputation as a leading proponent of "one-stop shopping"—a single city agency that satisfies business clients' needs on problems that invariably cut across dozens

Sears needed, and to provide multiple offers and eventually meet Sears's asking price. Due to Sears's identification as the symbol of Chicago's strong retail business, and Thompson's determination not to let Sears leave, the Sears saga attracted national and international attention. Should Illinois lose 6,000 jobs, Illinois officials publicly proclaimed that it would cost the state $411 million in personal income tax revenue, $19.4 million in other state and local taxes, 2,200 indirect jobs, and nearly $1 billion in total direct and indirect costs. The saga concluded on June 26, 1989, when Sears announced the move of its Merchandise Group to Hoffman Estates, a northwest Chicago suburb in the so-called "Golden Corridor," at an estimated incentive package of $107 million.

The city of Charlotte demonstrated how to handle a loss only one month after Hoffman Estates was awarded the prize. The city ran a full-page ad with the headline "You've heard about the incentives that kept Sears in Chicago. Now read about the ones that almost brought them to Charlotte." The ad then recited a long list of new acquisitions ranging from a National Basketball Association team to Okuma Machine Tools. Charlotte understands that a competitive environment demands an optimistic viewpoint and a witty copy editor.

Sources: Merrill Goozner, "City Meets Sears to Save Jobs," *Chicago Tribune*, November 11, 1988, p. 1; and Charlotte ad in *Crain's Chicago Business*, July 31, 1991, p. 13.

of city agencies: taxes, regulation, permits, utilities, parking, snow and trash removal, employee security, access roads, and so forth. This concept of concentrated customer service and intraorganizational marketing became the foundation on which many successful business retention programs have been built.

The shift to business retention strategy did not immunize places from getting involved in retention mega-deals comparable to the ones used to attract companies. Civic pride and political incumbent survival lead many places to "overpay" for retaining companies that threatened to leave (see exhibits 9–3 and 9–4).

Localities, in emphasizing retention strategies, need to distinguish between companies worth retaining and those that are not. Such distinctions are easier with hindsight than factual determinations made at

EXHIBIT 9–4

Arlington and Ypsilanti Fight to Retain a GM Plant

In December 1991, following record losses, General Motors Corporation's president announced that the nation's largest automobile producer would reduce employment by 74,000 jobs and close 21 plants. In consolidating production, GM would close one of its two rear-wheel car plants: either Arlington, Texas, twenty miles west of Dallas–Ft. Worth, or the Willow Run plant in Ypsilanti, Michigan, twenty miles west of Detroit.

Opened in 1950, when Arlington was a small farm town of 7,800 people, the GM plant is the largest private employer and local taxpayer in what is now Texas' seventh largest city. Arlington's closure could cost the Texas economy more than $1 billion, $208 million in income, 3,750 GM jobs, and 7,800 non-GM jobs. Ypsilanti's Willow Run plant had a 1990 payroll of nearly $180 million and 2,600 jobs. Its closure would cost the 60,000 people in Ypsilanti $50 million in personal income and $35 million in retail sales, and the loss of another 10,000 non-GM jobs in Michigan. Previously, both communities had made tax concessions to protect their GM plants.

the time when emotions run high. By subsidizing inefficient, technologically laggard, noncompetitive businesses in the name of business retention, states and localities simply delay the inevitable—plant closings, business failures, and job loss. In providing grants and loans to workers to buy a company or facility, places assume considerable risk should the firm fail later. Some places sought to restrain or delay change by enacting plant closing legislation, severance and site clean-up requirements, tax penalties for closing, and the like. While business retention and expansion strategies offer more potential than conventional business attraction strategies, they also invite abuses that can harm investment and discourage businesses from locating or starting in a particular place. Thus, retention policies and programs should be

In a classic zero-sum game, two communities more than 1,000 miles apart were pitted against one another for survival of their largest manufacturing employer. While GM officials maintained that they were not going to whipsaw the communities or states for concessions, these governments fought desperately for their survival. The threatened loss of Texas' only automobile plant mobilized the governor and the state's congressional delegation. In Ypsilanti, the stakes were even greater due to GM and Ford auto parts plants in the community that could go down with the GM plant closing. While Michigan officials were committed to fighting for jobs at Willow Run, a spokesman for Republican Governor John Engler insisted, "What we are not going to do is get into an incentives war to pay them to work here." Texas Governor Ann Richards later noted that her state wanted to make GM an offer it couldn't refuse. Governor Engler responded that he would "match anything Texas offers." Arlington, with an aggressive package of inducements including crucial labor concessions, was the victor.

Would this situation be a harbinger of the next round in state incentive wars, not over the location of a new plant or even beggar-thy-neighbor moving a plant from one state to another, but rather a form of industrial triage? An ailing business giant seeking to remain competitive downsizes and consolidates and, in so doing, decides among the various wounded plants and communities, whom to let live and whom to let die.

Sources: See Thomas Hayes, "A Crusade to Save the Soul of Arlington," *New York Times*, January 12, 1992, sec. 3, pp. 1–2; Donna Rosato, "GM Rebuffs Bids," *USA TODAY*, February 6, 1992, p. B1; and Hayes, "Making a Difference," *New York Times*, March 1, 1992, p. 10F.

compatible with market forces and trends, rather than be antimarket or simply punitive.

PROMOTING SMALL BUSINESS AND FOSTERING NEW BUSINESS START-UPS

By the mid-1980s, place development strategies turned a third time, from attraction and retention to helping new businesses start and expand. In seeking to promote new business start-ups, place strategists worked with the marketplace to support new technologies, improve job training and employee education, and fill in financing gaps in capital markets. This focus constituted a new phase in place development, one not built on an abundance of incentives, but rather around quality schools and universities; quality workers; quality airports, telecommunications, and infrastructure; and quality government. This shift from quantity (land, labor, incentives) to quality spawned new and innovative place improvement strategies (see exhibit 9-5).

In *Laboratories for Democracy*, David Osborne found that places adapting to this new focus increasingly sought to improve their intellectual infrastructure by upgrading their universities and creating programs to stimulate the development and commercialization of new technologies. At least four models emerged: (1) research parks which numbered more than 300 in 1990; (2) business-academic research consortia of which scores of thriving entities now exist; (3) matching public research grants to businesses for the development of new technologies with high commercial applications and for new manufacturing processes which many states and a number of localities now provide; and (4) the much emulated Ben Franklin Partnership that Osborne calls the comprehensive model insofar as each of its Advanced Technology Centers works through public-private partnerships geared to a particular local market, businesses, and education needs.[29]

Nearly all place-development programs geared to enterprise development have sought to overcome the aversion of private capital markets to funding start-up firms. To overcome these market deficiencies and the control costs imposed by private venture capital, place developers started their own seed capital programs in Pennsylvania, Michigan, and elsewhere. New public-private partnerships for risk lending emerged to help new companies at various start-up-stages.

The task of getting major corporations, universities, and entrepreneurs together has taken on several distinctive forms: technology centers, business incubators, and research consortia. Few places could replicate what MIT has done for Massachusetts's economy in spinning off hardware and software companies. Situated next to MIT, East Cambridge, an area of one square mile, created an estimated 17,000 new jobs between 1983 and 1990—more jobs than produced by eight states over the same period.[30] Ranging from major universities to networks of local community colleges, examples abound of how places have used educational programs to bring together business, academia, entrepreneurs, financiers, and others to promote new business development.

EXHIBIT 9–5

Omaha Turns Talk into a Dominant Industry

A classic example of how a Midwestern city has taken advantage of its location, trained labor force, and other assets is Omaha—a telemarketing–telecommunications center with more than twenty-five telemarketing and reservation systems, and more than 10,000 jobs in this growth field.

Besides its location in the Central time zone, the city of 350,000 people has inexpensive real estate, moderate wages and living costs, a reliable labor force, and a twentieth-century state-of-the-art telecommunications center, bolstered by the Defense Department's Strategic Air Command. Omaha's advantages lie not only in being one of the first junctions of east–west and north–south fiber optic lines, but also in supporting the new equipment with concentrated "know-how"—training programs that have produced a pool of managerial and service personnel unmatched by any other medium-size city in the United States.

Other places around the world have joined the telecommunications competition. The scramble among London, Zurich, Frankfurt, and Paris to be Europe's financial capital turns largely on who is first to develop a state-of-the-art telecommunications center. In the telecommunications war, time zones have become more important than geographic boundaries. Information networks in the 1990s are as important as railroad lines were in the 1890s. Thus, the decentralizing forces of the Information Age are making possible opportunities for places that simply did not exist two decades ago, when the place competition game first accelerated.

Source: Barnaby J. Feder, "Omaha: Talk, Talk, Talk of Telemarketing," New York Times, July 20, 1991, p. 1.

David Birch's writings have given a boost to practitioners seeking alternative strategies to the fading allure of business attraction. In *The Job Generation Process*, Birch found that for the 1969–1976 period, companies employing fewer than 100 had created 82 percent of net new U.S. jobs.[31] This finding, *that small business had become the dy-*

namic engine behind job growth, has been revised and refined over time
due to considerable variances among states and places, and several
business-economic cycles. Birch's findings, nevertheless, have remained essentially intact. He provided the data and support that place
practitioners and others needed to change strategies, approaches, and
programs to move from business attraction to retention, and from retention to growing a place's own businesses.

The small business as the salvation of the U.S. economy thesis needs
to be qualified. Small businesses that grow often require a decade or
more to develop. Furthermore, most do not grow, but their failure rate
may not be as high as commonly believed. Based on his analysis of 9
million companies in Dun & Bradstreet and Small Business Administration files for the 1970–1988 period, Birch found that 40 percent of all
new business start-ups survived at least six years; and, in fact, at least 66
percent of those that survived that long, added jobs.[32] These data became important for identifying new or emerging growth-oriented companies and assisting them wherever possible in their efforts. In tracking
17 million firms since 1969, Birch identified some 700,000 firms that
have experienced growth levels of 20 percent or more per year which
he labeled "gazelles." In contrast, "elephants" comprised 7,000 or so
publicly listed, larger firms, whose growth rates were minimal, while
"mice" constituted another 16 to 17 million firms of four or fewer employees that didn't grow at all, or failed. The implication for local place
developers is clear, namely, find the gazelles and do what you can to
help them grow or remain where they are.[33]

Yet, distinguishing among gazelles, elephants, and mice is not a simple task. While places may create a more entrepreneurial environment,
foster new technologies, and help new businesses start, these activities
are no guarantee of success. Investment and lending programs can be
costly, the incubation of new businesses may take years to materialize,
and efforts to pick winners can run against competitive market forces
and technological advances. Both the much emulated Silicon Valley
and Boston's Route 128 experience boom and bust cycles, and dozens
of research parks have turned into highly subsidized real estate ventures. Efforts to target public pension fund investments (whose assets
approximated $800 billion in 1990) to geographically defined busi-
nesses (e.g., state, county, or city) can limit returns, run against diversification, and increase risks of poor returns. States are better positioned
and usually can draw more talent than a locality, while partnerships
between public and private organizations that syndicate risks are pref-

erable to a single government unit going it alone. For many places, the amount of risk-lending capital is so small that it is unlikely to have much impact on local or state economy, while one bad loan or experience can greatly detract from future expansion. Most places are well advised to think before acting.

Whether or not a place is actively supportive of new business development can be better assessed by answering the questions developed for places and shown in exhibit 9–6. Anything less than a passing score on this imperfect, but still useful, litmus test probably warrants a reassessment by a place of its commitment to new business development.

CONCLUSION

The worldwide competition for attracting and retaining business has forged new directions for place-development practices. What practices, approaches, incentives, or policies work, and which do not? We believe that under certain conditions, some policies work better than others and the following seeks to sort out some of the differences.

Starting in the 1970s, sweeping economic changes led to a strong public demand for government action. Economic transformation constituted an enormous challenge. The task was compounded by a realignment of political and governmental responsibilities which thrust places—states and localities—into new roles in place development.

The decade of the 1970s vastly accelerated the fortunes of specific industries and the places to which they were tied. A painful economic transition occurred for places from a stable industrial economy that dominated global markets to a rapidly changing, knowledge-intensive economy subject to fierce global competition. Without an underlying understanding of market dynamics or industry competitive structures, places rushed in to replace lost jobs and business by reaching out to capture relocators, whether home or abroad. When that strategy either failed, fell short of expectations, or proved prohibitively expensive, places next turned to retaining those industries or businesses they already had, or emphasized helping existing businesses to grow or expand. That, too, proved to be only moderately successful and fell short of expectations. This approach alone could not stem the tide of new technologies, competitive forces, and industrial restructuring. Finally, places moved to a third generic strategy, one broader and more compatible with market forces, namely developing their own economies and businesses. This latter approach embraced vast experimentation with

EXHIBIT 9-6

A Business Climate Test to Measure Your Place's Entrepreneurial Climate

Background: Since the late 1980s, nearly all places embrace a strategy of promoting new business start-ups and small business growth and development. While no definitive test exists to measure a favorable climate or culture conducive to grow your own businesses, the following ten-question quiz developed by *Inc.* magazine provides a rough approximation of where your community stands. With ten points for each favorable answer, a passing grade is sixty points. Places can periodically use the test to measure goals and achievements in new business development.

1. When the mayor of the city meets with business leaders, are there as many chief executive officers of mid-size growth companies as bankers and corporate executives?
2. Are entrepreneurs invited to join the best athletic, social, and country clubs?
3. Does the local newspaper follow the fortunes of start-ups and mid-size growth companies with the same intensity and sophistication as it does large corporations?
4. Are innovative companies able to recruit nearly all of their professional work force from the local area?
5. Is there a sizable, visible venture capital community?
6. Does the local university encourage its faculty and its students to participate in entrepreneurial spin-offs?
7. Do growth-company CEOs and venture capitalists hold even a quarter of the seats on the boards of the three largest banks?
8. Does the city's economic-development department spend more time helping local companies grow than it does chasing after branch facilities for out-of-state corporations?
9. Is there decent, affordable office and factory space available for businesses in the central business district?
10. Can you quickly think of 10 recent spin-offs—growth companies started by entrepreneurs—who have left large companies?

Source: "The Business Climate Test," *Inc.*, March 1988, p. 81. Reprinted with permission, *Inc.* magazine, March 1988. Copyright 1988 by Goldhirsh Groups, Inc., 38 Commercial Wharf, Boston, MA 02110.

new programs that used public and private resources to help mature industries adapt; to develop and apply new technologies; to improve work force skills; to foster new business start-ups, and to facilitate new business growth.

One lesson learned was that places could not bend the marketplace to respond to what government wanted, but had to respond positively to the trends and forces that directed the marketplace.[34] Reactive policies and actions to stem market forces proved unsuccessful, while proactive and interactive responses enabled places to work with business in creative ways that accommodated market forces. In this learning process, government responses lagged market changes and policies failed to adjust quickly enough to industry changes.

A second related lesson is that places, like investors, often felt that they could outperform the market; pick winners and losers; carve out and retain market niches; successfully target industries and technologies for growth and expansion; select the right foreign investments; identify the best industries for retention; or create the optimum environment for entrepreneurship to flourish. Although this approach offered certain advantages over smokestack chasing or indiscriminate efforts to capture footloose industries, places like businesses still faced the unpredictability of markets. A place's comparative advantages provided some useful insights and clues to opportunities, but competitive forces were still far beyond a place's influence or control.

A third lesson is that place development far transcends narrowly defined economic development programs, policies, agencies, and institutions. The Committee for Economic Development refers to these broader place roles and responsibilities as the foundations on which an economy needs to grow, adapt, and compete: a capable and motivated work force; sound physical infrastructure; well-managed environment and natural resources; universities and other research institutions; a system of regulation, capital, and technical assistance that encourages business growth and development; a quality of life attractive to business and their employees; and fiscal stability. As Scott Fosler observed, "The new strategies conceive of a state or local jurisdiction as a far more complex unit of production, in which numerous parts—social and political, as well as those strictly defined as economic—are integrally related to one another."[35] Following on this bigger picture of place development, or the economic-foundations approach, is the blurring of relationships and responsibilities between public and private sectors. These include new partnerships, new institutions, and new approaches to carry out multiple, complex place-development activities. A broader, more inclusive view of place development proves more dynamic, catalytic, interactive, and responsive than a top-down agency-program model of development.

A fourth lesson involves balance, stability, and an incremental approach to place development. Once places learned that what works is ambiguous and uncertain, and that no magical panaceas existed for place development, many recognized the folly of betting the ranch on a single approach, a single investment, or even a single industry to ride to prosperity. Those places that had a diversified economy or the potential to move to diversify were motivated, like the prudent investor, to develop a mixed and diversified portfolio to hedge against dependency on a single industry or sector. A place's economic incentives and approaches should not so distort location choices that they foster inequities in tax policies, skew expenditures away from public services, neglect infrastructure, or underinvest in human capital. A narrow focus on policies or actions could well yield beneficial consequences for a specific business or industry, but may have far more detrimental consequences on existing businesses, other firms, and household decisions about where to live. Consequently, places would be better off adopting balanced strategies (retain, attract, grow new businesses), emphasizing basic services, and looking after amenities rather than subordinating everything to economic development.

Incentives should be seen as a limited technique to be evaluated on its merits. As a generalization, one can think of incentives as costs to the provider and benefits to the receiver. In most cases involving the subsidization of capital and credit (loans, grants, tax abatements tied to capital investments), the cost to the government providing the subsidy exceeds the benefits to the firm. Similarly, the cost-benefit ratios for places generally overstate immediate benefits and, depending on choice of economic multipliers used, often exaggerate the ripple effect of secondary benefits from business attraction or retention.[36] On the other hand, one can point to incentives and programs where costs are minimal, leverage great, and distortion potential low. For example, programs that reduce information costs—where to obtain capital, location specific data, labor force availability, how to facilitate exports, technology transfer, and the like—can be extremely beneficial to places and businesses.

Finally, the reality of the incentives race is that no place can long eschew their practical use. In late 1991, New Jersey, Connecticut, New

York State, and New York City signed a non-aggression pact to prevent companies from playing one part of the New York Metro region against another and reduce public subsidies aimed at encouraging this. The four governments also pledged to cooperate on regional marketing and regional development. Within a year even this modest joint effort had fallen into disrepute as all four had greatly increased their incentives, raided each other's businesses, and invited retaliation. In this case, economic development had triumphed over neighborliness.[37]

10

Expanding Exports and Stimulating Foreign Investment

Sweden is an unlikely place to place-brand an alcoholic product. The country has a strong tradition of temperance; as late as 1955 the use of alcohol had been severely rationed. Nonetheless, the success of state-owned Absolut Vodka is one of the great export stories, capturing more than half of the large, highly competitive United States market for imported vodka in the last ten years. When consumers now think of vodka, they think of Sweden and that, of course, is crucial to their large export success.[1]

Clearly, places can improve their economy by attracting tourists and business, but places can also grow by encouraging their businesses to export. This chapter is about how state and local governments and their officials can promote trade and foreign investment. Export promotion has emerged as a major place development strategy and it is likely to command an even more important position in the years ahead. We examine the following questions in this chapter:

- How important are exports to a place's economy?
- What firms currently export, and what goods and services produced in a place's economy have the greatest export potential?
- What programs, services, and activities can be offered that most effectively assist existing exporters to expand, and nonexporters to export?
- What strategies can a place use to enhance the image of its export-

able products, and to transfer a positive place identification to these products?

• What evidence is there that export promotion programs work?

HOW IMPORTANT ARE EXPORTS TO A PLACE'S ECONOMY?

Exports are the amount and value of goods and services produced in one place that are sold and shipped to another place. A place without exports is almost unimaginable because it would be a place that consumes everything it produces. Imagine a place that grows only apples and consumes all of the apples locally. The place would need to import other goods that it did not produce: food stocks, computers, automobiles, and so on. But then, how is the place to pay for the goods it imports? Ultimately, the place would have to develop some exports to pay for its imports.

For many cities, regions, and nations, exports are their lifeblood. Singapore and Hong Kong live or die by their exports. Their wealth depends on aggressively exporting their products—shoes, consumer electronics, bank loans, and clothing—to be able to pay for the goods they import. Somewhat larger countries such as Finland, Sweden, Norway, Denmark, Belgium, and the Netherlands have achieved a high proficiency in foreign trade because their domestic markets are too small. Overall, the twelve European Community nations' exports averaged more than 30 percent of their GNP in 1989. Historically, the living standards in these nations are closely linked to their export success.

Exports not only serve to pay for imports but, in many countries, they are also the foundation for the country's power and prosperity. This is certainly the case for Japan, Taiwan, and South Korea. Japan represents the extreme case of a country that produces many goods the world wants—consumer electronics, automobiles and motorcycles, watches, musical instruments, and computers. Japan's export strength did not occur accidentally but through the careful and sophisticated encouragement and support of exports by the central government and its financial institutions.

Two decades ago. U.S. firms produced nearly 100 percent of the home electronics bought in America; today they make less than 5 percent. Twenty years ago foreign-made automobiles commanded only a 10 percent share of the U.S. auto market; today, foreign imports plus

EXHIBIT 10-1

Buffalo: Resurgence from Trade

In 1991, the *New York Times* declared that Buffalo was now certifiably recovered. An editorial conceded that the put-down from the musical *A Chorus Line*—"a place where suicide would be redundant"—and the endless jokes about being snowbound are now out of favor. The evidence of a turnaround is everywhere. For the first time since the late 1970s, the city's unemployment rate fell below the state average in 1990. Runner-up in Super Bowl XXVI, Buffalo waged a fanatical crusade to win a major league expansion baseball team, and can point to new growth in business expansion, shopping malls, and small business development. The reason for this revival is the 1988 U.S.-Canadian Free Trade Pact that changed the way business operates in North America and is the largest and most complex trading relationship in the world.

Victimized in the past by its frost-belt geography, Buffalo is now the beneficiary of its location across the Niagara River from Canada, our nation's largest trading partner. With relatively inexpensive real estate, affordable labor, and good transportation access, Buffalo and Erie County have become a new gateway to the

Japanese transplants now command nearly 40 percent. In 1970, some 20 percent of American-made goods faced foreign competition. In the 1990's, 75 percent face competition. Globalization had become a reality to U.S. business, leaving no place unaffected.

The importance of export trade cannot be underestimated. Buffalo's recent revival is largely attributable to its international position as a gateway to Canada's largest markets and the United States–Canadian Free Trade Agreement of 1988 (see exhibit 10–1). Houston is a classic example of a U.S. city that has newly positioned itself between New York and Los Angeles as an international world-class city, port, and gateway to world commerce (see exhibit 10–2).

The benefit that a place gets from foreign trade largely depends on whether its industries are export-oriented or import-competing. Places

huge American market. Within viewing distance of the abandoned Bethlehem Steel Mill that employed 22,000 workers at its
peak before closing in 1983, commercial and industrial parks are
expanding with plans underway for a 1.5-million-square-foot factory outlet mall—arguably a new world size leader. Cross-border
shopping, as measured by same-day trips, jumped by more than 20
percent in 1990–91 amounting to as much as $2 billion a year
across the 4,000 mile U.S.-Canadian border. Canadian shoppers
take advantage of lower prices, cheap fuel, and the weaker U.S.
dollar. Since 1988, more than ninety Canadian companies have
relocated or expanded in the Buffalo area due to taxes, wages, real
estate, and market access opportunities. Similar prosperity and diversification is also occurring in Port Huron, Michigan, and Platts-
burgh, New York. In the trade wars, one place's resurgence is
another's collapse; Buffalo's rise is at Canada's expense.

Sources: John Pettibone Mackenzie, "Editorial Notebook; Buffalo Finally Fa-
vored," *New York Times,* January 23, 1991, p. 18; Kevin Sack, "Buffalo Moves
from Rust Belt to Money Belt," *New York Times,* July 20, 1990, p. A14; Bernard
Wysocki, "Canada Suffers Exodus of Jobs and Shoppers," *Wall Street Journal,*
June 20, 1991, p. 1; and Alan Freeman, "Ottawa Foresaw Effects," *The Globe and
Mail,* September 18, 1991, p. 1.

strong in export-oriented industries—aircraft, business services, chemicals, and computers—benefit directly and through the ripple effects of
these exports on local employment and purchasing power. Places
strong in import-competing industries—auto, textiles, consumer electronics, metal products, and tires—are likely to be hurt by growing imports. Some places seek to export more (export promotion). Others
seek to reduce current imports by making goods and services at home
(import substitution).[2]

An example where the two basic strategies coincide is the new emphasis states and cities give to small business matchmaking. Matchmak-
ers basically are brokers who uncover local businesses that can provide
goods and services to purchasers who are currently buying from suppliers out of the state or area. A centralized matchmaking program can be
more efficient, effective, and less costly than private piecemeal under-
takings. For example, matching enables an Oregon producer to replace
an out-of-state or foreign supplier with a local one (import substitution)

EXHIBIT 10-2

Houston: A New International Place

- International business as core—service, financial, medical, and manufacturing center;
- Port of Houston, largest U.S. port (1988) based on foreign trade tonnage, valued at $22 billion in annual export/import trade;
- 53 foreign consulates and 61 foreign banks—largest number in South and Southwest;
- 574 Houston companies with operations in 108 foreign countries; 623 foreign companies from 51 nations;
- Houston's Texas Medical Center is the largest collection of medical institutions in the world, and largest concentration of doctors, scientists, and researchers in the United States;
- Fourth largest U.S. city, located in third largest state, and sixth fastest growing U.S. state;
- Gross Metropolitan Area Product approaches $100 billion; with a 500-mile metro-area of 29 million people or 12 percent of the U.S. population;
- 13 Fortune 500 company headquarters; 21 companies on the Forbes 500 list.

Source: Exhibits and testimony of the city of Houston and the Greater Houston Chamber of Commerce before the U.S. Department of Transportation, Washington, D.C., U.S. Japan Service Case Docket 46438, April 1990.

and puts a foreign or out-of-state producer in touch with an Oregon supplier (export promotions). Matchmaking programs expand small businesses' access to new markets (local, out of state, and abroad), and often tap unused skills, resources, and engineering capabilities where new products are developed to meet a procurement need.[3] Oregon, Washington, Colorado, Tennessee, and New York have adopted matchmaking programs.

As places adapt to global competition, they may encounter indifference and even resistance. Pollster Daniel Yankelovich observed that "over 80 percent of Americans say they have heard or read something about competitiveness, and equal numbers are aware of our trade deficit, but genuine understanding is absent."[4] Polls conducted in 1991 by the Council on Competitiveness found that Americans blame the country as a whole for not responding to economic competitive challenges, and specifically government itself as being responsible for the greatest blame.[5] Exhibit 10-3 describes how state leaders are waking up to globalization.

ASSESSING A PLACE'S EXPORT POTENTIAL

Export promotion begins with identifying who exports and who can potentially export. One tool, *economic base analysis*, measures the relative presence of a particular industry in a place compared to the nation as a whole. If the *export base ratio* in a place is greater than one, this suggests that the industry exports its goods or services outside the region; a ratio less than one suggests that the industry's goods or services are partly imported. Thus if 15 percent of Detroit's workers are in the auto industry, and only 5 percent of the nation's workers are in the auto industry, we can assume that Detroit's auto industry exports some cars, based on the premise that Detroit does not buy disproportionately more cars than the United States as a whole. This rough measuring device provides some indication of the export side of a place's economy as well as where it might have a competitive advantage.

The other task is to identify nonexporting companies and industries that have export potential. These companies can offer products or services that would possess some competitive advantage in another market, such as unique features or styling, high quality, high value for the money, or brand image strength. Some of these companies start exporting on their own for a variety of reasons: excess capacity, unsolicited orders from abroad, a competitive attack from abroad, or the pursuit of production economies of scale. At the same time, some managements hesitate because of perceived high cost, risk, or lack of export management know-how. Here, place officials can play a positive role. They can help identify foreign opportunities for companies, assist them in finding distributors or importers, provide export training, and provide export insurance and credit.

In 1991 exports accounted for 7.5 percent of the U.S. economic activity, compared to 31 percent for China, 28 percent for Germany, 27 percent for Korea, and 13.5 percent for Japan. President Bush champi-

EXHIBIT 10-3

Hitting the Road: Changing Attitudes Toward Foreign Investment

Trade promotion and foreign investment attraction emerged as place development strategies in two stages: 1969–85, and the post-1985 period. In the earlier stage, foreign activities by states and localities were largely overseas extensions of smokestack-chasing, namely attracting overseas industries with various inducements much like attracting out-of-state companies to a specific location. Virginia is credited as being the first state to go global when, in 1969, it stationed public employees in Brussels to promote the state's economic development programs. Neither states nor the U.S. Government then viewed trade and investment as very important, as evidenced by reports that the U.S. Department of Commerce had only a single employee assigned to foreign investment matters.[1] Over the next several years, a number of places touted the job benefits of this strategy: Scranton, Pennsylvania, and Volkswagen; Chesterfield County, Virginia, and Imperial Chemical Industries; Greenwood, South Carolina, and Fuji Film; Swepsonville, North Carolina, and Honda lawnmowers, to name a few.

Equally important, places sought foreign investment in the early 1980s as the U.S. dollar soared against major foreign currencies under the tight monetary and strong fiscal stimulus policies of the Reagan Administration. Imports surged, exports faltered, and huge foreign investments flowed into the United States. Where the United States had been a net exporter of foreign investment for eighty years, it became a net importer throughout the 1980s. The result was that state and local officials traversed the globe in search of foreign funds. "The rivalries between cities and states to obtain foreign investments dwarf the Super Bowl," one observer of this period noted.[2]

The shift in strategy from foreign investment and business attraction to trade promotion after 1985 stemmed from two forces—economic and political. As the recession-stricken U.S. economy recovered and interest rates declined, the U.S. dollar weakened against major foreign currencies, which helped stimulate exports. Politically, the widespread use of incentives to attract foreign firms and to court foreign ownership generated its own backlash.

Public indignation rose not only over the "Selling of America," but over the use of taxpayer subsidies for foreign competitors on U.S. soil that could cost Americans their jobs. American business expressed alarm over unfair competitive advantages being offered to foreign firms at their expense.

In this second stage of global outreach, places responded to these economic and political trends by embracing trade promotion, namely providing multiple forms of assistance to local firms to penetrate and expand their export markets. Between 1984 and 1990, state spending on export promotion grew sixfold, while the number of overseas state offices increased threefold. In this process, not only had trade development emerged as a place development strategy, but also governors, mayors, and local officials had become place ambassadors, promoting their places' businesses and people.

The 1980s brought home the lesson of global competition to places as never before. Finally, the states undertook positive actions:

- By 1986, as many states had offices in Tokyo as in Washington, D.C.
- In 1987–88, North Carolina led the nation in new manufacturing plant start-ups and major expansions, largely on the strength of foreign investment.[3]
- In 1989, forty-one state governors made eighty-two trips abroad to thirty-five countries, excluding Canada and Mexico.
- In 1990, states were spending a reported $92 million on export promotion and foreign investment recruitment, and supported 161 overseas offices.[4]
- In 1991, California's World Trade Commission guaranteed nearly $100 million in export loans, the largest among twenty-six states with export finance programs.

1. Blaine Liner, "States and Localities in the Global Marketplace," *Intergovernmental Perspective*, Spring 1990, p. 13.
2. Martin Tolchin and Susan Tolchin, *Buying into America* (New York: Times Books, 1988), p. 13.
3. Hugh O'Neill, "The Role of the States in Trade Development," *The Academy of Political Science* 37, no. 1 (1990), pp. 181–82.
4. William E. Nothdurft, "The Export Game," *Governing*, August 1992, pp. 57–61.

oned the future U.S. position as an "export superpower," while the critic William Nothdurft calls the United States the "world's biggest export underachiever."[6] The problem is that only a small number of U.S. industries currently ship a significant portion of their output overseas. The bulk of U.S. exports are shipped by high profile, larger companies in aircraft, business services, electrical machinery, chemicals, computers, and cars and trucks. More than half of all U.S. exports are provided by just one hundred companies, and only a small percentage of U.S. companies sell in more than a few overseas markets. Take Illinois, for example, a state which ranked among the top eight in the 1980s. Five industries—machinery, food products, electrical items, chemicals, and transportation equipment—have accounted for 75 to 80 percent of the state's total export value over the past two decades. Among the state's 20,000 manufacturing firms, only about 5 percent, or 900 firms, export. Illinois officials are appropriately concerned by the concentration of the state's exports, the competitive position of their firms in these industries, and by the relatively low number of Illinois firms that export. Understandably, then, Illinois has invested heavily in export promotion strategies.

Contrary to conventional wisdom that large companies are more likely to export than small ones, David Birch analyzed a sample of thousands of companies broken down by employment size (1–19; 20–49; 50–99; 100–499; and 500 plus). He found that the second largest category of exporters consisted of companies employing 20–49, while more than one-half of all exporting companies had fewer than 100 employees.[7] Also, contrary to conventions that small business exporters are high-tech firms, he found small exporters concentrated in stable or declining industries, many in low-tech—jewelry, metal working, and specialized industrial machinery—who are niche players taking advantage of technology and large industry decline. Still, close to 90 percent of U.S. small businesses export neither goods nor services. Germany, the world's largest manufacturing exporter, has long capitalized on this by targeting small manufacturing companies for export assistance (see exhibit 10-4). Nothdurft found that European nations spend nearly eight times more than the United States on promoting exports.[8]

Until recently, many places assumed that service industries had far less potential for exporting than manufacturers. Not only has the service component of U.S. trade balances grown favorably over the years but services have also proven far more exportable than once thought. Take, for example, Arthur Andersen, the largest accounting and con-

EXHIBIT 10-4

Germany Grooms Its Smaller Companies For Export

In Germany, the middle-sized companies, called collectively *Mittlestand,* are a model for successful exporting. In contrast to Japan and the United States, where large companies dominate, the 300,000 middle-sized *Mittlestand* companies contribute almost one-third of the export revenue. Germany's strategy with these companies proceeds in three phases:

1. The various state and city agencies identify companies with export potential and estimate their possible sales.
2. The *Mittlestand* companies are assisted in getting their products to market fast.
3. *Mittlestand* companies are encouraged to invest in apprenticeship programs and research and development. The products tend to be more attractive to foreign markets because they are precise and durable.

The German model emphasizes cooperation, smallness, and niche marketing. The German government is not as crucial as the local agencies that directly assist in export.

Source: Gail E. Shares and John Templeman, "Think Small," *Business Week,* November 4, 1991, pp. 58–65.

sulting firm in the nation whose domestic market grows slowly and is highly competitive. In 1990, it experienced a 35 percent revenue growth from overseas offices compared to a 14 percent growth in U.S. domestic markets.[9]

Thus, export strategies apply equally to large and small businesses, goods producers and service producers, big places and little ones. Some small U.S. towns have been rescued when one of their companies moved into exports. Glennville, Georgia, was a small town best known for its alfalfa, sweet onions, and pecans. In 1966, it had only one manufacturing industry; lawn mower replacement parts were assembled and distributed regionally by the Rotary Corporation. Thirteen years later, Rotary was a $7 million company exporting lawn mower parts to thirty-eight countries, including Singapore, Canada, Europe, and New Zealand. The Glennville example of a small company generating job growth for a small community is repeated throughout the United States and among trading nations.

At the same time, public officials must not encourage the wrong companies to undertake exports. Some businesses are not prepared to export and they must be dissuaded from making a disastrous investment. The most common mistakes of first-time exporters include:

- Poor marketing plans, inadequate preparation, and choice of the wrong markets for entry;
- Insufficient attention and/or choice of overseas agents, distributors, and partners;
- Unwillingness to modify products to meet regulations and cultural preferences, or prices to meet competition and the products acceptance price;
- Failure to print instructions, sales, and warranty messages in locally understood languages and/or to provide servicing for the product;
- Making an insufficient investment to establish a toehold or market position or, the flip side, chasing orders instead of ordering growth;
- Failure to understand the risks of overseas markets, practices, and economic-political environment.

As in any service, government support for export development activities requires client satisfaction. Accordingly, places should direct their efforts on both selling the product and counseling companies to avoid common export pitfalls.

WAYS TO ASSIST COMPANIES IN EXPORT PROMOTION

Governments and their export promotion agencies face a difficult task in converting nonexporters to exporters, and in getting current exporters to expand their activities. Export promotion agencies play at least nine roles in assisting and stimulating exports. They are informer, broker, expediter, trainer and counselor, financier, host, targeter, promoter, and facility developer.

EXHIBIT 10-5

Sources of Export Information

The U.S. and Foreign Commercial Service (USFCS), the lead federal agency for export promotion activities, has offices in 120 foreign cities and more than sixty countries. Its district offices throughout the United States provide access to the National Trade Data Bank, a computerized source for market research information gathered by government agencies. It includes thousands of market research items from detailed country studies to a listing of 46,000 foreign agents and distributors. This information is supplemented by states that maintain their own data banks generated by their overseas offices and trade representatives and geared to the state's industries, products, and markets. Localities have their own reference lists, corporate leads, and ways of matching nonexporters with executives of firms that export.

The World Trade Center Association (WCTA), a private not-for-profit corporation, with more than 200 members in sixty countries, has its own NETWORK system, a computer-based communication and trade information service. The Small Business Foundation of America operates the Export Opportunity Hotline that answers questions on foreign market research, export financing, licensing and insurance, and how to obtain help. Foreign consulates and their trade representatives operating throughout the United States help on specific country questions. For instance, the Japanese Economic Trade Representative Organization (JETRO) has more than seventy offices in the United States, and provides assistance to our firms seeking information about access to Japanese markets.

The U.S. Commerce Department has other bureaus that provide specialized trade services. The Office of Export Promotion deals with export controls and licensing. The Small Business Administration (SBA) provides publications, technical and financial assistance, workshops and seminars, and other how-to services for small business. International Economic Policy has country specialists on foreign market conditions, tariffs and business prac-

(continued)

EXHIBIT 10–5
Sources of Export Information (continued)

tices, and the latest information on multilateral trade agreements. The Export-Import Bank, a separate government sponsored enterprise, provides assistance on supplier credit and buyer credit programs. The Foreign Agriculture Service in the U.S. Department of Agriculture provides a whole range of services, much like the Commerce Department, but geared to the agriculture export market. The Agency for International Development (A.I.D.) facilitates export opportunities arising from U.S. foreign aid, while the quasi-public Overseas Private Investment Corporation (OPIC) provides risk insurance (currency and expropriation of assets) for U.S. businesses in developing countries.

Informer

Would-be exporters need information about the marketplace. Yet they often lack the resources to assess carefully market size, competitors, and the quality and integrity of distributors. They face markets with different laws, culture, currency, and language, all of which contribute to uncertainty and risks. No wonder many companies hesitate to export.

These companies can reduce the costs and risks by turning to government agencies for help. Such agencies gather and make available mountains of information at very low cost. Exhibit 10–5 describes some of the main sources of export information.

Broker

A derivative of the informer role is the more specialized brokerage function places can perform. These involve specialized services for individual companies, industries, or even products. A would-be exporter may have a new or better product to export, but have little information on a specific region or country where a potential market exists. In such cases, brokering may entail finding names of specific contacts, agents, distributors, or foreign companies to serve as licensees or joint venture partners. The U.S. Commerce Department offers three brokerage services: (1) comparative shopping service—a quick assessment of how a company's product will sell in a given market including competitors and sales channels; (2) agent/distributor service—assistance in locating foreign representatives; and (3) *world traders* data report information for evaluating potential overseas partners.

Expediter

The export promotion agency tries to match local businesses with foreign trade missions and trade shows that have promising growth markets for their products. For example, Illinois focuses on missions and shows related to auto parts, electrical equipment, food processing, and scientific instruments. Places target specific companies to participate, sometimes offering to defray part or all of the costs of travel and displays, interpreters, and other required services. Foreign and domestic office staff help identify agents, distributors, shippers, and licensing partners in a particular country or region; arrange appointments; and target prospective customers.

Catalog shows provide a less expensive alternative to trade show participation whereby companies can display goods, provide information on products in various languages, and make accessible contacts between buyers and sellers without having to travel overseas. The U.S. Department of Commerce's *Commercial News USA* is a catalog of new U.S. products and services sent to more than 100,000 overseas buyers, agents, and distributors.

Trainer and Counselor

The U.S. and Foreign Commercial Service (USFCS) and the Small Business Administration (SBA) conduct how-to seminars for exporters, bringing government officials, business experts, and trade specialists to cities throughout the nation. Places can conduct their own seminars, workshops, conferences, and training sessions working through universities and colleges, chambers of commerce, industry councils, and nonprofit organizations. Some states provide job training assistance for new-to-export and new-to-market manufacturers, while others offer job assistance training as part of their foreign investment incentives. Education, training, and counseling have all become an integral part of trade promotion services offered by places seeking to promote export growth.

Ireland has turned its counseling expertise into a marketable export. The Irish export *target marketing:* they advise countries such as Costa Rica, China, Pakistan, Nigeria, and Panama as to where and to whom to sell their products. Recently they advised Panama to market food-processing and lower-level electronics to Spain, Italy, and France. In the future, businesses will seek training and counseling where they can find it, and will not limit themselves to their own state or nation.

Financier

In 1990, some twenty-six states provided loan guarantees and other financial aid to exporters to fill a gap in federal assistance and in commercial lending. The Export-Import Bank operates strictly in Washington with assistance mainly for large corporations, while SBA and the Overseas Private Investment Corporation (OPIC) assistance is limited to investment in developing countries.

States have filled this void through state financial intermediaries with authority to borrow funds, incur debt, discount, sell, or negotiate guaranteed and nonguaranteed notes. Illinois created an Export Development Authority in 1983 to help exports, while California's World Trade Commission is generally recognized as the largest state export finance agency. Some states have created their own export trading companies. XPORT, the first publicly sponsored trading company in the country, has been an affiliate of the New York and New Jersey Port Authority since 1982. On a contractual basis XPORT helps companies provide a full service menu of export services, including marketing, matchmaking, financing, insurance, and export licenses.

Two major deterrents to selling abroad involve the time required for collection and the risk of nonpayment. Banks generally require insurance to lend against foreign orders or receivables that provide an opportunity for government involvement in export promotion through lending, insurance, and good working relations with direct lenders. Banks are, however, reluctant to deal with small businesses and small transactions.

Host

Being a good host is a catchall designation from tourism and includes promoting foreign business visitors, sponsoring foreign delegations, and cultivating sister-city relations. The benefits of the tourism and hospitality business have multiple spillovers into trade and foreign investment as some places seek to convert tourists and guests to traders and investors. Places can actively promote foreign business visitation for local trade shows and exhibitions, and arrange for meetings and contacts with local business counterparts. Dating from the postwar period, "sister" relationships have expanded from ceremonial and cultural exchanges into place-to-place relationships (state-country; state-region; and city to city) where formal agreements are consummated to enhance bilateral trade, investment, tourism, technology, education and culture. Chicago has nine sister-city relations including Osaka, Kiev, and Prague, while Illinois has signed agreements with provinces in China, Japan, Russia, Spain, Israel, and Mexico. Hawaii has more than fifty sister-city or sister-nation agreements in Asia and the Far East. These relationships may not amount to much alone, and should be viewed as building blocks in opening up places to global opportunities, relationships, and exchanges.

Targeter

Rather than being all things to all businesses, more states and places have developed lists of target industries and target companies to pursue. Depending on organizational structure and resources, targeting can be by geographic area, industries, products, and by matching overseas market opportunities to specific companies and their products.

The USFCS targets companies that have the best chance of benefiting from government export promotion services. The U.S. Commerce Department currently focuses on infrequent exporters, companies that do a small amount of exporting to a limited number of markets. Typically, these companies are "reactors," with 5 to 10 percent of their sales overseas based on orders that come to them. Infrequent exporters, an estimated 86,000 small and medium-size firms, export to fewer than five foreign markets. They constitute 80 percent of U.S. exporting companies.[10]

Promoter

While all the aforementioned activities and programs involve trade stimulation, places need an overarching program for expanding public awareness of export opportunities. Just as some places invest heavily in tourism promotion, that same investment is required to reach broader audiences on trade. Such services include general ads, hot-line services, billboards, videos, newsletters, and promotional pieces. The marketing aspect of trade promotion, in many cases, is the weak link in export development strategies. Places tend to overinvest in providing services, and underinvest in marketing them.

No two places have identical or nearly identical international trade programs because they differ in their businesses, industries, location, and export markets.[11] Exhibit 10-6 provides an example of how one state, Illinois, carries out its trade promotion activities and plans.

Facility Developer

Obviously some places are better positioned for trade than others. They have coastal outlets, border on adjacent nations, or possess a basic international trade base with ports and airfields. Some places have exploited these advantages better than others: Hampton Roads, Norfolk, Seattle–Tacoma, and Los Angeles have outdone Chicago, Boston, or San Francisco in terms of ports. In air transport Chicago moved first to exploit technological change from prop to jet aircraft in building O'Hare Field in the 1950s. In the 1960s Dallas built a major new airport, Dallas–Ft. Worth, which today ranks only behind O'Hare in passenger traffic. New airport construction was not revived again until the 1980s. As airline deregulation led to major passenger hubs and major traffic increases for larger airports, airport expansion revived in the 1980s. Increasingly places viewed airport development as a necessary investment for job growth and for trading links to a global economy. Spurred by Federal Express' strategic use of Memphis, smaller communities and airports competed for shares of air cargo and small package markets. The point is that places can play many direct roles in helping companies export and an invaluable indirect role by developing and expanding physical assets to make exports possible, as illustrated by exhibit 10-7.

IMPROVING THE COUNTRY-OF-ORIGIN IMAGE OF PLACES

If all the brands within a particular product category were perceived by consumers to be equal in quality and price, buyers would probably favor buying the brand that is locally or domestically produced. In this way, consumers support local income and jobs and should receive faster producer redress if dissatisfied. However, brands in a product category are rarely perceived as delivering equal value. In fact, buyers make distinct evaluations of brands based on their image of the place of origin (see exhibit 10-8). An annual poll of 2,500 American consumers found that people are feeling more guilty about buying imports. Nevertheless, some 62 percent of the consumers agreed in 1990 with the

EXHIBIT 10–6

Illinois's Varied Efforts at Export Promotion

The objectives and activities of the state of Illinois in support and trade promotion include the following:

- Taking products and producers to customers or potential buyers by staging trade shows, trade missions, catalog shows;
- Bringing would-be customers to sellers or their intermediaries by sponsoring visiting trade delegations, buyers, and dignitaries;
- Brokering information between actual or would-be buyers and sellers through overseas offices and market studies; publishing directories of exporters, export agents, distributors, and trading companies; developing other trade leads and searches; and educating the broader public on the importance of foreign trade;
- Helping actual or would-be exporters to export by providing information, counseling, technical assistance, trading finance and insurance; facilitating access to banks; and conducting seminars, workshops, and conferences;
- Fostering better relationships and mutual access between places by sponsoring student internships and scholarships, and sister city, county, or state relationships; hosting events, ethnic festivals, and cultural promotions;
- Targeting specific regions and foreign countries for actual or would-be export industries and products by focusing and positioning a state or place in export markets.

Illinois recently set down its major export promotion strategies for the 1990s. They include:

- Increase the state's share of U.S. exports; focus on targets of opportunity

(continued)

EXHIBIT 10–6
Illinois's Varied Efforts at Export Promotion (continued)

- Increase the number of exporting companies; develop Canadian operations
- Assist EC exporting companies; respond to economic and market changes
- Establish a state presence in difficult markets with long-term potential: the former USSR and E. Germany, Hungary, and the People's Republic of China
- Expand the state's presence in Mexico
- Assist service companies; develop a program to promote services overseas
- Expand relations with foreign consultants, banks, trade associations, convention centers, and other trade promotion organizations in the state
- Continue low-cost opportunities; sponsor catalog shows
- Improve and increase printed materials to promote the state and its products
- Improve the export data base on exporters, and information exchange among overseas offices and Chicago.

Source: Illinois Department of Commerce and Community Affairs, various planning documents and publications, 1990.

statement that, "It is not worth it to me to pay more for a product just because it is American made," up from 57 percent in 1988.[12]

A product's place of origin can have a positive, neutral, or negative effect on nonresident buyers. Most buyers in the world are favorably disposed to apparel bearing the label "Made in Italy." They would also expect high quality and reliability from automobiles and consumer electronics made in Japan. (That, of course, was not the view thirty years ago.) At the other extreme, a car or stereo set produced in Poland would be negatively viewed. In between are those products, often raw materials and natural resources such as oil from Nigeria or timber from Canada, whose image is not much affected by knowing its country of origin.

Consumers have preferences for products from places, based on per-

EXHIBIT 10-7

Twilight Areas: Foreign Trade Zones (FTZ)

Congress passed the Foreign Trade Zones Act in 1934 to stimulate international trade and create jobs. An FTZ is a federally approved and state designated area within U.S. boundaries, typically at or near a U.S. Customs port of entry, where foreign and domestic merchandise is considered to be international commerce. Goods entering the enclave can be processed, repackaged, assembled, repaired, manufactured, and stored there and, if exported, can avoid customs duty or excise taxes. If the final product is imported into the United States, the duty paid is lower than that applicable to the product itself or its component parts.

Prior to 1970, only twelve zones existed, but the number grew thereafter once subzones were allowed for the purposes of manufacturing a specific product like automobiles, bicycles, typewriters, and ships. A general-purpose zone, like Miami's FTZ, functions like an industrial park and warehousing distribution facility which, in this case, is a center for European and Asian companies exporting into South America. By 1988, 138 FTZs and 106 subzones existed, used by 2,000 firms, with a $5.6 billion capital investment, providing an estimated total of 170,000 jobs, and handling nearly $80 billion in merchandise volume.

Used largely by coastal and Great Lake states, FTZs are advantageous to job retention insofar as they attract firms to a single place that might otherwise have gone offshore to manufacture, assemble, and store goods. Some twenty-four auto-assembly plants are located in FTZ subzones, which has sparked complaints of unfair competition by domestic suppliers of auto parts. Since 1991, regulations governing FTZs have been tightened, requiring demonstration of a significant public benefit to gain FTZ recognition.

Source: The National Association of Foreign Trade Zones, *An American Success Story* (Washington, D.C.: NAFTZ, 1989).

EXHIBIT 10-8

Swiss Knife Quality: A Launching Pad for Other Products

For less than $30 anyone can buy the Soldier, the original standard-issue knife Swiss manufacturer Victorinox Cutler Company has made for the Swiss Army since 1891. The Soldier is one of the 295 different models of almost indestructible pocketknives made by Victorinox and sold throughout the world. Swiss Army knives can be used for a number of different purposes such as sawing wood, trimming fingernails, driving screws, and opening cans. The models range from a slim, simple twin-bladed economy model to the full-featured SwissChamp, an eight-ounce model with twenty-nine different functions.

In 1989, $33 million of red-with-silver-cross Swiss Army knives were sold in the United States, with virtually no advertising. This is certainly a big jump from $1 million in sales just sixteen years before. The knives have reached almost a cult status all over the world and personal testimony from users is legendary.

The country of origin, Switzerland, is regarded as a major factor in the appeal of this brand. Recently, the brand's name strength has been lent to sell Swiss Army watches, compasses, and sunglasses "hoping the knives' allure will transfer to these items." All these products are made in Switzerland. The manufacturer is vigorously prosecuting brand infringements by manufacturers in other countries making inferior imitations. The success of the Swiss Army name in marketing a range of products owes to their ability to produce high quality in keeping with the country's image for other items such as Swiss watches, Swiss candy, and Swiss machinery.

Source: Fleming Meeks, "Blade Runner," *Forbes*, October 15, 1990, pp. 164–67.

sonal experience and inferences about quality, reliability, and service. Johny Johansson contends that consumers use the made-in label as a cue to draw inferences about the product's worth.[13] Thus, buyers assume that a new printing machine made in Germany has higher quality than one made in Bulgaria. Several country-of-origin studies have found the following:

- The impact of country of origin varies with the type of product (e.g., car versus oil).
- In highly industrial countries, consumers tend to rate their domestic goods high, whereas consumers in the developing world tend to rate foreign goods more favorably. Industrial countries tend to have a bias against products produced in developing countries and in Eastern Europe.
- Campaigns to get people to buy the goods in their country rarely succeed when these goods are perceived to be inferior to foreign goods.
- Certain countries have established a generally good reputation regarding certain goods: Japan for automobiles and consumer electronics; the United States for high-tech innovations, soft drinks, toys, cigarettes, jeans; France for wine, perfumes, and luxury goods. Some of this reputation may be attributable not simply to a product's characteristics but also to its accessibility and service reliability.
- The more favorable a country's image, the more prominently the country of origin should be displayed in promoting the brand.
- Attitudes toward country of origin can change over time. Note how Japan improved its quality image since pre–World War II days, and how Korean products are receiving higher regard.[14]

What can a place do when its products are competitively equal or superior but its place of origin turns off consumers? The place may resort to co-production or even a joint venture, where the product is to be finished at another place that carries a more positive image. Thus South Korea makes a fine leather jacket that it sends to Italy for finishing. The final jacket is then exported with a Made in Italy label and commands a much higher price. A joint venture, AT&T and Gold Star in Korea, creates a broader market for a finished good that meets AT&T standards but is made in Korea. A portable telephone or pager made by Motorola in Kuala Lumpar overcomes consumer misgivings about a little known city in Malaysia.

Another strategy a place may pursue is to hire a well-known local

celebrity to endorse the product to overcome local consumers' appre-
hensions. Thus when Mazda Motors of America was less known and
Japan less well-thought of, Mazda hired the American actor James Gar-
ner to tout the Mazda in U.S. commercials. In seeking to introduce
athletic footwear to Europe, Nike used America's best-known professional basketball star, Michael Jordan, to attract huge crowds to his performances at Nike's exhibits. A variation of this approach is the iconic
visits. Britain's Queen Elizabeth and Prince Philip visit various countries to build goodwill; following in their wake are British salespeople
touting everything from tours to British linen and sweaters. Places and
their companies often use similar strategies in sponsoring art exhibits,
artistic tours, and cultural shows.

In *The Competitive Advantage of Nations*, Michael Porter argues
that nations succeed in particular industries because their home environment is the most forward-looking, dynamic and challenging. Based
on a four-year study of competitive successes in ten leading trading nations, Porter found that companies facing tough, effective competition
at home are more likely to be successful abroad. Competitive advantages
are generated whenever rivals are geographically concentrated and are
vying for supremacy in innovation, efficiency, and quality.[15]

This competition also allows places to align a name or region to its
products: Italian jewelry companies around the towns of Arezzo and
Valenza Po; cutlery companies around Solingen, Germany; motorcycle
and musical instruments around Hamamatsu, Japan. Porter's argument
accounts for how places' names become associated with consumable
products: Belgian chocolates, French wine, Irish whiskey, Polish ham,
Colombian coffee, and German beer.

Once a place's name becomes identified with a product category, it
can seek to protect the integrity and exclusiveness of the product's benefits through regulatory and legal protections. For example, since 1937
the U.S. Department of Agriculture has encouraged marketing orders
that define specific growing areas for specialty products. Vidalia onions, a sweet Georgia onion has its labeling restricted to thirteen central Georgia counties and parts of six others. Once producers agree on
a designated area and obtain USDA approval for a marketing order,
regulations typically govern quality factors such as grade, size, and
other product characteristics (e.g., California almonds and wines, Idaho
potatoes, Wisconsin cheeses, Hawaiian papayas).[16] States spare no expense in going after packagers that fraudulently label products as coming from their state.

An interesting variation of aligning a place's name with its products involves cross-national, ethnic marketing. Due to historical, cultural, and current ties between certain American states and regions and their European counterparts, certain states target their export promotion and foreign investment strategies to these places: Minnesota to Scandinavian countries; Wisconsin to Germany; Rhode Island to Italy; Massachusetts to Ireland. Such marketing currently operates in both directions. Ethnic identification with products and place of origin can be a positive force in cross-national sales and marketing efforts.

DO EXPORT PROMOTION PROGRAMS WORK?

Governors, legislators, the media, business, and taxpayers are all interested in knowing whether or not export promotion programs and services are effective. The evidence is mixed. The overall impact of these programs is hard to measure, although some specific programs clearly have contributed to export development.

State and local officials defend public investment in overseas activities and trade programs on the basis of observed paybacks: direct and indirect jobs created or retained; foreign dollars invested; business start-ups and expansions; sales, output, and income. For example, the value of foreign-owned assets in the United States increased fourfold to $1.8 trillion from 1980 to 1988. Illinois officials assert that from 1977 to 1988, its Brussels office guided 262 European firms to invest more than $1 billion in Illinois business start-ups and expansions, creating more than 8,300 new jobs. Virginia's former Governor Gerald Baliles noted that 76 new foreign companies started or expanded in his state between 1986 and 1988, investing $535 million and creating more than 6,000 jobs.[17] Thus, the payback, according to the Congressional Research Service, is that every $60 states invest in promoting foreign investment attracts $40,000 in foreign capital and creates one new job.

On the other hand, critics, like economic development expert David Osborne, argue that "most of the states' trade promotion activities, overseas offices . . . and goodwill missions, don't do much good."[18] Others contend that public-sponsored trade programs are over-ambitious, unfocused, and spread too thin. CED's former vice-president, Scott Fosler, argues that promotion programs are untested and need evaluation over time.[19] Even with data and evaluations, the Urban Institute's Blaine Liner cautions that "what works [is] fraught with difficulties in establishing cause and effect, attribution, appropriate lag time for outcomes to occur and with other uncertainties."[20]

Martin and Susan Tolchin, for example, could find no clear relationship between the percentage of a state's national product derived from exports, and its spending on overseas activities. Nor could they find a connection between a state's success in generating foreign investment and the quality or quantity of its overseas branch offices.[21] Tennessee, the state that achieved a record among mainland states for attracting the most Japanese manufacturing plants in the shortest time, had no overseas office (although its governors led several trade missions to Japan). Under then Governor Ronald Reagan, California closed its London and Tokyo trade offices in 1970 to save $105,000; these were not reopened until 1986. In the interim, more than one-third of all Japanese investment in U.S. real estate occurred in California. Conversely, California's trade imbalance rose from a $2.1 billion deficit in 1980 to a $37 billion deficit in 1986, an amount equal to 13 percent of the entire U.S. trade deficit.[22]

Aggregate state spending on developing trade by forty-five states amounted to only $50 million, according to a survey by the National Association of State Development Agencies.[23] Even in a big export spender state such as Illinois, trade programs cost $9 million out of a $26.5 billion state budget in 1990–91, an amount that is less than 1 percent of the state's principal economic development agency's budget. The Tolchins found that average state expenditure on foreign investment and trade climbed from $235,000 per year in 1979 to $980,000 by 1986, a significant increase but hardly a major state expenditure.[24] A 1990 survey found that California, Illinois, New York, and Michigan had the largest trade budgets; Illinois and California the largest staffs; New York and California conducted the most seminars and conferences; and Michigan ran the most trade shows.[25]

On the individual program level, results are easier to measure. Most states keep annual records of trade missions, catalog shows, seminars, contacts, and businesses assisted. Illinois, for example, listed the following accomplishments for the international business division of its economic development agency in fiscal year 1990: twenty-eight catalog shows assisted 525 companies; twenty-three trade shows and missions assisted 105 companies and were likely to result in $50 million in first-year sales; overseas investor referrals helped 67 foreign firms to expand or locate in the state.[26] If the activity involves a lead-generation program, the number of leads can be measured as can frequency of contacts between buyers and sellers, and contacts resulting in sales. However, few places keep records beyond a single year, and all face the problem of documenting what ultimately is a private business transaction.

Governor Baliles established a reputation as the traveling governor "peddling chicken feet in Hong Kong, wines in Taipei, lumber in Tokyo, coal in Seoul."[27] Illinois' former Governor Jim Thompson opened eleven trade offices abroad, the most of any state. In 1989–90, he led six separate trade missions to Germany, Canada, Mexico, Israel, Japan, Poland, the Soviet Union and the United Kingdom. For each mission he established objectives—investment, sales, sister-state relations, cultural exchanges, trade office openings—that were reported to the legislature, the media, and the public. However, this strategy can be politically delicate. The governor's travels became so controversial that his successor cut back the state's overseas offices and trade budgets and, other than a low-key Mexican trade mission, he has eschewed foreign travel.[28] Most states reduced their economic development budgets significantly in light of the 1990–92 recession, and also curtailed overseas travel by their chief executives, representing the latest turn in the efforts of states to manage exports and foreign investment. (See exhibit 10–9.)

CONCLUSION

Promoting foreign trade and investment has emerged as an important place development strategy that has gained equal footing with business attraction, retention, start-up, and tourism-hospitality activities. What began in the 1970s as an overseas extension of traditional place approaches to economic development, namely industrial attraction through incentives, grew into a broader, more balanced approach to economic globalization.

As in other aspects of place development, businesses responded to globalization and economic interdependence faster than governments. The significance of governors and mayors as new actors on the international scene is that they have become advocates, surrogates, and brokers for making places more competitive.

In 1989, President George Bush noted that the "governors are becoming our economic envoys—restoring American international competitiveness and expanding world markets for American goods and services."[29] These officials are now being consulted on trade policies such as the Uruguay Rounds, GATT agreements, and U.S. free trade pacts

EXHIBIT 10-9

Remarketing Trade Programs

In state after state, legislatures are cutting back on international export trade programs for the following reasons:

1. Export programs tend to exaggerate their benefits or take credit for successes that would have happened anyway.
2. Many export promotion activities are mere political tools which are more appropriate to campaigning than to trade. The governor's visits, trade missions, and exchanges are good public relations but rarely yield sales.
3. The objectives of the export programs are not clearly stated and therefore hard to substantiate.

These charges, coupled with the budget crisis of many states, call into question the entire enterprise. However, many valuable programs find themselves seriously wounded by cutbacks. To turn their situation around, export programs need to do a better job of marketing benefits. As William E. Nothdurft has noted, "Until recently, states had little reason to think strategically about their international

with Canada and Mexico. They have generally been less protectionistic than their national counterparts who often blame foreigners for America's trade problems. State and local leaders have been more creative, flexible, and imaginative in addressing trade problems than has the federal establishment.

As the world economic forces move toward more defined trading blocks in North America, Asia, and Europe, national borders are likely to blur.[30] Federalism still divides these efforts, the debate over states' rights or central control, and freer trade within but greater barriers to those outside.[31] Nevertheless, large multination markets will continue their integration. The effect is that places will become more identifiable in competitiveness: South Florida to Latin America; Los Angeles and the Pacific Northwest to the Pacific Basin; New York City to Tokyo and London; northern border towns and cities to Canadian provinces.[32]

programs: Promotion was the objective, and salesmanship overshadowed the questionable economics of the game." Instead, he offers advice on exporting modeled on successful European efforts.

- The major problem in exporting is targeting the "export-ready" firm. Many market factors can be solved if the firm has the right attitude and skills.
- The best export companies are totally committed and view the process as long-term and not as a single conquest.
- The best export assistance comes from a combination of private or quasi-private sources. The role of the government is best as an enabler and not the primary source.
- The exporting businesses should be profitable: companies should pay for advice.

States have poorly marketed their export programs to their own citizens. They must reenergize their export programs by convincing their legislatures that investment will produce new jobs, satisfied workers, and better opportunities for companies.

Successful exporters understand that a good audit, vision, infrastructure, and execution are parts of a successful marketing program, while an underdeveloped, high-profile export program will fail.

Source: William E. Nothdurft, "The Export Game," *Governing*, August 1992, pp. 57–61.

As interests diverge and economic differentiation occurs at the regional or subnational level, place development strategies will increasingly require more global thinking, and strategic marketing to set apart a place, its people, and business from other places or regions. Local response to economic change will increasingly become a vital component of national competitiveness.

We conclude with a simple test places might use to audit how they measure up to the challenge of export promotion (see table 10–1). With ten points for each favorable answer, a passing grade is sixty points.

TABLE 10-1

A Way to Measure Your Place's Export Climate

1. Can you name your place's leading manufacturing and service industry exporters?
2. Does your local chamber of commerce offer a program for members on export trade at least annually?
3. Does your local college or university provide any help to would-be exporters on identifying overseas markets and opportunities?
4. Is your major financial institution familiar with export financing, letters of credit, and foreign exchange protections?
5. Does your local economic development agency sponsor trade seminars, trade shows, and catalogs, or provide marketing assistance?
6. Does your local export development agency/organization identify, target, and contact potential export companies to support trade facilitation?
7. If your place has a sister-city relationship with an overseas counterpart, has it produced any new contacts or business ties between them?
8. Does your mayor or do local officials organize trade missions to visit Canada or Mexico, or to travel overseas to promote contacts and trade?
9. Does your community/place have a well-defined understanding of its local economy as to trade composition or potential?
10. Can you identify any trade facilitation strategies of your business community and/or economic development agency? Does it have a plan?

11

Attracting Residents

Places not only try to attract tourists, businesses, and investors—they also undertake to shape a policy toward residents as part of building a viable community. Places seek to attract certain groups, and by the same token, discourage other groups. The targeted groups typically include professionals, investors, the wealthy, young families, retirees, and those with specific skills such as physicians. At the same time, they may try to discourage low-income families, the homeless, criminal types, and illegal immigrants. Understandably, efforts to attract certain people or exclude others remain controversial.

Consider the following examples from recent news stories at the international level:

- The United States triples visas (140,000) to highly skilled professionals and, for the first time, sets aside 10,000 visas for special immigrants who plow at least $1 million into the economy, create ten full-time jobs, or who invest $500,000 in designated areas.
- Italians send boatloads of would-be Albanian asylum seekers back home.
- Britain doubles the fine on foreign airlines that fly foreigners into England without proper identification.

At the national and state level:

- California governor proposes to pare the state's budget deficit by a 25 percent reduction in welfare payments.

- New York's residency law for welfare recipients held to be unconstitutional.
- Michigan cuts off general assistance payments for able-bodied citizens to avoid tax increases.
- Legislator charges that the University of Wisconsin is subsidizing too many out-of-state-students.
- Northwesterners (Oregon and Washington) make obscene gestures to tourists and visitors with California license plates.

And at the local:

- Clinton, New Jersey, pays bounties to new employees to overcome labor shortages.
- Koochiching County, Minnesota, provides forty free acres of wilderness or abandoned farmland for anyone who builds a home and lives there for ten years.
- Yonkers, New York, City Council refuses court order to make affordable housing available for poor and minorities.
- Ohio, Illinois pays newcomers $3,000 in property taxes for purchase of existing homes and $5,000 for new homes.[1]

Together, these stories are about how places—nations, states, and local governments—develop policies whose purpose is to attract/exclude, encourage/discourage, and market/de-market geopolitical areas to certain publics or identifiable groups. At the nation-state level, the issue is immigration policy: whom to admit, on what basis, and for what period of time. At the state level, the issues largely involve taxes, spending, and regulatory considerations. Most localities, in contrast, share the preceding responsibilities with states, but have direct responsibility for land use, zoning, building codes, health, and safety standards. The actions government takes, the policies they pursue, the programs they adopt or expand are rarely neutral regarding people attraction. They have impacts and consequences which, although sometimes difficult to determine, usually benefit some population segments more than others.

In discussing people attraction/detraction, this chapter addresses the following:

- Why has people attraction become important for place marketing?
- Whom do places want to attract and why? Within applicable laws, whom do places wish to encourage to relocate elsewhere?

• What policies/programs can places use to attract/discourage certain population segments, and how do they market them?

WHY PEOPLE ATTRACTION IS IMPORTANT IN PLACE MARKETING

Even before governments and law, places competed for people—traders, settlers, homesteaders, herders, and workers. Whether by conquest, slavery, or feudal systems, nations' policies were frequently directed at exploiting cheap labor or populating new markets. England populated the United States with those fleeing religious prosecution, Australia with criminals and misfits, and India with its army. The United States opened its western lands by giving 160 free acres to those who tilled them and the railroads imported tens of thousands of Chinese laborers to build western railroads. The industrialized cities of the North, Chicago and Detroit particularly, recruited black workers in the South to fill jobs in the labor-intensive meat packing and auto industries. Farmers of southwestern states utilized Mexican workers to harvest their crops. Postwar Europe is replete with examples of efforts to attract cheap labor, known as "guest workers": the Turks and Yugoslavians to Germany, the Algerians to France, and the Italians to Switzerland. However, people-attraction policies change with the economy, as amply illustrated by changing U.S. immigration policies over the last 200 years (see exhibit 11–1).

A World Problem: Competing for Talent and Identity

Demography is the statistical study of human population. In the information age, demographics provide places with valuable data to affect the flow of people and resources. Places are appropriately concerned about their demographic condition. In Third-World countries, where fast-growing population exceeds economic growth, concerns abound about famine, unemployment, and social unrest. In slow population growth regions—United States, Europe, and East Asia—population growth is deemed essential to economic progress tied to markets, jobs, economies of scale, and rising standards of living. "Birth-dearthers," concerned that the birth rates of modern nations are insufficient to reproduce themselves, anticipate the loss of economic and geopolitical power by Japan and Germany. Ben Wattenberg, the modern Cassandra of this view, stated in 1987 "no nation or group of nations without a

EXHIBIT 11-1

Immigration Policies: America's Four Major Shifts

Under international law and nation sovereignty, each nation sets its own immigration policies. These policies typically change through history as a nation's needs, values, and attitudes toward immigrants also change. No nation has been as much populated by immigrants as the United States. Immigration, for example, accounted for one-third of the U.S. population growth in the 1980s, with a greater increase of immigrants from 1980 to 1990 than in any twentieth century decade except 1900–1910 when 8 million immigrants came to this country.

U.S. attitudes toward immigrants have been mixed and contradictory; sometimes welcoming and, at other times hostile. This nation did not even have a general immigration law until 1882, when it enacted its first major change that barred convicts and mental incompetents and limited Chinese immigration (due to a 200,000 increase from 1850 to 1882). The second major change occurred in 1924 when a quota law limited admissions from any country to a percentage of the foreign-born persons of that nationality already living in the United States. Prior to the limited restrictions just cited, the United States operated on open admissions: "Give me your tired, your poor . . . The wretched refuse of your teeming shore." The generous sentiment of the Emma Lazarus poem inscribed on the Statue of Liberty was very much part of our value system and egalitarian spirit until the 1924 change.

In 1965, a third change occurred when the United States abolished "the national origins" system, replacing it with "preference," a priority system favoring the close relatives of people already in this country plus professionals, scientists, artists, and others whose talents made them desirable. This 1965 shift to skilled and unskilled workers in short supply in this country marked a gradual, but conspicuous recognition of recruiting "value adding" immigrants based on U.S. economic needs.

In the early 1980s, the U.S. Congress faced the mounting immigration crisis of an illegal population that had been growing by nearly 1 million per year since 1977, and whose total population estimates ran as high as 12 million, more than one-half estimated to be from Mexico. The widely debated issue pitted diverse groups and interests: Hispanics, labor unions, state and local governments, religious groups, farmers, and business organizations. Tangible concerns centered on money and taxes, working standards and wages, unemployment rates, and public services. The debate also sparked more fundamental visceral notions of America's identity and its ideals. Because no consensus existed on whether the mass illegal population benefited or hurt the U.S. economy, the Immigration Reform and Control Act of 1986 provided a sweeping amnesty program for those who arrived in the country before 1981, and included employer sanctions on those who hired illegal workers. The 1986 act pleased few, but the compromise represented an attempt to seal our southern borders on the one hand, yet provide for the civil liberties and citizenship transition of those who had illegally entered the United States prior to 1981 on the other.

In late 1990, the country adopted its fourth major shift in immigration policy, a conspicuous departure based largely on efforts to increase the economic benefits from immigration, including the following provisions:

- Raised the cap on legal immigrants by 40 percent from 500,000 to 700,000;
- Provided 40,000 visas for priority workers with extraordinary ability in arts, sciences, education, business, or athletics; and another 40,000 visas for other skilled workers, such as professionals holding basic degrees;
- Provided 10,000 visas for investors meeting certain economic criteria.

The 1990 act was widely criticized as a repudiation of U.S. values. "The U.S. is trying to get all the brains in the world," noted one foreign diplomat, while another commented the United States was "trading greenbacks for green cards." Supporters responded that the

(continued)

EXHIBIT 11–1
Immigration Policies: America's Four Major Shifts (continued)

United States was not selling citizenship with its investor-immigrant provisions, but simply competing with Canada and Australia that previously adopted such provisions to attract wealthy Asians, particularly those fleeing Hong Kong. Labor economists defended the new law citing differences in performance between skilled and unskilled immigrants in the 1960s and 1970s, noting growing disparity in earnings, welfare costs, and contribution to the U.S. economy, between the two groups. With the 1990 act, this nation joined the global competitive race for skills, talent, and wealth that now characterizes most of the world's immigration policies.

Sources: Dianna Solis and Pauline Yoshihashi "Immigration Bill Expands Access to U.S.," *Wall Street Journal,* November 15, 1990, p. A16; also see George Borjas, *Friends or Strangers: The Impact of Immigration on the U.S. Economy* (New York: Basic Books, 1990).

substantial population can hope for lasting global influence."[2] At the same time, several nations are resisting adding to their population growth through immigration (see exhibit 11–2).

Nations are strategically positioning themselves on their ability to attract human and physical capital regionally and globally. Singapore, for example, aims to be the "brain capital of Southeast Asia." It advertises around the world for professionals (e.g., lawyers, physicians, engineers, architects, accountants) with the objective of wedding Singapore's future to its ability to export expensive services to the rest of Asia. Korea seeks to persuade expatriots currently employed in the United States to return home for high-paying technical and scientific job opportunities. In contrast, Japan, with its extremely homogeneous population, faces growing labor shortages and a cultural crisis as it modifies its immigration policies by introducing foreign workers. Thus, immigration policies affect a nation's foreign and domestic politics and, as a consequence, have a significant impact on how places market themselves.

Resident Attraction Policies: Reactive to Proactive

Resident attraction/exclusion policies are not the same as a nation's immigration policy, which usually is uniform throughout a country.

EXHIBIT 11-2
Handling Major Waves of New Immigrants

Following the collapse of the Iron Curtain and vast unrest in Eastern Europe, millions of new immigrants flooded Germany, Austria, Finland, Poland, and Western Europe, touching nerves of old hostilities and nationalism. Coming at a time of recession and high unemployment in the West, the influx sparked fears of job displacement and increased economic and social costs of settling the new immigrants. Practically overnight, West German unification with East Germany transformed West Germany's demographic makeup in size, composition, and future labor supply. Inundated by a record number of Soviet Union immigrants, Israel, internally and externally, seeks to cope with changes that will dramatically change that nation. Austria's settlement of 600,000 refugees since 1945 has given rise to right-wing political parties desiring to limit immigration and to expel recent refugees.[1] Indeed, the massive immigration from Eastern Europe to the West has raised the specter of prolonged instability, social dissent, and even the creation of a new Iron Curtain in Western Europe.[2] Just as immigration has changed the composition of the U.S. population, so it is vastly transforming Europe. Britain's nonwhite population in 1945, for example, was fewer than 20,000; in 1990 it was nearly 5 percent of the population, or 2.6 million people. In 1960, Berlin had only 22,000 non-Germans. In 1990, it had 312,000, nearly half of whom were Turkish.

European nations have long extended citizenship to people of their former colonies, while Germany's constitution grants citizenship to people of German ancestry. Britain first embraced, and then largely stopped immigration from its former colonies. Just as Athens debated nearly 3,000 years ago who is an Athenian, today whom to admit and to exclude have become a world problem of unprecedented scope. It has been compounded by the terms of the 1951 United Nations convention that the United States and European Community pledged to uphold, that asylum as grounds for refugee status be granted to someone who can prove a "well-founded fear of being persecuted for reasons of race, religion, na-

(continued)

EXHIBIT 11-2
Handling Major Waves of New Immigrants

tionality, membership in a particular social group, or political opinion." With more than 500,000 people applying for political asylum in Western Europe in 1991, each country makes its own, albeit often narrow interpretation of what constitutes persecution.[3]

Sources: [1]Brenda Fowler, "With New Look, Far Right Makes Gains in Austria," New York Times, October 7, 1990, p. 3.
[2]Robert D. Hormats, "Don't Let the West Erect A New Iron Curtain," Wall Street Journal, December 27, 1990, p. A16.
[3]Craig Whitney, "Europeans Look for Ways to Bar Immigrants," New York Times, December 29, 1991, p. 1.

Prior to the extension of federal civil rights to voting, housing, employment, and public facilities for U.S. minorities, some state and local governments enacted laws excluding certain population segments from full participation in their civic, social, and economic life based on race, ethnicity, political beliefs, religion, physical or mental condition, and economic means. Segregation *de jure* existed in most southern states; segregation *de facto* elsewhere. Some states used nonpayment of taxes, and swift property foreclosure laws to force out those of lesser means. Vagrancy and loitering laws, literacy tests for voting, residency requirements for welfare, and trespass laws are but a few of the devices places have used to discourage people from living in a place, or forcing out those unwanted.

Today, states and localities are proactively competing for residents who meet certain characteristics and profiles. Several trends help explain this phenomenon:

- Labor shortages have increased the demand for skilled rather than unskilled workers.
- An aging America has a vastly expanding retirement market whose spending exceeds the costs of state and local services consumed.
- The wage gap is growing between U.S. college graduates and the less-educated.

Thus, as human capital has become an increasingly important determinant of a place's economic well-being, policymakers often must choose between developing that capital within or attracting it elsewhere. Some places do both, while others do neither. So, too, places have awakened to the vast benefits from attracting retirees, a new form of place competition for people.

Population Imperative: Growth, AntiGrowth, and Growth Loss

A number of places seek to attract outsiders simply due to significant depopulation. Koochiching County, Minnesota, and Ohio, Illinois, are typical of rural places whose population loss threatens their viability. Resident attraction policies are essential to develop land, settle homes, and provide kids for schools. This use of incentives is predicated on attracting modern pioneers with the means to buy a house, invest, pay taxes, or start a business. Four states lost population in the 1980s—West Virginia, Iowa, Wyoming, and North Dakota—each has taken specific actions to reverse this decline. Wyoming, for example, targets specific industries with the lure of a low-tax environment and advertises nationally in *Plants & Sites* and *Newsweek*. The hope is that the new companies will attract newcomers and retain the old ones (see exhibit 11–3 for Hollywood's version of attraction).

Conversely, certain high growth places in the 1970s and 1980s now find they must deal with an antigrowth sentiment of residents. In some cases, population growth failed to produce presumed benefits of more jobs, higher incomes, and lower taxes. On the contrary, the dynamics of growth produced rising taxes for infrastructure and schools, traffic congestion, and pollution that many sense detracts from quality of life. DuPage County, Illinois, the fastest growing county in Illinois and the Midwest during the 1970s with its massive sales-tax generator, the Woodfield Shopping Mall, finds itself struggling with various combinations of antitax, antidevelopment, and antigrowth sentiments. The Pacific Northwest flirted with no-growth policies when its economy boomed in the 1970s, then faltered, only to have this sentiment reignite again in the mid-1980s in the midst of renewed growth. Residents of growth cities in Washington—Seattle, Olympia, Bremerton—have become openly hostile to the influx of post-earthquake Californians. The fear of being "Californianized" has added impetus to Washington's environmental actions aimed at limiting growth, albeit people. Those fleeing California frequently cashed out high-cost housing there using the funds to buy cheaper housing in Washington, Oregon, Nevada, and Ar-

---

EXHIBIT 11-3

Paramount Discovers Small Town Attraction

In the film *Baby Boom*, Diane Keaton plays the role of a burnt-out New York City advertising executive who moves to a small New England town. The new resident meets all the expected nightmares as her well runs dry, pipes freeze, locals are suspicious and unfriendly, and she becomes morose and lonely. In short movie time, she discovers a handsome doctor, invents a wholesome line of baby foods, and learns to love the small-town life.

Chevy Chase, playing the role of a burnt-out New York City sports writer in the film *Funny Farm*, endured even more small-town hazing than Keaton. But he became the local sports writer and beloved coach of the town baseball team.

The struggling small towns of America are aware of the need to entice entrepreneurial city types. In the late 80s the town of Rolfe, Iowa, population 700, offered free land and $1,200 cash bonus to anyone who would build a house worth $30,000 or more. The results are encouraging as seventy people moved in and are self-supporting. A few immigrants still wonder where the bagel shop is or long for a small theater performance of *Peer Gynt*, but the trend seems permanent.

Source: For Rolfe, Iowa, see Roger Munns, "Iowa Farm Town Gets Its Wish: People," *Chicago Sun Times*, January 2, 1990, p. 44.

---

izona, driving up prices. These California expatriates, or "equity exiles," have met with a chilly reception, particularly in the Northwest.

Northern Californians today seek statehood for residents and the forty counties north of San Francisco to limit growth and stem migration to new growth areas of Chico, Santa Rosa-Petaluma, Stockton, and Sacramento. The same phenomenon is occurring in New Mexico, the seventh fastest growing state during the 1980s, where Las Cruces and Santa Fe have emerged in the top 50 growth areas among the 320 officially designated U.S. metropolitan areas. In many cases, these places seek growth restriction through environmental laws governing land use, zoning, and housing; others use court-approved extraction and development fees from developers for infrastructure and public services. By raising the cost of development up front, advocates hope either to discourage development or to get new homeowners to pay the real costs of growth. Such regulatory restrictions on property use—in cases where the state takes property without full compensation to owners—are finding their way to the federal courts for resolution.

Another category of places may be termed "flatliners." These older places—cities, towns and metro areas—are neither growing nor greatly shrinking, and although desiring growth, realistically must learn to live with very limited growth prospects. The nation's 320 metropolitan areas increased their share of the U.S. population by 1 percent from 1980 to 1990, from 76 percent to 77 percent. While one-quarter of these metro areas grew at twice the population growth rate of the nation as a whole over the last decade, largely in the South and West, nearly 60 percent grew more slowly than the national levels. In effect, most metro areas are experiencing slow growth and are likely to do so in the future because the only two sources of growth—natural increase and in-migration—have diminished.[3]

Slow growth, no growth, and growth loss can result in economic stagnation for those places whose manufacturing base has failed to change with the U.S. economy or places largely dependent on declining industries. However, several older places that have made an economic transition to more stable industries, possess a well-trained labor force, or are advantaged by good location fall into the flatliner category. These include in the East and Midwest, Binghamton, New York; Sioux Falls, South Dakota; Rockford, Illinois; Louisville, Kentucky; and Toledo, Ohio. They have reasonably good prospects of remaining healthy in the absence of significant population growth. With rural migration to these areas depleted and attraction of immigrants from places elsewhere limited, their tasks are largely to attract and retain skilled labor—their principal asset.

Thus, a wide difference exists among places in their efforts to increase, decrease, or stabilize their resident populations. With the nation's overall population growth slowing and major metro center growth slowing as well, growth occurs from (1) natural increases: birth less death rates; (2) largely slowed migration from nonmetro areas; (3) migration from other metropolitan areas; and (4) migration from abroad. High population growth areas such as Naples, Florida; Riverside and San Bernadino, California; Fort Pierce, Florida—the three fastest growing areas in the 1980s—gained new residents largely at the expense of other metro areas. In contrast, a flatliner, such as Nassau and Suffolk counties, New York, aims at keeping its aggregate population at current levels by stemming out-migration, hoping that birth and death rates remain near constant, and attracting enough in-migration to offset out-migration. Thus, stabilization depends largely on a place's economic-business mix, and the quality of its labor force.[4]

DEFINING THE POPULATION GROUPS TO ATTRACT

Places vary in the groups they can and want to attract. They may reach out for retirees, skilled professionals, high-income earners, and in some cases, unskilled workers. Here we examine efforts made to attract retirees and a few other classes of residents.

Targeting Retirees

In targeting a retired population segment, Florida leads the nation, with 90 percent of its population growth in the 1980s attributable to the retired. It experienced a net gain of $5 billion between in-migration and out-migration of the elderly from 1985 to 1990 with Arizona a weak second at a $1 billion net gain. In contrast, New York was a net loser with elderly move-outs worth $2.9 billion, and Illinois the second biggest net loser at $1 billion during this period.[5]

With the aging of America, competition for elderly residents has increased. Median household income typically peaks for householders aged forty-five to fifty-four, while median net worth peaks among householders aged sixty-five to sixty-nine.[6] Home equity captures the largest share of total net worth for most people. Little wonder, then, that certain place marketers target the elderly: income, net worth, high consumption, and often low service demands. Because retirement migration boosts spending and broadens the tax base, place planners view this phenomenon as a new growth industry for small towns. Besides Florida, Arizona, New Mexico, and California, all of whom have been leaders in retirement communities, no state has better positioned itself for attracting this population than South Carolina (see exhibit 11–4).

Between 1970 and 1980, many rural counties became hot retirement areas as net in-migration of people sixty and older grew by at least 15 percent in some 500 communities. Rural havens grew faster than metropolitan areas in the 1980s. These hot spots are located in all U.S. re-

EXHIBIT 11-4

South Carolina Pitches to the Elderly

South Carolina, seeing itself as a state with opportunities to attract the retirement community, set out systematically to improve its position. While not yet a significant leader in percentage of retirees, South Carolina has some unique advantages to attract the retirement community: a warm climate, mountains and the ocean, and—most significantly—a low tax rate and cost of living.

In recognizing the potential of retirees, South Carolina bought more than 3,000 acres of land near a sparsely settled stretch of the Savannah River in 1986. The state put in roads and other infrastructure, and then sold the property to a developer to build a retirement community for 12,000 people; it represents a good example of how states have entered into the retirement promotion business.

Set against major competitors such as Florida and California, South Carolina seeks to exploit the critical advantage it enjoys in cost of living differences. California and Florida taxes have increased significantly to pay for their large population increases, infrastructure, and public services. Should South Carolina maintain this cost advantage, that difference alone is likely to prove attractive in reaching larger segments of retirees over time.

To enhance its retirement positioning, a nonprofit organization called the South Carolina Retirement Communities Association (SCRCA) was formed in 1987 to market South Carolina. The nonprofit association is a consortium of forty private firms, including the South Carolina Parks, Recreation, and Tourism Department; and the South Carolina Commission on Aging. In setting its sights on making the state a retirement capital, the association "estimated that 70 percent of its growth is generated by retirees who move to South Carolina [and] who spend $100,000 each to purchase housing and in getting settled."

South Carolina has audited and polled its potential retirement community's visitors which revealed some interesting insights on retirement objectives. For example, it takes at least three visits before people buy, indicating clearly that a retirement area needs

(continued)

EXHIBIT 11-4
South Carolina Pitches to the Elderly (continued)

to work hard in courting this audience on its multiple visits. A direct link exists between tourism and what is euphemistically called the senior living industry, namely that visitors are often turned into residents. The South Carolina poll also revealed that 58 percent of the prospective retirees were interested in a rural environment. That information has been capitalized on by South Carolina's marketing efforts, which extol the state's reputation for being rural and small townish. South Carolina's small towns are finding what many before already discovered—that their viability depends on social security, pensions, annuities, and the assistance income of the elderly.

The root mission of the SCRCA is to improve South Carolina's competitive position as an excellent retirement destination in comparison to strong competitors such as Florida, California, and Arizona. This means not only offering the retiree a better deal in housing, infrastructure, and tight control over real estate companies but also in sustaining the progress over the next hundred years. That involves a possible contraction between attracting retirees and their wealth, and dealing with the associated growth costs that afflict retirement areas in Florida and California.

South Carolina is trying to appeal to many of the values that marked the retirement decade just after World War II to win over new retirees. The city of Kingstree in Williamsburg County is a good example of this approach. A local columnist listed ten qualities that differentiate his county in South Carolina from Florida: "(1) historic Williamsburg County; (2) the slow, easy pace of small-town living; (3) low taxes and reasonable real estate values; (4) a friendly atmosphere; (5) hunting and fishing paradise and golfing; (6) easy accessibility to mountains and seashore; (7) opportunity for continued education at a two-year college; (8) commercial and entertainment activities at Florence and Charleston; (9) places of worship for all denominations; (10) commercial airports at Myrtle Beach and Charleston, also county airport."

Sources: "South Carolina Group Seeking to Attract Retires," *Charlotte Observer*, March 22, 1987, p. 26; Charles Walker, "Williamsburg Is a Great Place," *The News*, May 11, 1988, p. 2B.

gions, frequently areas of scenic beauty and recreation, revitalizing these communities and expanding business and employment opportunities.[7]

Not to be left out, cold-climate out-of-the-way places also sought retirees—places such as Michigan's upper peninsula, Minnesota's Iron Range, western Massachusetts, and upstate New York. Silver Bay, Minnesota, after losing its major industry, Reserve Mining Corporation, placed ads throughout the nation for retirees with some success.[8] Massachusetts helped promote the Mount Greylock area in the Northern Berkshires with a retirement development which includes ski trails, golf, tennis courts, and other amenities.

Retirees generally seek places offering recreation activities where they can pursue hobbies such as painting, handicrafts, or writing. They can be attracted by medical care facilities, home health care, and some form of senior transportation such as golf carts, trolley cars, or special buses. Some businesses greatly benefit from the aging population and are willing to help a place attract retirees. Businesses oriented to the home, health care, leisure, counseling, education, managing finances, and slowing the aging process are some examples.[9] A growing retiree population brings with it a demand for certain services which a place can both market to and help develop.

A warm climate and picturesque surroundings are not the only factors in attracting retirees. For example, at least six states have organized efforts to court a projected 1.6 million military service people who will start retiring in much larger numbers after the turn of the century, not to mention nearly 700,000 military personnel who are scheduled to be severed from military employment from 1992 to 1995. Many seek opportunities for a second career (the average retirees are in their forties following twenty years of military service) and locations near military bases so they can utilize discount retailers and medical facilities. Like other affluent retirees, ex-soldiers are sought because they are typically well-educated and in good health, have higher-than-average disposable income, and become involved in civic projects. According to *Governing* magazine, California, Michigan, New Jersey, New York, Pennsylvania, and Texas are leaders in seeking ex-military for key jobs. The most aggressive is Florida, which has designated $500,000 for what is described as a "second careers" office.[10]

Some places that market to retirees seek to exclude families with young children. Such private developments expressly prohibit children or seek their exclusion through restrictive leases and covenants. Sun

City, Arizona, was one of the first residential retirement communities to pursue such policies, as has Long Boat Key in Naples, Florida. To keep taxes down and recreational/cultural amenities geared to an older generation, demarketing to young families has caught on with other retirement places.

A place containing a college or university can easily make itself attractive to the elderly. Amherst, Williamstown, and North Hampton, Massachusetts; Palo Alto, California; Ann Arbor, Michigan; and Williamsburg and Charlottesville, Virginia, today contain large retirement communities. The quality of life in these communities is directly associated with university life and resources. Their increased attractiveness to senior citizens has a downside to students: Property values rise, driving off-campus students back to less-expensive dormitories on campus.

The importance of effective place marketing to retirees is underscored by potential foreign competition. Should the anticipated U.S.–Mexican Trade Agreement permit foreigners to own Mexican land, one can expect a tremendous push by Mexico to attract U.S. retirees to reside there. Another incipient trend over the last several years has been for U.S. retirees to return to their native European countries such as Poland, where the cost of living is low and extended care is available at modest prices.

Targeting Other Life-Style Groups

The increased mobility of the population is a major factor in the business of people attraction. In the information age, people are able to define where they live to work rather than where they work to live. The modern city is the creation of the nineteenth century. For example, every single means of public transportation had been invented by 1914. As Peter Drucker observed, "It is now infinitely easier, cheaper and faster to do what the 19th century could not do: move information, and with it office work, to where the people are."[11]

Futurists ponder on a world consisting of an officeless city, a new era of electronic cottage industries with more people employed at home as independent contractors than at centralized workstations. The exodus from cities to suburbs as a place of residence and work is a phenomenon in the United States, United Kingdom, the Continent, and Japan. The marketing challenge for large cities, then, is how to accommodate these technological and life-style trends to slow the exodus and retain

certain segments of urban dwellers. In addition, large cities seek to capture a share of the city-to-city migration of professionals, attract new
city migrants, and bring certain suburbanites back into the city.

Places must accommodate to a nation of movers. Roughly 20 percent of Americans move each year. From 1960 to 1989, more than 91
percent of the nation's households moved, and nearly one-half of all
households moved from 1985 to 1989 alone.[12] The vast majority of
moves are within the same community, county, or state. Roughly 10 to
20 percent of movers migrate to another state or abroad. Job change is
the driving force in out-of-state moves. People change jobs and also ca-
reers. According to the U.S. Bureau of Labor Statistics, 9 to 12 percent
of workers change the type of work they do each year, a figure that
amounted to 10 million people in 1986.[13]

To attract and retain a mobile population, places must learn to market to various individual life-styles. Demographics and life-style proliferation have led to an entire language characterizing attitudes and be-
haviors. The YUPPIE (young urban professional), a small segment of
baby boomers, multiplied into a variety of races, ethnicities, life-styles,
and age cohorts: buppies (blacks), guppies (gays), huppies (Hispanics),
and juppies (Japanese). Middle-aged yuppies become muppies. DINKs
are the family version of yuppies (dual income, no kids), who, when
they have children, become DEWKS (double earners with kids).[14] Marketers constantly segment markets according to consumer attitudes
and behavior labeling them as strivers, achievers, pressured, adapters,
and traditionalists. As American households have fragmented, marketers have devised all kinds of denominations to distinguish the traditional nuclear family from other life-styles.

Viewing households from a statistical vantage, recent changes have
been enormous. In 1970 married couples with children dominated the
consumer market; by 1990 no household type was dominant. Instead,
there are childless married couples, young singles, single parents,
empty nesters, retirees, and cohabitant households.[15]

Changes in household size and income are critical to place marketing. Life-styles are associated with, but not necessarily determined by,
household size and income. Places seeking to attract or retain people
by skills, income, or other characteristics must also accommodate the
life-style needs of these population segments. In *The Rating Guide
to Life in America's Small Cities,* G. Scott Thomas ranks the nation's
219 "micropolitan areas" largely because they have many of the good
things of big-city life (sports, art, shopping, etc.) without the problems.

These are cities in counties of at least 40,000 that are not part of a metro area. Five of Thomas's top ten eastern cities are in New York State, while five of the western top ten are in Washington. A sampling includes Ithaca, New York; Ames, Iowa; Mankato, Minnesota; Fredericksburg, Virginia; and Hattiesburg, Mississippi.[16] Indeed, scores of places can market themselves as an alternative to the big-city hustle— all the benefits, and none of the costs. Quality-of-life factors—air, natural beauty, recreational facilities, and cultural and social amenities— can be valuable assets in attracting people. Small towns also are being rediscovered by mass marketers who have found major metro markets too crowded and too competitive. Following the lead of Wal-Mart Stores into more rustic locations, more companies are pursuing micromarketing strategies into new, smaller markets.[17]

Large cities are by no means defenseless in this competition. For example, Canada's three largest cities and metro areas—Toronto, Montreal, and Vancouver—continue to grow. Years ago, urbanists detected a small trickle of suburban empty nesters (couples with kids gone) returning to the cities. The attractiveness of urban life compared to suburbia for young singles, dual income earners with no kids, and older retirees is a real phenomenon to which cities are learning to adjust. In some cases, revitalization occurs when more affluent newcomers buy and refurbish homes in run-down neighborhoods and, in other cases, incumbent upgradings occur when low and moderate-income residents rehabilitate deteriorated neighborhoods themselves. In still other cases such as Dearborn Park, an entirely new residential community has been built by a public-private partnership in downtown Chicago on the edge of the city's central business district.

In *Edge City: Life on the New Frontier,* Joel Garreau found 200 places that met his edge city definition: 5 million square feet of leasable office space; 600,000 square feet or more of leasable retail space; more jobs than bedrooms; and perceived by people as being one place. According to Garreau, "Edge cities are the culmination of a generation of individual American value decisions about the best ways to live, to work, and play—about how to create home."[18] Edge cities began 10 miles from downtown, spread to 20 miles and, in the case of the San Francisco area, now spread halfway across the state. Edge cities, a product of the information age, contain all the functions a central city offers with shopping malls as the equivalent of the village square. They are a new and growing phenomenon, a new place competitor between cities and their more traditional suburbs.

ATTRACTION/DISCOURAGEMENT POLICIES AND PROGRAMS REGARDING RESIDENTS

It is tempting to assume that consumers live in those communities that best satisfy their preferences,[19] but it is not always the case. People find it difficult and risky to move even when their community has become unattractive and other communities appear more attractive. In addition, they may feel unwelcome and even discouraged from moving into certain communities. The fact is that various places develop policies to attract, retain, or discourage certain people from moving. The National Commission on Affordable Housing concluded in 1990 that "exclusionary, discriminatory, and unnecessary regulations constitute formidable barriers to affordable housing, raising costs by 20 to 35 percent in some communities."[20] For example, Florida's tax and regulatory structure— no income tax, no inheritance tax, and rather lax bankruptcy laws—are highly geared to the elderly, while its relatively low education expenditures are not particularly attractive to a young family looking for the best public education for their children. At the other extreme, Winnetka, Illinois, is attractive to young upper-income families because of its fine public school system. Annual property taxes typically range from $6,000 to $12,000, but can run as high as $30,000. More than half of the property taxes are allocated to support the school system. Obviously, empty nesters are less happy about paying these high taxes.

A place's attractiveness is influenced by its bundle of public services and taxes that must be levied to provide these services. A place must decide how much to spend on building a good public school system, providing services to its senior citizens, and providing welfare payments to its indigent population. For example, welfare spending differences among the ten largest states is more than 3 to 1. Wisconsin overhauled its above-average welfare payments and grants in the late 1980s to stem welfare migration from northern Illinois to southern Wisconsin. California currently seeks to reduce its national leadership in welfare assistance to deal with its exploding welfare costs (see exhibit 11–5).[21]

The larger the provided service bundle, the higher the place's taxes. When those population groups that provide the bulk of the taxes receive disproportionately less of the benefits, they tend to move. Thus, in search of better schools, many young middle-class families relocate from the city to the suburb where their high property taxes yield at least proportional benefits.

EXHIBIT 11-5

California: Taxpayers versus Taxeaters

Governor Pete Wilson claims that our nation's largest and most diverse state is running into a fiscal train wreck. He argues that too many immigrants and welfare recipients are consuming state benefits and that the income-producing middle class is moving to lower-cost places. The middle class are leaving California in their prime earning years; the "producers" are being replaced by people who receive more in-state services than they pay in taxes—the consumers. According to state computations, tax receivers will outnumber taxpayers by 1995. California, with 12 percent of the nation's population and 26 percent of total state spending going to welfare, seeks to cut back its welfare programs drastically and to discourage needy migrants from locating there. The Golden State has run out of gold.

Sources: Andrew Pollack, "Cracks in California's Economy," New York Times, February 9, 1991, p. 17; and Pollack, "California Dreams: Moving In, or Out," New York Times, December 29, 1991, p. 1.

Attracting new residents goes well beyond a place's public service mix and taxation. Although nearly all places claim to be friendly, warm, and welcoming to out of towners, the facts may be quite different. The informal fabric of a place—its places of worship, civic and fraternal groups, social clubs, educational and business organizations—go a long way toward shaping a place's real hospitality norms. In seeking to attract a certain segment of residents, how a place develops, nurtures, and mobilizes these marketing resources may be as important in resident attraction as formal policies.

Demarketing Places

Entering the 1990s, two interacting trends point toward even greater competition among places: One involves the influx of immigrants, and the other relates to the conflict between environmental concerns and employment opportunities. These two trends often collide when governments seek to attract certain groups and avoid others.

The racial composition of the United States changed more dramatically in the past decade than at any time in the twentieth century. Such changes were not uniformly distributed by states, cities, or even metropolitan areas throughout the country. The racial composition in northern New England and the upper Midwest changed hardly at all, remaining 95 percent or more white. In contrast, California, the nation's fastest growing state and location of the largest segment of immigrants, moved from two-thirds of its population being from European ancestry to 57 percent.[22] Ninety percent of immigrants chose to live in metro areas: New York City—Dominican Republicans, Jamaicans, and Chinese; Los Angeles—Mexicans, Filipinos, and South Koreans; Chicago—Mexicans; Miami—Cubans; San Francisco—Chinese; Baltimore—South Koreans; Atlanta—Vietnamese; Detroit—Indians; Denver—Mexicans and Vietnamese; Seattle—Filipinos, Vietnamese, and South Koreans.[23]

The changing race and class composition of places is raising the question of whose responsibility it is to pay for the homeless, the unskilled, the education of children, a growing prison population, and other social and economic costs. For example, estimates of homeless people range from 230,000 (1990 census) to as high as 3 million. Their concentration in major urban centers has produced a bewildering array of government actions, from limiting their access to public facilities or property, to the enforcement of vagrancy and loitering laws, to transporting them out of town to other jurisdictions.[24]

One way to solve the problems of unskilled immigrants and the homeless is to attract industrial businesses that can employ them. However, the more environmentally conscious a place—as defined by its environmental policies governing land use, density, zoning, housing codes, pollution standards, and the like—the more such policies work against attracting low-income populations, blue-collar manufacturing, and affordable housing. The less environmentally conscious a place, the more likely it is to pursue a different set of business attraction-retention policies. The latter may seek to attract the less skilled or be amenable to accepting a solid waste dump, a prison, a power station, or disrupting physical investment. The more unconstrained the place competition game, the more likely are vast differences to be found among places and in their resident marketing.

As places decide whom they wish to attract, retain, or otherwise accept, they generally confront an identity crisis involving values, traditions, and ethical concerns. Unlike a commercial business seeking to meet consumer needs and bound by a unitary purpose of making a profit, the people-attraction business is unlikely to produce a common consensual basis for action. It can be highly divisive and openly conflictual.

CONCLUSION

The people-attraction business and its flip side, demarketing for purposes of cost avoidance, are place phenomena that have increased in visibility and importance over the years. What the national government's responsibility should be for income distribution and setting standards of social equity has swung in pendulum fashion between concern for greater equity and concern for greater efficiency.[25] How these issues are resolved depends a great deal on economic growth for the nation as a whole. In the absence of a growth economy, some observers see an even greater tendency for places to sort themselves out in seeking to attract some population segments and exclude others. The same tendencies may be found in European nations where newly arrived immigrants have met open hostility and nationalistic pressures to seal borders.

Thus, attracting people, whether it be a nation's immigration policies, a state's tax structure, or the bundling of taxes and public services at the local level, is a complex and complicated business in a democratic society. It is contentious, conflictual, and divisive. Just as national immigration policies have changed to reflect global competition for the skilled, talented, and wealthy, so places have entered the contest in competing for residents. That competition is largely carried out through various place-marketing efforts targeted to attract and retain specific groups and population segments. People attraction is likely to become an even more important aspect in place competition in the years ahead.

12

Organizing for Change

In this book, we have argued that places—cities, states, regions, entire nations—are facing a growing crisis. Unlike periodic challenges produced by normal business and economic cycles, places now face new developments in the global marketplace, on the technological frontier, in the political-economic environment. These developments raise fundamental questions about what places can do to survive, let alone prosper.

As the information society advances, people and businesses are becoming more mobile. These trends and changes necessitate that places more routinely reassess whether they are meeting the needs of their citizens. What value are they adding? As *Fortune* magazine's 1991 survey of the best cities for business noted, "the best . . . are those offering the best value."[1] Places have to visualize a clearer sense of the functions they perform and the roles they play in the local, national, and global economy. They have to answer: Who will want to live and work here, under what conditions, and with what expectations? A place that fails to examine its prospects and potential critically is likely to lose out to more attractive competitors.

In this last chapter, we summarize the key challenges facing places and suggest ways in which they might meet these challenges. Specifically, we address three issues:

- What key challenges are places facing?
- How can places respond positively to these challenges?
- Why is marketing places necessary?

WHAT KEY CHALLENGES ARE PLACES FACING?

The world economy is undergoing a major transformation that has and will continue impacting places everywhere. Those responsible for leading and planning a place's future need to apply fresh thinking to the task. Old one-shot or quick-fix formulas for attracting businesses or building sports stadiums and convention centers or increasing tourist advertising expenditures typically fail to deal with the root causes of contemporary place predicaments.

Places, in essence, face these four major challenges:

Challenge One: Places are increasingly at risk as a result of the accelerating pace of change in the global economic, political, and technological environment.

There was a time when place residents expected their city, state, or region to retain its business and industrial character for life. Tomorrow would be much like today. Pittsburgh would remain the nation's steel capital, Detroit the auto capital, New England the shoe capital, and so on. Today, place residents have learned that change, not stability, is the only constant. More U.S. steel is being produced outside Pennsylvania than inside, more U.S. autos are being produced outside Michigan than inside, and more shoes are produced outside than within New England. Soon U.S. multinationals will produce more steel, autos, and shoes outside the United States than inside.

The fact is that the locations of global industries keep shifting. Mobile companies are drawn to places with either lower costs or better skills and/or quality of life. Companies have moved from the high-labor-cost northern states to the lower-cost southern states; now more of them are moving their production to Mexico, the Far East, and Eastern Europe. The gnawing question becomes: What industries and businesses are available to the communities once these migrating companies and industries leave?

Local companies move not only in search of lower costs but also because they are outperformed on the demand side. Local companies that once had assured markets now face tough competition from invading multinational possessing greater resources and offering better products at lower prices.

The heightened mobility of industry is largely due to dynamic advances in communication, transportation, and information systems; these, in turn, have facilitated the movement of goods, services, technology, and capital across national borders. The result is a dramatic shrinkage in distances over time and space. Places can no longer expect to retain all of their major industries and businesses. They must be ready to abandon shrinking or noncompetitive ones, replacing them with new and more value-adding businesses.

In the old economy, goods were produced in certain places due to least-cost advantages. They had distinctive national and often even specific place identities. In the new economy, goods can be produced in several locations and assembled at various places. As Robert Reich observed,

> Precision ice hockey equipment is designed in Sweden, financed in Canada, and assembled in Cleveland and Denmark for distribution in North America and Europe, respectively, out of alloys whose molecular structure was researched and patented in Delaware and fabricated in Japan.[2]

The same principle holds true for service producers who draw information from multiple places; process, interpret, and analyze the information in other places; and disseminate the information to still other places. Initially, corporations moved their back office operations from cities to suburbs, next they moved to low-cost regions, such as Citicorp moving its credit card operations to Tampa, Florida, and Sioux Falls, South Dakota. Today, clerical services in industries such as insurance, banking, and publishing are moving offshore to the Caribbean, Ireland, Portugal, and the Philippines where labor costs are much lower. An increasing number of large companies are outsourcing their in-house information systems to capture value from specialized firms and technologies whose location may be inside or outside the United States.

Places are further influenced by significant political developments. The end of the Cold War has meant that defense-dependent cities, states, and regions—those with military bases or heavy defense production—must develop new strategies and programs to soften the impact of the defense wind down on jobs and facilitate commercial conversion to serving new markets. Southern California, for example, seeks to reposition itself as the emerging global center for electrical vehicle technology. The whole balance of global power is shifting. Asia is booming, ready to take the step toward the level of industrialization achieved in Japan and the West. Western Europe is moving toward becoming the world's largest consumer bloc. Certain Latin American nations—particularly Mexico, Chile, and Argentina—have suddenly turned on their economic engines and are now attracting strong investment and new industries.

If the post–Cold War period had any leading characteristic, it is the shortage of capital. Most nations, states, and cities are burdened by debt and cannot generate sufficient internal or external funds to make the investments necessary for gaining competitive advantages and satisfying the consumption needs of their people. The rapid rate of urbanization has strained the limited resources of the public sector in every developing country. The main sources of capital—the United States, Japan, and Germany—each face enormous capital demands to meet their own internal needs, let alone the growing international commitments to Eastern Europe, the former Soviet Union, and developing nations.[3]

The fundamental point is that external forces change rapidly and often unexpectedly, transforming in turn, the fate and fortunes of places. Add industry cycles, trade policies, and fluctuating national currencies to these uncertainties, and one understands why places function in a turbulent external environment.

Challenge Two: Places are increasingly at risk as a result of normal processes or urban evolution and decay.

Places normally start off as rural-agricultural communities, become towns, and then grow into cities and metropolitan areas. In the modern period, cities move from centers for trade, to industrial centers, and next to service producers. As problems within the city increase—pollution, crime, congestion, traffic gridlock, poor schools and services, higher taxes—movement to the suburbs expands. Initially, suburbanites commute to the cities for work, but then work and employment opportunities move to the suburbs—a pattern repeated in nearly all major U.S. metro areas.

Left with a concentration of poorer people and higher service costs, and unable to tap sufficient resources from higher government levels, the city must live within its financial resources, reducing both services and maintenance of its fixed environment. In a spiraling fashion, infrastructure deteriorates, service gaps grow wider, and blight spreads. Meanwhile, metropolitan growth continues from inner-ring suburbs to outer-ring exurbs. Factories and offices also move further out. Soon clean and well-functioning "edge cities" emerge around the core city. The core city struggles with a declining economic and job base which results in reduced quality of life.

A century ago, major technological changes occurred that transformed and benefited urban growth: electricity, the internal combustion engine, subways, indoor plumbing and sanitation systems, elevators, and steel structured buildings. A century later, new technologies have emerged that are not captives of urban places, but rather lend themselves to applications allowing economic activity to occur most anywhere—satellite communications, microprocessors, robotics, lasers, fiber optics, microcomputers, and integrated circuitry. In the 1970s and 1980s, some cities made the successful transition from a manufacturing to a service economy only to discover that new technologies had reshaped not only office work but also the location decisions of service firms and industries. Nearly twenty years ago, the father of urban economics, Wilbur Thompson, stated that cities have failed to recycle fast enough, unloading aging urban capital and industries as well as depopulating to enable the next cycle of stabilization or growth to occur.[4] While much agreement exists on the need for places to accelerate their response to change, far less can be found on those specific factors that explain why some metropolitan areas grow faster than others, and some do not grow at all.[5] We understand the components of decline much more than the rapidly changing factors related to growth.

Challenge Three: Places are facing a growing number of competitors in their efforts to attract scarce resources.

In the face of mounting problems, places responded with a proliferation of economic development agencies to specialize in distinctive tasks—planning, financing, marketing, tourism, exports—all related to place improvement. These agencies spend public funds for advertising and send salespeople on missions at home and abroad to attract resources to their area. But other places, they soon discover, are matching or exceeding their efforts and level of sophistication. The stark reality is that there is a superabundance of place sellers hunting for a very limited number of place buyers. The buyers have available a growing amount of information about places—including place raters, real estate interests, consultants, and new software technologies that provide highly sophisticated and usable data about places. They make careful comparisons of what each place seller offers in the way of costs of doing business, inducements, and quality-of-life benefits. Place buyers may demand such high concessions from sellers that even the final winner may turn out to be a loser. Place-inducement battles similar to those in the United States during the 1970s and 1980s have already become part of a global phenomenon in the 1990s.

Competition will only intensify in the future. The lure of low-cost, highly-skilled goods and service producing areas in Eastern Europe, Latin America, and Southeast Asia will inevitably draw resources away from high cost, low-skilled labor areas. The United States contains more than 25,000 geopolitical towns, counties, cities, and states competing for resources; extrapolating this number to a global basis, the staggering figure of actual or would-be competitors exceeds 700,000.

Places have to rethink the premises on which they base their future. They have to learn more about target customers if they are to successfully attract and retain businesses and people, export their products, promote tourism and investments. Every place must recognize this contest among rivals and hone its skills as a competitor. Since the writings of David Ricardo nearly 200 years ago, economists have embraced the benefits of reducing trade barriers, namely that lower prices and higher growth outweigh the loss of jobs and income that some workers and places experience in this process. The difference today is that we have a much better idea of whom and where gains and losses will occur.

Places must respond to rather than resist change, adapt to rather than ignore market forces. In 1985, the President's Commission on Industrial Competitiveness defined competitiveness as "the degree to which a nation can, under free and fair market conditions, produce goods and services that meet the test of international markets, while simultaneously maintaining and expanding the real income of its citizens."[6] This challenge applies not simply to nations but to all regions and places.

Challenge Four: Places have to rely increasingly on their own local resources to face the growing competition.

Trends and forces pull business, much like nations, in two directions simultaneously. "Think globally; act locally" represents the new paradigm in which businesses must both face globalism in outlook and operation, and localism in business practices and market differences. Nation-states are pulled together by the imperatives of trading blocs and the need for common rules, but pulled apart by parochial interests and provincial needs. Places, too, encounter the full force of these centripetal and centrifugal pressures from business and higher government levels, producing a certain reversal of the preceding maxim; namely, "Think locally; act globally." That paradigm requires first an understanding of what they have or can have that someone else needs or wants, and second a translation of those advantages to broader selected audiences. What places need to do to become more competitive may differ both in degree and kind from what nation-states or specific industries and businesses must do to be competitive. Their actual or potential resource base turns on a combination of factors differing from place to place.

Because many national governments are preoccupied with a huge debt burden, they are less able to provide substantial direct aid to local communities in their competitive struggle. Even were such resources to exist, the ability of national governments to target and tailor specific resources to meet individual place needs is fraught with distributional and equity considerations. Furthermore, a worldwide trend exists toward national fragmentation, characterized by greater local choices and empowerment. New nations are still being formed, old boundaries changing, and hundreds of nationalities seeking their identities through greater autonomy and nation status. Even the much vaunted movement for European integration has incurred setbacks in voting for the Maastricht Treaty of greater political and economic unity due to economic fears of German control and popular concern about loss of natural sovereignty. We may see the rise once again of powerful city-states—Singapore and Hong Kong are examples of this. The wealth of nations is produced by the sum of its parts: industries, people, and places. Nations enhance their competitiveness when their individual cities and regions become more competitive.

In view of powerful new forces reshaping the world such as global competition, technological acceleration, and political splintering, places simply have no choice but to be more strategic and entrepreneurial in managing their futures.

HOW MUST PLACES RESPOND TO THESE CHALLENGES?

We have seen how places can be transformed: Massachusetts from textiles to computers; Texas from natural resources to aerospace and new technologies; and the Carolinas from textiles and agriculture to goods production.

"Many states now believe," notes Scott Fosler, "that actions they take, or do not take, can significantly affect the extent to which businesses start, grow, innovate, develop and market new products, improve their productivity, develop export markets, contract, decline, relocate and fold."[7]

Generally, the smaller the jurisdiction, the clearer the evidence of what places can do to effectuate their own fortunes. Older industrial cities such as Pittsburgh, Baltimore, St. Paul, and Glasgow have remarkable achievements to show for their efforts over the last thirty years. A place's condition need not be hopeless because, as we have argued, all places have some actual or potential resources to exploit in place competition. To turn fortunes around, places must think longer term, and still build short-term actions into a broader, long range perspective.

Yet those who seek to improve a place's or region's competitive position are inundated by advice-givers: planners, consultants, economists, investment bankers, real estate, and other business professionals. The late media commentator, Eric Sevareid once observed that "the chief cause of problems is solutions," which, for place improvers, translates into whom do I listen to, or how do I deal with the experts?

To assist place development in the years ahead, we propose the following ten responses that constitute a framework for navigating place development in the twenty-first century.

Response One: Places need to establish a strategic vision to face these challenges.

Few places today can articulate a strategic vision of what they are aiming to be in the next ten or twenty years. They all want prosperous industries, rising real incomes, and more quality jobs. But this wish or hope is not a vision. A vision defines a realistic picture of what they can become in the next decade and beyond as a place to live, work, and play. A vision goes beyond simply targeting specific businesses that the public would like to see locate in a place. According to the Committee for Economic Development, "An effective vision can give direction and cohesion to specific government actions and help avoid the pitfalls and tempting quick-fixes that can undermine long-term performance."[8]

Minneapolis provides a good illustration of a city that has hammered out its vision for the twenty-first century. Its goals are to be:

1. A city with a safe environment for all citizens.
2. A city where jobs are available for all who want to work.

3. A city that seeks fairness, celebrates diversity, and works to strengthen civic values.
4. A city in which all children are school-ready and work-ready and in which networks of support are available to all families within their neighborhoods.
5. A city in which neighborhoods are revitalized through citizen participation and neighborhood specific service delivery via a twenty-year Neighborhood Revitalization Plan.
6. A city with decent and affordable housing for all who seek it.
7. A city that is clean, healthful, and attractive.
8. A city that has a vital and economically healthy downtown.
9. A city featuring a rich variety of cultural, entertainment, and recreational opportunities.
10. A city that is financially sound and well-managed.

These goals are straightforward and readily understandable. Getting the public to formulate and buy into a vision moves the debate beyond "what to do" into the more conflictual territory of "how to" and "who pays for what." Mayor Donald M. Fraser of Minneapolis said of the city's goals: "With strong shared leadership, . . . elected officials can give form and substance to this vision. . . . The process of moving toward a vision is, in the final analysis, as important as the vision itself. Perhaps more so."[9]

Another example of the power of vision is provided by the state of Tennessee:

Governor Lamar Alexander (1979–87) of Tennessee approached economic development by combining a highly successful industrial recruitment effort with improved public services to attract and retain businesses. The latter included a focus on three major public services and amenities: the environment, roads, and schools. Alexander's Better Schools Program made sweeping changes in the state's educational system from primary and secondary education through the public universities. In raising taxes and educational standards, these programs linked increased education funding to performance—a precursor to national school reform. Such innovations catapulted Alexander to a leadership position among fellow governors and later to his appointment as U.S. Secretary of Education in 1990. Tennessee's emphasis on education enhancement paid handsome dividends by creating a positive climate for General Motors which located its multibillion dollar Saturn plant in that state.[10]

Response Two: Places need to establish a market-oriented strategic planning process to face these challenges.

All places engage in some form of planning whether driven by fiscal, physical, or social needs. These include multiyear budgets, public works, school enrollments, and the like. Many places suffer from too many plans; too many planning groups' surveys of public managers indicate that many employ some form of strategic planning as a management tool to help shape basic directions, goals, and resource allocations. However, strategic planning has proven more useful for organizational units with a unified sense of mission rather than a highly diversified and fragmented municipal or metropolitan jurisidiction as a whole.

At the same time, fundamental differences exist between the public and private sectors in their relation to resource allocation. As David Osborne and Ted Gaebler note, "Most public agencies don't get their funds from customers. Businesses do."[11] Public agencies are funded by legislative bodies and boards—elected public officials beholden to their constituents, often organized groups. Not only does this perspective work against long-term planning but it also may neglect the broader interests of a place.

Consequently, in a place's desperation to find planning answers, various quick fixes emerge to span a short-term planning horizon and placate various interest groups that seek immediate action. The most common ones are business attraction such as a new plant; major capital projects from sports stadiums to convention centers; a new tourist attraction such as a festival market; reorientation of retail operations into a mall; or now, casino gambling, which, according to one hotel chain leader, will be in every major U.S. city by the end of the 1990s. Often they are forced by those outside government—a developer, an entrepreneur, a relocating firm—where the prospect of lost opportunities compels immediate decisions.

These proposals have the virtue of appearing to address one or more problems. They often deliver symbolic comfort to the citizens that some specific action will secure a better future. After all, the message of jobs now is often far more persuasive than one of more durable or higher paying jobs later. Yet, many turn out to be boondoggles or white elephants. More often than not, they fail to meet most tests of a viable plan for improving the community. Often such stopgap measures offer vague hope for triggering a host of other improvements that may or may not follow. "Build and they shall come" turned out to make no more sense for real estate development than it did for overall place development in the 1980s. Rarely do these proposals deliver a full solution to the community's problems. They do not deal with, albeit seek to avoid, more basic issues such as suburban flight, increasing crime rate, deteriorating educational and transportation systems, and inadequate housing. As Osborne noted,

> the economic development question of what works, begets a wrong focus on incubators, research parks, venture capital funds, small business loans and the other business programs. [He concludes that] the specific programs chosen are far less important than the way in which each program is carried out; how it fits into an overall strategy, what principles underlie that strategy, and how the different pieces fit together.[12]

Clearly, places need to assign higher importance to the strategic planning process that moves beyond meeting electoral needs of the moment to incorporating the broader perspectives of the marketplace into place planning. Strategic market planning can serve as the guiding force in developing the place's future—a screen both for filtering and ranking specific actions or proposals that inevitably arise. Places need to defend themselves against constantly reacting to proposals for change, and be proactive in what they can do. This is not to ignore the reality of politics, but rather to balance political needs with market forces. The place needs to identify its resources, opportunities, and natural customers. The place must understand its potential customers' needs, perceptions, preferences, and buying decisions. The place must construct scenarios of its potential futures and determine a path that confers the place with competitive advantages.

Places also must understand their current and prospective competitors. They must see themselves as competing with specific places that are trying to attract many of the same tourists, business firms, and investors. Because place competition has been fundamentally altered by the inescapable forces of technology and globalism, place rivalry extends far beyond city and suburbs, centers within a region, or even between regions. It is now international in scope. These target customers inevitably make comparisons and choose locations that serve their best interests.

Response Three: Places must adopt a genuine market perspective toward their products and customers.

The world is moving rapidly toward a more market-oriented, consumer-driven economy. The aim is a democratic one—to place power and choice in the hands of citizens as perhaps never before done. A public sector bent on serving its own needs, taxing and spending without a sense of the new competition, comes up short in place development. Citizens who see the costs but not the benefits of public spending are unlikely to be persuaded that certain investments are necessary for the future.

In an era when the public sector is asked to do more with less, governments are compelled to think and plan more like businesses. They need to calculate the actual costs of their services, often apportioning them through prices to determine demand levels. They must generate more of their own resources through sale of services, and seek to reduce costs but not service quality through user fees and contracted services. They also may need to get out of certain public businesses and eliminate programs that no longer meet the public's needs. They are learning the business of converting spending-thinking into investment-thinking, whether through preventive actions to avoid more costly remedies later or putting resources where they have highest returns. With a market-orientation, a place sees itself as serving and meeting the needs of customers and directing resources toward citizen welfare.[13]

Places ultimately thrive or languish on the basis of what they do to create skilled, motivated, and satisfied citizens—workers, teachers, inventors, entrepreneurs, managers. Human capital is emerging as the most vital resource places possess or can develop in place competition. Places that turn unskilled workers into skilled labor, promote innovation and entrepreneurship, and provide lifelong education and training gain a competitive advantage in the new economic order.[14] The most important industries of the future where commercial application of new technologies will locate are likely to be in those places having a supply of skilled workers. Places that do little else but nurture an educated and trained labor force may do far more to enhance their competitive advantages over the longer run than those making a series of one-time investments in a single employer or a single capital investment.

Much of the public mindset turns on resource allocating decisions. Capital decisions that require debt to be incurred spreads physical costs and benefits over multiyear periods, whereas operating decisions involving human resources spending generally are annualized decisions in which the multiyear benefits are subordinated to meeting this year's needs now. We must view human capital in much the same way that we look at physical capital—investments whose costs and returns are spread over time. Because competitiveness demands producing goods for international markets and raising people's real incomes, education and training have assumed an increasingly important role in this development process.

Response Four: Places have to build quality into their programs and services to compete with other places.

On a day-to-day basis, people judge a place not as much by its grand vision as they do by the quality of its everyday services. Their impressions come from how easily the traffic moves, how clean the city air and streets are, how good the education system is, and how accessible cultural and recreational amenities are. Quality services are noted not only by the residents and business firms but also by those considering moving to, visiting, or investing in a place. The same principle holds true for the tourism-hospitality business where competition intensifies as more places make the physical investments necessary to enhance their relative attractiveness. Beyond infrastructure, success turns increasingly on the service quality provided by industry and governments alike.

When standards of living rise, citizens generally develop higher expectations of performance. In weighing relocation decisions, businesses place increasingly more value on quality-of-life considerations than cost factors alone. Service quality, therefore, requires continuous investments in infrastructure as well as in various amenities—museums, theaters, sports, entertainment, recreation—to maintain a competitive posture. The fact that tax revenues and borrowing costs may not always accommodate such needs necessitates even more the need for a planning and market perspective. Those places that figure out how to create and deliver high quality in their various services are much more formidable competitors in place competition.

For many places, the transition to a strategic planning process and market perspective for their products and services is an evolutionary one. It often begins with opening up public services to competition, moving to some privatization, and adopting total quality management (TQM) principles in service delivery. Once the skills of greater competitiveness and customer orientation are internalized, places are far more likely to adopt a customer orientation in marketing themselves externally. Not that the former necessarily leads to the latter, but rather the mindset of markets and meeting identifiable needs can carry over from one to the other. (See exhibit 12–1, Privatization and Other Answers to Improving Public Sector Service Quality)

Response Five: Places need skill to effectively communicate and promote their competitive advantages.

Having quality and being an attractive place is one thing; communicating the special quality of a place to others is quite another. Places must skillfully position themselves to those various publics who may wish to locate, invest, live, visit, or do business there. They must adapt their messages to highly differentiated buyers while at the same time developing a core image of what the place basically offers. Take, for example, Brownsville, Texas, whose "By the sea, by the border" positioning delineates the place as a port access to the Gulf of Mexico, where the nation's largest free trade zone is located, and as a border access to Mexico. One also thinks of Indianapolis as a sports center, Pittsburgh as a service and research center, Mexico as a parts-assembly center for North America, Hong Kong as a regional source for low-tech production and cheap labor, and Seattle as a software development center. It is not enough for a city to select a slogan such as "Pleasantville—A Nice Place to Live and Do Business." The place must develop a concept infusing energy, direction, and pride into the place's citizens. It must be a concept that is true of the place, where the conveyed image is congruent with the reality.

In today's tough competitive market, combinations of industry, universities, government, and venture capitalists have created a growth synergy in such seemingly diverse places as Salt Lake City, suburban Philadelphia, Champaign-Urbana, Illinois and Tucson, Arizona. In Minnesota's "Medical Alley," some 300 makers of medical devices find 30 percent of their revenues now driven by exports and companies in other growth regions are matching that rate. Places and businesses are learning what chemistry best facilitates growth—a mixture that differs from place to place, but with many common elements.[15] These places have congruity between image and reality as employment is increasing in new technologies and businesses.

Exhibit 12-1

Privatization and Other Answers To Improving Public Sector Service Quality

The public sector, being largely monopolistic in character, often lags behind the private sector in being responsive to the needs and service requirements of its citizens. A number of mechanisms can help the public sector become more responsive to its private citizens:

1. *Privatization,* where more use is made of the private sector to carry out formerly publicly provided services. Outside the United States, privatization involves the sale of publicly owned assets to the private sector and denationalization or commercialization of government enterprises. In this country, it commonly involves government contracting out for services. In the latter case, privatization often provides full-cost pricing which allows citizens to make more informed choices as to whether they want more, less, or about the same amount of service and quality. Choice begets competition among service providers which, in turn, means meeting customer satisfaction or else losing the renewal of service contracts.

2. *Voucherization,* where citizens receive a basic credit that they can choose to spend on the public service or a competing private service.

3. *Warranties,* where a public agency is required to compensate aggrieved citizens for personal losses or inconveniences caused by that agency. Here are some warranties that the current British government is thinking of implementing:

   • If British Rail cancels trains or runs them excessively late, passengers may get compensated for their ticket cost by receiving a voucher for off-peak travel.
   • If garbage is not collected in a timely fashion, households can call in private contractors at the city's expense.

(continued)

Exhibit 12–1
Privatization and Other Answers To Improving Public Sector
Service Quality (continued)

- If National Health Service patients wait too long for operations, they receive vouchers whose value would be
  equivalent to the government's cost in rendering that
  service.

The point is that public agencies need to adopt the identical
concern for service quality found in private industry. This calls for
researching citizen needs and expectations, setting up the service
delivery system, training and motivating public employees to
meet the expected standards, and implementing a continuous service delivery improvement process. The real gain in public service
competition is that public officials are learning to deal with constituents as consumers, and choice as a way of meeting various
citizen demand levels. The public sector must move from simply
being responsive to competing public demands to becoming *entrepreneurial and innovative* in marketing and delivering new services.

**Response Six: Places need to diversify their economic base and
develop mechanisms for flexibly adapting to changing conditions.**

Places cannot rely on one or a few miscellaneous industries or businesses on which to base their future. Industries quickly rise and fall due
to technological changes, and globally can respond quickly to cost advantages found elsewhere. Places must view as their challenge building
a well balanced portfolio of businesses.

"Nations succeed not in isolated industries, but in clusters of industries connected through vertical and horizontal relationships."[16] This
phenomenon, seen in California's Silicon Valley and Boston's Route
128, is being replicated elsewhere in goods and service producing industries both in the United States and abroad through networks, alliances,
joint ventures, and product development. Diversification became a
major objective of places seeking to avoid the business-industry cycles
of the 1970s and 1980s while clustering has become a key concept of
the 1990s. More than the agglomeration of old in which similar indus-

tries clustered in one place to benefit from economies of scale, modern clustering involves sharing of new technologies and applications across industries.

Places must develop better competitive intelligence and forecasting abilities to recognize trends and emerging needs. Feast and famine defense spending since 1945 provided cyclical comfort to defense-dependent areas, but also gave a clear signal of what life might be like should more permanent demobilization occur. The Canada–U.S. Free Trade Pact of the late 1980s constituted a precursor to a North American pact with Mexico—well understood trends that would affect places and industries throughout the United States. Both small and large developmental choices impact on a place. Consider the following:

The futurist John Naisbitt in his *Megatrends 2000* cites certain indicators that suggest "during the 1990s art will gradually replace sports as society's primary leisure activity."[17] If he is correct, this change may have vast consequences for those places that narrow their portfolios of amenities to sports stadiums and franchises. The new sports stadiums of the 1980s may well be the white elephants of the late 1990s.

An effective mechanism for enacting change is the community development corporation (CDC). From the South Bronx to the Mississippi Delta, from Appalachia to South Central Los Angeles, more than 2,000 CDCs have been started over the past 20 years whose services are geographically targeted to low-income people. These non-profit CDCs often involve a partnership among business, government, foundations, and local organizations as a mechanism to invest in people, property, and businesses in impoverished areas. These organizations seek to empower people in distressed urban and rural communities providing new opportunities whether through job skills, housing, or business ownership. CDC goals are often to create stable places or neighborhoods where disinvestment has occurred and opportunities exist for reinvestment in local jobs and economic activities. Like their larger geopolitical counterparts—cities and counties or states—CDCs are flexible responses to situations where neither government nor the private sector alone are likely to work, and where a geographically specific area needs economic revitalization.

Exhibit 12-2

St. Paul: Small Business Development

No middle American city has so consistently pursued a business development strategy as has St. Paul, Minnesota, (pop. 264,000).When George Latimer became St. Paul's mayor in 1976, St. Paul was the lesser of the twin cities, a waning blue-collar, ethnic community which was also the state capital. Latimer made entrepreneurship the focus of St. Paul's economic development strategy with his Homegrown Economy Project as the centerpiece of a self-reliant city. At a time when other cities sought to attract outside business or emphasized basic retention, St. Paul's emphasis on *small business revitalization,* with strong support from banks, corporations, foundations, and academic institutions, emerged as a unique development approach.

St. Paul's economy already had been moving in the direction of service sector growth and high-technology firms. However, under Latimer, city officials sought to identify its strengths and weaknesses in self-reliant activities, crafting new programs and mechanisms to overcome weaknesses and to fill gaps. In August 1983, St. Paul issued its strategy document, *The Homegrown*

Response Seven: Places must develop and nurture entrepreneurial characteristics.

Place development is spurred by entrepreneurial people and organizations. It can be accelerated by entrepreneurial governments. Neil Peirce and Robert Guskind, building on Tom Peters' best-seller, *In Search of Excellence,* identified the nation's ten best-managed cities. The ten cities should come as no surprise: Baltimore, Dallas, Indianapolis, Minneapolis, St. Paul, Seattle, Charlotte, Phoenix, San Antonio, and San Diego. (See exhibit 12-2 for St. Paul's small business development story.) These cities demonstrated direct involvement in economic activities. They acted as lenders, brokers, land developers, job trainers, and facilitators for business and real estate development.

City, that identified how private cooperative activities could better promote homegrown economic enterprises. The plan emphasized local ownership, the creation of skilled jobs, local economic diversification, high inter-industry dependence, benefits for workers and neighborhoods, and the attraction of capital and funds from outside the area.

Latimer gained national recognition as a place development guru. His and St. Paul's success derived from results; new partnerships, investments, programs, and ventures fit together into an overall strategy. Labor, neighborhood advocates, citizen activists, foundations, business and financial leaders bought into this new approach to stimulate the community's economy. It was a win-win situation rather than the zero-sum game that many places faced with business attraction or choosing between projects benefiting downtown or city neighborhoods.

George Latimer finished six terms as St. Paul's mayor in December 1989. He achieved recognition nationally as an entrepreneurial mayor—a pioneer in using public funds to leverage private resources. He made St. Paul a coequal partner, not a stepchild of Minneapolis. Latimer left a legacy of a well-run government and revitalized neighborhoods, innovations in energy conservation and housing for the homeless, and proved himself a national leader in place development.

Sources: Neal Peirce and Robert Guskind, "Hot Managers, Sizzling Cities," *Business Month*, June 1989, pp. 36–53, and Dorothy Parr Riesen, "Mayor of St. Paul to Head Law School," *City and State*, May 22, 1989, p. 16.

Beyond the ability of delivering a wide range of services, while keeping taxes modest and bond-ratings high, the ten best cities reflected an entrepreneurial spirit, their mayors and managers every bit the equals of their private sector counterparts. "Most important," noted the authors, "all of the nation's best-run cities are characterized by managerial leadership that has set the stage for economic advances that make these cities masters of their own destiny."[18] Their leaders are risk-takers. Some characteristics of entrepreneurial places and governments are shown in tables 12–1 and 12–2.

TABLE 12–1
Entrepreneurial Places: Characteristics

Economy	Open, fluid, low barriers to start-ups
Social structure	Dynamic, mobile, outsiders welcome
Business	No dominant employer, competitive
Financial	Competitive banks, venture capital access
Labor	Skilled labor, professional work force, support
Government	Support small business, start-ups
Innovation	Large university, corporate research center
Media	Attention to entrepreneurs, new business
Jobs	Grow new businesses, small business growth
Amenities	Good quality of life, culture/recreation

Sources: David L. Birch, "Thriving on Adversity," *Inc.*, March 1988, pp. 80–84; and Joel Kotkin, "City of the Future," *Inc.*, April 1987, pp. 56–60.

TABLE 12–2
Entrepreneurial Governments: Characteristics

Finances	Modest taxes, high bond ratings
Managers	Thinkers, visionaries, politicians, salespersons
Services	High quality, innovative, competitive
Culture	High citizen participation, open
Styles	Professional, results oriented
Bureaucracy	Entrepreneurial, new ways to do things
Spending	Investments, performance, outcomes
Citizens	Consumers, stockholders
Planning	Anticipation, multiyear, strategic
Responsiveness	Good listeners, negotiators, accountability

Source: Adapted fromNeil Peirce and Robert Guskind, "Hot Managers, Sizzling Cities," *Business Month*, June 1989, pp. 36–53.

Response Eight: Places must rely more on the private sector to accomplish their tasks.

The business community must actively participate in helping plan the place's future. In many places, local chambers of commerce or their equivalents assume the lead business role, functioning as place boosters and promoters externally, and watchdogs on place spending and taxation internally. In much of the South, chambers provide political as well as economic leadership. Ivan Allen, Jr., led Atlanta's meteoric rise, moving from president of Atlanta's chamber to mayor (1961-69). Probably no large city is more closely identified with its business community than Dallas, where Goals for Dallas—eighty-six goals for the educational, social, recreational, and physical development of the city— guided that place's growth during the 1960s, 1970s, and much of the 1980s. Minneapolis's Five Percent Club—those major corporations that contributed 5 percent of pretax earnings to local philanthropic causes—constituted the core of Minneapolis's civic activities. The Indianapolis Chamber of Commerce provided the initial impetus for that city's turnaround in the early 1970s.

In the 1960s and 1970s, public/private partnerships emerged at the city level; initially they focused on central city development, and later on neighborhoods, education, and social services. In the late 1970s and into the 1980s, partnerships covered larger geographic groupings of places—metropolitan, regional, and statewide—with broader focuses and greater emphasis on strategies. Take the case of Michigan in the early 1980s; observers generally agree that its Path to Prosperity is "one of the best economic strategy documents produced by any state."[19] This document's uniqueness stems from its bold departure from previous state plans—by targeting advanced manufacturing —and the extent to which state leaders followed its recommendations. (Exhibit 12-3 describes Michigan's Path to Prosperity.) Other states also produced well-received blueprints for development: Pennsylvania's Choices; Illinois' Corridors of Opportunity; Nevada's Plan for Economic Diversification and Development; and Indiana's In Step with the Future.

From the early 1950s to the mid-1970s, cities produced no end of master plans for their physical redevelopment: Forward Atlanta, Pittsburgh's Renaissance II, and Chicago 21. However, the Allegheny Conference on Community Development in Pittsburgh was one of the first to develop an overall economic development strategy and plan that included not just downtown improvement but also the advance-

EXHIBIT 12-3
Michigan's Path to Prosperity

In 1983, former Congressman James Blanchard succeeded William Milliken as Michigan's governor at a time when the state's economy had been devastated by recessionary forces and global competition. In the preceding four years, the state's manufacturing had shrunk by 25 percent, or nearly 300,000 jobs, mostly in auto and steel-producing firms. Business and government alike recognized that maintaining the status quo would be indefensible.

Governor Blanchard immediately slashed budgets and raised income taxes to avoid state bankruptcy. Following an extensive study of Michigan's economy, Blanchard issued a comprehensive economic development plan, *The Path to Prosperity*, whose underlying concept was that manufacturing should remain the focus of the state's economic base because it not only drove the state's export products but also fed its service industries. To become a center for the automated factory of the future and new companies producing related technologies, Michigan's manufacturers would have to be transformed by: (1) entrepreneurs bringing new technologies to market; (2) research industries excelling in engineering and industrial technology; (3) creation of new labor-management relationships; and (4) government providing the financial, legal, tax, and other support systems necessary to speed this transition or, at least, cushion inevitable disruptions caused by this transition.

The report outlined several themes that would later guide specific state actions and initiatives including: a concentration on the

ment of the Pittsburgh region. The Allegheny Conference agenda expanded to cover improved schools, health care cost containment, and neighborhood development.

Cleveland's Tomorrow: A Strategy for Economic Vitality, Miami Beacon Council's Strategic Plan for Dade's Economic Future, and Metro Denver's Strategic Economic Development Plan represent new place blueprints built on economic analysis, place strategies, and a state's economic base, a future based on having innovative firms developing new products and product technologies, private industry leadership, state investments in education and research, and reducing state related business costs.

These principles constituted a dramatic departure from past state practices and ran contrary to how other industrialized states responded to the 1980–83 recession. Blanchard and Michigan's bold venture turned not simply on a well-crafted strategy but also on the political sophistication of its implementation.

The task force's 1984 report, *The Path to Prosperity*, gained support from prominent corporate, labor, and political leaders. It avoided the many pitfalls of grand plans such as great fanfare and hype. Based on an objective examination of the state's economy and what state actions might alter the economy, the report avoided the problems faced by earlier commissions that had named leaders with set positions and agendas that had to be moderated, mediated, and compromised to gain a working consensus. It was written with relative anonymity as to authorship.

Implementation required dozens of specific tax, regulatory, spending, and investment decisions whose success turned on getting key groups and leaders to buy into change rather than characteristically vetoing change. Blanchard got his programs through the state legislature, while key actors in the state's political and economic communities bought into a multiyear development plan to reposition the state's economy.

Sources: Charles Bartsch, "Michigan Reaching For Recovery," *Economic Development Commentary*, 10 (Fall 1980), pp. 8–12, and John E. Jackson, "Michigan," in *The New Role of American States*, ed. R. Scott Fosler (New York: Oxford University Press,1988), pp. 91–140.

range of public/private investment to position a place in the new economy.

Various communities demonstrated the benefits of developing strong public/private partnerships. Each included a comprehensive plan as well as one or two key ideas that captured the public's imagination: Pennsylvania's Ben Franklin Partnerships, Tennessee's emphasis on education, Indianapolis's concentration on sports and associations,

Pittsburgh's amenities and new industries formula, Wichita's diversification program (see exhibit 12–4), Fairfax County, Virginia's successful business attraction marketing, Baltimore's waterfront and downtown redevelopment, and Cleveland's pursuit of growth industries (see exhibit 12–5).

What worked in the 1970s and 1980s, of course, may be inappropriate in the 1990s and in the decade beyond. In the early 1990s, public sector budget constraints have crippled many a state-local government's economic development efforts. Agencies and programs have been eliminated and, following the trend of privatizing nonessential public services, others have been transferred to the private sector. The trends toward increased privatization of place development are powerful.

The Utah Economic Development Corporation, for example, was created out of necessity in 1987 to overcome jurisdictional fragmentation, to pool public and private resources, and to generate greater corporate participation. More states and places are contracting out their marketing and business contact activities to private organizations and professional staffs: Advantage Minnesota, the Arizona Economic Development Council, and Enterprise Florida are just a few among many major organizational changes underway that reflect the migration of place development activities from the public to the private sectors.

The accelerated trend toward privatizing economic development activities is being driven not simply by disillusionment or despair at results, but by learning experiences and the four fundamental factors which follow:

- *Resources*—Privatization is driven by the imperative of cost savings. In Utah, the state's Economic Development Commission offered the prospect of overcoming the competition among dozens of public county agencies and chambers of commerce through resource pooling into one large expanded development organization.
- *Fragmentation*—In the 1990s, the drive to consolidate development agencies and blunt neighboring rivalries will give rise to local, metro, multiregional, and statewide private organizations better able to promote economic market areas than specific political subdivisions operating independently and competitively with one another. Consolidation and resource pooling also are driven by the forces of globalism in which competition across nation-states requires broader orchestra-

EXHIBIT 12-4

Wichita's Successful Diversification

Wichita, Kansas, (pop. 290,000) constitutes another civic model of vision, people working together, and strategies to diversify a place's industries. Business leaders, public officials, and economic planners recognized the necessity to move Wichita away from dependence on past cyclical and unstable industries: agriculture, oil and gas production, and aviation firms (Boeing Company, Cessna Aircraft Company, LearJet Corporation, and Beech Aircraft Corporation). The community found a need for a new structure, new leadership, and public-private capital to reposition itself against other urban areas, to diversify its economy, and to create a new image of Wichita. The Wichita/Sedgwick County Partnership placed the city and county's economic development activities under the chamber of commerce in 1987, bringing together leadership from government, business, labor, and education to focus on strategies and investments required to attract and to grow new businesses.

Specific actions included projects to revitalize downtown, to upgrade regional transportation, to strengthen K–12 education and Wichita State University, and to create a Center for Creative Capital and other investments to make the city and metro area more attractive to business investment and new businesses. Between 1987 and 1990, Wichita could claim several successes: the expansion of local businesses, relocation and expansion of outside firms, and a corporate home for telemarketing and franchising industries.

Wichita's progress stems not simply from putting the pieces together—organization, education, infrastructure, technology, and capital availability—but in marketing these products within the community and outside. Based on a study done by Stanford Research Institute, Wichita's *Blueprint 2000* provided a plan for developing new business technology, improving the local education system, and for redeveloping the downtown. The city and private sector, county, and suburbs all working together have pledged nearly $400 million in investments over the next several years to

(continued)

EXHIBIT 12–4
Wichita's Successful Diversification (continued)

complete the comprehensive strategy. A five-year, $4 million marketing program using advertising, public relations, and direct mail techniques provided Wichita with favorable coverage in trade magazines, periodicals, and national media. These activities have paid off.

Sources: John T. Bailey, *Marketing Cities in the 1980s and Beyond: New Patterns, New Pressures, New Promise* (Chicago: American Economic Development Council, 1989), pp. 41–45; and Todd Sloane, "New Images Paves Way for Wichita," *City & State,* August 13, 1990, pp. 11, 13.

tion of markets rather than narrow, geopolitical boundaries of towns or cities.

- *Continuity*—Discontinuity has been more characteristic of place development than continuity. Leaders come and go; programs are started and stopped; strategies change. As place development responsibilities and financing devolve from public to private, continuity is likely to increase both in leadership, programs, and personnel. Independent agencies and partnerships are likely to be less vulnerable to political vicissitudes and annual budget battles. The lower profile and posture that a private sector agency provides enhances greater confidentiality in searches, contacts, and negotiations.
- *Private sector expertise*—The fact is that the private sector has far greater experience and knowledge in selling, marketing, strategic planning, and customer orientation than the public sector. The involvement of corporate leaders and officers in place development is critical because they know, far better than public officials, the factors involved in relocating, starting, or expanding a business. It perhaps goes without saying that business sells best to business.

We have demonstrated that sectoral roles are fluid, dynamic, and at times, interchangeable. Partnerships between the public and private sectors vary according to what each brings to the table. What the private sector may offer to create a partnership in one situation may be contributed by the public sector in another. Either sector, for example,

EXHIBIT 12-5

Cleveland's Drive for High-Growth Industries

Cleveland Tomorrow, a civic organization of forty corporate chief executives, commissioned McKinsey & Company, the international management consulting firm, to analyze Cleveland's changing economic base—a quarter of a century of decline—to help answer the critical question: What basic and effective actions can be taken by the Greater Cleveland community to assure its broad-based economic vitality? Based on a full year of study, analysis, and a survey of the learning experiences of other frost-belt cities, the Cleveland Tomorrow committee embraced six long-term programs designed "to cure causes rather than treat symptoms." These included two to assist the anchor or basic industries, three to foster growth industries, and one to address both. Cleveland Tomorrow: A Strategy for Economic Vitality constitutes one of the most thoughtful action plans put together by any place; it includes implementation mechanisms that have been followed since 1981. Cleveland's turnaround is now well established as a tribute to a business community which, after years of inactivity, rallied Cleveland's citizens behind a strategy for renewal.

Cleveland's efforts to turn around its faltering and cyclical economy to become an emerging center for management, technology, and production involved much more than long-term strategies, investments, and new partnerships. Cleveland suffered from a poor image—a rust-belt city, racially divisive politics, poor leadership and, in fact, a city that defaulted in 1979 on its debt obligations. Since 1981, city leaders led by major corporations (Cleveland is home to 22 Fortune 1,000 headquarters) have done much to reshape a new city image under the New Cleveland Campaign, and have aggressively marketed the city nationally. Downtown renewal is occurring, health and new technology businesses are growing, and Cleveland appears to have fully turned the corner on transition from manufacturing to services.

Sources: Cleveland Tomorrow: A Strategy for Economic Vitality (Cleveland: The Cleveland Tomorrow Committee, December 1981), quotation from introduction to report; and John T. Bailey, *Marketing Cities in the 1980s and Beyond: New Patterns, New Pressures, New Promise* (Chicago: American Economic Development Council, 1989), p. 17.

can build infrastructure by contributing land or money. Other contributions may be unique to one sector or another, but both bring various resources and skills to the negotiating table.

The private sector can contribute specialized knowledge, information, or skills, while the public sector may offer unique powers to assemble land, access tax exempt markets, secure zoning and permits to ensure that projects move, and provide various incentives necessary to attract private capital. What and how much each sector contributes depends on overall goals, specific objectives, resources, and economic circumstances. The fact is that no one sector—government or business—acting alone and without the cooperation and support of the other is likely to be very successful over the long term in turning around a place's economy or in making it more competitive.

Response Nine: Each place needs to develop its own unique change processes as a result of differences in the place's culture, politics, and leadership processes.

Different places cannot be expected to develop the same approaches in adapting to change and planning their future. Each place has its own history, culture, values, government and business institutions, systems of public and private decision making and leadership. Strategic market planning inevitably takes a different form in Amsterdam than in New Orleans. Each place has to sort out how best to promote innovation, to take the actions necessary to produce change, and to form alliances and coalitions to get various publics to buy into change. The Goals for Dallas program, for example, reportedly involved more than 100,000 people in planning committees and neighborhood gatherings during the 1966–77 period.

In contrast to St. Paul and Michigan—two examples of places where vision, leadership, and strategies combined to produce action plans to guide development—a multitude of examples can be cited as initial failures. We have selected the two in exhibit 12–6, Rhode Island and Louisiana, due largely to their national prominence in the 1980s and because they had much in common. Both represented a top-down approach to economic development and pitted elite organizations against blue-collar ethnic resistance to change. Both packaged great efforts into a single plan presented to the electorate for a decisive vote. Both schemes were oversold, required major tax increases, and failed to get a majority of voters to buy into change. Both ran counter to major vested interests, antitax sentiment, and gave rise to demagogic responses. Finally, each plan repre-

EXHIBIT 12–6

Failures: Rhode Island and Louisiana

In the summer of 1984, following one of the largest public selling campaigns in any state's history, Rhode Island voters overwhelmingly defeated a major bond proposal as part of a $250 million economic development package to overhaul the state's economy. Although backed by the media, bankers, industrialists, labor, and major elected officials, the state's blue-collar and ethnic population wreaked vengeance against the state's elites over what had been billed as the most ambitious state-sponsored economic development program anywhere in the United States. The Greenhouse Compact was a 1,000-page grand plan to produce more jobs and higher wages for Rhode Islanders. It cast the nation's smallest geographic state into national prominence as a test of a state-generated industrial policy. Rhode Island was to be a national model—a laboratory for testing bold, fresh economic ideas to overhaul older industries, and develop new businesses and technologies.

Once the little giant of nineteenth-century industry, Rhode Island experienced decades of gradual decline resulting in low growth, high unemployment, low wages, and a declining standard of living. In 1982, four-term Governor Francis Garrahy appointed a ten-member Strategic Development Commission that undertook the most comprehensive study of a state's economy and businesses to date. To reverse the state's decline, the report called for a far-reaching $250 million rescue plan. With the warning message to voters that failure to adopt the plan would result in a bleak economic future, the commission and its supporters packaged tax increases and bond issues into a single referendum rather than piecemeal actions to be approved sequentially over several years. Following nine months of a hard-sell campaign led by Garrahy and many of the state's leaders, the much publicized compact referendum went down in flames by a 4 to 1 margin. This defeat was not lost on other state and local officials seeking public support for their economic development policies. Blue-collar voters could not resist the opportunity to kick the state's elite in the teeth, and the overwhelming vote against the compact did just that.

(continued)

EXHIBIT 12–6
Failures: Rhode Island and Louisiana (continued)

By most any standard, Louisiana has a less than favorable business climate: high unemployment and corruption, low level of education and public services, and an inequitable tax system. Unlike some other Deep South states, Louisiana is asset-rich: mineral resources, a well-developed ocean port, a melting-pot culture that is a magnet for tourism, low-cost labor, and ample water supplies. However, Louisiana has yet to make the cultural, economic, and social transformation to become a significant factor in attracting new business and expanding into the service sector.

Old ways seemed to be passing when, in late 1987, Harvard MBA and reformer Charles E. "Buddy" Roemer III became governor. Having inherited $2 billion in accumulated deficits that only could be closed by overhauling the state's antiquated tax structure, Roemer rallied support from the state's major business leaders, media, and influentials for a tax and business reform package that cut sales, property, and business taxes and raised income taxes. Because the Louisiana Constitution requires a public referendum to raise taxes, Roemer and his business supporters had to sell voters on this comprehensive plan to break away from the state's past. However, on April 29, 1989, Louisiana voters rejected by a 55 to 45 margin these proposed tax changes. A reinvigorated populist alliance of antibusiness and antitax voters brought together blue-collar, poor white, and middle-class taxpayers to defeat what Roemer called "the state's best hope for creating jobs."

Sources: For Rhode Island, "The Greenhouse Compact," (Report published in full) *The Providence Journal Bulletin*, October 18, 1983, pp. 1–20. For Louisiana, Peter Passell, "The Last Laugh of the King Fish," *New York Times*, May 3, 1989, p. 26; Glenn Simpson, "Voters to Roemer: It's Not Worth It," *Insight*, May 29, 1989, p. 28; and Robert Suro, "In the Inside and Looking Within," *New York Times*, January 20, 1991, p. 16.

sented a radical departure from a place's political culture and a dramatic break with the past without a real public understanding of the advantages or benefits of an alternative future.

Different formulas have worked in different places at different times—Goals for Dallas, the Minneapolis Five Percent Club, the Chicago Civic Committee of the Commercial Club, the Hartford Bishops, and so on. Such places as Indianapolis, Baltimore, Dallas, Atlanta, and Raleigh may enjoy a certain continuity of leadership, while others may experience a rapid changing of the guard as businesses falter, downsize, or relocate as has occurred in Hartford, Chicago, Philadelphia, and elsewhere. Continuity of political leadership is even less assured given demographic changes and the high political risks of being a big-city mayor. Unlike business, where planned succession is a common feature, places are democratic institutions where succession and continuity may be sporadic, unpredictable, and unexpected. Michigan's strategic plan and innovative programs in the 1980s have been scaled back and overhauled in the 1990s due to a change of administration and more pressing budgetary priorities but, arguably, achieved their goals of making the state's manufacturers more competitive. Pennsylvania's Ben Franklin Partnerships have had a more durable legacy.

Most places experience common barriers to change: inertia, lack of vision and political consensus, resource scarcity, and inadequate organizational machinery to lead change. Overcoming them depends on favorable events, trends, and various catalysts for change—an election, new leaders, the media, and new organizations or evolution of older ones.

In spite of place differences, all places have to pay attention to certain basic imperatives: First, resource scarcity necessitates a certain consolidation of place development activities both within government and between government and the private sector. Consolidation provides opportunities to pool and better leverage resources, refine and focus place development strategies, and broaden participation.

Second, places need greater continuity and consistency in their approaches to place development which means more institutionalized ways for leadership to emerge. Through consolidation, partnerships, and the emergence of lead organizations, professionalization of both public and private leaders can develop. Place development is frequently associated with recognized leaders who come from a variety of sectors—Bernard Berkowitz, Martin Millspaugh, and James Rouse in Baltimore; R. K. Mellon in Pittsburgh; Felix Rohatyn in New York; George Latimer in St. Paul; J. Erik Jonsson in Dallas; Richard Lugar in Indianapolis. Whether from business, elected office, or appointed officialdom, they initiated organizational developments and agencies that helped sustain leadership over time.[20]

Third, places need to reach beyond their geopolitical boundaries to leverage their resources, attack common problems, and share collective benefits. Tourism and convention businesses are consolidating their activities in large places, while transportation planners seek multimodal terminals that improve links between rail and bus, air and ground transport, making the hospitality business more user friendly. The reinvigorated Dallas Chamber of Commerce unites under one privately funded umbrella six counties and thirty-three cities, business attraction and retention, export trade, tourism and conventions, and marketing for the region. Each of the thirty-three cities has designated a single point person to process and coordinate requests for information by firms interested in the Dallas area. Such requests are identified by and cleared centrally through the chamber's marketing efforts. Like Dallas, the Metropolitan Economic Development Council of Richmond embraces three counties and the city of Richmond, Virginia. Some of our best-managed cities are those that have reached out across their boundaries to solve problems in transportation, solid waste disposal, and water resources. This process is now occurring in place development.

Response Ten: Places must develop organizational and procedural mechanisms to sustain place development, and maintain momentum once it has begun.

Strategic market planning requires patience and persistence. It may take years for specific small businesses to reach their potential, new technologies to reap their commercial benefits, and investments in human capital to bear fruit. The danger is that an impatient public becomes discouraged, changes elected leaders, and reverts to preferences for quick fixes that invariably promise more jobs now. Because no magic panaceas or quick-fix elixirs exist for place development, we can only learn from history that place marketing requires cumulative learning from the past successes and mistakes of others. Historians have long noted that democracies rise effectively to meet crises, enabling leaders to lead, and power temporarily to be concentrated. But democratic institutions often work poorly in noncrises where checks and balances can create stalemate, if not paralysis. So, too, places may be galvanized to action under crisis conditions, but momentum wanes as the crisis recedes. The public can be easily bored by a single issue or problem; their attention is quickly diverted by more pressing problems. A classic example of how one organization and region has sustained momentum is the Allegheny Conference in Pittsburgh in exhibit 12-7.

The flip side of sustaining momentum is that initial successes can be

EXHIBIT 12-7

The Allegheny Conference: Implementation

With more than fifty years of experience, the Allegheny Conference on Community Development spearheaded Pittsburgh's downtown redevelopment, moved to issues of job training and racial discrimination in the 1970s, and on to regional economic development in the 1980s. To provide direction to Pittsburgh's regional development, the conference created a strategy to deal with global changes focusing on economic diversification. That strategy had five premises:

- Never again should the region depend so strongly on primary metals and other durable goods producers.
- Diversification should come through a mix of both product-oriented and service-oriented industries, and a mix of mature and new activities.
- No short-term fixes should be adopted for the region.
- Solutions should be private sector-oriented and market-driven.
- Planning should be coordinated rather than centralized through a master planning agency.

In its 1984 report, *A Strategy for Growth*, the conference focused on three intermediate objectives: (1) business and job development; (2) improving the economic environment; and (3) upgrading the infrastructure. Each year since, the conference has issued a report widely distributed throughout the Pittsburgh region, including the media, neighborhoods, and business and civic organizations, to document yearly progress. In 1990 the conference also issued a five-year report so that longer-term developments could be seen in perspective.

The Allegheny Conference's methods for sustaining public interest in and commitment to achieving long-term goals is considered among the best in the country. Modelled on the lines of a public company's annual report to stockholders, the Allegheny Conference helps maintain its momentum by sustaining the allegiances of the region's stakeholders in collective economic progress.

Sources: The Allegheny Conference on Community Development: *A Strategy for Growth* (Pittsburgh: ACCD, November 1984), and *Five Year Economic Development Report: 1984–1989* (Pittsburgh: ACCD, 1990).

their own worst enemies. A danger exists that as the community makes some initial progress, it becomes complacent and relaxes its efforts. Soon longer-term goals are forgotten. The momentum fizzles out. Here the challenge to the community's leaders is to keep the goal foremost in the public's mind, allowing them to revisit the strategic plan, and to provide a constant flow of information to the public on progress achieved to date. Regrettably, implementation may be the least exciting but remains the most important aspect of strategic planning.[21] To sustain interest and approval means the public must be convinced that various investments are producing results, accountability is being maintained, and further progress will be achieved.

Take, for example, Fairfax County, Virginia, once a rural, agricultural, residential bedroom community for Washington, D.C. Practically overnight it became a high-tech mecca and the fastest growing county east of the Mississippi River. Its well-financed business attraction strategies and marketing campaigns achieved national acclaim. Between 1977 and 1985 Fairfax County attracted 800 new companies, $1 billion in investments, and 50,000 new jobs. In that period it attracted over half of the new technology firms in the United States—electronics, data processing, telecommunications, and biotech and biomedical research firms.[22]

Such phenomenal success also produced a litany of new problems: soaring home values, traffic congestion, huge infrastructure needs, speculative real estate ventures, and a tarnished quality of life. By 1990 Fairfax County faced a vastly different situation and strategic challenge—growth management. In addition to the problem of curbing growth and development, officials allowed the infrastructure to catch up with an urban county whose population approached 700,000, as they balanced quality-of-life considerations with other service demands.

Growth management introduces the new challenge of demarketing a place in ways that discourage the rate of in-migration of people, raise the costs of relocation for new businesses and developers and, at times, simply aim to stop growth. In ancient times, cities and even nations constructed walls to keep undesirables out. Today, places are not only more subtle in the ways they demarket but they also operate within the rules that protect property and citizens' civil rights. Examples include

Santa Fe, New Mexico, which refuses to build a modern airport to keep from being inundated with tourists and new residents. Santa Barbara, California, refuses to increase its water supply to support further land development. Algonquin, Illinois, petitioned the Interstate Commerce Commission to abandon its train stop so that fewer people could reach it by train. Development fees are frequently used by high-growth areas to get residential and commercial real estate developers to pay for the related infrastructure costs that accompany development—streets, sewers, and schools. Rigid zoning and land-use requirements can be effectively used for growth constraint. Citizens themselves take anti-growth actions from sporting unfriendly bumper stickers to rude behavior to an extreme example such as Bolinas, a town in Marin County California, where townspeople repeatedly remove state highway marker signs so people cannot find it.

WHY IS MARKETING PLACES NECESSARY?

A marketing approach to place development is the overriding response places need to compete effectively in our new economy. Places must produce products and services that current and prospective customers want or need. Places must sell products and services internally and externally, nationally and internationally. Place marketing is a continual activity that must be adjusted to meet changing economic conditions and new opportunities.

The task of marketing places to actual or potential customers undergoes constant change as new industries form; new technologies emerge; companies expand; and old businesses shrink, merge, or consolidate. As conditions and customers change, products must be upgraded and refined, and new products must be designed to meet new needs. As New York City has learned painfully, just having multi-million dollar tax incentive packages to retain industry is not enough.[23] Some place features have a permanent staying power in the new economy: a trained and skilled labor force, basic infrastructure, place amenities, good schools and universities, and support for research and development. However, the tools and programs necessary to support these products undergo constant evaluation, reformulation, and change.

Selling abroad is vastly expanding as global markets grow. Places are becoming more aggressive in assisting, financing, and facilitating exports through information assistance, trading companies, and trade centers. Communities help their local business firms develop market opportunities in specific national and international markets; do on-line searches for buyers and agents; and engage in cultural, scientific, and educational exchanges. They need the support of commercial banks, chambers of commerce, trade clubs, and other export intermediaries. Sister-city and place relationships are growing in number and in relative importance. Tourism and travel are becoming the nation's largest service industry.

However, the single greatest challenge places face involves marketing their various activities to their own residents and voters. Europe's experience provides ample lessons on how countries can focus assistance that is specific to their regions and sectors geared to those firms that are "export ready." Marketing to the internal consumers is not as much a technical marketing problem of methods, messages, and targets as it is a political problem of defining place development in the values of the public's own framework.

Now we are back to the point at which we began. All places are in trouble now, or will be in the near future. The globalization of the world's economy and the accelerating pace of technological changes are two forces that require all places to learn how to compete. Places must learn how to think more like businesses, developing products, markets, and customers. This shift is a major contribution that modern Japan and several East Asian countries—Singapore, Hong Kong, Thailand, South Korea, and Taiwan—have made to our new economy and the challenges of place competition. The collaborative benefits of business and government working together, shaped by different cultures, traditions, and institutions, are compelling leaders at all place levels and sizes to rethink their responses. If the trends toward collapsing economic borders among nations accelerates as we think they will, economic regions and places will transcend political boundaries. In a borderless economy, they will emerge as the new actors on the world scene.

The central tenet of *Marketing Places* is that in spite of the powerful external and internal forces that buffet them, places have within their collective resources and people the capacity to improve their relative competitive positions. Their responses to the new, bottom up economic order should be placed on an equal footing with national responses to the competitiveness challenge. A strategic market planning perspective provides places with the marketing tools and opportunities to rise to that challenge.

NOTES

Chapter One: Places in Trouble

1. Rich Miller, "Financial Gap Plagues Most Cities," *Chicago Tribune,* June 23, 1991, sec. 7, p. 8B.
2. National League of Cities, "News," July 8, 1991, p. 1.
3. Marlise Simons, "As Its Problems Mount, Rio Declares Bankruptcy," *New York Times,* September 18, 1988, sec. 1, p. 8.
4. Multiple definitions of sickness exist on defining and characterizing place health, stress, and hardship. See, for example, U.S. House of Representatives, Subcommittee on the City, "City Need and the Responsiveness of Federal Grant Programs," 95th congress, 2nd session, 1978. See also Robert W. Burchell, et al. *The New Reality of Municipal Finance: The Rise and Fall of the Intergovernmental City* (New Brunswick, N.J.: Rutgers University Press, 1984.)
5. Andrea Stone, "City Verges on Bankruptcy," USA TODAY, October 11, 1990, p. 8A. Also see Bill Turque, et al., "Cities on the Brink: Philadelphia Is Not the Only One Going Broke," *Newsweek,* November 19, 1990, pp. 44–45. In 1992, under a new mayor, Philadelphia's fortunes showed improvement, although it still faced formidable recovery problems.

6. William Van Dusen Wishard, "The 21st Century Economy," *The Futurist*, May-June 1987, p. 23.

7. David L. Birch, "The Changing Rules of the Game," *Economic Development Commentary*, Winter 1984, p. 13.

8. Ibid., p. 12.

9. David Osborne, *Laboratories of Democracy* (Boston: Harvard Business School Press, 1988), ch. 1.

10. David Hale, "For New Jobs, Help Small Business," *Wall Street Journal*, August 10, 1992, p. 10A.

11. Raymond Vernon, "Global Interdependence in a Historic Perspective," *Interdependence and Cooperation in Tomorrow's World* (Paris: Organization for Economic Cooperation and Development, 1987), p. 14.

12. David L. Birch, "The Rise and Fall of Everybody," *Inc.*, September 1987, pp 18–20.

13. Christopher Farrell and Michael J. Mandel, "Industrial Policy," *Business Week*, April 6, 1992, pp. 70–76.

14. Robert B. Reich, "Corporation and Nation," *Atlantic Monthly*, May 1988, pp. 76–81.

15. Thomas J. Lueck, "New York Gives Bank a Break: The Return Is Uncertain," *New York Times*, November 13, 1988, p. 6E.

16. George N. Miller, "Cleveland's Marketing and Communication Program," *Public Management*, June 1986, p. 12.

Chapter Two: How Places Market Themselves

1. Stanley Ziemba, "Indianapolis Lands United Repair Plant," *Chicago Tribune*, October 24, 1991, p. 4.

2. Interview with Gerald J. Roper, president of the Chicago Convention and Tourism Bureau in April 21, 1992.

3. Donald Groves, "Who Should Be Marketing Bethlehem?" *Bethlehem Globe-Times*, December 10, 1987, p. A1.

4. David Birch, *Job Creation in America: How Our Smallest Companies Put the Most People to Work* (New York: The Free Press, 1987).

5. Bill Powell, "War between the States," *Newsweek*, May 30, 1988, p. 44.

6. Robert Guskind, "Games Cities Play," *National Journal*, March 18, 1989, pp. 635–36.

7. See Richard Kern, "Marketing Indianapolis: Sports and Statistics to Numb the Mind," *Sales and Marketing Management*, May 1987, pp.

45–47. "A Port in a Storm," *U.S. News and World Report*, December 16, 1985, pp. 50–51. Neil Peirce and Robert Guskind, "Hot Managers, Sizzling Cities," *Business Month*, June 1989, pp. 36–53.

8. Interviews with Bill Chandler, Lions Club contact to town hall on January 13, 1992, and Ken Storey, St. Mary's town clerk on January 14, 1992.

Chapter Three: How Target Markets Make Their Choices

1. Leon Festinger and Dana Bramel, "The Reactions of Humans to Cognitive Dissonance," in *Experimental Foundations of Clinical Psychology*, ed. Arthur J. Bachrach (New York: Basic Books, 1962), pp. 251–62.

2. Tim Urbonya, "Pleasant Prairie, Wis.: A Utility's Industrial Park Grows in the Cabbage and Corn Fields," *New York Times*, May 15, 1988, sec. 13, p. 32, and David Young, "'Border Bandits' Raid Illinois," *Chicago Tribune*, May 12, 1992, sec. 7, p. 2.

3. Kerry Hannon, "There He Goes Again," *Forbes*, October 31, 1988, p. 130.

4. Interview with Mike Prendergast, public relations, Figgie International, January 2, 1992.

5. J. D. Reed, "All Riled Up About Ratings," *Time*, March 11, 1985, p. 76.

6. David Gertner conducted research on place rating systems at Northwestern University during the winter of 1991.

7. Laura Van Tuyl, "City Ratings Confuse, Confound," *Christian Science Monitor*, November 7, 1989, p. 14.

8. Tom Walker, "What Do Businesses Look for in a City?" *Atlanta Constitution*, July 24, 1989, sec. B, p. 1.

9. See Sandra McIntosh, "Atlanta Again Named Crime Capitol: Mayor Disputes Report," *Atlanta Constitution*, August 7, 1989, sec. A, p. 1; Charles Seabrook, "Atlanta Flunks EPA Ozone Tests for Smog," *Atlanta Constitution*, August 17, 1990, sec. A, p. 3; Jane O. Hansen, "Georgia Babies Dying at Third Highest Rate in South, Study Finds," *Atlanta Constitution*, September 23, 1989, p. 1; Robert Levine, "City Stress Index: As Best, As Worst," *Psychology Today*, November 1988, pp. 52–58.

10. Reed, "All Riled Up," p. 76.

11. Ibid.

12. "Chicago 16th Among U.S.'s 'Best' Cities," *Chicago Tribune*, July 24, 1988, p. 6.

Chapter Four: The Place Auditioning and Strategic Market Planning Process

1. See Milton Kotler, *Neighborhood Government: The Local Foundations of Political Life* (Indianapolis: Bobbs-Merrill, 1969).
2. John S. DeMott, "My Name Is on the Building," *Time*, October 12, 1987, p. 56.
3. See John T. Bailey, *Marketing Cities in the 1980s and Beyond: New Patterns, New Pressures, New Promise* (Chicago: American Economic Development Council, 1989), pp. 14–18.
4. Ibid., p. 15.
5. Ibid., p. 16.
6. Sudhir H. Kale and Katherine Weir, "Marketing Third World Countries," *Journal of Travel Research*, Fall 1986, p. 6.
7. Haya El Nasser, "Tinsel Town Has Lost Its Luster," *USA TODAY*, January 3, 1992, p. 2A.
8. See Abraham Shama, "Analysis of New Mexico's Strategic Plan for Economic Development" (Paper presented at the Second International Conference on Marketing Development, Karl Marx University, Budapest, Hungary, July 1988).

Chapter Five: Strategies for Place Improvement

1. Daniel H. Burnham, Jr., and Robert Kingery, *Planning the Region of Chicago* (Chicago: Chicago Regional Planning Association, 1956), p. 18.
2. Donald J. Olsen, *The City as a Work of Art: London, Paris, Vienna* (New Haven: Yale University Press, 1986), p. 4.
3. Jane Jacobs, *The Death and Life of Great American Cities* (New York: Random House, 1961), p. 3.
4. LeCorbusier, *The City of Tomorrow and Its Planning* (New York: Dover Publications, 1987). The book was originally published in French in 1929.
5. Allan Jacobs and Donald Appleyard, "Toward an Urban Design Manifesto," *Journal of the American Planning Association*, Winter 1987, pp. 112–20.
6. James Holston, *The Modernist City: An Anthropological Critique of Brasilia* (Chicago: University of Chicago Press, 1989), p. 107.

7. Ruth Eckdish Knack, "Visiting Firemen," *Planning*, May 1987, pp. 8–16.

8. Ed Zotti, "Design by Committee," *Planning*, May 1987, pp. 22–27.

9. William Hoffer, "Main Street Revisited," *Nation's Business*, January 1989, pp. 36–40.

10. Ruth Eckdish Knack, "Designing Mayors," *Planning*, August 1990, pp. 20–25.

11. Oliver Gordon, "Portland Goes for Broke," *Planning*, February 1989, pp. 10–15.

12. Ed Zotti, "River North Urban Design Plan," *Planning*, April 1988, pp. 8–9.

13. David Dillon, Ed Zotti, and Tracy Burrows, "Outstanding Planning Process: Arlington Comprehensive Plan; Honorable Mentions: North Philadelphia Plan; San Francisco Rezoning Study; Forsyth County Comprehensive Plan; Oakland County Community Projects Program," *Planning*, March 1989, pp. 10–15.

14. Jack Wynn, "The Growing Lure of the Suburbs," *Barron's*, June 8, 1987, p. 75.

15. Emily Lau, "Hong Kong: Don't Hold Your Breath," *Far Eastern Economic Review* (Hong Kong), August 4, 1988, pp. 20–21. Carl Goldstein and Mark Clifford, "Cash from Trash; Choking on Plastic; Arsenic and Oil Waste; Down in the Dump," *Far Eastern Economic Review*, September 21, 1989, pp. 80–85.

16. Bruce McDowell, "Public Works for Tomorrow," *Intergovernmental Perspective*, Summer, 1992, p. 23.

17. See Samia El-Badry and Peter K. Nance, "Driving into the 21th Century," *American Demographics*, September 1992, pp. 46–53.

18. See Clifford J. Levy, "New $100 Million Sensor System to Monitor New York Traffic Congestion," *New York Times*, August 29, 1992, p. 16.

19. See Matthew L. Wald, "12 States Consider Smog Curb," *New York Times*, July 15, 1991, pp. C1, C3.

20. Steven Vale, "Red Light on Road Traffic," *Management Today* (UK), March 1990, p. 24.

21. Daniel Machalaba, "Cities Try to Link Trains, Buses, Planes," *Wall Street Journal*, August 6, 1992, p. B1.

22. David C. Couper and Sabine H. Lobitz, *Quality Policing: The Madison Experience* (Washington, D.C.: Police Executive Research Forum, 1991).

23. Peter Ohlhausen, "Security in Paris: Views of the Rues," *Security Management*, 32, no. 6 (October 1988), pp. 27–29.
24. "Education," *Business Week*, September 14, 1992, pp. 70–71.
25. Kathleen Sylvester, "Business and the Schools: The Failure and the Promise," *Governing*, September 1992, pp. 23–29.
26. PHH Fantus, December 21, 1992. Incentives and infrastructure also played a role in the plant location decision.
27. Committee for Economic Development, *Investing in Our Children* (New York: CED, 1985).
28. June G. Naylor, "Reservations Needed if You're Going to San Antonio," *Chicago Tribune*, August 23, 1992, sec. 12, p. 9.
29. Carol McGraw, "Wrecking Ball Falls on Famed Schwab's Store," *Los Angeles Times*, October 7, 1988, p. 3. Interview with Alan Schwab, son of one of the original owners, January 10, 1992.
30. Karen Ann Coburn, "The Malling of Downtown Business," *Governing*, October 1991, pp. 31–32.
31. James Rouse, "Festival Marketplaces: Bringing New Life to the Center City," *Commentary*, Summer 1984, pp. 3–8.
32. Peter D. Waldstein, "Re-Streeting Revives Oak Park Biz District," *Crain's Chicago Business*, July 27, 1992, p. R3.
33. See Bernard J. Frieden and Lynne B. Sagalyn, *Downtown, Inc. How America Rebuilds Cities* (Cambridge, Mass.: MIT Press, 1989); John Fondersmith, "Downtown 2040," *The Futurist*, March–April 1988, pp. 105–14.
34. See Pete Axthelm and Andrew Muir, "RX for Cities: Build a Dome," *Newsweek*, December 28, 1987, p. 21; William C. Symonds, "Take Me Out to the Cleaners," *Business Week*, May 6, 1991, p. 40.
35. See Christi Harlan and Marj Charlier, "Denver Hopes to Spend into Recovery," *Wall Street Journal*, March 18, 1991, p. 6.
36. Cecile Sorra, "Next Year, the Tourists Will Get to Bury City Officials in the Sand," *Wall Street Journal*, June 19, 1989, p. B1.

Chapter Six: Designing the Place's Image

1. Interview conducted by Mark Rothchild at Northwestern University in April 1988.
2. See Philip Kotler and Alan R. Andreasen, *Strategic Marketing for Non-Profit Organizations*, 4th ed. (Englewood Cliffs, N.J.: Prentice Hall, 1991), p. 202.

3. Des Kilalea, "Marketing to the Affluent: Natural Treasure Attracts Repeat Business," *Advertising Age* 58, March 11, 1987, pp. S12–S13.
4. See Kotler, *Strategic Marketing,* pp. 169–70.
5. Bonnie D. Davis and Brenda Sternquist, "Appealing to the Elusive Tourist: An Attribute Cluster Strategy," *Journal of Travel Research,* Spring 1987, p. 129.
6. The material in this section is drawn from Kotler, *Strategic Marketing,* pp. 203–4.
7. C. E. Osgood, G. J. Suci, and P. H. Tannenbaum, *The Measurement of Meaning* (Urbana: University of Illinois Press, 1957). Other image-measuring tools exist; on object sorting, see W. A. Scott, "A Structure of Natural Cognitions," *Journal of Personality and Social Psychology* 12, no. 4 (1969), pp. 261–78. On multidimensional scaling, see Paul E. Green and Vithala R. Rao, *Applied Multidimensional Scaling* (New York: Holt, Rinehart and Winston, 1972), and on item lists, see John W. Riley, Jr., ed., *The Corporation and Its Public* (New York: John Wiley, 1963), pp. 51–62.
8. Jack L. Nasar, "The Evaluative Image of the City," *Journal of the American Planning Association,* Winter 1990, p. 44.
9. John T. Bailey, *Marketing Cities in the 1980s and Beyond: New Patterns, New Pressures, New Promise* (Chicago: American Economic Development Council, 1989), pp. 22–23. The concept of slogans, themes, and positions as applied to places was developed by Bailey.
10. John T. Grace, "Singapore: The Vision of a Global Image," *Vital Speeches of the Day,* November 15, 1989, pp. 76–79.
11. Interview with Lisa Daily from the Welcome Center, an office in the Johnstown Chamber of Commerce, April 13, 1992.
12. Clare Ansberry, "Johnstown Offers a Lot to the Devotees of Floods This Year," May 31, 1989, *Wall Street Journal,* p. 1.
13. Interview with Lisa Daily.
14. Gregory Jensen, "Glasgow—A City Reborn," *Chicago Sun-Times,* July 1, 1988, p. 143.
15. Ibid.

Chapter Seven: Distributing the Place's Image and Message

1. See Sidney J. Levy, *Promotional Behavior* (Glenview, Ill.: Scott, Foresman, 1971), chapter 4 for some of the characteristics of advertising, personal selling, and sales promotion to follow.

2. Thomas L. Harris, *The Marketer's Guide to Public Relations* (New York: John Wiley & Sons, 1991).

3. Anthony R. Pratkanis, *Age of Propaganda: The Everyday Use and Abuse of Persuasion* (New York: W. H. Freeman, 1992), p. 3.

4. Donna Dawson, "Direct Marketing: Home Sweet Home," *Marketing* (UK), October 5, 1989, pp. 55–56.

5. Lisa Gubernick, "Doing the Bellevue Shuffle," *Forbes*, October 24, 1988, pp. 86–88.

6. Melina Hung, "Boat Races Sail via Satellite," *Communication World*, March 1987, pp. 21–22.

7. Pat Ross, "Low-Cost Marketing Magic," *Association Management*, November 1988, pp. 115–18.

8. Joanne Y. Cleaver, "Regional Profiles: Chicago," *Advertising Age*, November 9, 1988, pp. 20–28.

9. Daniel Drosdoff, "Amnesty International Ends Rock Concert Tour," United Press International, October 17, 1988.

10. "Carson Dedicates Radiation Center," United Press International, October 16, 1988.

Chapter Eight: Attracting the Tourism and Hospitality Business Markets

1. Peter Elsworth, "Too Many People and Not Enough Places to Go," *New York Times*, May 26, 1991, p. F4.

2. Susan Carey, "Tourist Spots Developing 'Green' Images," *Wall Street Journal*, May 10, 1991, p. A7.

3. Jonathan Dahl, "It Seems that Nothing Is Certain Except Taxes—and More Taxes," *Wall Street Journal*, March 4, 1991, p. B1.

4. Boom Timi, "Thailand's Economy Surges and Country Is Feeling Strain," *Wall Street Journal*, June 12, 1991, p. 1.

5. Robert Reinhold, "Fearing Recession, Americans Skimp on Vacation Costs," *New York Times*, August 13, 1990, pp. 1, 11.

6. Steven Morris, "The New 'In' Vacation: Shorter, Closer to Home," *Chicago Tribune*, September 1, 1991, pp. 1, 5.

7. *1988 Annual Research Report*, Hawaii Visitors Bureau.

8. Cathy Grossman, "More Baby Boomers Find Tours Just the Right Speed," *USA TODAY*, May 2, 1991, p. 4D.

9. Rogers Worthington, "Rural U.S. Courting Tourists," *Chicago Tribune*, June 3, 1990, p. 25.

10. Steven Greenhouse, "Disney's Only Fear with European Park Is Too Successful," *Chicago Tribune*, March 17, 1991, p. 9D.
11. Carey, "Tourist Spots," p. A7.
12. Marj Charlier, "Troubled U.S. Ski Resorts Hope to Cure Ills with an Infusion of Foreign Tourists," *Wall Street Journal*, November 25, 1991, p. B1.
13. Carla Marinucci, "San Francisco Pitching Itself as Tourist Utopia," *Chicago Tribune*, March 17, 1991, p. 9C.
14. Anne Spiselman, "New York's Woes May Ease Visit Expense," *Crain's Chicago Business*, January 21, 1991, p. t8; and Sarah Bartlett, "Lag in U.S. Tourists Hurts New York," *New York Times*, June 5, 1991, p. 16.
15. For a list of frequently read travel newsletters and magazines see, "Newsletters and Magazines to Help You Travel Smarter," *USA TODAY*, March 21, 1991, p. 13E.
16. Brian Downes, "Remembering Ireland," *Chicago Tribune*, March 17, 1991, sec. 12, p. 1.
17. Bob Dyer, "Booming Atlanta," *Chicago Tribune*, May 5, 1991, sec. 12, p. 17.
18. Tom Dunkel, "New Sources of Wealth Put Vegas in the Chips," *Insight*, March 5, 1990, pp. 8–19.
19. U.S. Travel Data Center, Washington, D.C., January 15, 1991.
20. "Executive Summary," *KPMG Peat Marwick Marketing and Impact Study on McCormick Place Expansion* (Chicago: Metropolitan Pier and Exposition Authority, 1989), p. 2.
21. "Meetings and Conventions," *Crain's Chicago Business*, July 14, 1986, pp. T1–3.
22. Linda Paustian, "How Some Cities Got Looted," *Wall Street Journal*, October 5, 1987, p. 22 and N. R. Kleinfield, "The Latest Municipal Malady," *New York Times*, February 24, 1991, p. 10F.
23. Metropolitan Pier and Exposition Authority, "McCormick Place Expansion Site and Concept Plan Overview," Chicago: Metropolitan Pier and Exposition Authority, June 1990.
24. Anne Spiselman, "New York's Woes May Ease," *Crain's Chicago Business*, January 21, 1991, pp. T8–9.
25. Ibid., T10.
26. Joanne Clever, "Shaking Off All-Work Image," *Crain's Chicago Business*, January 21, 1991, p. T1.

Chapter Nine: Attracting, Retaining, Expanding, and Starting Businesses

1. Roger Schmenner, *Making Business Location Decisions* (Englewood Cliffs, N.J.: Prentice Hall, 1982).
2. David Birch, "The Changing Rules of the Game," *Economic Development Commentary* 4, Winter 1984, pp. 12–16.
3. Christopher Duerksen, "Industrial Plant Location: Do Environmental Controls Inhibit Development?" *Economic Development Commentary*, Winter 1985, pp. 17–21.
4. *Fairfax Prospectus* 6 (Vienna, Va.: Fairfax County Economic Development Authority, December 1985), pp. 1–2.
5. See Robert M. Ady, "High-Technology Plants: Different Criteria for the Best Location," *Economic Development Commentary*, Winter 1983, pp. 8–10; Ann Markusen, "High-Tech Plants and Jobs: What Really Lures Them?" *Economic Development Commentary*, Fall 1986, pp. 3–7; and Charles F. Harding, "Location Choices for Research Labs," *Economic Development Quarterly*, August 1989, pp. 223–34.
6. Alan S. Gregerman, *Competitive Strategy* (Washington, D.C.: National Council for Urban Economic Development, 1984), pp. 7–8.
7. Mark Satterthwaite, "Location Patterns of High-Growth Firms," *Economic Development Commentary*, Spring 1988, pp. 7–11.
8. See Thomas Stanback, *Services: The New Economy* (Tatowa, N.J.: Allenheld, Osmun, 1981).
9. See Helen F. Ladd and John Yinger, *America's Ailing Cities* (Baltimore, Md.: Johns Hopkins University Press, 1989), chap. 2.
10. John Case, "The Disciples of David Birch," *Inc.*, January 1989, pp. 39–45.
11. John Case, "The Invisible Powerhouse," *Inc.*, September 1989, pp. 25–26.
12. M. Ross Boyle, "Corporate Headquarters," *Economic Development Commentary*, Winter 1990, p. 30.
13. George Judson, "Moving from Greenwich to Georgia with the Employees' Needs in Mind," *New York Times*, December 15, 1991, p. 15.
14. Urban Land Institute, *Land Use Digest* 1, January 1989, p. 1.
15. Anne Kates, "Dallas on the Rebound: City Lures Firms Seeking Land Bargains," *USA TODAY*, November 29, 1989, p. B1.

16. Carl Patton, "Jobs and Commercial Office Development," *Economic Development Quarterly,* November 1988, p. 324.
17. "Office Glut Will Take Years to Work Off," *Wall Street Journal,* December 20, 1990, p. B1.
18. George Sternlieb and James W. Hughes, "The Demise of the Department Stores," *American Demographics,* August 1987, pp. 31–33, 59.
19. John Handley, "New Chicago Woodfield Mall Spawned a Revolution," *Chicago Tribune,* April 3, 1991, sec. 8, pp. 18–19.
20. See Richard Corrigan, "The Debate Continues," in *The National Journal,* Special Edition: "Smokestacks and Silicon" (1984), pp. 10–14.
21. National Governors Association, *Governors' Roundtable on Industrial Incentives: A Briefing Book* (Washington, D.C.: NGA, February 1992), pp. 14–19. The definitive source on incentives is provided by National Association of State Development for Agencies, *Directory of Incentives, Business Investment, and Development in the United States, A State-by-State Guide,* 3rd ed. (Washington, D.C.: Urban Institute Press, 1991).
22. Mei-Mei Chan, "Saturn Race Heads into Final Stretch," *USA TODAY,* March 20, 1985, p. 1.
23. Kent Gibbons, "States Offer Big Bucks to Land United Hub: A Tale of Many Cities," *USA TODAY,* March 21, 1991, p. 8E.
24. Nonna Notta, "Trying to Understand the ED Official's Dilemma," in *Competition among States and Local Governments,* ed. Daphne Kenyon and John Kincaid (Washington, D.C.: Urban Institute Press, 1991), pp. 247–50.
25. "Saturn's Beneficial Fallout," *Chicago Tribune,* March 22, 1985, p. 30.
26. David L. Birch, *Job Creation in America* (New York: The Free Press, 1987).
27. David Osborne, *Laboratories of Democracy* (Boston: Harvard Business School Press, 1989), pp. 43–82; and National Council for Urban Economic Development, *The Ben Franklin Partnership,* (Washington, D.C.: National Council for Urban Economic Development, November 1985).
28. Ralph R. Widner, "The Philadelphia Experiment Unifying Economic Development," *Economic Development Commentary,* Winter 1983, pp. 16–19.
29. Osborne, *Laboratories of Democracy,* pp. 264–66.

30. David L. Birch, "The Q Factor," *Inc.*, April 1987, p. 53.
31. David L. Birch, *The Job Generation Process* (Cambridge, Mass.: MIT Press, 1979).
32. David L. Birch, "Who Survives," *Inc.*, July 1988, p. 22; and Birch, "Live Fast, Die Young," *Inc.*, August 1988, pp.23–24.
33. David L. Birch, "The Booming Hidden Market," *Inc.*, October 1987, p. 15; and Birch, "Down, But Not Out," *Inc.*, May 1988, pp. 20–21.
34. See Committee for Economic Development, *Leadership for Dynamic State Economies* (New York: CED, 1986).
35. F. Scott Fosler, "Does Economic Theory Capture the Effects of New and Traditional State Policies on Economic Development?" in *Competition among States* (Washington, D.C.: Urban Institute Press, 1991), p. 248.
36. William Hamilton, Larry Ledebur, and Deborah Matz, *Industrial Incentives: Public Promotion of Private Enterprise* (Washington, D.C.: Aslan Press, 1985); and Douglas P. Woodward and Norman J. Glickman, *The New Competitors* (New York: Basic Books, 1989).
37. Steven Prokesch, "Despite Pact, New York and Region Spar over Jobs," *New York Times*, November 30, 1962, p. C6.

Chapter Ten: Expanding Exports and Stimulating Foreign Investment

1. "Swedish Export Vodka but Frown on It at Home," *Chicago Tribune*, November 6, 1988, sec. 7, p. 4.
2. See President's Commission on Industrial Competitiveness, *Global Competition: The New Reality*, vols. 1 and 2 (Washington, D.C.: U.S. Government Printing Office, 1985); and Susan Dentzer, "The Coming Global Boom," *U.S. News and World Report*, July 16, 1990, pp. 20–25.
3. Sue Shellenbarger, "Cities and States Help Local Businesses by Matching Them," *Wall Street Journal*, March 7, 1991, p. B1.
4. Daniel Yankelovich, "The Competitiveness Conundrum," *American Enterprise*, September–October, 1990, p. 43.
5. *Challenges:* Monthly Newsletter of the Council on Competitiveness, December 1991, p. 7.
6. Stuart Auerbach, "Export the Unexported from America," *Washington Post National Weekly Edition*, September 28–October 4, 1992, p. 9.

7. David L. Birch, "Trading Places," *Inc.*, April 1988, pp. 42–43.
8. William E. Nothdurft, *Going Global: How Europe Helps Small Firms Export* (Washington, D.C.: Brookings Institution, 1992).
9. Michael Mandel and Aaron Bernstein, "Dispelling the Myths that Are Holding Us Back," *Business Week*, December 17, 1990, p. 66.
10. "Schwab Leads New Era in U.S. Export Promotion," *Challenges: Council on Competitiveness*, May 1991, pp. 1, 6.
11. Blaine Liner, "States and Localities in the Global Marketplace," *Intergovernmental Perspective* 16, Spring 1990, pp. 11–14; Louis T. Wells and Alvin G. Wint, *Marketing a Country: Promotion as a Tool for Attracting Foreign Investment* (Washington,D.C.: World Bank, 1990).
12. *Challenges*, January 1991, p. 3.
13. Johny K. Johansson, "Determinants and Effects of the Use of 'Made In' Labels," *International Marketing Review* (UK) 6, no. 1 (1989), pp. 47–58.
14. See Warren J. Bilkey and Erik Nes, "Country-of-Origin Effects on Product Evaluations," *Journal of International Business Studies* 13, Spring–Summer 1982, pp. 89–99; P. J. Cattin et al., "A Cross-Cultural Study of 'Made-In' Concepts," *Journal of International Business Studies*, Winter 1982, pp. 131–41; and Gary M. Erickson, Johny K. Johansson, and Paul Chao, "Image Variables in Multi-Attribute Product Evaluations: Country-of-Origin Effects," *Journal of Consumer Research*, September 1984, pp. 694–99.
15. Michael Porter, *The Competitive Advantage of Nations* (New York: The Free Press, 1990), pp. 131–78.
16. Rodd Zolkas, "States Rush to Defend Home Products," *City and State*, June 5, 1989, pp. 3–4.
17. Lisa Goff, "States Map Sales Strategies," *City and State*, May 22, 1989, pp. 11–12, and Goff, "Making It Happen Overseas," pp. 11–15.
18. "Local Efforts in States Support Exports," *Challenges*, July 1991, p. 6.
19. Ibid.
20. Liner, "States and Localities," p. 12.
21. Martin Tolchin and Susan Tolchin, *Buying into America* (New York: Times Books, 1988), p. 53.
22. Ellen Hoffman, "Overseas Sales Pitch," *National Journal*, January 16, 1988, pp. 129–33.
23. "Local Efforts," p. 6.

24. Tolchin and Tolchin, *Buying into America*, p. 53.

25. Report to the Governor, *Illinois Economic Board*, December 1990.

26. Illinois Department of Commerce and Community Affairs, International Business Division, *1990 Report* (Springfield, IL: DCCA, 1991).

27. Jonathan Kendall, "U.S. Governors Wooing Foreign Investors," *Wall Street Journal*, December 15, 1988, p. A10.

28. Mark Hornung, "Edgar's Overhauled DCCA," *Crain's Chicago Business*, November 25, 1991, p. 2.

29. Liner, "States and Localities," p. 14.

30. Louis Uchitelle, "Blocs Seen Replacing Free Trade," *New York Times*, August 26, 1991, p. C1; and "The Stateless Corporation," *Business Week*, May 14, 1990, pp. 98–104.

31. Craig Forman, "Europe Crossroads," *Wall Street Journal*, December 6, 1991, p. 1.

32. Hugh O'Neill, "The Role of the States in Trade Development," in *International Trade: The Changing Role of the U.S.*, *The Academy of Political Science* 37, no. 1 (1990), p. 194; Susan Dentzer, "Business without Borders," *U.S. News and World Report*, July 16, 1990, pp. 29–31; and Robert Reich, "Corporation and Nation," *Atlantic Monthly*, May 1988, pp. 76–81.

Chapter Eleven: Attracting Residents

1. For a compilation of these stories, see Susan C. Falundi and Marilyn Chase, "Surging Welfare Costs, Struggle to Control Them, Join Health-Care Expense as Hot Political Issue," *Wall Street Journal*, December 11, 1991, p. A18; Daniel Kagan, "Free Acres in Northern Wonderland," *Insight*, February 6, 1989, p. 56; Martin J. Moylan, "Cold Minnesota Offers Warm Welcome," *Chicago Tribune*, February 12, 1989, p. 29; and "Town Solicits Settlers with Success," *New York Times*, December 28, 1989, p. 13.

2. Allen L. Otten, "Birth Dearth . . . Mr. Wattenberg's Crystal Ball," *Wall Street Journal*, June 18, 1987, p. 17. Also, Ben J. Wattenberg, *The Birth Dearth* (New York: Pharos Books, 1987).

3. Joe Schwartz and Thomas Exter, "This World Is Flat," *American Demographics*, April 1991, pp. 34–39.

4. Ibid.

5. Charles Langino and William Crown, "The Migration of Old Money," *American Demographics*, October 1989, pp. 28–31.

6. "Elderly Households: Low Income, High Net Worth,"*American Demographics*, April 1991, p. 11.

7. Nina Glascow, "A Place in the Country,"*American Demographics*, March 1991, pp. 24–30. See also, Peter Kerr, "Rural Towns to Lure Retirees," *New York Times*, September 22, 1991, p. 1.

8. Bill Richards, "The Influx of Retirees Adds New Vitality into Distressed Towns," *Wall Street Journal*, August 5, 1988, p. 12.

9. Jeff Ostroff, "An Aging Market: How Businesses Can Prosper," *American Demographics*, May 1989, pp. 26–28.

10. Frederick Day and Charles Jackson, "How to Reach Military Retirees," *American Demographics*, April 1991, pp. 41–44.

11. Peter F. Drucker, "Information and the Future of the City," *Wall Street Journal*, April 4, 1989, p. A14.

12. Felicity Barringer, "18% Households in U.S. Moved in '89," *New York Times*, December 20,1991, p. A10. Also, Larry Long, "Americans on the Move," *American Demographics*, June 1990, pp. 46–49.

13. Paula Mergenhagen, "Doing the Career Shuffle," *American Demographics*, November 1991, pp. 42–53.

14. Diane Crispell, "Guppies, Minks, and Tinks," *American Demographics*, June 1990, p. 51.

15. For the sizes of these different groups, see *American Demographics*, October 1991, p. 38.

16. G. Scott Thomas, *The Rating Guide to Life in America's Small Cities* (New York: Prometheus Books, 1990).

17. Bruce Hager and Julia Siler, "Podunk Is Beckoning," *Business Week*, December 23, 1991, p. 76.

18. Joel Garreau, "Edge City," *American Demographics*, September 1991, p. 30. See also, Garreau, *Edge City: Life on the New Frontier* (New York: Doubleday, 1991).

19. For an economic model based on this assumption, see Charles M. Tiebout, "A Pure Theory of Local Expenditures," *Journal of Political Economy*, October 5, 1956, pp. 416–24.

20. Patrick Reardon, "Suburbs Pressed to Build Affordable Housing,"*Chicago Tribune*, December 29, 1991, sec. 4, p. 1.

21. Jane Gross, "Poor Seekers of Good Life Flock to California," *New York Times*, December 29, 1991, p. 11.

22. Felicity Barringer, "Census Shows Profound Changes in Racial Makeup of the Nation," *New York Times*, March 11, 1991, p. 1.

23. James Allen and Eugene Turner, "Where to Find the New Immigrants," *American Demographics*, September 1988, pp. 26–27.

24. "Homeless Shelters Turn Away 1 out of 6," *USA TODAY*, December 17, 1991, p. 3A.
25. Ronald C. Fisher, "Interjurisdictional Competition: A Summary Perspective," in *Competitors among States and Local Governments* (Washington, D.C.: Urban Institute, 1991), pp. 261–73.

Chapter 12: Organizing for Change

1. John Huey, "The Best Cities For Business," *Fortune*, November 4, 1991, p. 52.
2. Robert Reich, "The Myth of 'Made in America'," *Wall Street Journal*, July 5, 1991, p. 14; see also Reich, *The Work of Nations: Preparing Ourselves for 21st Century Capitalism* (New York: Knopf, 1991).
3. Lester Thurow, *Head to Head: The Coming Economic Battle among Japan, Europe, and America* (New York: Morrow, 1992).
4. Wilbur Thompson, "Economic Processes and Employment Problems in Metropolitan Areas," in *Post Industrial America*, ed. George Sternlieb and James W. Hughes (New Brunswick, N.J.: Rutgers University Press, 1975), pp. 192–94.
5. Edwin S. Mills and John F. McDonald, eds., *Sources of Metropolitan Growth* (Piscotaway, N.J.: Center for Urban Policy Research, Rutgers, 1992).
6. The President's Commission on Industrial Competitiveness, *Global Competition: The New Reality*, vol. 1 (Washington, D.C.: U.S. Government Printing Office, 1985), p. 6.
7. R. Scott Fosler, ed., *The New Economic Role of American States* (New York: Oxford University Press, 1988), p. 319.
8. Committee for Economic Development, *Leadership for Dynamic State Economies* (New York: CED, 1986), p. 28.
9. The complete report is reprinted in Donald M. Fraser, "State of the City: Minneapolis as a City for the 21st Century," *Futurics*, vol. 14, no. 2, 1990, pp. 1–13.
10. Timothy J. Bartik, "Tennessee," in Fosler, *The New Economic Role*, pp. 141–202.
11. David Osborne and Ted Gaebler, *Reinventing Government* (Reading, Mass.: Addison-Wesley, 1992), p. 167.
12. David Osborne, *Laboratories of Democracy* (Boston, Mass.: Harvard Business School Press, 1988), p. 259.
13. Osborne and Gaebler, *Reinventing Government*, chap. 10.

14. Committee for Economic Development, *An America that Works: The Life Cycle Approach to a Competitive Work Force* (New York: CED, 1990).
15. Kevin Kelly et al., "Hot Spots: America's New Growth Regions are Blossoming Despite the Slump." *Business Week,* October 19, 1992, pp. 80–88.
16. Michael E. Porter, *The Competitive Advantage of Nations* (New York: The Free Press, 1990), p. 73.
17. John Naisbitt and Patricia Aburdene, *Megatrends 2000: Ten New Directions for the 1990s* (New York: Avon Books, 1990), p. 62.
18. Neil Peirce and Robert Guskind, "Hot Managers, Sizzling Cities," *Business Month,* June 1989, p. 38.
19. Osborne, *Laboratories,* p. 171.
20. See, R. Scott Fosler and Renee A. Berger, eds. *Public-Private Partnerships in American Cities* (Lexington, Mass.: D.C. Heath, 1982), chap. 2–3, and Perry Davis, ed., *Public-Private Partnerships* (New York: Academy of Political Science, 1986).
21. John Gunther-Mohr and Bert Winterbottom, "Implementation Strategies: Turning Plans into Successful Development," *Economic Development Commentary,* Summer, 1989, pp. 23–31.
22. Fairfax County Economic Development Authority, *Fairfax County: 1985 Annual Report* (Tysons Corner, Va.: FCEDA, 1985); and Wanda Norton, "Interview: John Siddall," *Virginia Review* 60, September–October 1982, pp. 22–34.
23. Stephen Kagann, "New York's Incentives, the Wrong Incentives," *Wall Street Journal,* October 6, 1992, p. 14.

INDEX